Perspectives on Taste

This book offers a sustained, interdisciplinary examination of taste. It addresses a range of topics that have been at the heart of lively debates in philosophy of language, linguistics, metaphysics, aesthetics, and experimental philosophy.

Our everyday lives are suffused with discussions about taste. We are quick to offer familiar platitudes about taste, but we struggle when facing the questions that matter—what taste is, how it is related to subjectivity, what distinguishes good from bad taste, why it is valuable to make and evaluate judgments about matters of taste, and what, exactly, we mean in speaking about these matters. The essays in this volume open up new, intersecting lines of research about these questions that cross traditional disciplinary boundaries. They address the notion of aesthetic taste; connections between taste and the natures of truth, disagreement, assertion, belief, retraction, linguistic context-sensitivity, and the semantics/pragmatics interface; experimental inquiry about taste; and metaphysical questions underlying ongoing discussions about taste.

Perspectives on Taste will be of interest to researchers and advanced students working in aesthetics, philosophy of language, linguistics, metaphysics, and experimental philosophy.

Jeremy Wyatt is Senior Lecturer in Philosophy at the University of Waikato. He is an editor or co-editor of *Pluralisms in Truth and Logic* (2018), *The Nature of Truth: Classic and Contemporary Perspectives, 2nd ed.* (2021), and *Truth: Concept Meets Property* (*Synthese*, 2021). His articles have appeared in *Philosophical Studies*, *The Philosophical Quarterly*, *Synthese*, *American Philosophical Quarterly*, and *Inquiry*.

Julia Zakkou is Assistant Professor of Philosophy at the University of Bielefeld, Germany. She is the author of *Faultless Disagreement* (2019) and a co-editor of the *Inquiry* special issue *Semantic Variability* (2021). Her articles have appeared in *Philosophers' Imprint*, *Philosophical Studies*, *Synthese*, *Semantics and Pragmatics*, *Mind and Language*, *Philosophy Compass*, *Inquiry*, and *Thought*.

Dan Zeman is Adjunct Professor at the University of Warsaw. He is a co-editor of *Relativism about Value* (2012) and *New Work on Disagreement* (*Synthese*, forthcoming). His articles have appeared in *Thought*, *Dialectica*, *Linguistics and Philosophy*, *Philosophia*, *Critica*, *Inquiry*, and *Theoria*. His monograph *Disagreement in Semantics* (co-authored with Mihai Hîncu) is forthcoming with Routledge.

Routledge Studies in Contemporary Philosophy

The Single-Minded Animal
Shared Intentionality, Normativity, and the Foundations
of Discursive Cognition
Preston Stovall

Autonomy and Equality
Relational Approaches
Edited by Natalie Stoljar and Kristin Voigt

Contractarianism, Role Obligations, and Political Morality
Benjamin Sachs

Force, Content and the Unity of the Proposition
Edited by Gabriele M. Mras and Michael Schmitz

John Rawls and the Common Good
Edited by Roberto Luppi

Philosophy of Love in the Past, Present, and Future
Edited by André Grahle, Natasha McKeever, and Joe Saunders

Time in Action
The Temporal Structure of Rational Agency and Practical Thought
Edited by Carla Bagnoli

Perspectives on Taste
Aesthetics, Language, Metaphysics, and Experimental Philosophy
Edited by Jeremy Wyatt, Julia Zakkou, and Dan Zeman

For more information about this series, please visit: www.routledge.com/
Routledge-Studies-in-Contemporary-Philosophy/book-series/SE0720

Perspectives on Taste
Aesthetics, Language, Metaphysics, and Experimental Philosophy

Edited by Jeremy Wyatt,
Julia Zakkou, and Dan Zeman

NEW YORK AND LONDON

First published 2022
by Routledge
605 Third Avenue, New York, NY 10158

and by Routledge
4 Park Square, Milton Park, Abingdon, Oxon, OX14 4RN

Routledge is an imprint of the Taylor & Francis Group, an informa business

© 2022 selection and editorial matter, Jeremy Wyatt, Julia Zakkou, and Dan Zeman; individual chapters, the contributors

The right of Jeremy Wyatt, Julia Zakkou, and Dan Zeman to be identified as the authors of the editorial material, and of the authors for their individual chapters, has been asserted in accordance with sections 77 and 78 of the Copyright, Designs and Patents Act 1988.

All rights reserved. No part of this book may be reprinted or reproduced or utilised in any form or by any electronic, mechanical, or other means, now known or hereafter invented, including photocopying and recording, or in any information storage or retrieval system, without permission in writing from the publishers.

Trademark notice: Product or corporate names may be trademarks or registered trademarks, and are used only for identification and explanation without intent to infringe.

Library of Congress Cataloging-in-Publication Data
A catalog record for this book has been requested

ISBN: 978-1-032-00317-7 (hbk)
ISBN: 978-1-032-02619-0 (pbk)
ISBN: 978-1-003-18422-5 (ebk)

DOI: 10.4324/9781003184225

Typeset in Sabon
by Apex CoVantage, LLC

Contents

List of Figures and Tables	vii

1 Introduction 1
JEREMY WYATT, JULIA ZAKKOU, AND DAN ZEMAN

PART I
Aesthetics 17

2 The Trajectory of Gustatory Taste 19
KEVIN SWEENEY

3 Over-Appreciating Appreciation 40
REBECCA WALLBANK AND JON ROBSON

4 Aesthetic Taste: Perceptual Discernment or Emotional Sensibility? 58
IRENE MARTÍNEZ MARÍN AND ELISABETH SCHELLEKENS

PART II
Experimental Philosophy 75

5 De Gustibus *Est* Disputandum: An Empirical Investigation of the Folk Concept of Aesthetic Taste 77
CONSTANT BONARD, FLORIAN COVA, AND STEVE HUMBERT-DROZ

6 Contextualism Versus Relativism: More Empirical Data 109
MARKUS KNEER

vi *Contents*

PART III

Metaphysics

141

7 Disagreements and Disputes About Matters of Taste

143

DAN LÓPEZ DE SA

8 How to Canberra-Plan Disagreement: Platitudes,
Taste, Preferences

163

JEREMY WYATT

PART IV

Philosophy of Language and Linguistics

191

9 Non-Indexical Contextualism, Relativism, and Retraction

193

ALEXANDER DINGES

10 Perspectival Content and Semantic Composition

207

MALTE WILLER AND CHRISTOPHER KENNEDY

11 Exploring Valence in Judgments of Taste

231

ISIDORA STOJANOVIC AND ELSI KAISER

12 Differences of Taste: An Investigation of Phenomenal and
Non-Phenomenal Appearance Sentences

260

RACHEL ETTA RUDOLPH

13 Individual- and Stage-Level Predicates of Personal Taste:
Another Argument for Genericity as the Source of
Faultless Disagreement

286

HAZEL PEARSON

14 Tastes and the Ontology of Impersonal Perception Reports

319

FRIEDERIKE MOLTMANN

Notes on Contributors

342

Index

348

Figures and Tables

Figures

5.1	Percentage of participants' definitions of *good taste* falling into each category	95
5.2	Percentage of participants' definitions of *bad taste* falling into each category	95
6.1	Mean agreement with the statement that an original taste claim was false at the context of utterance and that it must be retracted given preference reversals across different scenarios. Error bars denote standard error of the mean	113
6.2	*Left*—Proportions of participants who judged a justified claim *x* assertible and true across conditions (true v. false); *Right*—Proportions of participants who judged a claim assertible and justified across conditions (good v. poor evidence)	115
6.3	Mean ratings for the nonmodal and modal condition. Error bars designate standard error of the mean	116
6.4	Mean ratings by condition. Error bars show 95% CI	117
6.5	Likelihood of uttering a contextualist (true) response and a relativist (false) response across directions of preference reversal. Error bars denote 95% confidence intervals	122
6.6	Proportion of responses (forced-choice) across direction of preference reversal. Error bars denote 95%-confidence intervals	124
6.7	Likelihood of uttering a contextualist (true) and relativist (false) response across directions of preference reversal. Error bars denote standard error of the mean	127
6.8	Agreement with proposed retraction across formulation ("retraction appropriate" v. "retraction required"). Error bars denote standard errors	130
8.1	The nature of taste disagreement	179
11.1	Difficulty class (Average valence: 5.56, average arousal: 4.09. Range for valence: 3.78–7.47, range for arousal: 2.71–5.75)	247

viii   *Figures and Tables*

11.2   Excess class (Average valence: 5.84, average arousal: 5.07.
     Range for valence: 4.37–7.45, range for arousal: 3.73–6.6)   248
11.3   Surprise class (Average valence: 5.69, average arousal: 4.86.
     Range for valence: 4.41–7.72, range for arousal: 3.5–6.05)   248
11.4   Middling adjectives (Average valence: 4.93, average
     arousal: 3.12. Range for valence: 3.63–6.17, range
     for arousal: 2.29–4)   250
11.5   Average valence and arousal ratings for the 34 neutral
     adjectives (collapsing all three classes) and the 14 middling
     adjectives (error bars show +/-1 SD)   251

Tables

5.1   Participants' definitions of good taste   85
5.2   Participants' definitions of bad taste. The indications for
     the columns are the same as for Table 5.1   90
5.3   Demographic predictors of participants' definitions of
     good taste   94
5.4   Demographic predictors of participants' definitions of
     bad taste. The indications for the columns are the same
     as for Table 5.3   94
5.5   Means and SDs for participants to our four questions about
     domains (*say, distinguish, important, knowledgeable*)   99
5.6   Participants' methods to improve taste. The indications
     for the columns are the same as for Table 5.1   102
6.1   Mixed ANOVA for the likelihood of uttering a
     contextualist or relativist response   121
11.1   Average valence and arousal ratings (standard deviation
     provided in parentheses)   251

1 Introduction

Jeremy Wyatt, Julia Zakkou, and Dan Zeman

Our everyday lives are suffused with discussions about taste. These happen in a diverse array of situations, such as when we are enjoying a new drink at a café, discussing the avant-garde pieces that just arrived at the local gallery, comparing the grandeur of the Dolomites to the austerity of the Sahara, or determining whether an item of clothing is nice enough to warrant the price.

A characteristic aim of philosophy is to pinpoint issues that are prominent in our everyday thought and discourse but which, in ordinary contexts, we rarely take care to examine in a systematic way. Taste is a paradigm example of such an issue. We are quick to mouth the familiar platitudes about taste, but we struggle when facing the questions that matter—what taste is, how it is related to subjectivity, what distinguishes good from bad taste, why it is valuable to make and evaluate judgements about matters of taste, and what, exactly, we mean in speaking about these matters. This volume is a sustained, cross-disciplinary examination of these and related questions about taste. In designing and preparing the volume, our central aims have been to work toward unifying the extensive bodies of research on taste, whose major themes intersect in rather interesting ways, and to stimulate further cross-disciplinary research on this topic.

Taste is a long-standing occupation of philosophers. The notion of aesthetic taste, with its complex relationship to the notion of gustatory taste, came to the fore in 18th-century aesthetics and has continued to interest aestheticians until the present day.[1] Moreover, during the past 20 years, discourse about taste has been at the heart of lively debates among philosophers of language and linguists. A thorough study of taste discourse has promised illumination in connection with major topics such as the natures of truth and disagreement; the natures of and norms governing assertion, belief, and retraction; linguistic context sensitivity; and the semantics/pragmatics interface.[2] Additionally, while armchair inquiry has played a dominant role in these aesthetic and linguistic debates, many theorists have come to appreciate the relevance—indeed, the necessity—of experimental investigations into the phenomena that are discussed therein.[3]

DOI: 10.4324/9781003184225-1

2 Jeremy Wyatt, Julia Zakkou, and Dan Zeman

In this volume, we bring together 13 state-of-the-art essays on taste by leading experts and up-and-coming scholars in the philosophy of language, linguistics, metaphysics, aesthetics, and experimental philosophy. In doing so, we wish to demonstrate how considering questions about taste that arise within neighbouring disciplines can spur new lines of research which would otherwise remain invisible. We also want to illustrate just how robust and exciting contemporary research on taste is, putting on display the ways in which it enables us to better understand ourselves and our evaluations of the world that we inhabit.

Part I: Aesthetics

The papers in Part I are devoted to issues that arise in connection with *aesthetic taste*, including the nature and aesthetic potential of gustatory taste, the value of aesthetic appreciation as a component of our aesthetic practices, and the nature of aesthetic taste.

Kevin Sweeney's chapter (Chapter 2) examines the physiological trajectory that is involved in tasting something that one has consumed. He begins by offering a brief historical overview of theories of taste, focusing on the theories of Kant and Brillat-Savarin. Kant distinguishes the *taste of sense* from the *taste of reflection*, maintaining that the latter, in contrast to the former, is exercised in aesthetic judgement. He also maintains that it is impossible to make aesthetic judgements about the tastes of foods and drinks, since our evaluations of their tastes are based on immediate, rather than reflective and imaginative, hedonic reactions. By contrast, Brillat-Savarin emphasises that gustatory experience involves an interplay between taste and smell as well as an analysable temporal trajectory. In light of its complexity, Brillat-Savarin maintains that gustatory experience can in fact support reflective and imaginative gustatory evaluations of foods and drinks.

Sweeney takes Brillat-Savarin's emphasis on the multisensory nature, temporal trajectory, and ensuing aesthetic potential of gustatory experience to be highly insightful, though he points out that contemporary scientific evidence indicates that there are some significant limitations in Brillat-Savarin's account. Drawing on Brillat-Savarin's insights, Sweeney argues that the integrity of the gustatory, or alimentary, trajectory is a highly important feature of gustatory experience, applying this view to the practice of wine tasting and, in particular, to the discernment of a wine's *terroir*.

Rebecca Wallbank and Jon Robson (Chapter 3) direct our attention to the characteristic values and goals of our aesthetic practices, exploring the status that *aesthetic appreciation* has within these practices. Their central aim is to argue that we should not take aesthetic appreciation to be the *sine qua non* of our aesthetic practices but should instead recognise that these practices are underwritten by other values and goals that have unique roles to play. Among the values and goals that they discuss are having true aesthetic beliefs, including ones that are based on testimony, as well as having interpersonal aesthetic interactions that are prompted by engagement with artworks. In emphasising the significance of these goals and values, Wallbank and Robson aim to resist the tempting picture of aesthetic practice according to which it canonically consists of an individual solitarily and autonomously exercising their aesthetic taste in an attempt to appreciate artworks. On their alternative picture, our aesthetic practices are highly social insofar as they are underwritten by essentially social values and goals.

Irene Martínez Marín and Elisabeth Schellekens (Chapter 4) explore the nature of aesthetic taste itself. Martínez Marín and Schellekens' primary goal is to reconcile two compelling ideas about aesthetic taste. The first is that aesthetic taste is subjective, insofar as one's aesthetic taste involves one's personal preferences, likings, and dislikings and the resultant emotional responses that one has to the perceived aesthetic character of artworks. The second is that aesthetic taste is objective, insofar as it involves the perception of distinctively aesthetic properties that are possessed by artworks.

Their proposed reconciliation rests on the idea that an aesthetic agent can *attune* themselves more or less well to an artwork by adjusting their emotional dispositions to the aesthetic properties that the artwork exhibits. On this account, aesthetic taste involves perception, as we must rely on perception in coming to know which aesthetic properties artworks exhibit. Aesthetic taste also involves emotion, as developing one's aesthetic taste doesn't just consist in the ability to perceptually recognise artworks' aesthetic properties but also in the disposition to have emotional responses that are appropriate in light of those properties. Martínez Marín and Schellekens emphasise that this process of attunement is meant to be bi-directional in that improving one's aesthetic perception can improve one's emotional dispositions towards artworks and vice versa.

Part II: Experimental Philosophy

The papers in Part II represent significant contributions to the experimental literature on taste. Constant Bonard, Florian Cova, and Steve Humbert-Droz (Chapter 5) investigate a puzzle that arises in light of what extant empirical research has taught us about ordinary subjects' attitudes towards aesthetic issues. This research strongly indicates that ordinary subjects are *aesthetic subjectivists* in the sense that they are disinclined to posit objective aesthetic facts and that when it comes to aesthetic disagreements, they are also disinclined to describe either party as being mistaken. On the other hand, it seems that when engaging in aesthetic evaluation, we routinely describe some persons as having either 'good taste' or 'bad taste' with respect to certain matters. In this regard, our

4 *Jeremy Wyatt, Julia Zakkou, and Dan Zeman*

ordinary aesthetic practices seem to involve tendencies that can be fairly described as *objectivist*. The puzzle is whether we can resolve the apparent conflict between our subjectivist and objectivist aesthetic tendencies. This conflict is closely related to the 'paradox of taste' that was highlighted by Hume (1757/1875) and Kant (1790), and it is also clearly related to the tension between the subjectivity and objectivity of aesthetic taste that is detailed by Martínez Marín and Schellekens.

To investigate this conflict, Bonard, Cova, and Humbert-Droz performed an experiment that was designed to determine whether their participants, a representative sample of the US population, in fact exhibited both subjectivist and objectivist aesthetic tendencies. They report a range of interesting findings. Two particularly important findings are (i) that 93% of their participants reported that they have said that one person has better taste in works of art than another person and (ii) that when asked to provide open-ended answers explaining how they think about good and bad taste, the participants' answers were split between more subjectivist and more objectivist conceptions of good and bad taste. The latter finding indicates that the subjectivism–objectivism tension is indeed a feature of our ordinary aesthetic practices, especially if we think of this tension as arising at the population level.

Lastly, it is worth noting that 92.5% of Bonard, Cova, and Humbert-Droz's participants agreed that people can improve their aesthetic taste and that when asked how people could improve their taste, only 4.5% emphasised perception. This means that a rather small minority of their participants associated perceptual improvement with the improvement of aesthetic taste. It is also notable that Bonard, Cova, and Humbert-Droz don't mention any associations by their participants of taste improvement with the improvement of one's emotional responses to artworks.

This suggests that Bonard, Cova, and Humbert-Droz's participants weren't inclined to think of the improvement of aesthetic taste as involving what Martínez Marín and Schellekens call 'attunement.' It is of course open to Martínez Marín and Schellekens to respond that the improvement of aesthetic taste does involve attunement even though ordinary subjects aren't typically aware of this fact. It may also be that if the participants' responses are reanalysed with Martínez Marín and Schellekens's views in mind, the responses will turn out to fit well with their views.

Markus Kneer's discussion (Chapter 6) begins with the observation that over the past fifteen years, philosophers of language and linguists have put forward many analyses of *perspective-dependent expressions*, including *predicates of personal taste* (e.g. 'fun,' 'tasty,' and 'cool') and *epistemic modals* (e.g. epistemic 'might' and 'probably'). This much is common knowledge. However, what is observed less often is that these analyses generate interesting *empirical* predictions which can be properly evaluated only by way of empirical inquiry. Kneer offers a survey of the relatively few experimental studies concerning people's judgements about truth assessment and retraction in connection with these expressions. He also describes the results of a battery of new experiments.

Kneer first presents the crux of the debate between contextualists and relativists, noting that the majority of extant empirical studies have favoured contextualism. The remainder of Kneer's chapter consists of an in-depth discussion of two studies that have yielded divergent results—those by Knobe and Yalcin (2014) on retraction and by Dinges and Zakkou (2020) on truth assessment. Kneer's aim is to show that contextualists shouldn't worry about these results.

In connection with the latter study, he traces the divergent result to what he takes to be a flawed formulation of one of the sentences to be evaluated. After running a novel experiment with a new formulation, Kneer reports that none of the effects found by Dinges and Zakkou were replicated, and the contrast with previous results is taken to be merely the effect of a design choice. In relation to the former study, Kneer replicates the results of Knobe and Yalcin's main experiment and runs a novel experiment involving what he takes to be a more relevant question (whether retraction is required as opposed to appropriate). Finally, Kneer observes that permissive norms of assertion have no dialectical significance vis-à-vis retraction and concludes that extant experimental results, including the novel results that he reports, provide unequivocal support for contextualism over relativism.

Part III: Metaphysics

The papers in Part III focus on metaphysical questions underlying ongoing discussions in aesthetics, philosophy of language, and linguistics. Dan López de Sa (Chapter 7) investigates disagreements and disputes about taste, our understanding of which is still highly incomplete, despite the fact that they have received ample attention in semantics and pragmatics. He stresses that when studying such disagreements and disputes, we must take care to keep mental and linguistic questions separate from one another. *Disagreement*, in his preferred understanding, is a phenomenon that hinges upon features of mental states, whereas *dispute* should be seen as the overt linguistic expression of this phenomenon. He goes on to show how this distinction has significant and underappreciated metaphysical impact in connection with extant theories of taste disagreement.

Thus, in connection to the disagreement challenges that have been offered for contextualist views, López de Sa maintains that the objection from "lost disagreement" is spurious and that it is problematic for the contemporary literature to continuously emphasise it. He suggests that this objection rests on a conception of disagreement, according to which disagreement requires exclusionary contents, that both armchair and experimental investigations of disagreement have shown to be overly narrow.

6 *Jeremy Wyatt, Julia Zakkou, and Dan Zeman*

López de Sa agrees, however, that there is a challenge for the contextualist in the vicinity: namely, that of explaining the felicity of denial (and related phenomena) involving predicates of taste. Luckily, he points out that the answer to this problem can be found in previous work and is compatible with several contextualist views (including his own 'presupposition of commonality' approach). Accordingly, López de Sa concludes that while it is often said that contextualists face serious problems related to disagreement, this charge is ultimately misdirected.

Jeremy Wyatt (Chapter 8) likewise examines disagreement, and specifically taste disagreement, from a metaphysical perspective. He addresses three main questions:

- What methods should we use when thinking about the nature of taste disagreement?
- What are the relata of the relation of taste disagreement?
- What is the nature of the relation of taste disagreement itself?

Wyatt argues that we can make significant progress on these issues by 'Canberra-planning' disagreement—that is, by offering an account of taste disagreement that draws on the resources of the Canberra Plan, which has been previously used to investigate other important metaphysical issues. Wyatt starts by offering a series of platitudes about disagreement, which detail structural features of the disagreement relation as well as connections between our ordinary concept of disagreement and other concepts such as that of the incompatibility of attitudes and that of mistaken judgement. He uses these platitudes to generate a Ramsey sentence, which expresses the functional role that a disagreement relation must play.

With this Ramsey sentence in hand, Wyatt turns to investigate the nature of taste disagreement. The question that he raises is: which relations with relata that pertain to matters of gustatory taste make this Ramsey sentence true? Wyatt first considers *doxastic* accounts of taste disagreement, arguing that they are undermined by experimental results such as those of Cova and Pain (2012). He then goes on to defend a preferential account of taste disagreement, according to which taste disagreement consists in a relation that he calls *preferential type-noncotenability*. By way of defending this account, Wyatt shows that—with one caveat—preferential type-noncotenability makes the Ramsey sentence for disagreement true. He then develops his account a bit further by explaining why we should take preferential type-noncotenability to be grounded in a further relation, *paralysis-inducement*. Lastly, Wyatt describes some upshots of his account of taste disagreement for ongoing debates about taste discourse, including (i) that we should be wary of arguments about taste discourse which assume that taste disagreement is doxastic; (ii) that expressivism about predicates of personal taste may deserve more attention than it has

Introduction 7

received; and (iii) that pluralism about disagreement is highly plausible and fits nicely with the machinery of the Canberra Plan.

Part IV: Philosophy of Language and Linguistics

The papers in Part IV approach the issue of taste from the vantage points of the philosophy of language and linguistics—that is, they focus on the *meaning* of the expressions we use when speaking about matters of taste and on the *contents* we entertain when speaking and thinking about such matters. Matters of taste have been widely discussed in semantics, with a plethora of positions being proposed and many healthy debates being pursued. Broadly speaking, four kinds of view are currently on the market:

- *Contextualist* views take semantic content to include perspectival information
- *Relativist* views take perspectival information to figure not in semantic content but in postsemantics
- *Absolutist* views take perspectival information to play no semantic or postsemantic roles
- *Expressivist* views take perspectival information to be expressed as part of the non-doxastic attitudes of speakers.

While some of the contributions in Part IV can be easily placed into one of these camps, others are dedicated to addressing more foundational issues, providing new and useful categories, and tackling less discussed phenomena. Among the issues tackled in Part IV are the following:

- What types of predicates of personal taste (*PPTs*) and similar expressions are there?
- What is the relation between the semantic contents of PPTs and the attitudes of speakers?
- What exactly do notions like evaluativity and valence come to in connection with PPTs and similar expressions?
- Are seemingly synonymous expressions like 'tasty' and 'tastes good' actually semantically equivalent?
- Are PPTs and similar expressions inherent generics?

Alexander Dinges (Chapter 9) takes up the issue of how non-indexical contextualism—one of the most prominent analyses of PPTs—can account for the retraction of taste claims. After presenting both non-indexical contextualism and one of its rivals, assessment relativism, and spelling out their corresponding assertion and retraction norms, Dinges puts forward a novel non-indexical contextualist retraction norm. He defends this norm from several objections, showing, perhaps most importantly, that its adoption doesn't cause non-indexical contextualism to collapse into assessment relativism. This leads Dinges to provisionally conclude that when it comes to taste claims, the phenomenon of retraction doesn't favour the more radical assessment relativism over the simpler non-indexical contextualism.

That said, Dinges goes on to note that his non-indexical contextualist retraction norm holds only given certain views about time and location. In particular, he argues that if one adopts either temporalism or locationism (according to which propositions vary in truth-value with time and location, respectively), then this norm yields the wrong predictions. Dinges' overall conclusion, then, is that the choice between non-indexical contextualism and assessment relativism turns on whether one endorses temporalism or locationism. He holds that if one endorses either of the latter, then one should also endorse assessment relativism. By contrast, if one rejects both temporalism and locationism, then one should endorse non-indexical contextualism. While Dinges favours the second approach, he indicates that he takes both approaches to be acceptable.

Malte Willer and Christopher Kennedy (Chapter 10) address the question of how perspectival content is grammatically encoded. Following Sæbø (2009), they contrast *syntactic* accounts, which explain data about embeddability under the subjective attitude verb *find* syntactically or by way of a special semantic type (such as contextualism), with *non-syntactic* accounts, which account for the relevant data as a matter of contingency rather than syntactic argument structure or semantic type (such as relativism). Willer and Kennedy provide a two-step argument against the former accounts and in favour of the latter. First, they show that syntactic approaches have difficulties accounting for the embeddability of certain perspectival predicates under a further subjective attitude verb, *consider*. Second, drawing on their earlier work in Kennedy and Willer (2016, 2019), they present an alternative theory that accounts for the embedding behaviour of perspectival expressions under *find* and *consider* pragmatically. Crucially, this theory has it that subjective attitude verbs presuppose their complement to be contingent across a set of doxastic alternatives, where the set of doxastic alternatives arises from our assumption that matters of fact do not fully determine what we say and think.

Isidora Stojanovic and Elsi Kaiser (Chapter 11) address a widespread assumption in the linguistic literature on taste: that judgements of taste are evaluative. They note that evaluativity and related notions such as valence haven't received much attention from a semantic point of view, and the aim of their paper is to remedy this. As a first step, they argue that the division between positive and negative PPTs is too simplistic and that a third category—that of *neutral PPTs*—needs to be introduced. They then go on to investigate how neutral PPTs differ from evaluative PPTs. On the one hand, they examine how they differ among themselves, suggesting that they come in at least three subtypes: the difficulty class, the excess class, and the surprise class. On the other, they look into how they

Introduction 9

differ from yet another category of predicates, which they call *middling*, exemplified by 'average.' Stojanovic and Kaiser propose novel linguistic tests to distinguish neutral PPTs from valenced PPTs, helping themselves to findings on pre-existing psychological norms of valence. By investigating crucial aspects of PPTs like evaluativity and valence, Kaiser and Stojanovic's paper offers valuable insight into these predicates' semantic life.

Rachel Etta Rudolph (Chapter 12) raises the question of how simple and widely investigated PPTs such as 'tasty' compare to more complex expressions like 'tastes good.' She notices that while they can be used interchangeably in many contexts, there are also contexts in which they behave differently, such as when a wine expert identifies a good wine by taste but doesn't enjoy it. Rudolph argues that this phenomenon arises systematically with complex sensory-evaluative predicates (such as 'looks splendid' and 'sounds nice') and investigates two strategies for explaining it. One strategy is to posit an ambiguity in the appearance verb, and the other involves appealing to an independently motivated flexibility in the adjective's meaning. Rudolph argues that while both approaches can account for a range of data, the second faces a challenge concerning sentences like 'The cake tastes like it's good' that the first strategy seems to avoid.

Hazel Pearson (Chapter 13) also takes up the issue of how the behaviour of 'tasty' compares to that of 'tastes good.' Based on a well-known distinction in linguistics between *individual-level* and *stage-level predicates*, she argues against taking these predicates to be synonymous. In particular, she observes that while 'tasty' and its ilk are individual-level predicates, 'tastes good' and its ilk are stage-level predicates, thus undermining the case for synonymy. Furthermore, Pearson argues that the covert experiencer argument of a simple PPT can only receive a generic interpretation, while the covert experiencer argument of a complex PPT can receive either a generic, bound variable, or referential interpretation. Additionally, Pearson investigates the consequences of this difference for disagreement involving such expressions, thus entering the ongoing debate between contextualism and relativism. She concludes that the data support the view that some PPTs are inherent generics while others are not, and favours a version of contextualism.

The idea that PPTs are inherent generics is also at the core of Friederike Moltmann's contribution (Chapter 14). In previous work, Moltmann has proposed to treat PPTs as involving a form of first person–based genericity, which is overtly expressed by generic 'one' and conveys a personal experience (or simulated experience) generalised to anyone with whom the agent identifies. In her chapter, she focuses on impersonal taste reports (and impersonal perception reports in general) and devises a different semantics for PPTs, based on a richer ontology.

The ontology that Moltmann describes involves *taste occurrences*, which depend on a particular perceptual experience and thus essentially

10 *Jeremy Wyatt, Julia Zakkou, and Dan Zeman*

involve an experiencer, and *taste objects*, which have neither of these features. This ontological distinction is reflected in semantic differences between impersonal perception verbs ('taste,' 'look,' 'sound,' 'smell,' etc.) and nouns ('the taste of coffee,' 'the sound of the violin,' 'the smell of the perfume,' etc.). Criticising Pearson's reliance on the individual-level/stage-level distinction, Moltmann shows how the distinction that she introduces can be put to work in accounting for a variety of linguistic phenomena while showing that appeals to both first person–based genericity and genericity in agent-centred situations are needed. In the final section of her chapter, Moltmann takes up the issue of faultless disagreement as it appears in connection with impersonal taste verbs and nouns, arguing that the apparatus that she develops accounts for faultless disagreement satisfactorily.[4]

Notes

1. A sampling of major work on this topic includes Aagaard-Mogensen and Forsey (2019), Allison (2001), Baker and Robson (2017), Bender (1997), Carroll (1984), Carruthers (2013, ch. 4), Chignell (2007), Cohen (1973, 2004), Dickie (1996), Fenner (2020), Gigante (2005), Ginsborg (1990, 2015), Goldman (2018), Guyer (1997, 2005, ch. 2, 2008, ch. 5), Hume (1757/1875), Kant (1790), Kivy (2015), Korsmeyer (1976, 1999, 2002, 2007, 2013, 2016, 2018), Kulenkampff (1990), Levinson (2002), Lopes (2008, 2017), Mothersill (1984, 1997), Perullo (2016), Plakias (2021), Schaper (1966), Schellekens (2004, 2006, 2009), Shiner (1996, 1997), Sibley (2001), Smith (2007, 2013), Sweeney (2018), Wieand (1984), Wiggins (2002, Essay V), and Zemach (1997).
2. The central contributions to these debates include Beddor (2019), Cappelen and Hawthorne (2009), Clapp (2015), Egan (2010, 2014), García-Carpintero and Kölbel (2008), Glanzberg (2007), Huvenes (2012, 2014), Kennedy (2013, 2016), Kennedy and Willer (2016), Kindermann (2019), Kneer et al. (2017), Kölbel (2002, 2004, 2015a, 2015b), Lasersohn (2005, 2016), López de Sa (2008, 2015), MacFarlane (2009, 2014), Marques (2014), Marques and García-Carpintero (2014), Meier and van Wijnbergen-Huitink (2016), Moltmann (2010), Pearson (2013), Richard (2008), Schafer (2011), Schaffer (2011), Silk (2016), Stephenson (2007), Stojanovic (2007), Sundell (2011), Wright (2006, 2008), Wyatt (2018, 2021), Zakkou (2019), and Zeman (2020).
3. Representative work includes Andow (2021), Beebe (2014), Beebe et al. (2015), Beebe and Sackris (2016), Bonard, Cova, and Humbert-Droz (this volume); Cohen and Nichols (2010), Cova (2019), Cova et al. (2015), Cova and Pain (2012), Cova and Réhault (2019), Cova et al. (2019), Currie et al. (2014), Dinges and Zakkou (2020), Foushee and Srinivasan (2017), Goodwin and Darley (2008, 2012), Kaiser (2015, 2021), Kaiser and Lee (2017a, 2017b), Kaiser and Rudin (2020), Kneer (2021, this volume), Kuhn et al. (2000), Liao et al. (2016), Liao and Meskin (2017, 2019), McNally and Stojanovic (2017), Meskin et al. (2017), Murray (2020), Nichols and Folds-Bennett (2003), Rabb et al. (2020), Rudin and Kaiser (2022), Sarkissian et al. (2011), Schellekens (2012, 2019), Schellekens and Goldie (2011), Solt (2016, 2018), Stojanovic (2019a, 2019b), Stojanovic and Kaiser (this volume); Stokes (2009), and Wyatt (2018, 2021).
4. Dan Zeman would like to acknowledge the financial help of an OPUS 17 grant (no. 2019/33/B/HS1/01269, "Semantic Relativism about Perspectival Expressions: A Reassessment and Defense") from the National Science Centre, Poland.

References

Aagaard-Mogensen, L., & Forsey, J. (Eds.). (2019). *On taste: Aesthetic exchanges*. Cambridge Scholars Publishing.

Allison, H. (2001). *Kant's theory of taste: A reading of the critique of aesthetic judgment*. Cambridge University Press.

Andow, J. (2021). Further exploration of anti-realist intuitions about aesthetics judgment. *Philosophical Psychology*, doi:10.1080/09515089.2021.2014440.

Baker, C., & Robson, J. (2017). An absolutist theory of faultless disagreement in aesthetics. *Pacific Philosophical Quarterly*, 98(3), 29–48.

Beddor, B. (2019). Subjective disagreement. *Noûs*, 53(4), 819–851.

Beebe, J. (2014). How different kinds of disagreement impact folk metaethical judgments. In H. Sarkissian & J. Wright (Eds.), *Advances in experimental moral psychology* (pp. 167–187). Bloomsbury.

Beebe, J., Qiaoan, R., Wysocki, T., & Endara, M. (2015). Moral objectivism in cross-cultural perspective. *Journal of Cognition and Culture*, 15(3–4), 386–401.

Beebe, J., & Sackris, D. (2016). Moral objectivism across the lifespan. *Philosophical Psychology*, 29(6), 912–929.

Bender, J. (1997). On Shiner's "Hume and the causal theory of taste". *The Journal of Aesthetics and Art Criticism*, 55(3), 317–320.

Cappelen, H., & Hawthorne, J. (2009). *Relativism and monadic truth*. Oxford: Oxford University Press.

Carroll, N. (1984). Hume's standard of taste. *Journal of Aesthetics and Art Criticism*, 43(2), 181–194.

Carruthers, M. (2013). *The experience of beauty in the middle ages*. Oxford University Press.

Chignell, A. (2007). Kant on the normativity of taste: The role of aesthetic ideas. *Australasian Journal of Philosophy*, 85(3), 415–433.

Clapp, L. (2015). A non-alethic approach to faultless disagreement. *Dialectica*, 69(4), 517–550.

Cohen, J., & Nichols, S. (2010). Colours, colour relationalism, and the deliverances of introspection. *Analysis*, 70(2), 218–228.

Cohen, T. (1973). Aesthetic/nonaesthetic and the concept of taste: A critique of Sibley's position. *Theoria*, 39(1–3), 113–152.

Cohen, T. (2004). The philosophy of taste: Thoughts on the idea. In P. Kivy (Ed.), *The Blackwell guide to aesthetics* (pp. 167–173). Blackwell.

Cova, F. (2019). Beyond intersubjective validity: Recent empirical investigations into the nature of aesthetic judgment. In F. Cova & S. Réhault (Eds.), *Advances in experimental philosophy of aesthetics* (pp. 13–32). Bloomsbury.

Cova, F., Garcia, A., & Liao, S. (2015). Experimental philosophy of aesthetics. *Philosophy Compass*, 10(12), 927–939.

Cova, F., Olivola, C. Y., Machery, E., Stich, S., Rose, D., Alai, M., Angelucci, A., Berniūnas, R., Buchtel, E. E., Chatterjee, A., Cheon, H., Cho, I.-R., Cohnitz, D., Dranseika, V., Lagos, Á. E., Ghadakpour, L., Grinberg, M., Hannikainen, I., Hashimoto, T., . . . & Zhu, J. (2019). *De pulchritudine non est disputandum?* A cross-cultural investigation of the alleged intersubjective validity of aesthetic judgment. *Mind and Language*, 34(3), 317–338.

Cova, F., & Pain, N. (2012). Can folk aesthetics ground aesthetic realism? *The Monist*, 95(2), 241–263.

Currie, G., Kieran, M., Meskin, A., & Robson, J. (Eds.). (2014). *Aesthetics and the sciences of mind*. Oxford University Press.

Dickie, G. (1996). *The century of taste: The philosophical odyssey of taste in the eighteenth century*. Oxford University Press.

Dinges, A., & Zakkou, J. (2020). A direction effect on taste predicates. *Philosophers' Imprint*, *20*(27), 1–22.

Egan, A. (2010). Disputing about taste. In R. Feldman & T. Warfield (Eds.), *Disagreement* (pp. 247–286). Oxford University Press.

Egan, A. (2014). There's something funny about comedy: A case study in faultless disagreement. *Erkenntnis*, *79*, 73–100.

Fenner, D. (2020). Developing aesthetic taste. *The Journal of Aesthetic Education*, *54*(2), 113–122.

Foushee, R., & Srinivasan, M. (2017). Could both be right? Children and adults' sensitivity to subjectivity in language. In *Proceedings of the 39th annual conference of the cognitive science society, London, UK* (pp. 379–384). https://cogsci.mindmodeling.org/2017/index.html.

García-Carpintero, M., & Kölbel, M. (Eds.). (2008). *Relative truth*. Oxford University Press.

Gigante, D. (2005). *Taste: A literary history*. Yale University Press.

Ginsborg, H. (1990). *The role of taste in Kant's theory of cognition*. Garland Publishing.

Ginsborg, H. (2015). *The normativity of nature: Essays on Kant's critique of judgement*. Oxford University Press.

Glanzberg, M. (2007). Context, content, and relativism. *Philosophical Studies*, *136*(1), 1–29.

Goldman, A. (2018). *Aesthetic value*. Routledge. First published in 1998 by Westview Press.

Goodwin, G. & Darley, J. (2008). The psychology of meta-ethics: exploring objectivism. *Cognition*, *106*(3), 1339–1366.

Goodwin, G. & Darley, J. (2012). Why are some moral beliefs perceived to be more objective than others? *Journal of Experimental Social Psychology*, *48*(1), 250–256.

Guyer, P. (1997). *Kant and the claims of taste* (2nd ed.). Cambridge University Press.

Guyer, P. (2005). *Values of beauty: Historical essays in aesthetics*. Cambridge University Press.

Guyer, P. (2008). *Knowledge, reason, and taste: Kant's response to Hume*. Princeton University Press.

Hume, D. (1757/1875). Of the standard of taste. In *Essays moral, literary, and political*. Grant Richards.

Huvenes, T. (2012). Varieties of disagreement and predicates of taste. *Australasian Journal of Philosophy*, *90*(1), 167–181.

Huvenes, T. (2014). Disagreement without error. *Erkenntnis*, *79*(S1), 143–154.

Kaiser, E. (2015). Perspective-shifting and free indirect discourse: Experimental investigations. In S. D'Antonio, M. Moroney, & C. Little (Eds.), *Proceedings of SALT 25* (pp. 346–372). Linguistic Society of America. https://doi.org/10.3765/salt.v25i0.3436.

Kaiser, E. (2021). Consequences of sensory modality for perspective-taking: Comparing visual, olfactory, and gustatory perception. *Frontiers in Psychology*. https://doi.org/10.3389/fpsyg.2021.701486

Kaiser, E., & Lee, J. (2017a). Experience matters: A psycholinguistic investigation of predicates of personal taste. In D. Burgdorf, J. Collard, S. Maspong, & B. Stefánsdóttir (Eds.), *Proceedings of SALT 27* (pp. 323–339). Linguistic Society of America. https://journals.linguisticsociety.org/proceedings/index.php/SALT/article/view/27.323

Kaiser, E., & Lee, J. (2017b). Predicates of personal taste and multidimensional adjectives: an experimental investigation. In W. Bennett, L. Hracs, & D. Storoshenko (Eds.), *Proceedings of the 35th West Coast conference on formal linguistics* (pp. 224–231). www.lingref.com/cpp/wccfl/35/index.html.

Kaiser, E., & Rudin, D. (2020). When faultless disagreement is not so faultless: What widely-held opinions can tell us about subjective adjectives. *Proceedings of the Linguistic Society of America*, 5(1), 698–707.

Kant, I. (1790). *Critique of the power of judgment* (Paul Guyer, Ed. & Trans.). Cambridge University Press, 2000.

Kennedy, C. (2013). Two sources of subjectivity: Qualitative assessment and dimensional uncertainty. *Inquiry*, 56(2–3), 258–277.

Kennedy, C. (2016). Two kinds of subjectivity. In C. Meier & J. van Wijnbergen-Huitink (Eds.), *Subjective meaning: Alternatives to relativism* (pp. 105–126). de Gruyter.

Kennedy, C., & Willer, M. (2016). Subjective attitudes and counterstance contingency. In M. Moroney, C. Little, J. Collard, & D. Burgdorf (Eds.), *Proceedings of SALT 26* (pp. 913–933). Linguistic Society of America. https://journals.linguisticsociety.org/proceedings/index.php/SALT/article/view/26.913

Kennedy, C., & Willer, M. (2019). *Evidence, attitudes, and counterstance contingency: Toward a pragmatic theory of subjective meaning* [Manuscript]. University of Chicago. https://semanticsarchive.net/Archive/jhkYzk3M/counterstance-draft.pdf.

Kindermann, D. (2019). Coordinating perspectives: *De se* and taste attitudes in communication. *Inquiry*, 62(8), 912–955.

Kivy, P. (2015). *De Gustibus: Arguing about taste and why we do it*. Oxford University Press.

Kneer, M. (2021). Predicates of personal taste: Empirical data. *Synthese*. https://doi.org/10.1007/s11229-021-03077-9

Kneer, M., Vicente, A., & Zeman, D. (2017). Relativism about predicates of personal taste and perspectival plurality. *Linguistics and Philosophy*, 40(1), 37–60.

Knobe, J., & Yalcin, S. (2014). Epistemic modals and context: Experimental data. *Semantics and Pragmatics*, 7(10), 1–21.

Kölbel, M. (2002). *Truth without objectivity*. Routledge.

Kölbel, M. (2004). Faultless disagreement. *Proceedings of the Aristotelian Society*, 104(1), 53–73.

Kölbel, M. (2015a). Relativism 1: Representational content. *Philosophy Compass*, 10(1), 38–51.

Kölbel, M. (2015b). Relativism 2: Semantic content. *Philosophy Compass*, 10(1), 52–67.

Korsmeyer, C. (1976). Hume and the foundations of taste. *The Journal of Aesthetics and Art Criticism*, 35(2), 201–215.

Korsmeyer, C. (1999). *Making sense of taste: Food and philosophy*. Cornell University Press.

Korsmeyer, C. (2002). Delightful, delicious, disgusting. *Journal of Aesthetics and Art Criticism*, 60(3), 218–225.

Korsmeyer, C. (2007). Tastes and pleasures. *Romantic Circles Praxis*. https://romantic-circles.org/praxis/gastronomy/korsmeyer/korsmeyer_essay.html.

Korsmeyer, C. (2013). Taste. In B. Gaut & D. McIver Lopes (Eds.), *The Routledge companion to aesthetics* (3rd ed., pp. 257–266). Routledge.

Korsmeyer, C. (Ed.). (2016). *The taste culture reader: Experiencing food and drink* (2nd ed.). Bloomsbury.

Korsmeyer, C. (2018). Taste and other senses: Reconsidering the foundations of aesthetics. *The Nordic Journal of Aesthetics*, 26(54). https://doi.org/10.7146/nja.v26i54.103078

Kuhn, D., Cheney, R., & Weinstock, M. (2000). The development of epistemological understanding. *Cognitive Development*, 15(3), 309–328.

Kulenkampff, J. (1990). The objectivity of taste: Hume and Kant. *Noûs*, 24(1), 93–110.

Lasersohn, P. (2005). Context dependence, disagreement, and predicates of personal taste. *Linguistics and Philosophy*, 28(6), 643–686.

Lasersohn, P. (2016). *Subjectivity and perspective in truth-theoretic semantics*. Oxford University Press.

Levinson, J. (2002). Hume's standard of taste: The real problem. *Journal of Aesthetics and Art Criticism*, 60(3), 227–238.

Liao, S., McNally, L., & Meskin, A. (2016). Aesthetic adjectives lack uniform behavior. *Inquiry*, 59(6), 618–631.

Liao, S., & Meskin, A. (2017). Aesthetic adjectives: Experimental semantics and context-sensitivity. *Philosophy and Phenomenological Research*, 94(2), 371–398.

Liao, S., & Meskin, A. (2019). Experimental philosophical aesthetics as public philosophy. In F. Cova & S. Réhault (Eds.), *Advances in experimental philosophy of aesthetics* (pp. 309–326). Bloomsbury.

Lopes, D. (2017). Disputing taste. In J. O. Young (Ed.), *Semantics of aesthetic judgments* (pp. 61–81). Oxford University Press.

López de Sa, D. (2008). Presuppositions of commonality: An indexical relativist account of disagreement. In M. García-Carpintero & M. Kölbel (Eds.), *Relative truth* (pp. 297–310). Oxford University Press.

López de Sa, D. (2015). Expressing disagreement. A presuppositional indexical contextualist relativist account. *Erkenntnis*, 80(1), 153–165.

MacFarlane, J. (2009). Nonindexical contextualism. *Synthese*, 166(2), 231–250.

MacFarlane, J. (2014). *Assessment sensitivity: Relative truth and its applications*. Oxford University Press.

Marques, T. (2014). Doxastic disagreement. *Erkenntnis*, 79(S1), 121–142.

Marques, T., & García-Carpintero, M. (2014). Disagreement about taste: Commonality presuppositions and coordination. *Australasian Journal of Philosophy*, 92(4), 701–723.

McNally, L., & Stojanovic, I. (2017). Aesthetic adjectives. In J. O. Young (Ed.), *Semantics of aesthetic judgments* (pp. 17–37). Oxford University Press.

Meskin, A., Robson, J., Ichino, A., Goffin, K., & Monseré, A. (2017). Philosophical aesthetics and cognitive science. *WIREs Cognitive Science*, 9(1), 1–15.

Moltmann, F. (2010). Relative truth and the first person. *Philosophical Studies*, *150*(2), 187–220.

Mothersill, M. (1984). *Beauty restored*. Clarendon Press.

Mothersill, M. (1997). In defense of Hume and the causal theory of taste. *The Journal of Aesthetics and Art Criticism*, *55*(3), 312–317.

Murray, D. (2020). Maggots are delicious, sunsets hideous. False, or do you just disagree? Data on truth relativism about judgments of personal taste and aesthetics. In T. Lombrozo, J. Knobe, & S. Nichols (Eds.), *Oxford studies in experimental philosophy* (Vol. 3, pp. 64–96). Oxford University Press.

Nichols, S., & Folds-Bennett, T. (2003). Are children moral objectivists? Children's judgments about moral and response-dependent properties. *Cognition*, *90*(2), B23–B32.

Pearson, H. (2013). A judge-free semantics of predicates of personal taste. *Journal of Semantics*, *30*(1), 103–154.

Perullo, N. (2016). *Taste as experience*. Columbia University Press.

Plakias, A. (2021). The aesthetics of food. *Philosophy Compass*, *16*(11), https://doi.org/10.1111/phc3.12781

Rabb, N., Han, A., Nebeker, L., & Winner, E. (2020). Expressivist to the core: Metaesthetic subjectivism is stable and robust. *New Ideas in Psychology*, *57*, Article 100760.

Richard, M. (2008). *When truth gives out*. Oxford University Press.

Rudin, D. & Kaiser, E. (2022). Connoisseurial contradictions: expertise modulates faultless disagreement. In N. Dreier, C. Kwon, T. Darnell, & J. Starr (Eds.), *Proceedings of SALT 31*. Linguistic Society of America. https://doi.org/10.3765/salt.v31i0.5099.

Sæbø, K. (2009). Judgment ascriptions. *Linguistics and Philosophy*, *32*(4), 327–352.

Sarkissian, H., Park, J., Tien, D., Wright, J., & Knobe, J. (2011). Folk moral relativism. *Mind and Language*, *26*(4), 482–505.

Schafer, K. (2011). Faultless disagreement and aesthetic realism. *Philosophy and Phenomenological Research*, *82*(2), 265–286.

Schaffer, J. (2011). Perspective in taste predicates and epistemic modals. In A. Egan & B. Weatherson (Eds.), *Epistemic modality* (pp. 179–226). Oxford University Press.

Schaper, E. (1966). About taste. *The British Journal of Aesthetics*, *6*(1), 55–67.

Schellekens, E. (2004). Review of *Aesthetics and Subjectivity: From Kant to Nietzsche*, 2nd ed. *British Journal of Aesthetics*, *44*(3), 304–307.

Schellekens, E. (2006). Towards a reasonable objectivism for aesthetic judgements. *British Journal of Aesthetics*, *46*(2), 163–177.

Schellekens, E. (2009). Taste and objectivity: The emergence of the concept of the aesthetic. *Philosophy Compass*, *4*(5), 734–43.

Schellekens, E. (2012). Explanatory dualism in empirical aesthetics: A new reading. *Journal of Consciousness Studies*, *19*(9–10), 200–219.

Schellekens, E. (2019). Psychologizing aesthetic attention. *Estetika: The Central European Journal of Aesthetics*, *56*(1), 110–117.

Schellekens, E., & Goldie, P. (Eds.). (2011). *The aesthetic mind: Philosophy and psychology*. Oxford University Press.

Shiner, R. (1996). Hume and the causal theory of taste. *The Journal of Aesthetics and Art Criticism*, *54*(3), 237–249.

16 *Jeremy Wyatt, Julia Zakkou, and Dan Zeman*

Shiner, R. (1997). Causes and tastes: A response. *The Journal of Aesthetics and Art Criticism, 55*(3), 320–324.

Sibley, F. (2001). *Approach to aesthetics: Collected papers on philosophical aesthetics* (J. Benson, B. Redfern, & J. Cox, Eds.). Oxford University Press.

Silk, A. (2016). *Discourse contextualism: A framework for contextualist semantics and pragmatics.* Oxford University Press.

Smith, B. (Ed.). (2007). *Questions of taste: The philosophy of wine.* Signal Books Limited.

Smith, B. (2013). Taste, philosophical perspectives. In H. Pashler (Ed.), *Encyclopedia of the mind: Volume two* (pp. 731–735). SAGE Publications.

Solt, S. (2016). Ordering subjectivity and the absolute/relative distinction. In N. Bade, P. Berezovskaya, & A. Schöller (Eds.), *Proceedings of Sinn und Bedeutung 20* (pp. 676–693).

Solt, S. (2018). Multidimensionality, subjectivity and scales: Experimental evidence. In E. Castroviejo, L. McNally, & G. Sassoon (Eds.), *The semantics of gradability, vagueness, and scale structure: Experimental perspectives* (pp. 59–92). Springer.

Stephenson, T. (2007). Judge dependence, epistemic modals, and predicates of personal taste. *Linguistics and Philosophy, 30*(4), 487–525.

Stojanovic, I. (2007). Talking about taste: Disagreement, implicit arguments, and relative truth. *Linguistics and Philosophy, 30*(6), 691–706.

Stojanovic, I. (2019a). An empirical approach to aesthetic adjectives. In F. Cova & S. Réhault (Eds.), *Advances in experimental philosophy of aesthetics* (pp. 221–240). Bloomsbury.

Stojanovic, I. (2019b). Disagreements about taste vs. disagreements about moral issues. *American Philosophical Quarterly, 56*(1), 29–42.

Stokes, D. (2009). Aesthetics and cognitive science. *Philosophy Compass, 4*(5), 715–733.

Sundell, T. (2011). Disagreements about taste. *Philosophical Studies, 155*(2), 267–288.

Sweeney, K. (2018). *The aesthetics of food: The philosophical debate about what we eat and drink.* Rowman and Littlefield.

Wieand, J. (1984). Hume's two standards of taste. *The Philosophical Quarterly, 34*(135), 129–142.

Wiggins, D. (2002). *Needs, values, truth: Essays in the philosophy of value* (3rd ed.). Oxford University Press.

Wright, C. (2006). Intuitionism, realism, relativism, and rhubarb. In P. Greenough & M. Lynch (Eds.), *Truth and realism* (pp. 38–60). Oxford University Press.

Wright, C. (2008). Relativism about truth itself: Haphazard thoughts about the very idea. In M. García-Carpintero & M. Kölbel (Eds.), *Relative truth* (pp. 157–186). Oxford University Press.

Wyatt, J. (2018). Absolutely tasty: An examination of predicates of personal taste and faultless disagreement. *Inquiry, 61*(3), 252–280.

Wyatt, J. (2021). The nature of disagreement: Matters of taste and environs. *Synthese,* https://doi.org/10.1007/s11229-021-03266-6

Zakkou, J. (2019). *Faultless disagreement: A defense of contextualism in the realm of personal taste.* Klostermann.

Zemach, E. (1997). *Real beauty.* Penn State University Press.

Zeman, D. (2020). Minimal disagreement. *Philosophia, 48*(4), 1649–1670.

Part I
Aesthetics

2 The Trajectory of Gustatory Taste

Kevin Sweeney

Gustatory experience, sensing the flavors and other qualities of what one is eating and drinking, often exhibits a vividness that captivates and focuses one's attention on what appears to be taking place in one's mouth and on one's palate. Nevertheless, even though one can acknowledge the forthright presentation of such experience, recent scientific research has proposed that gustatory sensing and focusing on one's mouth and palate are based on an illusion as to their origin. Yet one still commonly seems convinced that these qualities are experienced as being in one's mouth. True, there are qualities such as sweet, sour, salty, bitter, and the more recently discovered *umami* (sometimes referred to as "savory") that are sensed by taste receptors in one's mouth. However, most of the flavors that one believes to be in one's mouth and on one's palate are produced by olfactory sensing. A commonplace estimate is that 80% of what we sense as gustatory flavors are sensed by smell.[1] Specifically, when one breathes out through one's nose, vaporized molecules produced by ingesting or chewing what one has consumed are drawn and travel up through the nasopharynx at the back of the throat into the top of one's nasal passages, where they stimulate the olfactory epithelium and the olfactory bulb.

In light of this illusion, the project of this chapter is two-fold. First, an exploration of what gave rise to the recognition of this gustatory illusion, sometimes referred to as an "illusion of mislocation."[2] This will involve examining how classical theories of taste were replaced by positing the interdependence of taste and smell. In turn, this led to a recognition of the physiological trajectory involved in coming to sense and experience what we have ingested and consumed. Second, a critical examination of several attempts to short-circuit this trajectorial process and propose that there is a more limited way in which we sense what we have ingested. This abbreviated approach has led to a misunderstanding of the role that the trajectory of ingesting plays in gustatory experience. It has inhibited exploring and understanding some current concerns about what we taste, such as the nature of the qualitative character of a wine's *terroir*.

DOI: 10.4324/9781003184225-3

20 *Kevin Sweeney*

1. Taste and the Senses

As most commonly used, the word "taste" denotes one of the five basic modalities of sensory experience, along with sight, hearing, smell, and touch. With this sensory meaning, taste refers to the ability to register and experience gustatory qualities. A classical commonplace established in Western antiquity was that each of the five senses could be respectively distinguished and differentiated from the other senses by providing access to an exclusive set of qualities.[3] For example, sight exclusively provided access to qualities of light and color; smell provided access to qualities of scent and odor.[4]

Nevertheless, the five senses were divided into two separate groups. One group, sight and hearing, came to be called the "distal" senses because they provided qualitative experiences that were taken to refer to objects and events out in the world. Even though they were prone to illusion, the distal senses could be used to form the basis of knowledge about the world. The second group, consisting of taste, smell, and touch, was called the "proximate" senses because they registered qualities that were taken to be centered in or on the body (e.g., smells were registered as being in one's nose; tastes were registered as being in one's mouth). They were held to have a subjective character, unique to a single individual, which made them an inappropriate basis for deriving general knowledge. They also tended to exhibit a hedonic aspect, more so than qualities produced by the distal senses. For example, smells or odors were held to be pleasant or objectionable to some people but not so to others. Tastes provided qualities that were enjoyable or objectionable to some people but not to others.

The distinction between the distal and proximate senses was argued for by Socrates in Plato's *Phaedo*. When critically examined by Reason, the distal senses could provide some basis for knowledge of the world; however, the proximate senses were held to be inferior because they were concerned with the needs and subjective pleasures of the body (e.g., the pleasures of taste promoted bodily nutrition). They were not compatible with the intellectual pursuit of knowledge.[5] While this classical view continued to find supporters in later times, it was susceptible to several challenges. For example, the distal senses of sight and hearing were not always independent and exclusive. Both of those senses could provide an estimation of distance, how close or far away objects or events were. Rather than providing an independent and exclusive set of qualities, it seemed more appropriate to think of them as collaborative in their efforts to know and understand the world. This collaboration was further supported when one considered that the sense of touch, rather than solely exhibiting a proximate subjectivity of pleasing or objectionable feelings, could also support the distal sensing of distance, at least to the extent of how close an object was.

2. Taste in the Eighteenth Century

In eighteenth-century studies of the appreciation of the arts and nature, "taste" was the major term for making the judgment that something was or wasn't beautiful. This critical taste was held to be metaphorically based on the gustatory sense due to their both having a central hedonic nature. Sensing something to be beautiful was pleasing. David Hume observed the "great resemblance between mental and bodily taste . . . [the former taste being a] metaphorical [version of the latter]."[6] In the late eighteenth century, the most famous philosopher who supported the idea that taste was subjective and hedonic in nature was Immanuel Kant. In his *Critique of Judgment* (1987), Kant proposed that all judgments of taste, both bodily and critical taste, were subjective. He says that a judgment of taste and the accompanying hedonic feeling "is not a cognitive judgment and so is not a logical judgment but an aesthetic one, by which we mean a judgment whose determining basis *cannot be other* than *subjective*."[7] For Kant, there are no rules or principles that could prove or support a judgment of taste. Taste is based on an individual's own experience. He offers the following explanation of why judging something to be beautiful should be called an exercise in taste in this aesthetic or subjective way:

> It seems that this is one of the main reasons why this aesthetic power of judging was given that very name: taste. For even if someone one lists all the ingredients of a dish, pointing out that I have always found each of them agreeable, and goes on to praise this food—and rightly so—as wholesome, I shall be deaf to these reasons: I shall try the dish on *my* tongue and palate, and thereby (and not by universal principles) make my judgment.[8]

Kant referred to bodily taste, sensing the gustatory qualities of what one had orally ingested, as being the *taste of sense*; however, he referred to critical taste, the exercise of judging something to be beautiful, as being the *taste of reflection*.[9]

He differentiated the two tastes in the following way. In the case of the former sense, the sensory effect was an immediate and rather passive response to a gustatory stimulus. The exercise of this *taste of sense* produced a hedonic effect, either being pleasurable—what Kant called *agreeable*—or disliked and objectionable. The taste of sense merely showed an individual preference. Kant claimed that it "would be foolish if we disputed about such differences with the intention of censuring another's judgment as incorrect if it differs from ours."[10] On Kant's view, the object of an individual's agreeable preference could lay no claim to being beautiful.

However, the *taste of reflection* offered some basis for judging something to be beautiful. With this latter taste, there was no immediate

22 *Kevin Sweeney*

response that indicated something's being beautiful. Kant here parted company with Voltaire, who, in the middle eighteenth century, offered the following account of taste:

> *Taste*, then, in general is a quick discernment, a sudden perception, which, like the sensation of the palate, anticipates reflection; like the palate, it relishes what is good with an exquisite and voluptuous sensibility, and rejects the contrary with loathing and disgust. . . . [There must be] a quick and comprehensive discernment of the various qualities, in their several relations and connections, which enter into the composition of the object we contemplate.[11]

Instead, for Kant, the taste of reflection requires not a pleasurable "quick discernment" but an active engagement with the pleasure following some time later. The pleasure comes from enjoying a sustained contemplative activity with an object, one in which we bring to bear our imagination and cognitive powers of understanding. The harmonious integration of these mental faculties in the reflection, Kant claims, we find to be pleasurable. Finding something to be beautiful is not a case of cognitively identifying and merely knowing what the object is. That might be a very quick identification. Instead, the object under reflective consideration is enjoyed because of its indeterminate nature, at least in the case of what Kant calls "free beauty," which engages what he calls a *free play* of the imagination with the form of the object. This imaginative free play is stimulated because of the indeterminate character of the object; yet it still has what Kant calls a purposiveness without having a particular purpose or conceptual identity.[12]

Kant offers an example of how one might engage one's imaginative free play with the form of an object. He points out:

> Flowers are free natural beauties. Hardly anyone apart from the botanist knows what sort of thing a flower is [meant] to be; and even he, while recognizing it as the reproductive organ of a plant, pays no attention to this natural purpose when he judges the flower by taste. Hence the judgment is based on no perfection of any kind, no intrinsic purposiveness.[13]

Kant is claiming that no specific determinate concept (in his example, being a plant's reproductive organ) is the basis for one's finding a particular rose to be beautiful. Rather, he believes that one's imaginative play with the organization of its parts and petals and the pleasure that reflective engagement affords one is a basis for finding it beautiful.

One might suppose that Kant might allow the possibility of having an active and engaged experience with a complex dish that one was ingesting and savoring. However, he resists such an allowance for three reasons.

The first is the aforementioned view that one's reaction to food and drink is immediate and a hedonic preference, not the kind of experience that lends itself to an imaginative and extensive reflection that later is pleasurable. Second, Kant believes that judgments of beauty are not offered as individual preferences as would be the case with food and drink but instead lay claim to universal assent. He insists that if someone "proclaims something to be beautiful, then he requires the same liking from others; he then judges not just for himself but for everyone."[14] Kant believes that reflection that employs an active free play of one's imagination that is in harmony with one's cognitive powers of understanding would be similar for all human beings. He believes that we all have the same mental faculties for trying to understand the world, and he refers to this similar way of human beings cognitively understanding the world as their having a *common sense.*[15]

Finally, Kant believes that objects of gustatory experience cannot be beautiful because they do not adhere to a basic requirement that must be met by our experience with all beautiful things. Following in the eighteenth-century tradition, Kant believes that one must take a "disinterested" attitude toward all things held to be beautiful.[16] One must take pleasure only in the "presentation" or appearance of the object under consideration. If one's pleasure comes from an interest in something's existence (e.g., if the pleasure comes from the pride in owning the object), then it is not a disinterested pleasure. In the case of gustatory experience, Kant thinks that the pleasure we take in savoring the food we eat is based on our desire to satisfy our hunger. We are interested in consuming the food or the pleasure we would receive if we were to consume the food, not a pleasure just in its appearance.

Nevertheless, Kant does allow that if one were sated from having eaten one's fill, one might have a more disinterested appreciation of the food, since one would lose one's desire for the existence of the food. However, it is difficult to see how such a condition would make the food enjoyable. One would likely lose interest in a dish's nuances and flavors, interests that would be aroused if one were to approach prepared food and drink with a good appetite. Besides, Kant only seems to recognize that one's sensory taste in food and drink reflects an individual's preference rather than providing common ground for a universal assent to its being pleasurable.[17]

For Kant, food—especially fine cuisine—seems to provide only what would amount to a rather simple sensory experience. He does not seem to recognize the complexity of savoring fine cuisine. All sorts of culinary ingredients as found in the recipes of different cultures provide a vast array not only of flavors but also of other kinds of gustatory qualities that are perceived when we sense and encounter what we consume. However, the complexity of enjoying fine dining was about to be more fully recognized in the early nineteenth century.

24 *Kevin Sweeney*

3. Taste and Smell in the Nineteenth Century

Theorizing about taste began to change in the nineteenth century. Voltaire, as noted earlier, and Hume had both claimed that those possessing a high degree of critical—what Hume called "mental"—taste had to be able immediately to sense positive or negative features exhibited by an object. While he allowed for reflection in making critical judgments, Hume insisted that mental taste required "a quick and acute perception of beauty and deformity [and] must be the perfection of our mental taste."[18] By distinguishing the taste of sense from the taste of reflection, Kant had encouraged the uncoupling of one of the bases for the claim that there was a metaphorical connection between literal and critical taste, i.e., that both registered an immediate effect. As a result, critical immediacy began to lose prominence.

Another change that occurred was in the meaning of Kant's notion of the *aesthetic*.[19] Kant had used the term only to indicate that the experience of taste must be based on a person's own experience and that there were no general rules that could support judgments of taste. However, "*aesthetic*" gradually became a broad term for various aspects of critical appreciation, and taste subsumed a lesser role.

Nevertheless, although overthrown as the major critical category, *taste* at the same time emerged as a central concern of a new cultural inquiry, as the focus of a developing interest into the nature and values of cuisine or fine dining. A new term became popular, *gastronomy*, apparently coined by the poet Joseph Berchoux in 1801, and it quickly caught on as a culinary concept, generating a ballooning literary and cultural fascination with "the art and science of delicate eating."[20] With the nineteenth century's developing interest in gastronomy, theorists were soon looking for some underlying principles of gustatory experience that would support a genuine critical interest in cuisine. Two of the more famous theorists of that time were Alexandre Grimod de La Reynière (1758–1837) and Jean-Anthelme Brillat-Savarin (1755–1826), both of whom challenged the idea that cuisine was unworthy of critical appreciation. Their highly influential and popular writings prepared the way for what we would now hold to be *gustatory aesthetics*. Grimod de La Reynière introduced a *Tasting Jury* (*Jury Dégusteur*) composed of fellow gourmands whose role was to evaluate and judge the quality of Parisian culinary fare.[21]

4. Olfaction in Brillat-Savarin's Theory of Taste

In his ground-breaking work, *Physiologie Du Goût, ou Méditations De Gastronomie Transcendante* (1826), translated as *The Physiology of Taste, or Meditations on Transcendental Gastronomy*, Jean-Anthelme Brillat-Savarin proposed a model for appreciative gustatory experience that directly opposed the Kantian perspective on food and drink.[22]

The Trajectory of Gustatory Taste   25

Although he never specifically refers to or criticizes Kant in his discussion of gastronomy, he does use some of Kant's terminology when he discusses cuisine as an object of reflective pleasure, and his characterization of taste challenges Kant's distinction between the *taste of sense* and the *taste of reflection*.[23] In addition, as indicated in the subtitle of his book, *Meditations on Transcendental Gastronomy*, Brillat-Savarin presents his views on the gustatory pleasures of food and drink as a *transcendental* gastronomy, offering grounds that would serve as support for evaluative judgments of gustatory experience. (Brillat-Savarin's use of the term "transcendental" in the subtitle of his book is more than likely a reference to Kant, who popularized the term "transcendental.")

In his account, Brillat-Savarin proposes that gustatory experience is composed of both qualities that we taste and qualities that we smell. He urges that what we taste and smell both contribute to forming an object of a reflective gustatory hedonic experience. In addition, the term "physiology" in his book's title challenges Kant's view that an individual's gustatory pleasures are personal preferences and do not reflect a "common sense" that serves as a basis for critical evaluation. Instead, Brillat-Savarin insists that our distinctive physiology of how we smell and taste when ingesting and swallowing serves as the basis for our common appreciative experience of food and drink and its critical evaluation. He points out that the physiology of alimentation that all humans naturally have with its distinctive temporal sequence allows for a reflective experience rather than producing just an immediate response to a stimulus.

For Brillat-Savarin, tasting food, particularly fine food, can often lead to a complex and reflective experience. We frequently engage with a great variety of gustatory qualities, often coming upon new and different elements, in the successive stages of our ingesting encounter. We are able to sense this great variety of elements, as Brillat-Savarin recognized, because we engage with them not only by tasting them in our mouth but also by registering them with our sense of smell. In fact, Brillat-Savarin thought that taste and smell worked together to create qualities that in the now-common scientific parlance are referred to as "flavors."[24] He proclaimed that "I am not only convinced that there is no full act of tasting without the participation of the sense of smell, but I am also tempted to believe that smell and taste form a single sense."[25] Instead of thinking of taste as being a limited sense in keeping with the traditional view that a sense only registers an exclusive set of qualities that are differentiated from qualities sensed by the other four senses, Brillat-Savarin thinks of taste and smell as jointly forming a single complex sensory faculty. Because of the greatly expanded number of sensory inputs from both taste and smell, Brillat-Savarin proposed that the "number of tastes is infinite."[26]

Brillat-Savarin supports his belief that gustatory experience includes olfactory qualities by appealing to a common experience that many people would recognize. He calls on his readers to remember that when

26   *Kevin Sweeney*

their nasal passages were blocked because of congestion due to a head cold, their ability to taste was severely restricted. He also notices that when one holds one's nose closed so that one cannot breathe out through one's nose, one loses one's ability to taste as one could when one exhaled through one's nose.[27]

Contemporary scientific research supports Brillat-Savarin's claim about the integral nature of taste and smell and their contribution to the synesthetic experience of flavor. In fact a common scientific view is that around 80% of what one claims to taste in one's mouth is actually produced by one's sense of smell. True, there are simple tastes one senses without benefit of olfactory engagement such as sweet, sour, bitter, salty, and most recently, *umami*. Brillat-Savarin identifies several simple tastes: sweet, sour, and bitter, and, invoking the Kantian labels, he claims that such simple tastes provide us with hedonic experiences that are either "*agreeable* or *disagreeable*."[28] However, the majority of our gustatory experiences, he believes, involve a much broader range of flavors, ample resources for a complex aesthetic encounter.

Whereas Kant had characterized an instance of literal taste as producing a momentary hedonic reaction, Brillat-Savarin—to show that gustatory experience can allow for a reflective encounter—divides the temporal sequence of ingestion into three main stages. He claims that each stage, from the initial taste to final impressions after swallowing, features a particular set of sensory qualities. He refers to them respectively as *direct*, *complete*, and *reflective* sensory experiences. He describes his tripartite-stage process of appreciative ingesting with the following example of eating a peach:

> The *direct* sensation is the first one felt, produced from the immediate operations of the organs of the mouth, while the body under consideration is still on the forepart of the tongue.
>
> The *complete* sensation is the one made up of this first perception plus the impression which arises when the food leaves its original position, passes to the back of the mouth, and attacks the whole organ with its taste and its aroma.
>
> Finally, the *reflective* sensation is the opinion which one's spirit forms from the impressions which have been transmitted to it by the mouth.
>
> Let us put this theory into action, by seeing what happens to a man who is eating or drinking.
>
> He who eats a peach, for instance, is first of all agreeably struck by the perfume which it exhales; he puts a piece of it into his mouth, and enjoys a sensation of tart freshness which invites him to continue; but it is not until the instant of swallowing, when the mouthful passes under his nasal channel, that the full aroma is revealed to him; and this completes the sensation which the peach can cause. Finally, it is not until it has been swallowed that the man, considering what he

has just experienced, will say to himself, "Now there is something really delicious!"[29]

Brillat-Savarin also offers the following example about tasting a wine to illustrate his model of gustatory experience as being able to promote a reflective assessment of the wine:

> In the same way, in drinking, while the wine is in the mouth, one is agreeably but not completely appreciative of it; it is not until the moment when he has finished swallowing it that a man can truly taste, consider, and discover the bouquet peculiar to each variety; and there must still be a little lapse of time before a real connoisseur can say, "It is good, or passable, or bad."[30]

It is worth noting that this extended process of ingesting is developmental; it does not provide an immediate sensory response. Instead, the succession of gustatory stages provides a general temporal structure to what one tastes. After experiencing the aroma of the peach, one then tastes in the initial stage the sweet acidity of the fruit on one's palate. The process continues into a middle range of flavors that include further olfactory qualities. Finally, one swallows and enters the last third of the experience, the reflective phase, where a set of aftertastes provides both a final tonal development to the tasting of the peach and the opportunity for a reflective assessment of the structure and character of the whole experience.

Yet there might still be some doubts about whether such an experience is actually imaginative, as opposed to merely registering the sum of the sensations or conceptually fitting them into a particular determinate form (e.g., the taste of a peach). When we taste, how *actively* and *imaginatively* engaged are we? For Brillat-Savarin, such a successive experience is not merely a compounding of *direct* sensory details. The initial tastes, Brillat-Savarin's *direct* sensations such as sweet, sour, and bitter, might produce a temporally limited effect, but the full experience, in its successive developmental unfolding, encourages an extended period of inquisitive consideration. It is an occasion for contemplative reflection, an exercise of one's imagination, requiring one to compare the beginning, middle, and end of one's experience. One might even have to retaste what one has ingested to evaluate it more fully or to reassess an earlier evaluation. Such a reencountering involves an active engagement with one's imagination. The following section explores in more detail the imaginative nature of a gustatory encounter with a dish.

5. Brillat-Savarin's Physiology of Alimentation

In an extended reflective experience such as Brillat-Savarin is proposing for the process of alimentation, one imaginatively invests in the overall structure, shape, and character of what one tastes. One's experience is not just a sum of sensed qualities. We recall and imaginatively compare the flavors encountered, note complementary and contrasting qualities, and come to realize how these qualities form unities and other regional structures. One can even sense new stylistic and expressive features in tasting variations in popular dishes or in coming to savor a chef's creative efforts that highlight new emerging nuances.

Suppose a French chef from Marseille prepares the classic Mediterranean seafood dish bouillabaisse. The dish is a traditional fish stew that originated using local seafood, as well as being cooked with Provençal vegetables and seasonings. It was intended to be shared by several diners. It has since become very popular all over the world with many different variations in how it is prepared. Many contemporary recipes still try to maintain a connection to the traditional elements and roots of the original dish. It is not uncommon for a cook to start by simmering chopped onions, fennel, tomatoes, and garlic together with seasonings such as saffron, bay leaf, thyme, and the zest of some orange peel. Some fish or shellfish broth is then added to the simmering vegetables. Shellfish such as mussels, clams, and shrimp are added before putting in several different kinds of very fresh firm white fish. The tradition was to buy the seafood that day from the local fish market and to use monkfish and the local rare red scorpionfish (*rascasse*) that was only to be found in the waters around Marseille.

To serve the dish, a piece of grilled French bread was placed in the bottom of a soup bowl, and the bread was slathered with an emulsified paste of olive oil, garlic, and red pepper (called *rouille*). Some vegetables and broth were added to the bowl; however, a controversy developed about whether a portion of the fish and shellfish should be added to an individual diner's bowl or should be placed on a platter to be shared with other diners and eaten along with the broth, vegetables, and *rouille*.

The vegetable broth with the bread and *rouille* produce complex aromas that enliven our senses. As we take our first tastes, we note how the garlic and the heat of the cayenne pepper in the *rouille* combine and contrast with the tomatoes, fennel, and other vegetables as well as with the saffron, herbs, and other seasoning. Now as we further ingest, the different flavors of the seafood combine with the vegetable base. On swallowing, we note the way the spicy heat of the cayenne pepper lingers, and we are left with the rich and evolving flavors of the dish. There's a lot to taste and imaginatively reflect on in such a dish. Together, these flavors express some of the distinctive features of the seafood traditions of Marseille and Provençal cuisine. We are sensitive to the way the chef expressively shapes the dish, perhaps emphasizing qualities of the particular ingredients, their seasonal character, and the choice of seafood. All of these expressive and stylistic features are not simply identified; they imaginatively infuse the whole tasting experience.

The Trajectory of Gustatory Taste   29

In summary, Brillat-Savarin is proposing something like a reflective aesthetic in his account of appreciative tasting. It is a gustatory reworking of a Kantian experience of imaginative reflection. As human beings, we share a "physiology" that gives us a common form of alimentation, a trajectory of how we ingest and swallow our food and drink. Savoring and relishing, over and above direct stimulation, is not a simple reflexive act. We have to pay attention to what we are consuming. The ordered sequence of a gustatory encounter supports such a view, and it requires our imaginative attention. Of course, a skeptical critic of gustatory aesthetics might object that a shared physiology and an extended structure of imaginative experience will not overcome the problem of the subjectivity of individual preference. However, the quirkiness of preference is not a characteristic unique to taste. Individuals express their different preferences in a wide variety of other forms. We exhibit individual preferences towards objects encountered with each of our sensory modalities. Yet Brillat-Savarin has done a great deal to counter the view that culinary creations simply provoke a simple hedonic response. His account of taste demands that we think of the relishing experience produced by cuisine as affording a complex, evolving encounter worthy of imaginative involvement and reflective enjoyment.

Moreover, while it is certainly true that individuals have their personal preferences for what they like to eat and drink, there are social and cultural influences that mitigate gustatory idiosyncrasy and encourage more common forms of culinary preferences. A child's quirky tastes and preferences often change as the child matures. When young, there might be a preference for sweet things and a distaste for bitter vegetables like broccoli or spinach. When older, that same individual might come to like more bitter things, as happens when adults develop a liking for coffee and beer. In addition, a family's cooking style based on a mother's or grandmother's favorite recipes can influence children's tastes as they grow older. Broader social and cultural influences such as the traditional diet of a country or region also have their effect on creating some uniformity in people's food preferences. In virtue of these influences, an individual's preferences often change into a broader collective set of preferences reflective of that individual's cultural and national heritage.[31]

6.   Critical Reflections on Brillat-Savarin's Theory

Brillat-Savarin was certainly an innovative thinker for both championing the important role played by olfaction in gustatory experience and emphasizing the common human physiology and trajectory of alimentation; however, it is important to point out some of the limitations of his theory. First, while Brillat-Savarin acknowledges that olfaction makes a significant contribution to gustatory experience and that it combines with basic tastes, he only provides a sketch of the process. To be sure, it will be only in the next century that scientific research would discover and clarify how this process takes place. So, he does not mention that there are particular olfactory receptors in the roof of one's nasal passages—receptors that are now identified as the olfactory epithelium and the olfactory bulb—that respond to retronasally induced stimulation and initiate the process of affecting the brain and causing an olfactory sensory response.

Second, he also does not discuss how orthonasal sensing, which occurs when someone breathes in through their nostrils, and retronasal sensing, which occurs when someone has ingested food or drink and then breathes out through their nose, affect the same nasal olfactory receptors. Even so, the person senses the retronasally induced olfactory quality as a flavor in the mouth and not in the nose.[32] For example, vanilla is thought by most people to be a gustatory quality that is "tasted" in one's mouth. However, it is a quality that is not sensed by the taste receptors in one's mouth; instead, it is sensed retronasally by the olfactory receptors in one's nose. As a result, Brillat-Savarin offers no discussion of what contemporary science calls the "illusion of mislocation," where the origin of the flavor is produced retronasally but in an illusory way is felt as occurring on one's palate.

Third, Brillat-Savarin sketches the way that someone's gustatory experience proceeds through three stages in the trajectory of alimentation. However, some of what he describes as occurring in the first stage might give the impression that there are particular taste receptors in the forefront of one's mouth or on one's tongue that are dedicated to registering just one of the basic tastes. For example, it might seem that receptors in the taste buds on the forefront of one's tongue were dedicated to sensing sweet tastes and that one could only sense sweet tastes in that area of the tongue. Other taste buds in other parts of one's mouth would be dedicated to registering each of the other basic tastes.

Such a theory was developed and proposed at the beginning of the twentieth century and was popularly referred to as the *taste map* theory. The theory is now discredited, as there is ample evidence that receptors in the taste buds on one's tongue and throughout one's palate are sensitive to all of the basic tastes. For example, one can taste the sweetness of honey at the tip of one's tongue, but that taste also carries through into other areas of one's palate. Likewise, the bitterness of aspirin can be tasted on the tip of one's tongue, but that taste can also carry through to the back of one's palate.[33]

It should be pointed out that although Brillat-Savarin offers a developmental account of the gustatory trajectory, not all of the initial *direct* tastes are as distinct and specifically located as he suggests. For example, bitterness might seem an acceptable mild taste on the forefront of one's tongue but in some cases strike one as harsh and produce a gag reflex at the back of one's mouth. Marian Baldy explains:

The Trajectory of Gustatory Taste   31

Although taste receptor cells may not strictly specialize in receiving just one stimulus, the neural processing of taste stimuli from different parts of the tongue can be quite different, so our brains receive stronger information about specific tastes from different parts of the tongue. We know the most about the bitter taste mechanism in this regard: although the perception threshold for bitterness is actually lower in receptor cells on the tip of the tongue—making those cells sensitive to bitterness at lower concentrations—other receptor cells at the back of the tongue get more excited than tip-of-the-tongue receptors do by high levels of bitter stimuli and send more nerve impulses about that bitterness to the brain.[34]

As a consequence, there is sometimes more of a gustatory temporal evolution, even within the initial *direct* stage of the process, than Brillat-Savarin suggests.

7.   Contemporary Responses to the Gustatory Trajectory

Although the belief in the temporal trajectory of alimentation is now generally accepted, as is the multisensory nature of gustatory experience, there are still some fairly common practices in which some people engage that are believed to short-circuit the trajectory and diminish the third stage of the process. Professional wine tasters, when tasting and evaluating an extensive flight of wines, will often, after first sipping a wine, regularly spit out the rest and try not to swallow all of it. The reason for doing so is to limit the amount of alcohol that is swallowed so as to be more objective when tasting wines at the end of the flight. Some people, when tasting a wine at a winery or when they might be interested in evaluating several wines, have also adopted this practice. There seems to be a commonplace belief that when spitting out the mouthful before swallowing the wine, not only is one reducing the intake of alcohol, but the taster has diminished if not eliminated the third stage of the traditional trajectory. Instead, the taster will be evaluating the wine on the basis of the first two stages of the process.

While the belief in spitting some ingested wine in order to reduce the intake of alcohol has merit, there is a misconception that ordinarily, if one spits out the wine before swallowing, one has short-circuited the third stage of the trajectory. Now, if one senses or believes that what one has ingested is vile or poisonous, one can certainly expectorate what is in one's mouth in order to try to prevent swallowing it, but one will have to do this repeatedly. It will take many attempts to be effective. When eating and drinking, swallowing is a naturally induced biological reflex. If one makes a concerted effort not to swallow what has been ingested, one can resist this reflex, but only for a limited time. When one relaxes, one naturally starts to swallow. This is especially true if one's gastric juices have been stimulated in anticipation of eating something. With a buildup of saliva in one's mouth, swallowing naturally occurs. Swallowing is similar in certain respects to the natural process of blinking one's eyes. Of course, one can resist blinking, but only for a limited time. When one relaxes, one naturally blinks.

As a natural part of the trajectory of alimentation, usually, one need not swallow all of the contents of one's mouthful in order to be able to make a reflective assessment of the earlier stages of the trajectory. In fact, if one spits out a mouthful of wine, one usually does end up swallowing at least a slight amount of what has remained in one's mouth, enough to enable one to reflect on what one had ingested. Not only does swallowing even a slight amount of wine allow one to reflect on and assess the tastes and flavors of what one has ingested, but it prepares one for the next sip of what one was drinking.

8.   The Integrity of the Trajectory

In order to show the integrity of the gustatory trajectory as an important feature of the alimentary process, it is helpful to compare our aesthetic acquaintance with what we eat or drink with aesthetic encounters we can have with genres and media sensed by other modalities. One of the differences between gustatory experience and the aesthetic attention paid to other media is that it is sometimes difficult to immediately access a particular taste or flavor without having to traverse several stages of the trajectory to arrive at sensing that quality. Some gustatory qualities are so embedded within the trajectory's temporal structure so as to prevent the taster from having immediate sensory access to them. For example, there is an Italian red wine, Amarone, that comes from wineries northeast of Verona. The name "Amarone" in Italian refers to a pleasant bitter quality that is a feature of this kind of wine when vinified in a traditional way. One senses this quality just before swallowing some of the wine. It is not sensed on first sipping the wine. Instead, one needs to taste through the preliminary stages of the trajectory before one can sense the bitter quality; one cannot go immediately to it.

With literature, a reader can open a familiar text and go immediately to a word or a phrase without having to read the work from the beginning. Even with a temporally structured work like a film, by using some contemporary advances in video technology, a viewer can very quickly access a particular shot or image. With other visual media such as painting, the viewer has easy access to an image. This is not to claim that the particular elements of these readily accessible works do not derive their aesthetic character by their contextual relationship with the other elements in the work. Of course they do, as does the aesthetic character of the qualities of fine wines and works of cuisine. The point is to emphasize the heightened importance of the integrity of the gustatory trajectory in our aesthetic acquaintance with what we eat and drink.

The Trajectory of Gustatory Taste   33

To be sure, there are occasions when we do have an immediate acquaintance with a gustatory quality on first taking a sip of wine. Some wines such as the French white wine Picpoul are vinified in a style that accentuates a bracing initial acidity. However, the most noticeable examples of wines that foreground direct access to a characteristic contain what are called "wine faults." For example, instances of the abrasive taste of volatile acidity (the vinegar-producing acid) or the cooked quality of excessive oxidation, or excessive "Brett" (*Brettanomyces*, a spoiled yeast quality with a barnyard taste) are usually immediately noticeable.[35]

However, what might be a fault in some wines can in other wines be claimed to have a beneficial emergent effect. For example, oxidation in some wines is held to be a fault, but some sherries have a pleasant oxidized quality that works well with those wines' other qualities. Similar claims can be made for Brett. In some wines, it is a noticeable fault, but in other wines such as Italian old-style Barolos, it adds some beneficial complexity. Nevertheless, in fine wines that have a temporally extended character and an evolving finish, the taster is unable to immediately sense that evolving character. Only by concentrating and reflecting on the ingested wine as it proceeds through the trajectory will the taster be likely to discern and appreciate the overall aesthetic character of the wine.

A contemporary interest in the integrity of a wine's gustatory trajectory is revealed in the debate about the existence and importance of what has been called the *terroir* of a particular wine. On one side, there are those who champion the distinctive location or site—what the influential wine writer Matt Kramer has called the "somewhereness" of a wine—that constitutes its terroir.[36] The claim is made that it is a wine's particular terroir that makes possible the collection of qualities that constitutes that wine's greatness. Although the French root of the word refers to the particular soil of the place in which the vines were grown, the concept of "terroir" has come to have a much broader connotation. It indicates a relationship that includes not only the soil that provides nutrients to the vines but the climate of that location and the particular varietal of the grapes grown there. Noted University of Burgundy wine authority Jacky Rigaux points out that terroir includes the "complex interactions between geology, climate, topography, 'stoniness,' drainage, slope, altitude, soil, subsoil, microbes, soil fauna, vines, grapes, yeasts, and indigenous bacteria."[37]

However, critics of the emphasis on terroir claim that it is not so much location that determines a wine's greatness as it is the skill of the winemaker and the choices that she or he makes in producing the wine. They argue that even if grapes have been grown in a region that has been claimed to have a distinctive terroir but poor winemaking techniques have been employed, one ends up with a mediocre or worse—a bad—wine.

Nevertheless, those who promote the importance of a wine's terroir point out that over time, certain grape-growing regions have been identified as being especially able to produce outstanding wines. To cite only a

34   *Kevin Sweeney*

few of many examples, one thinks about areas in Burgundy and around Bordeaux in France, areas around the Mosel and Rhine rivers in Germany, as well as areas around Alba in Italy's Piedmont as being capable of producing great wines. These areas' distinctive terroirs enable them to make great wines, provided that careful and knowledgeable winemaking procedures that are respectful of the region's distinctive character are followed. Matt Kramer points out that in Burgundy, a winemaker's greed expressed by over cropping his vines and ignoring low yields will lead to disregarding the vineyard's terroir. In addition, he insists that in Burgundy, a wine's greatness will depend upon the "selective sorting of the grapes; and trickiest of all, fermenting and cellaring the wine in such a way as to allow the *terroir* to come through with no distracting stylistic flourishes."[38] In keeping with Kramer's concern to respect the terroir of a particular area, which might in the case of Burgundy be rather small, there is another concern: the tendency in today's worldwide wine market to make wine in what has been called an "international style" and to ignore making wines in styles that accentuate a region's distinctive character.

In the 1980s, there arose a number of wine writers who reviewed and rated the current year's wines that were produced not only in the Old World but also in developing regions in the New World. These wines were given a numerical rating, and wines with a high rating (above 90 out of 100) tended to be high-alcohol wines, overloaded with extract, approachable when released, and produced in a homogenous style that appealed to a broad popular taste. Regional differences in the wines tended to be downplayed, as did those wines' traditional distinctive terroir. Wines made in this way came to be seen as exhibiting an "international style." Another reason for making wines in this new way was that in shipping wines all over the world, higher-alcohol wines tended to be more stable following long voyages than did lower-alcohol wines. Popular grape varietals such as Cabernet Sauvignon, Merlot, Syrah, and Chardonnay were seen as more saleable and came to replace local varietals that did not have an international following.

Thankfully, this nonregional trend has been somewhat reversed, and there is now a developing interest in more unusual grape varietals and wines made from these varietals that exhibit their regional character. At least in the Old World, there came to be a recognition that a wine's local character and its particular terroir could only be perceived and respected after generations of winemakers learned what grapes and winemaking techniques were most suitable for making wine in that region. Randall Grahm, a California winemaker and astute champion of recognizing the evolving nature of a region's terroir, has described the process in this way:

> Soils (and microclimates) have in some sense taught vines what they might expect over a growing season. Over many generations a sort of stately, rhythmic dance has emerged. The most interesting wines

The Trajectory of Gustatory Taste 35

that arise from this dance are the ones that have captured this distinctive rhythm or waveform, this unmistakable signature, which we call *terroir*.[39]

What Grahm calls a wine's "signature" of terroir is often what emerges as a subtle structural arrangement of qualities that can be detected only after many generations' experience with tasting that wine.

While there is no single paradigm of qualities that all terroirs exhibit, there are grape-growing and winemaking practices that can inhibit revealing a wine's terroir. As Matt Kramer cautions, over cropping of grapes and ignoring low yields will certainly tend to do so. Adhering to stylistic choices commonly found in the creation of wines made in the international style will also ignore what will be the subtle flavors and gustatory qualities that reveal terroir. Over-oaking a wine and excessively manipulating its vinification—what is often referred to as not letting the wine speak for itself—will have a similar negative effect on allowing the qualities of a wine's terroir to shine through.

9. Conclusion

Current thoughts on the trajectory of taste highlight the amazing progress in our understanding of gustatory experience. Early days of thinking about taste focused on there being four elementary gustatory qualities (sweet, sour, salty, and bitter) centered in the mouth. It was a simple theory that ignored the complexity of our alimentary experience. A fuller account of taste was not achieved by Kant's insistence that gustatory experience primarily involves individual preferences and an immediate hedonic reaction to what was being ingested.

Brillat-Savarin's theory revolutionized our understanding of taste by showing that taste is not confined to an oral reaction to what was ingested but also includes olfactory sensing. This considerably broadened our understanding of the range of flavors that are created through retronasal olfactory sensing. Brillat-Savarin proposed that there is an alimentary trajectory as we ingest and swallow what we consumed that allows us to be acquainted with these flavors. As opposed to Kant's claim that gustatory experience could not provide one with an extended and imaginative reflection on what one had eaten, Brillat-Savarin claimed that the alimentary trajectory offers us the means to reflect on and assess what we have consumed.

Contemporary science has accepted Brillat-Savarin's olfactory extension of gustatory taste and has shown how retronasal sensing allows the brain to create flavors. Yet in doing so, science has identified what to some seems like a counterintuitive illusion, that the effect of retronasal olfactory sensing is experienced as a flavor taking place in one's mouth on one's palate. The complexity of gustatory experience has led some to

36 *Kevin Sweeney*

adopt the view that the alimentary trajectory can be short-circuited—at least with wine drinking—by spitting out and not swallowing the wine one has ingested. However, such a view ignores the basic integrity of the alimentary trajectory. For many of our experiences with what we eat and drink, it is difficult to separate out individual qualities of what we have tasted. This integrity of the process is also revealed when considering the complex but subtle character of a gustatory experience like that of sensing a wine's terroir. Rather than a simple sensory effect, the taste of a wine's terroir depends on many sources as well as on having to contend with many winemaking practices that would obscure its discernment.

Notes

1. One sees many general references to the 80% figure in discussions of the contribution that olfaction makes to gustatory experience. Murphy et al. (1977) give credence to that figure with some actual research. For further discussion of the olfactory relationship to gustatory experience, see Shepherd (2012, pp. 74–76, 109–125).
2. See Auvray and Spence (2008, p. 1016).
3. A classical exception to this view that the senses were differentiated one from another was Aristotle's view that taste was a form of touch. He held that it is only when we touch with our tongue and palate what we have orally ingested that we can taste what we have consumed. Nevertheless, he held that the sensory modalities of touch and taste were not identical, because while we can only taste what we have orally ingested, we can touch other areas of our body. See Aristotle, *De Anima [On the Soul]*, 422a10–20, in Aristotle (2011, p. 68).
4. The word "taste" is sometimes used to refer to a preference for a certain style or genre of objects (i.e., one's taste in music or one's taste in clothing). Sometimes there is an implied qualitative assessment such as holding someone to have "good" taste in having such a preference.
5. Plato, *Phaedo* 65b-66b, in Plato (1985, pp. 1001–1003). For further discussion of the distal/proximate division of the senses, see Korsmeyer (1999, pp. 11–26).
6. Hume (1987, p. 235).
7. Kant (1987, p. 44).
8. Ibid., p. 148.
9. Ibid., pp. 57–60.
10. Ibid., p. 55.
11. Voltaire (1764, p. 210).
12. Kant (1987, pp. 61–64).
13. Ibid., p. 76.
14. Ibid., p. 55.
15. Ibid., pp. 87–90. For further analysis and discussion of Kant's ideas about human beings having a *common sense*, see Crawford (1974, pp. 125–131).
16. Kant (1987, pp. 45–54). The role of "disinterestedness" in the history of aesthetic appreciation is discussed in Stolnitz (1961, pp. 131–143). For analysis of Kant's views on disinterestedness, see Crawford (1974, pp. 37–54). For further discussion of Kant's concept of disinterestedness, see Guyer (1997, pp. 148–183).
17. Kant (1987, p. 52). For further discussion of Kant's views on the role of appetite in the appreciation of gustatory experience, see Sweeney (2012).

18. Hume (1987, p. 236). For further discussion of Hume, see Sweeney (2018, pp. 100–108).
19. Although the concept of the aesthetic had its roots in the ancient Greek word for sensory perception, the term got its start in critical theory through the work of the German philosopher Alexander Baumgarten (1714–1762). Baumgarten introduced the term in his *Reflections on Poetry* (1735) to signify a perspective that brought together a sensory, emotional, and imaginative way of responding to poetry. He later went on to develop his idea of the aesthetic in his two-volume work, *Aesthetica* (1750–1758). For commentary on and critical analysis of Baumgarten's notion of the aesthetic, see Guyer (2014, pp. 318–340) and Shiner (2001, p. 146).
20. Mennell (1996, p. 266). For an English translation of part of Berchoux's poem, see Gigante (2005, pp. 275–281).
21. In his yearly publication *Almanach des Gourmands* (1803–1812), Grimod de La Reynière was at the forefront of this culinary revolution; see MacDonogh (1987). For an English translation of some of the *Almanach* and the writings of other writers in this movement, see Gigante (2005, pp. 1–55). For a discussion of Brillat-Savarin's influence on gastronomy, see MacDonogh (1992) and Korsmeyer (1999, pp. 68–71).
22. Brillat-Savarin (1978).
23. Brillat-Savarin (1978, p. 22).
24. In ordinary discourse, the words "taste" and "flavor" are commonly used interchangeably, and in later parts of this chapter, the terms will sometimes be used synonymously, particularly when informally discussing food or when analyzing gustatory theories before the nineteenth century. However, contemporary science has insisted on an important distinction between taste and flavor. Strictly speaking, "taste" refers to those five basic tastes sensed by taste buds on the tongue and throughout the mouth and throat. "Flavor" refers to a gustatory experience that is commonly described and experienced as a taste but can be a multisensory experience with a major contribution from olfactory receptors at the top of the nasal cavity. Charles Spence and Betina Piqueras-Fiszman note that in 2008, the International Standards Organization defined flavor as a "Complex combination of the olfactory, gustatory and trigeminal sensations perceived during tasting. The flavor may be influenced by tactile, thermal, painful and/or kinaesthetic effects." Spence and Piqueras-Fiszman prefer an even broader multisensory account; see Spence and Piqueras-Fiszman (2014, pp. 183–184).
25. Brillat-Savarin (1978, p. 39).
26. Ibid., p. 38.
27. Ibid., pp. 38–40.
28. Ibid., p. 38. Recently, the hedonic character of taste that had been supported by Kant and much of earlier eighteenth-century critical theory has been challenged. Robert Hopkins, in a chapter on taste, while recognizing the traditional role of pleasure and displeasure in taste, also points out that there can be other reactions such as "shock or boredom, sorrow or nostalgia" (Hopkins, 2009, p. 554).
29. Brillat-Savarin (1978, p. 40).
30. Ibid., pp. 40–41.
31. For further discussion of some of the objective influences on gustatory preferences, see Korsmeyer (1999, pp. 98–102).
32. Key research about the confusion of taste and smell was conducted by Paul Rozin. See Rozin (1982), and see also Shepherd (2012, pp. 16–18).
33. For further discussion of the taste map theory, see Bartoshuk (1993) and Sweeney (2018, pp. 10–11).

38   *Kevin Sweeney*

34. Baldy (1997, p. 24).
35. Three other notable wine faults include *trichloroanisole* (TCA), produced as a byproduct of mold in the cork or because of a lack of cleanliness at the winery; the nose-prickling sensation of sulfites that can also produce a burnt-match smell; and the rotten-egg smell of sulfides. I would like to acknowledge that John Buechsenstein brought these wine faults to my attention.
36. See Kramer (2018).
37. Rigaux (2008, pp. 24–25).
38. Kramer (2018, pp. 10–11).
39. Grahm (2018, p. 64).

References

Aristotle (2011). *De anima* (M. Shiffman, Trans.). Focus Publishing.

Auvray, M., & Spence, C. (2008). The multisensory perception of flavor. *Consciousness and Cognition, 17*(3), 1016–1031.

Baldy, M. (1997). *The university wine course.* The Wine Appreciation Guild.

Bartoshuk, L. (1993). The biological basis of food perception and acceptance. *Food Quality and Preference, 4*(1–2), 21–32.

Brillat-Savarin, J. (1978). *The physiology of taste, or meditations on transcendental gastronomy* (M. F. K. Fisher, Trans. & Ed.). Harcourt Brace Jovanovich. First published in 1825.

Crawford, D. (1974). *Kant's aesthetic theory.* University of Wisconsin Press.

Gigante, D. (Ed.). (2005). *Gusto: Essential readings in nineteenth-century gastronomy.* Routledge.

Grahm, R. (2018). The search for a great growth in the new world. In T. Patterson & J. Buechsenstein (Eds.), *Wine and place: A terroir reader* (pp. 63–67). University of California Press.

Guyer, P. (1997). *Kant and the claims of taste* (2nd ed.). Cambridge University Press.

Guyer, P. (2014). *A history of modern aesthetics. Vol. 1: The eighteenth century.* Cambridge University Press.

Hopkins, R. (2009). Taste. In S. Davies, K. Higgins, R. Hopkins, R. Stecker, & D. Cooper (Eds.), *A companion to aesthetics* (2nd ed., pp. 554–556). Blackwell.

Hume, D. (1987). Of the standard of taste. In E. Miller (Ed.), *Essays, moral, political, and literary* (pp. 226–249). Liberty Classics. Originally published in 1757.

Kant, I. (1987). *Critique of judgment* (W. Pluhar, Trans.). Hackett. Originally published in 1790.

Korsmeyer, C. (1999). *Making sense of taste: Food and philosophy.* Cornell University Press.

Kramer, M. (2018). The notion of terroir. In T. Patterson & J. Buechsenstein (Eds.), *Wine and place: A terroir reader* (pp. 36–44). University of California Press.

MacDonogh, G. (1987). *A palate in revolution: Grimod de La Reynière and the Almanach des Gourmands.* Robin Clark.

MacDonogh, G. (1992). *Brillat-Savarin: The judge and his stomach.* Ivan R. Dee.

Mennell, S. (1996). *All manners of food: Eating and taste in England and France from the middle ages to the present* (2nd ed.). University of Illinois Press.

Murphy, C., Cain, W., & Bartoshuk, L. (1977). Mutual action of taste and olfaction. *Sens Processes*, *1*(3), 204–211.

Plato (1985). *Five dialogues: Euthyphro, Apology, Crito, Meno, Phaedo* (G. M. A. Grube, Trans.). Hackett.

Rigaux, J. (2008). *Terroir and the winegrower* (C. du Toit & N. Morgan, Trans.). ICO.

Rozin, P. (1982). "Taste-smell confusions" and the duality of the olfactory sense. *Perception and Psychophysics*, *31*, 397–401.

Shepherd, G. (2012). *Neurogastronomy: How the brain creates flavor and why it matters*. Columbia University Press.

Shiner, L. (2001). *The invention of art: A cultural history*. University of Chicago Press.

Spence, C., & Piqueras-Fiszman, B. (2014). *The perfect meal: The multisensory science of food and dining*. Wiley Blackwell.

Stolnitz, J. (1961). On the origin of "aesthetic disinterestedness". *Journal of Aesthetics and Art Criticism*, *20*(2), 131–143.

Sweeney, K. (2012). Hunger is the best sauce: The aesthetics of food. In D. Kaplan (Ed.), *The philosophy of food* (pp. 52–68). University of California Press.

Sweeney, K. (2018). *The aesthetics of food: The philosophical debate about what we eat and drink*. Rowman & Littlefield.

Voltaire (François-Marie Arouet). (1764). An essay on taste. In A. Gerard (Ed.), *An essay on taste* (pp. 213–222). Millar.

3 Over-Appreciating Appreciation

Rebecca Wallbank and Jon Robson

Aestheticians have had a great deal to say recently in praise of (aesthetic) appreciation. This enthusiastic appreciation for appreciation may seem unsurprising given the important role it plays in many of our aesthetic practices, but we maintain that some prominent aestheticians have over-stated the role of appreciation (and, perhaps more importantly, understated the role of other elements we will discuss) when it comes to the exercise of aesthetic taste. This is not, of course, to deny the obvious fact that appreciation often plays an important role in our aesthetic practices but merely that it is a mistake to cast it in the role of the *sine qua non* of aesthetics. We will focus below on the following three claims, which we identify from the recent literature (though we don't mean to suggest that these are the only respects in which the value of appreciation has been overstated):

A1 We should reinterpret various influential claims in aesthetics in terms of appreciation.
A2 Aesthetic judgement in the absence of appreciation is (or is close to) worthless.
A3 The aim of engaging with artworks is appreciation.[1]

We will argue—with reference to examples from the ongoing debate concerning the Acquaintance Principle (*AP*) and related claims—that each of these theses is mistaken. In §§1–3, we address each claim in turn, before briefly offering some concluding remarks in §4.

Before moving on, it will be useful to say a little more to set up our discussion. Our focus in this chapter is on appreciation in aesthetics, but of course, the term 'appreciation' can be rather slippery. As such, it's important to make it clear that our focus will be on a particular species of appreciation which has garnered a great deal of focus in aesthetics and which has been taken to involve something like "perceiving [a work's aesthetic properties] as realized in the work" (Budd, 2003, p. 392) or "experiencing the qualities of a thing" in such a way as to find them "worthy or valuable" (Dickie, 1974, p. 40) or as an experience which "allows one to fittingly have the full range of affective and conative reactions"

DOI: 10.4324/9781003184225-4

appropriate for the entity (Lord, 2018, p. 76). The details of such a notion will, naturally, need to be spelled out in order to arrive at a full account of appreciation, but we will not attempt to do so here.[2]

1. Acquaintance and Exegesis

As mentioned, our discussion will focus on examples concerning the famous debate surrounding acquaintance and aesthetic taste. It has often been thought, as Carolyn Korsmeyer (2013, pp. 258–259) phrases things, that "both literal taste and taste for art require first-hand acquaintance with their objects" and that just "as one cannot decide that soup is well seasoned without actually sipping it, so one cannot conclude that music is moving without hearing it." However, this apparent truism has recently been subject to a number of challenges (see, e.g., Budd, 2003; Livingston, 2003; Robson, 2013).[3] In the aesthetic case, this debate has, of course, centred on Wollheim's influential claim that "judgements of aesthetic value, unlike judgements of moral knowledge, must be based on first-hand experience of their objects" (1980, p. 233). The debates surrounding Wollheim's 'Acquaintance Principle' (and parallel claims found in, e.g., Tormey, 1973; Pettit, 1983; Mothersill, 1994, p. 160) have concerned both the truth of the principle and various exegetical issues surrounding how it is best interpreted. Our focus in this section will be on a debate of the latter kind.

It may initially seem that to defend *AP* here someone would need to show that, contra recent criticisms, acquaintance of a certain kind is necessary for legitimate aesthetic belief. Some supporters of *AP* have, however, recently taken a rather different tack, arguing that the version of *AP* under attack was never one which Wollheim—or indeed many celebrated advocates of parallel principles—ever intended to defend. The most developed argument for a view of this kind is presented by Dominic McIver Lopes (2014, p. 170), who claims that "the controversy over the acquaintance principle ensues from an incorrect interpretation of it." According to Lopes (Ibid., p. 175), 'aesthetic judgement' can refer to both "experience-like states ascribing aesthetic value and non-experiential states ascribing aesthetic value" (Ibid., p. 175)—that is, roughly, appreciation-like-states and belief-like states, respectively. It is, Lopes maintains, the former with which *AP* is properly concerned, but many recent participants in the debate concerning *AP* have mistakenly taken it to be concerned with the latter.

If Lopes is right, *AP* should be reinterpreted in terms of appreciation and, thus redefined, it seems to at least come very close to rendering *AP* a truism. There may be a little housekeeping to do when it comes to spelling out precisely what acquaintance amounts to, but it seems clear that no one would want to allow that appreciation (of the kind outlined earlier) is available via testimony or via appeal to various other sources of aesthetic belief proposed as counterexamples to the spirit (and not merely the letter) of *AP*.[4] Indeed, Lopes's own understanding of appreciation appears intended to render the principle something of a truism. According to Lopes (Ibid., p. 179), aesthetic appreciation is "defined as a cognitive process where interpretation and clarification produce an ascription of aesthetic value." While this description is somewhat lacking in specificity, Lopes (Ibid.) suggests that we can fill in some of the details by claiming that aesthetic appreciation involves what he terms 'α-judgements'—that is, "experiential states ascribing aesthetic values" (Ibid., p. 175). Lopes is keen to stress here that the experiential states in question do not have to be (directly) caused by the objects themselves and that the relevant experience does not have to be a *perceptual* experience.[5] Still, though, it is clear that testimony and its ilk will have no place here, and so *AP*, once properly formulated, begins to look very close to being trivially true.

We are sympathetic to some aspects of Lopes's view. It does seem eminently plausible, for example, that *some* of the apparent controversy concerning acquaintance has been a merely verbal dispute between those who propose that it is a necessary condition for aesthetic appreciation and those who deny that it is a necessary condition for aesthetic belief. The phrase 'aesthetic judgement' is, after all, a notoriously slippery one, with some philosophers using it as a mere synonym for 'aesthetic belief' (Hopkins, 2006), while others set up a clear contrast between the two (Todd, 2004). Yet there are at least two reasons for believing that Lopes is mistaken in maintaining that his appeal to this appreciative interpretation of *AP* will dispel these debates entirely. First, regardless of historical exegesis, there are those (such as Hanson (2015) and Hopkins (2006, 2011)) who seem, at the very least, to be sympathetic to a version of *AP* explicated in terms of belief. Second, Lopes is mistaken in his exegetical proposal that we should interpret *AP* as concerned with appreciation rather than belief.

Immediately prior to his introduction of *AP*, Wollheim (1980, pp. 231–232) considers two different understandings of the nature of the aesthetic which he labels 'realism' and 'objectivism.'[6] The first of these is importantly distinct from realism, as it is now standardly understood in meta-aesthetic debates, and amounts to the claim that "attributions of aesthetic value have truth-value" and "the truth-value of such judgements depends entirely on the local character of that to which it is attributed" (Ibid., p. 231). This appeal to 'local character' is somewhat oblique, and it is unclear whether it would include, for example, facts about the artist's intentions or comparisons with the broader categories to which the work belongs. All that is relevant for present purposes, though, is that the realist takes aesthetic value to be "altogether independent of the psychological properties of human beings" (Ibid.). Objectivism, by contrast, makes direct reference to such properties. While the objectivist also accepts that judgements of aesthetic value have truth values, they claim that the truth

Over-Appreciating Appreciation 43

conditions for such judgements somehow concern "the experience of humanity at large."[7] As such, the objectivist would be committed to an absolutist—rather than a relativist or contextualist—understanding of the semantics of aesthetic judgement.[8,9]

So how does all of this relate to the alleged requirement that aesthetic judgements "*must* be based on first-hand experience of their objects" (Ibid., p. 233, italics ours)? It seems clear that the 'must' here is intended to be deliberately ambiguous depending on whether we are considering the view of the realist or the objectivist. Beginning with the realist, Wollheim asserts that they will find no place for a requirement for firsthand experience "as part of the truth-conditions of aesthetic evaluations" but, rather, that they are "highly likely to insist on some such experience as an epistemic condition of aesthetic evaluation" (Ibid.).[10] It is clear, then, that Wollheim is happy to countenance an epistemic, and so belief-focused, reading of *AP* and therefore that, contra Lopes, those who propose such interpretations have not misinterpreted Wollheim.

Still, while Wollheim takes the realist's commitment to *AP* to be an epistemic one, the same does not apply to his objectivist interpretation of the principle. Rather, Wollheim (1980, p. 232) suggests that the objectivist will hold that the special kind of experience she is concerned with "appears crucially in the truth-conditions of judgements of aesthetic value." It is difficult to see, though, precisely how we are to understand this claim. The most straightforward interpretation here—one made even more plausible by the fact that Wollheim contrasts the objectivist's view with that of the realist who believes that "aesthetic value has the status of a primary quality" (Ibid.)—is that the objectivist treats aesthetic properties as being constitutively response dependent. Yet such an interpretation would leave it mysterious why the objectivist should be committed to *AP*. After all, colour properties are frequently (though not uncontroversially) taken to be response dependent, but this isn't taken as a motivation for applying a version of *AP* to colour judgements. Indeed, it is a perennial aim of those proposing principles such as *AP* to draw a clear contrast between aesthetic and colour cases (see, e.g., Alcaraz León, 2008, p. 292; Pettit, 1983, p. 25).

A supporter of Lopes might propose, then, that we would be better placed interpreting this objectivist reading of *AP* along appreciative lines. However, while this interpretation may well render the principle considerably more plausible in itself, it would be considerably *less* plausible as an interpretation of Wollheim. It seems very much as if Wollheim takes the objectivist as offering a straightforwardly doxastic account of aesthetic judgement, one according to which these judgements are in no wise to be identified with any kind of experiential or appreciative state. He talks, for example, of aesthetic judgements of this kind having "truth-values" and "truth-conditions" (1980, p. 232). Further, he proposes (Ibid.) that certain kinds of experience (which seem very much to match the kinds of experience we are discussing under the heading of 'appreciation') provide justification for our aesthetic judgements and perhaps serve as a part of their truth conditions rather than being constitutive of the judgements themselves. Given this, it seems clear that, contra Lopes, both of the interpretations of *AP* which Wollheim himself proposes are focused on aesthetic belief.[11]

Lopes's exegetical claims don't stop with Wollheim, though, as he takes other famous advocates of principles such as *AP* to have been misrepresented as discussing belief when they are really concerned with appreciation. For example, he takes Philip Pettit to be expressing a view of this kind when he makes his (1983, p. 15), claim that "the state one is in when one sincerely assents to a given aesthetic characterisation is not a state to which one can have non-perceptual access". Again, though, we are unconvinced, and much of what Pettit says elsewhere in the same paper seems to clearly favour an epistemic (and, therefore, doxastic) interpretation of his view. Consider, for example, his (Ibid., p. 25) claim that in aesthetics "perception is the only title to the sort of knowledge which perception yields."

On a more concessive note, we do find Lopes's exegetical claims much more plausible with respect to some of the other authors he discusses. In particular, we are rather more sympathetic (for reasons we won't discuss here) with his (2014, p. 174) claim that Sibley should be interpreted as talking about appreciation rather than belief in his famous (2001, p. 34) claim that to suggest "that one can make aesthetic judgments without aesthetic perception [. . .] is to misunderstand aesthetic judgment."[12]

We do not take these concessions to be inconsistent with our argument in this section, however. Recall that our general aim in this chapter is not to deny that appreciation is important but merely to highlight ways in which this importance has been overstated. Lopes may be right—indeed, we suspect he *is* right—to maintain that claims about the importance of acquaintance are sometimes about appreciation. He is wrong, though, to maintain that those who have taken them to be about other things (most notably belief) are simply mistaken. This is a theme we will return to when we discuss other cases in which aestheticians have been too quick to move from the undoubted claim that appreciation matters in matters of aesthetic taste to the claim that it is (or at least is very close to being) all that matters.

2. The Value of Mere Aesthetic Belief

In this section we will turn to consider A2, the claim that there is little (if any) value to forming aesthetic judgements in the absence of appreciation. Before doing so, though, it's worth briefly pausing to consider two related positions: the position that such judgements are illegitimate and the position that they are impossible.

Over-Appreciating Appreciation 45

The most obvious motivation for the latter position would be the view—suggested by, e.g., Gorodeisky and Marcus (2018) and Todd (2004)—according to which aesthetic judgement is identical with (or at least constitutively requires) a certain kind of appreciative state. A view of this kind contrasts with an alternative, and we believe correct, position according to which aesthetic judgement is belief (or at the very least some belief-like state). Of course, some apparent disputes over this issue could merely be the result of different aestheticians stipulating different usages of 'aesthetic judgement.' In the cases we are concerned with, though, it is the result of a genuine and substantive disagreement—a disagreement which is, roughly, with how to identify the mental correlate of aesthetic assertions. According to one camp, this correlate is typically (Gorodeisky and Marcus explicitly allow exceptions, and they are by no means alone here) an appreciation-like state, while according to their opponents, it is a belief-like state. Our sympathies in this debate are, as we have indicated, with the latter camp (for reasons indicated in, e.g., Robson and Meskin (manuscript)), but we will not argue for this view here. Instead, we will merely highlight that even those who take aesthetic judgement to be identical with appreciation still allow that there is such a thing as aesthetic belief.[13] We will, therefore, focus in what follows on the legitimacy and value of certain kinds of aesthetic belief without taking any stance as to whether these count as aesthetic *judgements*. Those who hold that they do not can simply rephrase our claims accordingly.

What about the claim that the judgements in question are illegitimate? Let's consider someone who is the recipient of pure aesthetic testimony (that is, who merely receives testimony that some aesthetic claim, *P*, is the case without any access to supporting reasons, etc.). We already mentioned that we are unaware of any aesthetician who would want to claim that such an individual could legitimately *appreciate* (or indeed appreciate simpliciter) the object in question on this basis. The question of whether they could legitimately believe that the object is, say, beautiful on this basis is, by contrast, far more controversial. It is commonplace to divide the debate concerning aesthetic testimony into two broad camps. *Optimists* claim that testimony can serve as a legitimate source of aesthetic judgement, whereas *pessimists* deny this.[14] Some pessimists (such as Whiting, 2015) deny that judgements of this kind qualify as knowledge, while others (such as Hopkins, 2011) argue that they fall afoul of some kind of non-epistemic norm.

Importantly, our claim about the value of aesthetic judgement formed on the basis of testimony is neutral with respect to the optimism/pessimism debate. Some pessimists—those who take aesthetic judgements to be something other than beliefs—can allow that aesthetic beliefs formed on the basis of testimony are perfectly legitimate, and pessimists who take aesthetic judgements to be beliefs can take us to be merely highlighting the benefits of doing something illegitimate (after all, contra the cliché, crime sometimes does pay). Still, though, our claim is quite controversial. Indeed, it is commonly rejected by writers on both sides of the aesthetic testimony debate. As we will see, the particular reasons given for rejecting the claim vary, but the basic idea behind them seems to be that acquiring true aesthetic belief—or even *knowledge*—on the basis of testimony would be of scant value, given that such beliefs would not be accompanied by the richer kinds of mental state required for appreciation (with the further claim being, of course, that it is appreciation that we are really seeking in our aesthetic engagements). Despite the important differences between them, we take Ransom (2017), Lord (2018), Hills (2009), and Nguyen (2019) to all be offering suggestions along these general lines.

Ransom (2019) offers a Sosa-inspired account, which captures valuable epistemic inquiry in terms of the performative achievements which are not the mere production of a true belief but the production of true belief as a result of one's aesthetic competence. Here aesthetic competence is the skill set involved in a rich, appreciative grasping of the artwork and its aesthetic features attained via firsthand acquaintance. Ransom argues that a 'testimonial competence' can be attained via appeal to aesthetic testimony, where this is the skill set involved in ascertaining a true belief by judging whether a testifier is competent and sincere. Ransom also argues that testimonial competence can provide a form of aesthetic knowledge. However, she argues that only firsthand acquaintance will produce knowledge of the rich, appreciative kind. According to Ransom, during our aesthetic engagements, we most desire acquaintance with the relevant aesthetic object, as this enables a rich understanding of the matter in question: by being acquainted with the object, we can grasp how the relevant aesthetic properties have been ascribed and thereby develop our aesthetic taste. She explicitly denies that there is anything bad about acquiring the shallower kind of knowledge via testimony; nevertheless, the only means by which she justifies its value is in terms of pointing us in the right direction when we are developing the richer kind of knowledge. Arguing here (Ransom, 2019, p. 426) that aesthetic testimony is "an important source of training" for our aesthetic taste, she continues 'Aesthetic testimony can be vital for developing aesthetic competence as it can serve as a source of knowledge for novices who would otherwise be unsure of how to approach certain artworks, or even which artworks to engage with.'

Comparable moves are made, for example, by Lord (2018), who draws a distinction between 'appreciative knowledge' and 'know-how' and a basic propositional form of knowledge, only the latter of which can be acquired through testimony. Lord also claims that the appreciative kind of knowledge is the most valuable. He does allow that "given various pressures on our time, attention, and stamina," deference can be a valuable tool by which we can arrive at "various aesthetic truths." Nevertheless, he insists that it is a non-ideal (indeed, defective) means of engaging with an aesthetic object, because it doesn't allow us to appreciate the object in question. He argues that whilst we might attain beliefs in various aesthetic truths, and even knowledge, via deference, "[t]he primary downside is that deference cannot put us in a position to gain *appreciative* knowledge. This is because it does not put us in a position to be acquainted with the specific ways in which the aesthetic features are realized. This is a serious failing given the centrality of appreciation to our aesthetic lives." The main claim here is that deference is not conducive to appreciation, which is a central component of our aesthetic lives.

Nguyen (2019) argues that when we acquire beliefs via deferential testimony, far from enabling the training and development of appreciation, this mode of belief formation cuts short the opportunity for appreciative practice. In doing so, Nguyen suggests, it cuts short the opportunity to participate in that which is primarily valuable about this practice, that which our applications of aesthetic taste are *for*. To bring this out, Nguyen compares aesthetic appreciation to a game. He argues that "[w]hen we play a game, we try to win. But often winning isn't the point; playing is" (2019, p. 1127). Similarly, when we aesthetically appreciate, we try to form correct judgements, but forming correct judgements is not the point; the point is the process of engaging with the aesthetic object, i.e. the process of "interpreting, investigating, and exploring the aesthetic object" (Ibid.). Nguyen argues that this is evidenced by the fact that if we did merely aim for correctness, then it would make sense for us to simply defer to the testimony of experts. Yet he argues that it doesn't make sense for us to simply defer, as this defeats the point of the process in a similar manner to the shortcuts and cheats of a game. According to Nguyen, when we form appreciative aesthetic judgements, we require autonomy, that is to say our judgements must have been formed through our own cognitive efforts.

All of this seems very damning when it comes to the value of mere aesthetic belief. So why do we demur? We saw that Nguyen aims to explain an aspect of our aesthetic behaviour—our avoidance of merely deferring to experts—by appeal to our disregard for mere aesthetic belief. However, it is by no means clear that this is a genuine aspect of our aesthetic practice. Indeed, one of us has previously argued (in Robson, 2014) that there is good reason to think that we frequently *do* defer to others in aesthetic matters. Further, we believe that there are often significant benefits to doing so. One obvious benefit to having true aesthetic beliefs—whether acquired via testimony or otherwise—is that it will increase the number of true beliefs we have. And having true beliefs, whether about aesthetic matters or otherwise, is often a valuable thing in itself. This is not, of course, to suggest that all true beliefs are particularly valuable (perhaps memorising the first three digits of the phone numbers of everyone in Ottawa would, while being an impressive feat, have scant, if any, value). However, we think—given the importance we often attach to aesthetic matters—that it would (at the very least) be an oddity if it was *never* valuable for its own sake to have true beliefs in aesthetics.

Moreover, we think that it is not only possible to have true aesthetic beliefs via testimony but also aesthetic knowledge (of course, as we discuss in what follows, this aspect of our position isn't entirely neutral with respect to the optimism/pessimism debate). This would include what McShane (2018, p. 629), in a parallel discussion of moral testimony, terms "remedial" cases—cases in which we rely on testimony because we are concerned that our own judgement is compromised in some way. In such remedial cases, our aesthetic judgements may be too distorted by bias (imagine being asked to judge a beloved child's piano performance objectively), or they may be compromised because we lack the ability to engage with certain works (those with no appreciable sense of humour would be poor judges of the relative merits of sitcoms). Other limitations might apply not to an individual's ability to judge any particular work but, rather, to the range of works which any single individual can reasonably expect to be able to competently judge for themselves. Artforms are typically complex things (with long histories, litanies of conventions, etc.) such that acquiring the ability to properly judge artworks within a certain art kind, or even of a certain genre within that kind, can take a great deal of time and effort. Given this, it seems unlikely that any single individual will be able to develop a reasonable level of expertise in more than a fraction of the world's many and varied artforms. Testimony, by contrast, can give us access to the judgements of those who have expertise across the full gamut of cases. Finally, there will be cases in which we are prevented by historical contingencies or similar factors from properly applying our own judgements, the most prominent example here being 'lost work' cases, in which we have no choice but to rely on testimony when looking for knowledge concerning works that are no longer extant (and where no suitable photographs etc. are available).[15]

It could be objected that all of these epistemic advantages require that we abandon our feigned neutrality and commit to rejecting pessimism concerning aesthetic testimony. However, this is not the case. Recall that some pessimists are perfectly happy to allow that we *can* acquire aesthetic knowledge that is based on testimony while insisting that we should not do so (such pessimists could, therefore, just allow that we are once again considering the advantages available to us in violating their norms). Further, even many of those who *do* accept pessimism on epistemic grounds shy away from the hard-line view that aesthetic knowledge is *never* available via testimony (with cases involving lost works etc. being common areas for making concessions). Of course, we don't want to pretend that our epistemic claims here are entirely neutral—some pessimists would certainly reject them. What we want to emphasise is that they are rather less controversial than one might initially think.

Over-Appreciating Appreciation 49

Regardless of what we make of these epistemic claims, though, we can still appeal to the value of mere true belief. However, while we do think that the mere acquisition of true beliefs can be an important goal of some of our aesthetic practices, we don't want to overstate our case here. In particular, we are happy to concede that many cases in which we engage with artworks have nothing to do with the acquisition of true beliefs (aesthetic or otherwise). The person who relistens to a favourite musical work or rewatches a beloved film is rarely doing so with any aim to increase their store of true beliefs. And even if our initial engagement with a work leads us to the true belief that the work is beautiful, this is rarely taken to be of much importance in comparison to other factors such as, most obviously, appreciating that beauty.[16]

Still, we shouldn't be too hasty to denigrate the value of mere true belief in our aesthetic practices. Even if we bracket the intrinsic value of such beliefs, we can see that there are various important roles within the artworld which someone with true beliefs can perform regardless of their own appreciation of the works in question. As Nguyen (2017, p. 24) points out, a curator charged with, say, filling their museum with the best examples of impressionist works their budget can afford need not have any appreciation for impressionism themselves.[17] Merely having the right beliefs about the value of the works seems enough here. Similarly, truth (rather than personal appreciation) seems more important when it comes to which works are most worthy of preservation or of receiving various honours etc.[18]

Importantly, though, our claim is not merely that those who are interested (whether for practical purposes or otherwise) in increasing their store of true aesthetic beliefs can rely on testimony just as well as on firsthand judgement.[19] Rather, there seem to be some cases in which we *ought* to rely on testimony. Imagine that you are asked to choose which of a list of works are the most valuable artistic treasures and, therefore, in most urgent need of being protected in the face of some imminent conflict or natural disaster. We propose that there would be something wrong here with merely relying on your own judgement rather than (time permitting) doing your best to defer, via testimony, to the critical consensus. And we suspect that something similar will apply to at least some of the other cases we have discussed.

It could be objected at this stage, though, that in each of these cases the value of belief merely lies in promoting further aesthetic appreciation (either for the individual themselves or for others). The value of preserving great works, for example, is that it makes these works available as sources for appreciation to further generations. We suspect that, even in the cases we have highlighted, this objection overstates things and that there is, for example, a great deal of value to preserving masterpieces beyond their ability to furnish future appreciation. Rather than pushing this point here, though, we turn in the next section (as part of our response to A3) to consider a particular kind of value which, we will argue, frequently plays an important role in our everyday aesthetic practices. This kind of value is often manifested without our ordinary engagements with artworks (rather than merely for those in much less common roles such as curator) and doesn't reduce to the instrumental value of promoting future appreciation.

3. Testimony and Social Value

In the last section, we suggested that the value of mere aesthetic belief is often underestimated, leading to an endorsement of claims such as A2. These considerations also give us reason to reject a strong version of A3 which takes appreciation to be the sole aim of our engagement with artworks. Still, such an extreme version of A3 was never very plausible, since it is clear that there is a range of reasons—financial, educational, romantic, etc.— people engage with artworks. A more prima facie plausible version of A3 would, therefore, need to make a weaker claim. Perhaps the claim—as some of the views we've discussed seem to suggest—that appreciation is the *canonical* aim of engaging with artworks and that other aims we might have either fail to relate to our engagement with artworks as artworks (such as the financial aim of the person who trades impressionist paintings as if they were any other commodity) or else serve an enabling function in relation to appreciation (either that of the individual themselves or some target group such as visitors to their gallery). In this section, we will sketch a provisional account according to which even this weaker interpretation of A3 is mistaken.

To begin, let's return to the case of forming aesthetic beliefs based on testimony. In our view, the strongest reasons to think that there is considerable value to such a practice are social. Aesthetic practice has too frequently been treated by philosophers (and others) as a solitary pursuit when it is, in fact, frequently communicative, a form of intellectual or emotional sharing. This can encompass dialogue *with* the work but also, crucially, dialogue *about* it. The former involves an anthropomorphized view of aesthetic appreciation, which is fairly common within aesthetic literature (consider, for example, Anthony Cross's (2017) claim that we should treat artworks as friends), but we will have little to say about it, since the 'dialogue' here is, of course, typically metaphorical. The latter, by contrast, allows for a much broader range of dialogue (both metaphoric and literal). Focus on the way we engage with the artwork itself, while important, frequently overlooks the value of the engaged relationship which we have with the artist and the broader art community, a relationship between a collection of individuals created around the artwork, fostering connections and a sense of community. Interpersonal interactions with others are central to our aesthetic lives, and the formation of aesthetic beliefs on the basis of testimony can contribute to fostering these.

To see the importance of such deference here, return to the more mundane cases of testimony. When one accepts another's testimony, a bond is forged between the testifier and the receiver. This is reflected by work on 'testimonial insults' by, for example, G. E. M. Anscombe (1979), Olivia Bailey (2018), Finlay Malcolm (2018), and Allan Hazlett (2017). They argue that when one testifies, this can be understood as an extension of an invitation to one's audience, an invitation to take one's word for whatever it is that one is testifying to. The invitation is posed as an offer, and the audience is invited to believe in the truth of the proposition whilst being relieved of their "usual epistemic responsibility to review the evidence before making up one's mind about [it]" (Bailey, 2018, p. 141). If one were to reject the testifier's invitation and seek evidence, then this, they argue, would be received as an insult: when one testifies that p, one puts p forward as true, one *vouches* for it. To reject another's testimony and seek evidence is thereby to disparage either their competence or their sincerity, which reflects negatively on them in an insulting way. And this applies even if one's reasons to reject the testimony are justified, even if the testifier's competence or sincerity should be questioned.[20] This general picture, then, suggests that there is an important social role to the giving and receiving (or failing to receive) testimony in general. And it is, of course, by no means the only story which could be told concerning the social value of testimony. Given this, we see no reason those attracted to any of these general stories concerning the social role of testimony couldn't apply them in the case of aesthetics. Yet we think the defender of aesthetic testimony can go even further.[21]

Aesthetic testimony tends to be taken up, at least in part, because we trust the testifier, where this involves feeling some kind of respect towards them. We feel related to them and want to see things in the manner that they do. It arises alongside a desire to harbour a sense of community and belonging with others.[22] This sense of belonging is fundamental to the kind of trust involved in the reception of aesthetic testimony, and it is also fundamental to what we find aesthetically valuable about our engagement with artworks. Once we recognise the centrality of this interaction, we can see that, far from being detrimental to our aesthetic engagements, the formation of aesthetic beliefs via testimony is a manifestation of (at least one key aspect of) what we find valuable about such practices.[23]

We are now in a better position to understand where accounts such as Nguyen's go wrong. Nguyen argues that deference to aesthetic testimony strikes us as odd and wrong, and it strikes us so because it terminates our engagement with the work. Most significantly, he takes this to indicate that we do not value the mere formation of true beliefs in our aesthetic engagements and that we instead value the challenge of solving a puzzle, a persistent reassessment of aesthetic objects, which is part and parcel of an appreciative experience. In certain respects, Nguyen is on the right lines, but we believe that he overlooks some other important aspects of

52   *Rebecca Wallbank and Jon Robson*

our aesthetic practices. It is true that we enjoy the persistent reassessment of aesthetic objects, but we often do so, at least in part, because we value the interpersonal aesthetic interaction which this brings. Stopping at true belief and not investigating a work further may strike us as odd—in those cases in which it does strike us as odd—not simply because we think we should rise to the challenge of appreciatively solving a puzzle nor simply because we want the puzzle to continue but because we value interpersonal aesthetic interaction. And interactions of this kind are something which can be enhanced by a continuous aesthetic puzzle. We may enjoy viewing a beautiful meadow and relish it even more side by side with a friend, but the complex aesthetic properties found in the kind of 'puzzle' cases on which Nguyen focuses allow for a much richer range of social negotiations (a beautiful vista may be enchanting, but conversations about its beauty tend not to be).

This interpersonal interaction may be enhanced by our endeavours to solve an aesthetic puzzle, but such puzzle-solving endeavours are not the only means by which interpersonal interaction is enabled—it may equally well be enabled by discussion, debate, and even the simple acceptance of testimony. Moreover, the kind of isolated and autonomous puzzle-solving endeavour on which Nguyen often focuses may sometimes prove to be problematic in itself, since it can come to hinder richer interpersonal interactions. When autonomously engaging with the work for oneself, one will be able to achieve some interpersonal interaction, to the degree that one sees oneself as bonding with an artist or art community by discovering the aspects of an artwork laid out within it. Here one might see oneself as investigating an artwork in the manner that a treasure hunter might approach the deciphering of an ancient coded map. Still, there is something far more enriching about not going it alone, about thinking through and discussing the puzzle with a friend, sometimes relying on their insight and sometimes letting them rely on yours (even in cases where each of you would have solved the puzzle more quickly alone).

The portrayal of the aesthetic appreciator as a lone puzzle solver who ignores the word of others in a purist pursuit of aesthetic truth simply neglects the valuable interpersonal interactions that we can have with others in a shared pursuit of an aesthetic goal. Indeed, the more appropriate comparison will often be to that of team games, which function as a group exercise. This is not to claim that the lone puzzle solver does something illegitimate, nor, we believe, does the person who simply acquires true beliefs via testimony and leaves it at that. Nevertheless, in both cases we maintain that there is more of value to be had (though whether it will be worth seeking out these further values in a particular case will, of course, be a complex matter), since the opportunity for further dialogue and engagement with others is thwarted.[24]

On the kind of interpersonal model of aesthetic engagement that we are suggesting, the receipt of aesthetic testimony will rarely be a stopping point. Rather, it will be a spur to further investigation of the work itself and to comparisons and contrasts between a friend's taste and our own.[25] On the other hand, the proposed model is incompatible with a complete rejection of the value of aesthetic testimony and, more generally, with a push for autonomy in the exercise of our aesthetic taste.

Our appeal to interpersonal factors is, of course, in need of further development, and we don't mean to suggest that the sketch we have offered here captures anything like the full range of interpersonal benefits of engaging with artworks (and still less that it captures all the non-appreciative value in doing so). However, we think the points we have highlighted in this section are enough to motivate two claims. First, that our frequent practice of joining with other people to engage with an artwork is often as much and perhaps even more about our relationship to these individuals as it is about our relationship to the work. Second, that these interpersonal aspects of our aesthetic practice are not merely means to enabling appreciation (as is sometimes taken to be the case for other non-appreciative goals such as acquiring true aesthetic beliefs). We have seen that in many cases, we do come to a richer appreciation of artworks through our interactions with others, but this isn't a necessary condition of these activities being valuable. Imagine that, after having a long conversation with a friend about the putative merits of a film you have previously dismissed, you rewatch the film in question and still find nothing there to appreciate. This may be a disappointment, but we find it implausible to think that it is enough to render the whole process worthless.[26]

4. Concluding Remarks

We have argued that appreciation is over-appreciated when it comes to matters of aesthetic taste. Our primary aim in doing so, however, is not to denigrate aesthetic appreciation (we've been known to engage in it ourselves) but, rather, to highlight how an excessive focus on appreciation can lead to the neglect of other important aspects of our aesthetic practice. We have made some suggestions concerning what (some of) these aspects might be and the reasons for their importance, but we intend these far more as springboards for future discussion than as any kind of definitive account. In our views, the values and goals of our aesthetic practice are manifold, and fully exploring each of these (and the relationships between them) will prove to be a monumental task—a task that cannot make much progress if we are lured into taking a single goal amongst many as the *sine qua non* of all of our aesthetic activities.

Notes

1. Our discussion focuses on artworks, but many of the claims we discuss have also been applied to other objects of aesthetic judgement.

54 Rebecca Wallbank and Jon Robson

2. One such account is offered by Iseminger (1981, p. 389), who suggests that "S appreciates the Fness of a if and only if (i) a is F; (ii) S experientially takes a to be F; (iii) a's being F and S's experientially taking a to be F are "cognitively related"; (iv) S believes that the Fness of a is good."
3. We focus here on aesthetic taste. For some objections to acquaintance claims in relation to gustatory taste, see Meskin and Robson (2015).
4. It might be thought that Amir Konigsberg (2012) is an exception here, since he has argued that it is possible to transmit appreciation via testimony. According to Konigsberg (Ibid., p. 156), "it is not only possible to transmit declarative aesthetic knowledge through testimony" but also to transmit "aesthetically appreciative experiences." This would, however, be a mistake, since his concern is not with aesthetic testimony as this is standardly understood but, rather, with 'aesthetic testimony' understood as "aesthetic and non-aesthetic descriptions communicated from person to person" (Ibid., p. 154).
5. This allows him to avoid some well-worn objections to other formulations of *AP* concerning, for example, exact duplicates (Ibid., pp. 181–182) and literary works (Ibid., pp. 180–181). Discussion of these worries for principles such as *AP* date back at least as far as Tormey (1973, p. 39).
6. Wollheim also discusses two other views (Ibid., pp. 234–240), which he labels 'relativism' and 'subjectivism.' He takes the former to be incompatible with *AP* (though we found his argument here rather obscure) and leaves the relationship which the latter bears to it unexplored. So far as we can see, though, his discussion of these other two views provides no resources for defending the kind of account which Lopes proposes.
7. Wollheim does sometimes suggest (Ibid., pp. 233–234) that the objectivist should only be concerned with the experiences of those individuals who possess and are able to draw on a relevant level of understanding in relation to the work in question. We will not, however, attempt to resolve the apparent tension here, since it is irrelevant to our arguments.
8. For discussions of these different semantic views, see, e.g., Baker and Robson (2017, pp. 430–433), Schafer (2011) and Wyatt (2018).
9. Admittedly, it's not entirely clear that Wollheim's objectivist is committed to absolutism about aesthetic judgements. The letter of the view is compatible with taking a human's judgement that '*x*s are beautiful' to be equivalent to '*x*s are beautiful for human beings' and similarly taking a judgement that '*x*s are beautiful,' when made by the member of another species *s*, to be equivalent to '*x*s are beautiful for the members of species *s*.' Developed in this way, the objectivist's analysis of aesthetic judgements would be somewhat similar to the 'group contextualist' analysis of predicates of personal taste that is proposed by Glanzberg (2007).
10. Wollheim takes it for granted here that both the realist and the objectivist would *want* to accommodate *AP*.
11. At least provided we focus on something like what Neil Sinclair (2006) terms "minimal belief."
12. Chapter Two of Robson (manuscript) discusses some reasons for favouring this interpretation.
13. Todd (2004) is a possible exception here, but we think that a fully developed version of Todd's quasi-realist project would end up taking aesthetic judgements to be beliefs (at least in the minimal sense outlined in, e.g., Sinclair (2006)).
14. These distinctions, as stated, are very rough. For a more complete account, see Chapter One of Robson (manuscript).
15. One of us has also argued elsewhere (Robson, 2018) that testimony alone can provide us with a better epistemic position than first-hand acquaintance alone. However, we take no stance on that issue here.

Over-Appreciating Appreciation 55

16. A further argument against mere testimonial belief is presented by Howell (2014). Howell argues, in the context of a parallel argument pertaining to ethical testimony, that the possessor of such beliefs "might not understand how to apply" them nor be sufficiently motivated to act or be moved by them. Such beliefs will be "cognitively isolated" and "not introduced in a way that guarantees integration and coherence for the subject." We agree that these things *might* be the case (both in the moral and in the aesthetic case) but see no reason they need be so. In most domains, we can be motivated to act on the basis of testimony and can integrate our testimonial beliefs with our wider web of beliefs, etc., and we don't take Howell to have given enough of a reason to take the moral (or aesthetic) cases to be exceptional here.
17. Nguyen (2017) highlights a range of other useful examples here.
18. And something similar will apply when determining, e.g., which artists are most deserving of various endowments.
19. Of course, we don't mean to suggest that these are the only sources available to them.
20. Of course, in cases in which there is strong enough reason to take the testifier to be unreliable, we might judge that an insult of this kind is perfectly justified (both epistemically and otherwise).
21. Remember that we are focusing here on the person who defends reliance on aesthetic testimony as valuable. This is still compatible with the pessimist's denial that reliance on aesthetic testimony is legitimate.
22. Robson (2014) discusses empirical support for some of these claims.
23. McShane (2018) tells a similar story in relation to the social value of moral testimony.
24. And we suspect it will be very rare, though not unheard of, for there to be cases in which we are under any obligation to seek out these further values.
25. It is worth noting that using aesthetic testimony in this sense is something that even pessimists will often countenance (see Hopkins, 2011, p. 153).
26. Again, a comparison with gustatory taste can be made here when we consider how important social values often are when it comes to our engagement with food and drink.

References

Alcaraz-León, M. J. (2008). The rational justification of aesthetic judgments. *The Journal of Aesthetics and Art Criticism*, 66, 291–300.

Anscombe, G. E. M. (1979). What is it to believe someone? In C. F. Delaney (Ed.), *Rationality and religious belief* (pp. 1–10). University of Notre Dame Press.

Bailey, O. (2018). Empathy and testimonial trust. *Royal Institute of Philosophy Supplement*, 84, 139–160.

Baker, C., & Robson, J. (2017). An absolutist theory of faultless disagreement in aesthetics. *Pacific Philosophical Quarterly*, 98(3), 429–448.

Budd, M. (2003). The Acquaintance Principle. *British Journal of Aesthetics*, 43(4), 386–392.

Cross, A. (2017). Obligations to artworks as duties of love. *Estetika: The European Journal of Aesthetics*, 54(1), 85–101.

Dickie, G. (1974). *Art and the aesthetic: An institutional analysis*. Cornell University Press.

Glanzberg, M. (2007). Context, content, and relativism. *Philosophical Studies*, 136(1), 1–29.

56 Rebecca Wallbank and Jon Robson

Gorodeisky, K., & Marcus, E. (2018). Aesthetic rationality. *Journal of Philosophy, 115*(3), 113–140.

Hanson, L., (2015). Conceptual art and the Acquaintance Principle. *Journal of Aesthetics and Art Criticism, 73*(3), 247–258.

Hazlett, A. (2017). On the special insult of refusing testimony. *Philosophical Explorations, 20*, 37–51.

Hills, A. (2009). Moral testimony and moral epistemology. *Ethics, 120*(1), 94–127.

Hopkins, R. (2006). How to form aesthetic belief: Interpreting the Acquaintance Principle. *Postgraduate Journal of Aesthetics, 3*(3), 85–99.

Hopkins, R. (2011). How to be a pessimist about aesthetic testimony. *Journal of Philosophy, 108*(3), 138–157.

Howell, R. J. (2014). Google morals, virtue, and the asymmetry of deference. *Nous, 48*(3), 389–415.

Iseminger, G. (1981). Aesthetic appreciation. *The Journal of Aesthetics and Art Criticism, 39*, 389–397.

Konigsberg, A. (2012). The Acquaintance Principle, aesthetic autonomy, and aesthetic appreciation. *British Journal of Aesthetics, 52*, 153–168.

Korsmeyer, C. (2013). Taste. In B. Gaut & D. Lopes (Eds.), *The Routledge companion to aesthetics* (3rd ed., pp. 257–266). Routledge.

Livingston, P. (2003). On an apparent truism in Aesthetics. *British Journal of Aesthetics, 43*(3), 260–278.

Lopes, D. (2014). *Beyond art.* Oxford University Press.

Lord, E. (2018). How to learn about aesthetics and morality through acquaintance and testimony. In R. Shafer-Landau (Ed.), *Oxford studies in metaethics 13* (pp. 71–97). Oxford University Press.

Malcolm, F. (2018). Testimonial insult: A moral reason for belief. *Logos & Episteme, 9*(1), 27–48.

McShane, P. (2018). The non-remedial value of dependence on moral testimony. *Philosophical Studies, 175*(3), 629–647.

Meskin, A., & Robson, J. (2015). Taste and acquaintance. *The Journal of Aesthetics and Art Criticism, 73*, 127–139.

Mothersill, M. (1994). *Beauty restored.* Oxford University Press.

Nguyen, C. T. (2017). The uses of aesthetic testimony. *British Journal of Aesthetics, 57*(1), 19–36.

Nguyen, C. T. (2019). Autonomy and aesthetic engagement. *Mind, 129*(516), 1127–1156.

Pettit, P. (1983). The possibility of aesthetic realism. In E. Schaper (Ed.), *Pleasure preference and value: Studies in philosophical aesthetics* (pp. 17–38). Cambridge University Press.

Ransom, M. (2019). Frauds, posers and sheep: A virtue theoretic solution to the acquaintance debate. *Philosophy and Phenomenological Research, 98*(2), 417–434.

Robson, J. (2013). Appreciating the Acquaintance Principle: A reply to Konigsberg. *British Journal of Aesthetics, 53*, 237–245.

Robson, J. (2014). A social epistemology of aesthetics. *Synthese, 191*, 2513–2528.

Robson, J. (2018). Aesthetic testimony and the test of time. *Philosophy and Phenomenological Research, 96*(3).

Robson, J. (Manuscript). Aesthetic testimony: An optimistic approach.

Robson, J., & Meskin, A. (Manuscript). Comments on aesthetic rationality; or, why we haven't yet (fully) embraced the Auburn Programme.

Schafer, K. (2011). Faultless disagreement and aesthetic realism. *Philosophy and Phenomenological Research*, *82*(2), 265–286.

Sibley, F. (2001). Aesthetic and non-aesthetic. In J. Benson, B. Redfern, & J. Cox (Eds.), *Approach to aesthetics: Collected papers on philosophical aesthetics* (pp. 33–51). Oxford University Press.

Sinclair, N. (2006). The moral belief problem. *Ratio*, *19*, 249–260.

Todd, C. (2004). Quasi-realism, acquaintance, and the normative claims of aesthetic judgment. *British Journal of Aesthetics*, *44*(3), 277–296.

Tormey, A. (1973). Critical judgments. *Theoria*, *39*, 35–49.

Whiting, D. (2015). The glass is half empty: A new argument for pessimism about aesthetic testimony. *British Journal of Aesthetics*, *55*(1), 91–107.

Wollheim, R. (1980). *Art and its objects*. Cambridge University Press.

Wyatt, J. (2018). Absolutely tasty: An examination of predicates of personal taste and faultless disagreement. *Inquiry*, *61*(3), 252–280.

4 Aesthetic Taste
Perceptual Discernment or Emotional Sensibility?

Irene Martínez Marín and
Elisabeth Schellekens

I

What is aesthetic taste? What is the mental ability, state or process which enables us to engage with aesthetic value, perceive aesthetic qualities or experience aesthetic merit? These questions, widely regarded as triggering the emergence of aesthetics as a philosophical discipline almost three centuries ago, are still entirely apposite. For although contemporary philosophy of mind and epistemology no longer relies on positing 'faculties'[1] or an 'inner' and 'outer sense',[2] our understanding of the notion of aesthetic taste—broadly conceived as the ability to secure access to that which we deem aesthetically valuable—remains surprisingly sketchy. What is more, several functional roles tend to be ascribed to aesthetic taste, some of which converge while others pull in different directions. This, we shall argue, is in part due to a certain epistemological ambivalence inherent in the notion of taste itself. On the one hand, the term points to an agent-relative exercise grounded in sense experience, the outcome of which is best described in terms of preference, liking or disliking. On the other hand, aesthetic taste has been contrasted with gustatory taste[3] in virtue, precisely, of capturing qualities in objects not so contingent on appetite, bodily experience and personal inclination.[4] How are we to proceed?

Clearly, one simple way out of this quandary would be to adopt a deflationist or even reductivist approach. After all, if the notion of aesthetic taste is ridden with ambiguity and doesn't seem to sustain a viable aesthetic psychology, then why not abandon it altogether? While we are sympathetic to the view that the term 'taste' can be misleading and perhaps even otiose, we are committed to the idea that examining the complex process which enables at least some aesthetic experience is important not only to philosophical theorizing but also to how we relate aesthetically to our environment. Improving our understanding of our aesthetic abilities can feed directly into our aesthetic understanding of the world. But perhaps most importantly, an investigation of this kind can shed light on what is distinctive about grasping aesthetic character—a fine-grained discernment receptive to often volatile combinations of aesthetic qualities in

DOI: 10.4324/9781003184225-5

Aesthetic Taste 59

remarkably varied settings. For although aesthetic experience is far from unusual in our everyday lives, apprehending aesthetic qualities or value seems to work in a different way from, for example, ascertaining colour, size or shape. Grasping aesthetic qualities is not, or at least not always, quite as straightforward. Although aesthetic qualities do tend to rely on non-aesthetic qualities such as colour and shape (apprehended in ordinary sense perception) for their manifestation, they cannot be directly inferred from them.[5] To address this gap and better demarcate the aesthetic case, the question becomes what *kind* of ability or skill we need to perceive, enjoy or otherwise determine aesthetic character.

This discrepancy between aesthetic and non-aesthetic experience has long fuelled the numerous explanations philosophers have offered of the phenomenon of aesthetic taste. During most of the eighteenth century— sometimes referred to as the 'century of taste'[6]—taste was crucially under-stood as a kind of sense or faculty in its own right, separate from the other senses and central to how aesthetic perceptions, assessments and experi-ences differ from their non-aesthetic counterparts. According to Joseph Addison ([1712] 1970), for example, only taste can discern perfection in the visual representation of material objects, with a distinct pleasure of the imagination reserved for beauty. Also for Kant, famously, exercising our judgement of taste is key to unlocking the possibility of beauty, and it is taste and the uniquely disinterested pleasure it yields which sets the aesthetic apart from the cognitive. Somewhat more recently, Frank Sibley (2001) has claimed that aesthetic terms or predicates are to be defined in relation to taste, suggesting that "when a word or expression is such that taste . . . is required in order to apply it, I shall call it an aesthetic term or expression" (p. 1). For Sibley, it is "the exercise of taste, perceptiveness, or sensitivity, of aesthetic discrimination or appreciation" (ibid.) which distinguishes the application of aesthetic concepts and which differentiates them from non-aesthetic concepts. Aesthetic taste is, then, a susceptibility to recognize, discriminate and respond to the aesthetic.

Two particular questions about aesthetic taste will drive our critical discussion. First, how should we best conceive of this specific form (or manifestation) of perceptiveness or sensitivity? That is to say, if there is to be a distinctly aesthetic taste or a taste especially relevant to aesthetic experience, then how ought we to understand it? Second, what work can we reasonably expect the notion of taste to perform in aesthetic experi-ence (broadly construed)? Is the notion of taste, as at least one commenta-tor has suggested, in fact "a metaphor for aesthetic judgment"[7]?

Disentangling some of the roles ascribed to aesthetic taste will lead us to examine an epistemological ambivalence based on the idea that the notion of taste allows for both subjectivist and objectivist readings. Underly-ing this discussion will be a question about whether it is the object of appreciation or subject of experience that determines whether a particular experience is aesthetic or not. Building on our response to this question, we will investigate the extent to which the seemingly discordant elements of taste can be understood to work together in relation to objects of appreciation in ways connected to the nature of aesthetic value. It will be our claim that conceiving of aesthetic taste either as a perceptual ability or as an emotional skill leads to a conceptual incongruity which, in turn, prompts some philosophers to speak of aesthetic taste as an expression of personal likings, whereas others think of it as a kind of attention or observation. In an attempt to move the debate forward, we propose an understanding of the relation between affective response or emotion and perception in the exercise of aesthetic taste which relies on the concept of *attunement*. Attunement is here understood, roughly, as the process in which an aesthetic agent comes to adjust their sensitivity to the perceived aesthetic character of an object of appreciation in order to better grasp its content and evaluative significance. Aesthetic taste is, then, not simply a matter of perceptual discernment or emotional sensibility but is rather a rich psychological process capable of sustaining our aesthetic experience of the object of appreciation over time.

II

An expedient first step in the process of elucidating the notion of aesthetic taste is to reflect on the specific task (or tasks) we expect it to perform. In short, which role (or roles) do we tend to ascribe to taste in aesthetically relevant cases? To put it differently, what is the expected outcome of the exercise of taste?

Setting aside any characterization of taste purely in terms of more or less fashionable penchants or predilections, aesthetic taste can be conceived as a mental ability the exercise of which is required for:

(i)   discerning aesthetic qualities[8] (*aesthetic perception*);
(ii) responding affectively to aesthetic value[9] (*aesthetic (dis)pleasure*);
(iii) making judgements about aesthetic value[10] (*aesthetic judgement*);
(iv) applying aesthetic terms and predicates[11] (*aesthetic attributions*);
(v)   recognizing and enjoying aesthetic merit[12] (*aesthetic evaluation*).

Generally speaking, these different tasks are united in a coherent experiential whole which includes most, if not all, aspects of the aesthetic. Taste is thus cast as the capacity of adeptly ensuring the successful performance of all these aesthetic acts, ranging from our affective response to specific manifestations of aesthetic value to our perceptual identification of individual aesthetic qualities in objects of appreciation. Taste, in other words, is the very underpinning of the various forms of aesthetic engagement which are more or less directly dependent on it: where there is aesthetic activity, there is also aesthetic taste, and no such activity can occur without having been instigated (at least partially) by taste.[13] Let us call this the *holistic approach* to aesthetic taste's functional roles. On a holistic view, aesthetic experience is not made up of entirely separate and independent aesthetic events. Rather, it involves chain reactions between phenomeno-logically connected events that together constitute one coherent aesthetic experience. One of the main advantages of a holistic approach to aesthetic taste is, precisely, that it makes sense of how perception, pleasure, judge-ment, attribution and evaluation tend to agree or concur, aesthetically speaking.

Despite its intuitive appeal, at least two considerations speak against a simple version of the holistic approach. The first has to do with the inevi-table 'thinning out' which any such extension of the central notion brings about. If aesthetic taste is (by definition) instrumental to a range of diverse aesthetic acts, or if we use the notion of aesthetic taste in identifying any aesthetic skill or capacity, then our conception of that notion must remain fairly generalized. We shall return to this point. The second consideration, more serious perhaps, concerns the very possibility—or indeed advan-tage—of assuming that one single ability is capable of enabling aesthetic activity in all its variety. This worry gives us reason to reflect on the 'mechanics' of aesthetic experience and how such experience is supposed to be generated in the first place. It will be our claim that even though philosophers and non-philosophers alike tend to operate with a fairly generous interpretation of how the exercise of taste can manifest itself,[14] this causes problems for the status of aesthetic experience and confuses the various strands of the relevant concept of taste.

To examine whether we can reasonably assume that the notion of taste can perform all these roles meaningfully and without conflict, let us look more closely at aesthetic (i) perception, (ii) pleasure, (iii) judgement, (iv) attribution, (v) evaluation and how they relate to one another.[15] For even on a holistic approach, the aesthetic process initiated by taste must be seen to start somewhere, and as we shall see, much hangs on how we take aesthetic experience to be generated in the first place. Two main alternatives present themselves. If the exercise of aesthetic taste involves first and foremost perceptually discerning aesthetic qualities in objects of appreciation, then aesthetic judgements, attributions and evaluations can naturally be seen as recognitions or recordings of the presence of such qualities. If, on the other hand, the principal role of aesthetic taste is to respond emotionally to features of our environment, then aesthetic judge-ments, attributions and evaluations will tend to be understood as reports of those affective responses.

Let us begin by taking (i) as the opening task to be performed or the functional role emphasized in our philosophical accounts of aesthetic taste. This is the idea that taste initiates aesthetic experience by the dis-cernment of aesthetic qualities, a claim defended by many taste theorists.[16] On this line, for an agent to have aesthetic taste is first and foremost for them to be able to spot, pick out or detect aesthetic features in the objects that surround us. To use Sibley's words again, taste is the "ability to notice or see or tell that things have certain qualities" (p. 3) such as being graceful, delicate, balanced or garish. Underlining the significance of (i) thus suggests a chronology of aesthetic experience whereby exercising taste in the first instance opens up distinctly perceptual possibilities—that is to say, opportunities to identify and discriminate aesthetically relevant qualities. It is perception which grounds our aesthetic judgements, attributions and evaluations (iii–v) and which leads us to experience aesthetic pleasure (ii), and to the extent that (ii)–(v) can be said to be the products of the exercise of aesthetic taste, they are so mainly in virtue of the initial aesthetic act of perceptual discernment (i).[17]

If, however, the exercise of taste is primarily to be conceived in terms of (ii), and the occurrence of aesthetic pleasure is thought to generate aesthetic experience, then exercising our aesthetic taste is chiefly a matter of being sensitive to the ways in which objects of aesthetic appreciation can evoke affective states in us and being responsive in emotionally appropriate ways. Taste is here first and foremost the ability to feel or react affectively. This approach, which can be traced back to Hume and Kant (among others), tends to cash out such affective responses in terms of feelings, likings or sensations of pleasure.[18] As Hume writes in his essay *Of the Standard of Taste* ([1757] 1965), "beauty and deformity . . . are not qualities in objects but belong entirely to the sentiments" (p. 11). To grasp beauty or deformity is to respond with a sentiment of approbation or disapprobation to the object of appreciation.[19] Placing the onus on (ii) in aesthetic experience thus suggests that to exercise aesthetic taste is to activate an emotional sensitivity. Emotions ground our aesthetic judgements, attributions and evaluations (iii–v), and aesthetic perception (i) comes about as a result of our emotional states. To the extent that (i) and (iii)–(v) can be said to be the products of the exercise of aesthetic taste, they are so mainly in virtue of the initial aesthetic act of responding with affect (ii).[20]

Even this brief discussion of aesthetic taste's functional roles reveals two very different accounts of what exercising aesthetic taste *de facto* involves—perceiving qualities in objects on the one hand and responding affectively on the other. A liberal attitude to the work we expect aesthetic taste to be able to perform thus leads to a dilemma. When (i) is emphasized and the exercise of taste is conceived primarily in terms of perceptual discernment, the epistemology of aesthetic experience and judgement favours some sort of *aesthetic objectivism*. Roughly speaking, objectivism is the view that it is the object, whose qualities are perceived by us, which determines the nature and character of aesthetic experience.[21] However, when (ii) is stressed and taste is chiefly cast as an affective ability, then our epistemology supports some form of *aesthetic subjectivism*.[22] In contrast to objectivism, this approach holds that it is instead the subject, responding affectively, who settles the nature and character of aesthetic experience.

Aesthetic Taste 63

The deep-rooted tension between objectivism and subjectivism permeates the notion of aesthetic taste and weakens its explanatory power and epistemic standing by pulling it in opposite directions. Fundamentally, what is at stake here is whether aesthetic taste is a matter of personal attitude or expression (as many philosophers of language are inclined to hold)[23] or, rather, involves well-founded apprehension and observation. What, one may ask, is the promise of good taste: a more acute perception or a more pleasurable experience?

So far, we have suggested that although the exercise of aesthetic taste is best seen as a holistic enterprise, capable of encompassing various aspects of aesthetic experience, this holism leads to an ambivalent conception of aesthetic taste. One possible way forward takes a disjunctive guise: perhaps the exercise of aesthetic taste is *sometimes* a question of perceptual discernment and at *other times* a matter of emotional sensibility? Perhaps aesthetic taste is capable of spanning that wide a range. But if so, we seem to have doubled the work ahead of us by calling for an explication of not one but *two* notions of aesthetic taste. We also seem to have provoked a host of new questions calling for our attention. What determines whether aesthetic taste is a perceptual or an emotional operation in particular cases? Does a specific aesthetic quality always invite the same manifestation of taste? And how could this approach help us to better address the original brief, namely to explain what is unique about grasping that which is distinctly *aesthetic* in the first place? These questions take us back to our first concern about a simple holistic approach: the risk of the notion of taste being sliced so thinly that it fails to offer the level of specificity or detail required for a fuller account of what the notion of aesthetic taste really amounts to.

III

Examining the different tasks that the notion of taste may be said to perform has led us to pinpoint an irregularity about the epistemic status of aesthetic taste. On the one hand, we find *affect-based* accounts, according to which the exercise of aesthetic taste amounts to the expression of an emotional (or non-cognitive) response.[24] On the other hand, we have *perception-based* (or *cognitive*) approaches, for which to exercise taste is to perceptually track an aesthetic object's relevant aesthetic qualities.[25] The problem, in short, is that "the connotation of the term links taste as much with emotive response as with discerning perception" (Korsmeyer, 2013, p. 258), and this fluctuation, we suggest, reflects a damaging toing and froing between subjectivist and objectivist conceptions of aesthetic taste.

Although each approach provides us with resources that are adequate for making sense of certain instances of aesthetic experience, each also presents us with serious challenges as a general account of aesthetic taste.

Some of those challenges stem from the threat of reduction, the prospect that the notion we are seeking to explain in terms of either emotion or perception may be simply reducible to the very concepts employed to explain it. That is to say, whereas affective theories may be seen to jeopardize the independence of taste by reducing it to a fundamentally affective response, perceptual theories open up a possible reduction of aesthetic taste to a purely perceptual kind of discrimination. To put it differently, if taste is either all about emotion or all about perception, then why do we need taste in the first place?

Other challenges target what one might refer to as the normativity of taste. If affective theories are right, then all objects of appreciation—including artworks—which do not tend to arouse emotional responses are no longer straightforward candidates for being experienced with the help of aesthetic taste. Yet similarly, if the perceptual approach is to be preferred, then it is not entirely clear how objects of appreciation which evoke feelings or other sentimental reactions rather than presenting a distinct formal appearance can be picked up or recognized with the help of aesthetic taste. At any rate, taste's explanatory scope seems considerably trimmed.

The following case brings out the heart of the matter well. In one of the most famous passages of *À la Recherche du Temps Perdu*, Marcel Proust describes the workings of aesthetic taste. In this scene, the imaginary writer Bergotte, very animated by a critical review he has read in a newspaper, visits an exhibition of Dutch art. It is his intention to ignore most pictures and concentrate on a detailed examination of one of his favourite works, Vermeer's *View of Delft* (1660–61). Bergotte, who is in delicate health, engages with the work and then collapses in front of the painting.

> At the first few steps he had to climb, he was overcome by an attack of dizziness. He walked past several pictures and was struck by the aridity and pointlessness of such an artificial kind of art, which was greatly inferior to the sunshine of a windswept Venetian palazzo, or of an ordinary house by the sea. At last he came to the Vermeer which he remembered as more striking, more different from anything else he knew, but in which, thanks to the critic's article, he noticed for the first time some small figures in blue, that the sand was pink, and, finally, the precious substance of the tiny patch of yellow wall. His dizziness increased; he fixed his gaze, like a child upon a yellow butterfly that it wants to catch, on the precious little patch of wall. "That's how I ought to have written", he said. "My last books are too dry, I ought to have gone over them with a few layers of colour, made my language precious in itself, like this little patch of yellow wall". Meanwhile he was not unconscious of the gravity of his condition. In a celestial pair of scales there appeared to him, weighing down one of the pans, his own life, while the other contained the little patch

of wall so beautifully painted in yellow. He felt that he had rashly sacrificed the former for the latter . . . He repeated to himself: "Little patch of yellow wall, with a sloping roof, little patch of yellow wall" . . . A fresh attack struck him down; he rolled from the settee to the floor, as visitors and attendants came hurrying to his assistance. He was dead.

(Proust, [1923] 1981, Vol. 3, p. 185)

In the description of this fatal epiphany, Proust paints a vivid picture of the gradual yet rapid activation and improvement of Bergotte's aesthetic sensitivity. Bergotte, following the critic's recommendation, exercises his aesthetic taste in at least two instances. First, he comes to experience the human figures as blue, the sand as pink and then, crucially, the 'little patch' of wall not only as yellow but as 'precious in itself': one of the painting's non-aesthetic features suddenly acquires an aesthetic character of its own. Second, and in a more far-reaching manner, he takes the beauty of Vermeer's cityscape to urge him to reconsider his own professional efforts and long-established writing style. This in turn provokes a profound alteration of his aesthetic ambitions and goalposts. In the first instance, Bergotte discovers an important light source and thereby gains access to the overall tranquility of the depicted scene, as well as its sense of depth and distance. In the second instance, he comes to grasp the beauty of the work more fully while undergoing a profound conversion of his own aesthetic ideals. As a result, his aesthetic perspective is irreversibly altered, and his ability to capture aesthetic value is fundamentally transformed.

This fictional scene highlights some of the complexities associated with having to choose either of the two broad approaches outlined so far. From an affect-based or subject-oriented perspective, it seems that the already frail Bergotte is able to experience new aesthetic qualities because of the growing conformity between his own emotional sensibilities and the content of the work. To exercise aesthetic taste is here to be receptive and able to respond to features of the painting that were simply unavailable before the affective adjustment took place and to partake fully in the emotional dimension of the artwork. Bergotte's experiencing the patch of yellow wall as aesthetically valuable becomes a matter of reacting to or rejoining the painting with appropriate feeling, and it is the shift in his affective susceptibility which explains his new evaluation of the aesthetic significance of the luminous feature. The yellow stain is no longer merely a layer of colour on one of the background walls but an 'exquisite' way of creating light that seems to come from inside the painting.

From a perceptual or object-oriented point of view, however, there is more to aesthetic taste than being emotionally impressed by a feature that we deem valuable as a result of our having been affected by it. Instead, Bergotte's exercise of aesthetic taste involves seeing how the newly manifested feature helps to successfully realize one of the painting's artistic aims, that is, to create an interplay of light and shade in three horizontal bands (the cloudy sky, water and the city). On this approach, the activity of understanding *why* a work is aesthetically valuable can be detached from a subject's particular point of view and instead connected to the relation between the perceivable qualities of the work and the artist's overriding aspirations for it. Bergotte is able to reach an understanding of the work because he has acted in the same unprejudiced manner as the critic. The value of Vermeer's painting comes into sight as he interprets the purposes of the painting and, in that process, adds value to it. Bergotte dies with the conviction that he has finally understood what holds the key to Vermeer's painting, and it is the identification of specific observable features (such as "some small figures in blue, that the sand was pink") which grounds Bergotte's revised aesthetic experience.[26]

Where does this leave us? Perceptual or object-oriented theories of taste sit well with the appreciation of many artistic objects in general and specialized art criticism in particular. For we, like Bergotte, tend to think of critics as being able to appreciate artworks even if they are not to their liking and of critical evaluations of aesthetic objects' purposes as enabling comparisons, with the possibility of some judgments being better than others. Aesthetic evaluation may be seen to be cognitive in the sense that it can be backed up by reasons and grounded in observable evidence or in facts about the object of appreciation. If, in contrast, aesthetic taste is principally a matter of emotional sensibility, it is not clear how we should explain how a subject can consciously discover, as Bergotte does, that a previous judgement was not the appropriate one. To make subjective response (in the form of affect or pleasure) the single state that marks the appropriateness of one's aesthetic engagement seems to hinder at least some important instances of knowing *why* something is beautiful.

Of course, none of this is to say that aesthetic taste is necessarily exhausted by perception and cognition alone, for it seems equally misguided to suggest that the exercise of taste is simply a case of intellectual 'seeing' through perception. One important factor worth taking into consideration here has to do with the particular perspective from which such perceiving is done and the manner in which such a firsthand aesthetic perspective can also be affective. After all, our emotional sensibilities also have a say as to the kinds of objects with which we decide to engage aesthetically and the kinds of aesthetic items to which we feel perceptually attracted.

The aim of this section has been to shed light on how taste is an ability exercised by a subject yet firmly grounded in the object of appreciation. Our reflections lead us to the position that renouncing the central role of either seems both phenomenologically and philosophically problematic. And perhaps this goes some way towards explaining why we have tended to overlook the epistemological ambivalence described here—abandoning

Aesthetic Taste 67

either seems to create more problems than the apparent ambivalence may cause by itself.

IV

The account of aesthetic taste defended here (i) promotes a revised understanding of the subject- and object-oriented dimensions of taste, (ii) aims to make sense of the epistemic relationship between perceptual discernment and emotional sensibility as manifested in the process of experiencing aesthetic qualities and (iii) represents the proper exercise of taste as requiring both perceptual and emotional training. According to our view, aesthetic taste is object oriented or cognitive insofar as it depends on how the world presents itself to the subject in perceptual experience. But it is also subject oriented (in a non-subsidiary way) in that it includes an affective perspective on how that same world reveals itself to us. On our view, emotional sensibility is that which ensures that the subject has a predisposition to perceive certain qualities as valuable (or not). Perceptual discernment is a form of high-level perception able to account for the aesthetic character of objects of aesthetic appreciation. To exercise aesthetic taste adequately requires a prudent balance between these two.

In developing this idea, we shall make use of the notion of *attunement*, or the way in which aesthetic agents can align their emotional sensibility to the meaning of an artwork, say, in order to better grasp its content and worth. We shall claim that an aesthetic agent can attune herself more or less well to an artwork or object of appreciation insofar as she adjusts her emotional sensibilities to the aesthetic character and content that the artwork or object exhibits. This, in turn, renders a richer perceptual grasp of the object's aesthetic qualities possible and therefore also opens up the possibility of a more rewarding aesthetic experience overall.

Historically speaking, the notion of attunement plays an important role in the work of Ludwig Wittgenstein (*Übereinstimmung*) and Martin Heidegger (*Befindlichkeit*).[27] For both philosophers, attunement refers to a precondition or 'overall orientation' necessary for any form of meaningful engagement with the world. For Heidegger, this precondition takes the form of affective moods, where these moods make sense of the world and the way we relate to it. More importantly, however, they reveal features about an agent's environment that would otherwise be missed. Attunement does not merely capture a purely subjective experience but a phenomenon that enables genuine cognitive performance in relation to one's cares and concerns.[28] Similarly, Stanley Cavell refers to Wittgenstein's notion of 'agreement in form of life' as attunement.[29] According to Cavell (1976), this agreement works as the common ground for all our shared practices and evaluative judgments. To be attuned is "a matter of our sharing routes of interest and feeling, modes of response, senses of humour and of significance and of fulfilment, of what is outrageous, of what is similar to what else, what a rebuke, what forgiveness, of when an utterance is an assertion" (as cited in Egan, 2019, p. 65). What is characteristic of this understanding of attunement is that it is not a specific form of affect directed at an object but a kind of *feeling with* which marks an agent's general affinity with her surroundings.

How does this tie in with the aesthetic case? A discussion of the notion of attunement in connection with art has recently been offered by literary theorist Rita Felski (2020). Felski employs attunement primarily to explain why we are drawn to certain paintings, novels or pieces of music and not to others. Attunement is introduced as a way of describing the kind of attachment we can form with artworks.[30] Significantly, for Felski, this attachment is conceived as highly selective and based on personal affinities: to become attuned is to enter into a responsive affective relation with an artwork—a coordinating of the senses, affect, bodies and objects (p. 72). This response "can be a matter of stability but also surprise . . . collectively shaped but also idiosyncratic" (p. 77). Felski, inspired by Zadie Smith's essay on her experience of Joni Mitchell's music, takes this to be a paradigm of our aesthetic engagement with artworks. The aesthetic experience is described by Smith as a conversion which "took no time. Instantaneous. Involving no progressive change but, instead, a leap of faith. A sudden unexpected attunement" (Smith, 2012, p. 33). In other words,

> I didn't come to love Joni Mitchell . . . by knowing anything more about her, or understanding what an open-tuned guitar is or even by sitting down and forcing myself to listen and re-listen to her songs. I hated Joni Mitchell—and then I loved her. Her voice did nothing for me—until the day it undid me completely.
>
> (Smith, 2012, p. 35)

Two features in particular characterize this model of attunement. First, the appreciator is not aware of the different ways in which perceptual discernment and emotional sensibility depend upon and relate to one another in experience. Second, aesthetic acts do not (or at least do not always) arise out of an effort to develop or improve one's abilities and skills. Felski also goes on to stress that most of the time, the aesthetic experiences resulting from attunement are ineffable or hard to articulate (p. 41). Attunement is understood as a semi-conscious mental event that makes us 'fall' for artworks rather like a sudden infatuation or a slow, unwitting acclimatizing. Attunement is not, then, principally about the artwork's content or meaning but the connections one may find between the subjective self and the individual values we attach to some artworks.[31] Crucial for Felski is the idea that these attachments denote an emotional tie or a kind of falling in love, not only with the aesthetic value of the work but with other people or artworks linked to it.

Aesthetic Taste 69

Felski's notion of attunement highlights certain aspects of how we can connect to art and how art also can connect us to other things (such as other aesthetic agents). Yet it does not say much about what makes the target or object of appreciation valuable in the first place, nor about the psychological workings involved in recognizing such value. In the remainder of this chapter, we will outline a related yet distinct account of attunement more directly committed to the idea that our response to objects of appreciation is a matter of fine-tuned perceptual abilities which enable us to grasp those objects' aesthetically salient properties. Also, and in contrast with Felski, we do not hold that attunement tends to be uninformed or generally less than conscious. Rather, we conceive of it as an apperceptive and cognizant mental process dependent on the cultivation of our aesthetically relevant sensibilities.

Engaging aesthetically with our environment is not so much an act of conferring significance or value on artworks, say, in virtue of the meaningful personal associations we form with them. Rather, it is a way of discerning and relating to the aesthetically significant or valuable features of that environment. Attunement to an object of aesthetic appreciation is therefore not so much an expression of one's subjective affinity with an aesthetic object as, instead, a kind of emotional understanding grounded in the perception of that object. Emotional understanding is here fundamentally connected to a perceptual awareness of the relevant aesthetic properties of an object. It is also a matter of being properly directed or oriented towards the characteristics which may serve as reasons for an agent in explaining why she has ascribed certain properties (and not others) to the object of appreciation in question. This process of apprehension or detection is a proactive event that we tend to seek out consciously. And, crucially, it is our emotional sensibility that orientates us in our aesthetic engagement with that which is perceived. To exercise aesthetic taste is, then, both a matter of aligning emotionally with the character or content of the object of aesthetic appreciation and of ascertaining the aesthetic qualities thereby available to us.

Central to such an account is the idea that aesthetic taste can be improved or enhanced through the joint cultivation of our emotional and perceptual abilities, for such cultivation—like the evolution of our aesthetic taste—has no set endpoint.[32] To this extent at least, aesthetic taste is less something that we *have* and more something that we *develop*. Of course, famously for Hume ([1757] 1965), "good sense", "serenity of mind" and reflection allow the critic to perceive the "mutual relation and correspondence of parts" in a work of art, to grasp "the consistency and uniformity of the whole" or to calculate if the purpose of a work is "deemed more or less perfect, as it is more or less fitted to attain this end" (pp. 146–147). Yet it does not follow that the education of an agent's aesthetic taste is reducible to the training of her perceptual skills. Training her emotional sensibility complements the development of her perceptual discernment in important ways.[33] Certainly for Hume, good aesthetic appreciators are also endowed with emotional receptivity, openness and acumen. And even though our emotional character can at times be unstable or even unreliable, it benefits from the epistemic support of the continuous refining and calibrating of our sensitivities.

In the words of Catherine Elgin (2007), such training "increase[s] emotion's epistemic yield" and "amount[s] to fine-tuning" (pp. 37–47). Strategies such as these have to do with learning in which circumstances an affective response is or isn't appropriate, how to manage the intensity and duration of a particular response, how to ascertain which reactions should be avoided and which should be promoted and more. The goal is not merely to achieve a fitting aesthetic evaluation or experience (as when artworks prescribe a specific emotional response) but to bring about a non-accidental experience of value. In this sense, emotions are 'active' in that they appear to capture the position or point of view adopted by an aesthetic agent towards an object (one that can be favourable or disfavourable).[34] In exercising these emotional abilities, one is not 'disclosing' an object's aesthetic value but adopting a perspective and attaching value to what is perceived. In other words, cultivating our emotional sensibilities opens the door to a wider range of aesthetic experiences grounded in perception. The more trained our sensibility is, the more experiences we are open to; the more trained our discernment is, the more nuanced our aesthetic judgements and evaluations will be.[35]

In conclusion, the exercise of aesthetic taste is best thought of in terms of what we have referred to as the agent's emotional understanding, where such understanding is grounded in perception. Taste thus involves an adjustment of one's emotional sensibility to the aesthetic character of the object of appreciation, which, in turn, opens up a richer repertoire of perceptual possibilities. To that extent, activating aesthetic taste is a relational process where emotion and perception mutually influence one another. In exercising taste, aesthetic agents *attune* themselves to an aesthetic object insofar as they align or calibrate their emotional sensibilities to the perceived aesthetic character which that object exhibits. To be attuned is to feel that one stands in the proper relation to aesthetic value where this feeling is based on an understanding of the object's aesthetic character. Being both emotionally and perceptually receptive or available, so to speak, will be central to such alignment or adjustment, since it builds on a certain kind of openness of thought and feeling.

Emotion and perception, subject and object, expression and attention need not pull in opposite directions in aesthetic experience. Aesthetic taste need not be conceived *either* in terms of emotional sensibility *or* perceptual discernment. The epistemological ambivalence discussed at the opening of this chapter follows only from an insufficiently integrated conception of how these two abilities can interact in aesthetic experience. A holism regarding the range of aesthetic acts included in such experience

Aesthetic Taste 71

can be upheld, since an understanding of aesthetic taste in terms of attunement results in a properly integrated conception of these acts according to which they depend upon both perceptual and emotional training.

Notes

1. See, for example, Kant ([1790] 2000), Baumgarten ([1750] 1961).
2. Hutcheson ([1726] 2004)
3. E.g., Hume ([1757] 1965), Kant ([1790] 2000, §3), Hegel (1976, pp. 38–39).
4. See, for example, Hutcheson ([1726] 2004) and the idea that aesthetic taste is the way we come to know certain specific features of the world, such as 'uniformity in variety'. For Hutcheson, the ability to grasp beauty could not stem from the exercise of one of the five senses but rather directly from the mind.
5. E.g., Sibley (2001), Levinson (1996), Tormey (1973), Budd (1999). See also Dorsch (2013), who argues for a limited inferentialism.
6. For more, see for example, Dickie (1996).
7. Spicher (2017).
8. See, for example, Sibley (2001).
9. See, for example, Kant ([1790] 2000); Hume ([1757] 1965).
10. See, for example, Budd (2001).
11. See, for example, Sibley (2001).
12. See Levinson (2016) for a discussion on whether taste requires a positive response or reaction to an object's perceivable aesthetic features.
13. What is more, the exercise of taste is part and parcel of what renders these different acts distinctly aesthetic: it is arguably in virtue of deriving from taste that they can be deemed aesthetic.
14. The empirical study by Bonard, Cova and Humbert-Droz presented in this volume shows that people's definitions of taste are diverse, fluctuating between subjectivist and more objectivist interpretations of taste.
15. For more on this point, see, for example, Dickie (1973).
16. Most recently Sibley (2001).
17. In other words, (ii) can be seen to arise as a direct result of (i), and (iii)–(v) are dependent on (i) for their content. This is not to say that taste is no longer deployed at all once the process of aesthetic experience has been brought about but that the initial task in some way determines not only the aesthetic character of the experience (in virtue of the qualities perceived through the exercise of taste) but also the nature and ambitions of that process itself.
18. While Hume's account, as mentioned, relies on the notion of sentiments of approbation and disapprobation, Kant's theory builds on the disinterested pleasure that arises from the interaction of the imagination and the understanding.
19. E.g., Wiggins (1987) and Johnston (2001).
20. Again, this is not to say that taste is no longer employed at all once the process of aesthetic experience has been generated.
21. Interestingly, although Noël Carroll (2016) doesn't describe himself explicitly as an aesthetic objectivist, his theory of aesthetic appreciation reinforces the idea that aesthetic experience is primarily about the perceptual discernment of objects and their qualities. According to Carroll, it is by isolating a work's purpose and contemplating whether the artistic choices can realize the aims of the work that one can begin to appreciate it appropriately. (For a similar account, see Gilmore, 2011.) This act is also thought to be informed by (and sensitive to) the context of production, the category to which the item

belongs or the authorial intentions. Liking or disliking what is perceived is, in fact, secondary. Instead, what is key is that taste is not the causal effect of a stimulus on the subject but an expression of active understanding *via* perception. This means that instead of taking the recognition of aesthetic properties as being principally grounded in our affective responses, the focus is on our human *perceptual* capacities (where perception is understood in a broad sense).

22. A recent subjectivist account which fits this outline nicely is Hannah Ginsborg's Kantian aesthetic theory (2014). On this line, aesthetic pleasure is a (disinterested) feeling expressive of how the object is presented in experience to the subject. When the subject judges a work of art, say, to be beautiful, she is not claiming anything about how the work *is*. Rather, for a subject to judge a work to be beautiful is for that judge to express her liking for it. For Ginsborg, it "is the awareness that the object merits a very specific feeling of pleasure" (2014, p. 31) which allows for certain normative constraints.

23. E.g., Franzén (2020), Lasersohn (2011), MacFarlane (2014), Stephenson (2007).

24. For defences, see Hume ([1757] 1965), Ginsborg (2014), Gorodeisky & Marcus (2018), Wiggins (1987).

25. E.g., Carroll (2016), Sibley (2001), Danto (1997).

26. On a cognitivist account such as Carroll's (2016), for example, emotions can play a role in the identification of the object of appreciation's aims. Affective responses can, for instance, be used as guides in the discovery of hidden meanings and the recognition of patterns or themes (p. 6).

27. See Egan (2019), Mulhall (2011), Ratcliffe (2002).

28. See Mulhall (2011).

29. See Egan (2019).

30. Felski (2020) identifies three kinds of attachment to art: attunement, identification and interpretation.

31. See Nehamas (2007) for a similar account.

32. Felski (2020) also discusses aesthetic education, albeit mainly in relation to its potential to "shake up preferences and remake perception; one becomes attuned to what once seemed opaque or irrelevant, and one comes to admire what once seemed unworthy of affection" (p. 56). While it seems right to point out that an improvement of taste involves a shift in one's aesthetic preferences, we take it that this is first and foremost a *consequence* of taste education rather than what exercising such taste amounts to.

33. For a similar point on why aesthetic capacities are not simply perceptual, see Durà-Vilà (2014, pp. 93–95).

34. A salient account representing this idea is Mueller's (2018) agential or 'position-taking' view on emotions.

35. For an idea along similar lines, see Ted Cohen (2004): "When you, having more delicate taste than I, obtain pleasure from some object that leaves me unmoved, you therein exhibit your greater delicacy of taste, but your pleasure is the direct result of your identification of qualities of the object that escape me. That is, it is precisely because you can "perceive every ingredient in the composition" . . . that you are "sensible to [a pleasure that escapes me]" (p. 168).

References

Addison, J., & Steele, R. ([1712] 1970). In D. F. Bond (Ed.), *Critical essays from the spectator by Joseph Addison: With four essays by Richard Steel*. Oxford University Press.

Baumgarten, A. G. ([1750] 1961). *Aesthetica*. Georg Olms.

Bonard, C., Cova, F., & Humbert-Droz, S. (This volume). De gustibus est disputandum— An empirical investigation of the folk concept of aesthetic taste.

Budd, M. (1999). Aesthetic judgements, aesthetic principles and aesthetic properties. *European Journal of Philosophy*, 7, 295–311.

Budd, M. (2001). The pure judgement of taste as an aesthetic reflective judgement. *British Journal of Aesthetics*, 41(3), 247–260. https://doi.org/10.1093/bjaesthetics/41.3.247

Carroll, N. (2016). Art appreciation. *Journal of Aesthetic Education*, 50(4), 1 14. https://doi.org/10.5406/jaesteduc.50.4.0001

Cavell, S. (1976). The availability of Wittgenstein's later philosophy. In *Must we mean what we say? A book of essays* (pp. 44–72). Cambridge University Press.

Cohen, T. (2004). The philosophy of taste: Thoughts on the idea. In P. Kivy (Ed.), *The Blackwell guide to aesthetics* (pp. 167–173). Blackwell.

Danto, A. (1997). *After the end of art*. Princeton University Press.

Dickie, G. (1973). Taste and attitude: The origin of the aesthetic. *Theoria*, 39(1–3), 153–170.

Dickie, G. (1996). *The century of taste: The philosophical odyssey of taste in the eighteenth century*. Oxford University Press.

Dorsch, F. (2013). Non-Inferentialism about justification: The case of aesthetic judgements. *The Philosophical Quarterly*, 63, 660–682. https://doi.org/10.1111/1467-9213.12063

Durà-Vilà, V. (2014). Courage in art appreciation: A Humean perspective. *British Journal of Aesthetics*, 54(1), 77–95. https://doi.org/10.1093/aesthj/ayu001

Egan, D. (2019). Attunement and being-with. In *The pursuit of an authentic philosophy: Wittgenstein, Heidegger, and the everyday* (pp. 64–86). Oxford University Press. https://10.1093/oso/9780198832638.003.0003

Elgin, C. Z. (2007). Emotion and understanding. In G. Brun, U. Dogouglu, & D. Kunzle (Eds.), *Epistemology and emotions* (pp. 33–50). Ashgate.

Felski, R. (2020). Art and attunement. In *Hooked* (pp. 41–78). University of Chicago Press.

Franzén, N. (2020). Evaluative discourse and affective states of mind. *Mind*, 129(516), 1095–1126. https://doi.org/10.1093/mind/fzz088

Gilmore, J. (2011). A functional view of artistic evaluation. *Philosophical Studies*, 155(2), 289–305. https://doi.org/10.1007/s11098-010-9570-8

Ginsborg, H. (2014). Kant on the subjectivity of taste. In *The normativity of nature: Essays on Kant's critique of judgment* (pp. 15–31). Oxford University Press. https://doi.org/10.1093/acprof:oso/9780199547975.001.0001

Gorodeisky, K., & Marcus, E. (2018). Aesthetic rationality. *Journal of Philosophy*, 115(3), 113–140. https://doi.org/10.5840/jphil201811538

Hegel, G. W. F. ([1835] 1976). *Aesthetics: Lectures on fine art*, translated by T. M. Knox, Oxford University Press.

Hume, D. ([1757] 1965). *Of the standard of taste and other essays* (J. Lenz, Ed.). Bobbs-Merrill.

Hutcheson, F. ([1726] 2004). *An inquiry into the original of our ideas of beauty and virtue* (W. Leidhold, Ed.). Liberty Fund.

Johnston, M. (2001). The authority of affect. *Philosophy and Phenomenological Research*, 63(1), 181–214. https://doi.org/10.1111/j.1933-1592.2001.tb00097.x

Kant, I. ([1790] 2000). *Critique of the power of judgment* (P. Guyer & E. Matthews, Trans., P. Guyer, Ed.). Cambridge University Press.

74 I. Martínez Marín and E. Schellekens

Korsmeyer, C. (2013). Taste. In B. Gaut & D. M. Lopes (Eds.), *The Routledge companion to aesthetics* (3rd ed., pp. 257–266). Routledge.

Lasersohn, P. (2011). Context, relevant parts and (lack of) disagreement over taste. *Philosophical Studies, 156*(3), 433–439. https://doi.org/10.1007/s11098-010-9625-x

Levinson, J. (1996). Aesthetic supervenience. In *The pleasures of aesthetic: Philosophical essays* (pp. 134–158). Cornell University Press.

Levinson, J. (2016). Toward an adequate conception of aesthetic experience. In *Aesthetic pursuits: Essays in philosophy of art* (pp. 28–46). Oxford University Press.

MacFarlane, J. (2014). *Assessment sensitivity: Relative truth and its applications*. Oxford University Press.

Mueller, J. M. (2018). Emotion as position-taking. *Philosophia, 46*, 525–540. https://doi.org/10.1007/s11406-017-9905-1

Mulhall, S. (2011). Attunement and disorientation: The moods of philosophy in Heidegger and Sartre. In H. Kenaan & I. Ferber (Eds.), *Philosophy's moods: The affective grounds of thinking* (pp. 123–139). Springer.

Nehamas, A. (2007). *Only a promise of happiness: The place of beauty in a world of art*. Princeton University Press.

Proust, M. ([1923] 1981). *Remembrance of things past* (C. K. Scott Moncrieff, T. Kilmartin, & A. Mayor, Trans.) (3 vols.). Penguin.

Ratcliffe, M. (2002). Heidegger's attunement and the neuropsychology of emotion. *Phenomenology and the Cognitive Sciences, 1*, 287–312. https://doi-org.ezproxy.its.uu.se/10.1023/A:1021312100964

Sibley, F. (2001). *Approach to aesthetics: Collected papers on philosophical aesthetics*. Oxford University Press.

Smith, Z. (2012, December 17). Some notes on attunement. *The New Yorker*, pp. 30–35.

Spicher, M. R. (2017). Aesthetic taste. In *Internet encyclopedia of philosophy*. https://iep.utm.edu/a-taste/

Stephenson, T. (2007). Judge dependence, epistemic modals and predicates of personal taste. *Linguistics and Philosophy, 30*, 487–525. https://doi.org/10.1007/s10988-008-9023-4

Tormey, A. (1973). Critical judgments. *Theoria, 39*, 35–49. https://doi.org/10.1111/j.1755-2567.1973.tb00629.x

Wiggins, D. (1987). A sensible subjectivism? In *Needs, values, truth: Essays in the philosophy of value* (pp. 185–214). Clarendon Press.

Part II
Experimental Philosophy

5 De Gustibus *Est* Disputandum
An Empirical Investigation of the Folk Concept of Aesthetic Taste

Constant Bonard, Florian Cova, and Steve Humbert-Droz[1]

1. Introduction: The Search for Folk Aesthetics

In the past decade, experimental philosophers have been investigating how people think about aesthetics and aesthetic questions (Cova et al., 2015; Cova & Réhault, 2018). A lot of this research has focused on whether people tend to be *aesthetic objectivists*—i.e., whether they consider that aesthetic predicates (such as 'beautiful' or 'ugly') actually refer to mind-independent, objective properties of objects—or at least *aesthetic universalists*—i.e., whether they consider that aesthetic judgments are, as Kant put it, "universally valid" (1790/1914, p. 33).

So far, all studies seem to converge towards the following conclusion: most people seem to think that aesthetic properties only exist in the eyes of the beholder (Beebe et al., 2015, 2016; Cova, 2018; Cova & Pain, 2012; Cova et al., 2019; Goodwin & Darley, 2008, 2012; Murray, 2020; Rabb et al., 2020). Indeed, when presented with two people making contradictory aesthetic judgments, most people consider either that "both people are right" or that "neither is right and neither is wrong", because it makes no sense to speak of being right or wrong about such things. (For a methodological criticism of these studies, see Moss & Bush, 2021.)

However, as some have pointed out (Zangwill, 2018; Goffin & Cova, 2019), the fact that people *explicitly* reject the existence of objective, mind-independent properties doesn't mean that they don't endorse their existence at a more *implicit* level. After all, one could argue that a lot of our aesthetic practices only make sense if we suppose that, at some level, we do think that there are objective aesthetic properties.

An example of such practices would be our tendency to speak of people as having 'good' or 'bad' aesthetic taste. At first sight, it seems that the most obvious way of making sense of this tendency is to ascribe to us the beliefs that (i) certain objects are, aesthetically speaking, *objectively* better than others and (ii) some people are better than others at detecting and appreciating this objective aesthetic value.

However, this argument presupposes that people think about aesthetic taste as an ability to discriminate the value of works of art. But, as we

DOI: 10.4324/9781003184225-7

will see, ascribing such a conception of aesthetic taste does not go without some problems. Indeed, the notion of aesthetic taste raises an interesting paradox.

While contemporary philosophers have worked on elucidating notions such as knowledge, free will, or consciousness, very few have tried to provide an analysis of the notion of aesthetic taste that would help to shed light on our everyday use of this notion. This stands in contrast to the numerous studies conducted on aesthetic judgments, aesthetic experiences, or aesthetic properties. This is all the more surprising given that the classical philosophical debate in aesthetics was centered on taste and that, according to Schellekens, "[t]he paradox of taste, as found in Hume and Kant, is [. . .] highly relevant to contemporary metaphysical debate within aesthetics" (2009, p. 734).

2. Some Philosophical Questions about Aesthetic Taste

2.1. The Paradox of Taste

Though the notions of good and bad aesthetic taste are now part of our everyday language, the notion of aesthetic taste has a venerable history. In Europe, the use of the term 'taste' in relation to the appreciation of works of art arose through the sixteenth and seventeenth centuries, before becoming a topic of philosophical investigation in the eighteenth century (Korsmeyer, 2013).

In the beginning, the metaphor of taste was applied to our appreciation of aesthetic qualities to point to (and sometimes to explain) some of its peculiarities. The first was its *immediacy*: appreciation of works of art does not depend on prior reasoning, nor is it a conclusion reached through explicit rules and principles. The second was its need for *acquaintance:* in the same way one has to taste a certain kind of food to know whether one really likes it, one needs to experience a work of art to truly appreciate its value. Thus, aesthetic appreciation seems to be an immediate perception of aesthetic qualities in the same way that taste is an immediate perception of gustatory qualities.

However, as we will see, the metaphor of taste is double-edged. We will refer to this as *the paradox of taste* (Mothersill, 1989).

On the one hand, speaking of taste seems to emphasize the *subjectivity* of aesthetic preferences: as for food, we each have our *own* taste, our *own* preferences. If I like spinach but another person does not, who am I to think my taste is *better*? This idiosyncratic conception of taste is emphasized by sayings such as *de gustibus, non est disputandum.*

On the other hand, as one of our five senses, taste allows us to make certain distinctions: between sugary and salty or sour and bitter. A person whose sense of taste is well trained and developed is more capable of identifying the ingredients that compose a dish. From this angle, the

De Gustibus Est *Disputandum*   79

metaphor of taste seems to stress the objectivity of taste (we can be right or wrong in saying, e.g., that an object is very salty or very bitter) and the fact that certain individuals' tastes are better than those of other individuals. This idea comes out in Hume's famous tale about Sancho Panza's relatives. Their ability to detect a key tied to a leather thong in a barrel of wine shows their (objective) superiority of judgment regarding wine (1757/1987, p. 146).

The paradox of taste—as well as one solution of it—was famously introduced by Hume in *Of the Standard of Taste*. At the beginning of his essay, he introduces the all-too-familiar subjective conceptions of taste:

> All sentiment is right; because sentiment has a reference to nothing beyond itself, and is always real, wherever a man is conscious of it. [. . .] a thousand different sentiments, excited by the same object, are all right: Because no sentiment represents what is really in the object. [. . .] Beauty is no quality in things themselves: It exists merely in the mind which contemplates them; and each mind perceives a different beauty.
>
> (1757/1987, pp. 143–144)

However, just after observing that this deeply subjectivist point of view has passed into common sense as a proverb, he also observes that common sense doesn't seem ready to follow this line of thought down to its ultimate consequences:

> Whoever would assert an equality of genius and elegance between OGILBY and MILTON, or BUNYAN and ADDISON, would be thought to defend no less an extravagance, than if he had maintained a mole-hill to be as high as TENERIFFE, or a pond as extensive as the ocean. Though there may be found persons, who give the preference to the former authors; no one pays attention to such a taste; and we pronounce without scruple the sentiment of these pretended critics to be absurd and ridiculous. The principle of the natural equality of tastes is then totally forgot, and while we admit it on some occasions, where the objects seem near an equality, it appears an extravagant paradox, or rather a palpable absurdity, where objects so disproportioned are compared together.
>
> (1757/1987, p. 144)

Thus, according to Hume, the notion of aesthetic taste is Janus-faced, as common sense is torn between two ideas: on the one hand, it is tempted to think of aesthetic taste as a mere subjective preference, while, on the other hand, it cannot but recognize that certain aesthetic tastes are clearly better than others. This raises a first question: *Is common sense really torn between these two conceptions of aesthetic taste?* Or is it content to

80 C. Bonard, F. Cova, and S. Humbert-Droz

adopt a pure subjectivist stance according to which no taste is better than another, as previous studies in experimental philosophy might suggest?

2.2. Taste as an Active Ability

Hume's solution to the paradox of taste is to ground aesthetic properties in the abilities of *ideal judges*. Judgments of aesthetic taste can thus be said to be subjective—in the sense that they are mind-dependent, as their correctness is determined by the taste of these judges—as well as objective—in the sense that the ideal judges have the 'correct' opinion on these mind-dependent properties. To use Hume's own words:

> [A person of good taste possesses a] strong sense, united to delicate sentiment, improved by practice, perfected by comparison, and cleared of all prejudice.
>
> (1757/1987, p. 150)

A central idea of Hume is that the ideal judge is free from her bias, though her taste remains a passive trait, similar to sense perception. As Noël Carroll puts it:

> Hume portrays the aesthetic response as a passive response to the artwork [. . .] In "Of the Standard of Taste," the notion that the aesthetic response is a simple causal effect—a sentiment consequent to a stimulus—predominates.
>
> (1984, p. 186)

Edmund Burke, by contrast, insists on the active abilities that good taste requires. He also diverges from Hume—as well as Hutcheson (1727/2008)—by understanding taste to be a *kind of judgment* as opposed to a distinct faculty of the mind:

> I cannot help taking notice of an opinion which many persons entertain, as if the Taste were a separate faculty of the mind, and distinct from the judgment and imagination; a species of instinct by which we are struck naturally, and at the first glance, without any previous reasoning with the excellencies, or the defects of a composition. [. . .] *It is known that the Taste (whatever it is) is improved exactly as we improve our judgment, by extending our knowledge, by a steady attention to our object, and by frequent exercise.*
>
> (1757/1998, p. 25, our emphasis)

This raises a second question: *Does common sense think of taste as a passive or active ability?*

2.3. Judgments of Taste and of the Agreeable

Of course, no historical survey of philosophers' views on aesthetic taste would be complete without mentioning Kant's account. A key distinction in Kant's conception of aesthetic taste is that judgments of taste ("Roses in general are beautiful", see Kant, 1790/1914, p. 61) contrast sharply with mere judgments of the agreeable ("The rose is agreeable (to smell)", see Kant, 1790/1914, p. 62). Indeed, the judgment of taste is a "logical judgement based on an aesthetical one" (Kant, 1790/1914, p. 61; see also Ginsborg, 2019, §2.1). As an argument in favor of this distinction, Kant points out that we tend to claim universal validity for our aesthetic judgments (i.e., others *should* share our judgments). At the same time, we are happy to embrace diversity and relativity when it comes to judgments about what is agreeable. The distinction is also based on the idea that aesthetic judgments, unlike judgments of the agreeable, don't involve a desire for the object. This raises a third question: *When it comes to distinguishing good from bad taste, does common sense treat judgments about beauty and art differently from judgments of the agreeable?*

2.4. Bourdieu's High Taste

Finally, let's end this historical tour with ideas that are not often taken into account in analytical aesthetics but are relevant to our study: Pierre Bourdieu's sociological hypotheses on taste. In *Distinction* (1979/1984), Bourdieu observes that what is considered to be of good taste usually coincides with the taste of the dominant class. According to him, the reason is that "culture and aesthetics are used [structurally, but non-intentionally] by the dominant class as one of the means to naturalize (and thus perpetuate) their superiority in relation to the dominated class" (Lizardo, 2014, p. 336).

Moreover, for Bourdieu, 'high' aesthetic taste does not consist only in appreciating the 'right' objects but also in appreciating them in the 'right' way: good aesthetic taste requires a particular aesthetic outlook, a 'disinterested' contemplation that makes one able to appreciate the aesthetic value of an object without reference to other kinds of satisfaction, such as moral satisfaction.

Thus, both the kind of things we love and how we love them signal our socioeconomic status while justifying it. Given the success of Bourdieu's ideas, we wonder whether people might have developed a conception of aesthetic taste that serves as a socioeconomic marker. This raises a fourth question: *Do people define good aesthetic taste by referring to what it signals about people themselves rather than the objects of their enjoyment?*

82   C. Bonard, F. Cova, and S. Humbert-Droz

Such are the questions raised by past philosophical discussions of the notion of aesthetic taste. Of course, some of these discussions are rooted in everyday concepts of aesthetic taste from three centuries ago, and one may consider that common opinion has changed since then. For example, it could be that the contemporary concept of aesthetic taste is more subjectivist than the one that was common during the Enlightenment. Or maybe people's opinions have been influenced by postmodern philosophy. Either way, these questions only stress that we still have much to learn and understand about the folk concept of aesthetic taste. In this chapter, we present and discuss the results of a first study aiming at probing people's conceptions of good and bad aesthetic taste.

3.   Materials and Methods

Participants were redirected to an online questionnaire. After filling out an online consent form and answering a question about how much of a potential £100 bonus they were willing to give to a list of several charities, they were presented with the following question:

(Taste_Possibility) *When we speak of people's preferences about works of art (such as novels, paintings, music, songs, movies, TV shows, etc.), we sometimes make a difference between people who have "good taste" and those who have "bad taste".*

Has it ever happened to you to say or think that a certain person had better taste than another one in this sense? (YES/NO)

Participants who answered NO were then presented with the following open-ended question:

(NoTaste_Justification) *Please, explain why you never say or think this sort of things.*

Participants who answered YES were presented with the four following open-ended questions:

(GoodTaste_Def) *What do you mean when you say that someone has good taste? Please, explain in a few sentences.*

(BadTaste_Def) *What do you mean when you say that someone has bad taste? Please, explain in a few sentences.*

(GoodTaste_Example) *Can you think of a person who, according to you, has good taste? Describe in a few sentences why you think this person has good taste.*

(BadTaste_Example) *Can you think of a person who, according to you, has bad (or poor) taste? Describe in a few sentences why you think this person has poor taste.*

De Gustibus Est *Disputandum*   83

After that, we sought to explore in more detail participants' conceptions of good and bad taste by asking them about particular domains. Half of the participants received the following question:

(Domains_v1) *For each of the following domains, indicate whether (according to you), it makes sense to say someone has good or bad tastes in this domain:* (on a scale from -3 = "No sense at all" to 3 = "Completely sense")

The other half received the following question:

(Domains_v2) *For each of the following domains, indicate whether (according to you), it makes sense to distinguish between good or bad tastes in this domain:* (on a scale from -3 = "No sense at all" to 3 = "Completely sense")

In both cases, the full list of domains was beer, car races, clothing, comic books, food, graphic design, interior design, jewelry, literature, marijuana, movies, music, paintings, sculpture, sports, TV shows, videogames, wine, and wrestling.

After that, participants were once again presented with the same list of domains and asked:

(Importance) *For each of the following domains, indicate to which extent it is important to have good taste in this domain according to you:* (on a scale from 0 = "Not important at all" to 6 = "Extremely important")[2]

Then participants were asked the following question about the possibility of improving one's taste:

(Improve_Question) *Do you think people can improve their taste relative to fine arts (e.g. music, paintings, literature, cinema)?* (YES/NO)

Participants who answered YES were presented with the following open-ended question:

(Improve_Possible) *How can people improve their taste? Explain in a few sentences.*

Participants who answered NO were presented with the following open-ended question:

(Improve_Impossible) *Why can't people improve their taste? Explain in a few sentences.*

Finally, to better investigate participants' conceptions of a person with good taste, they were asked to rate their agreement with eight statements about the kinds of things a person who has good taste would like (on a seven-point scale ranging from "Strongly disagree" to "Strongly agree").

At the end of the questionnaire, participants were asked a series of questions about themselves. Some of them (such as those about participants' tendency to experience various positive emotions and the kinds of charities they usually give money to) were collected for other purposes and are not relevant for the current study. Others were more directly relevant. First, we asked participants to rate how knowledgeable they were in each of the 19 domains presented in the (Domains) and (Importance) questions (on a scale from 0 = "Not knowledgeable at all" to 6 = "Very knowledgeable"). Second, we asked participants to rate how often they went (i) to the museum, (ii) to art exhibitions, (iii) to classical music concerts, (iv) to popular music concerts, and (v) to the cinema (on a 5-point scale from "Daily" to "Never").

We also asked participants about their age, gender, native language, current country of residence, country of birth, job, study level, and political orientation. Participants who were still students were asked to provide their parents' highest education level. Participants' education level and/or their parent's education level served as a proxy for socioeconomic status.

All materials and data can be found at osf.io/ckx2z/.

4. Participants

A representative sample of the US population was collected through Prolific Academic. Participants were paid £2.38 for their participation. In total, 297 participants completed our survey. After exclusion based on four attention checks, we were left with 241 participants (124 identified as men, 114 as women, and 3 as 'other'; M_{age} = 44.92, SD_{age} = 16.12).

5. Folk Conceptions of Aesthetic Taste

To our first question (Taste_Possibility: *Has it ever happened to you to say or think that a certain person had better taste than another one in this sense?*), 224 participants (93%) answered 'YES' and 17 participants (7%) answered 'NO'. Thus, a crushing majority of participants acknowledged having already said or thought that one person had better aesthetic taste than another.

The 224 participants who answered YES were then asked to provide a definition of good taste (GoodTaste_Def) and a definition of bad taste (BadTaste_Def). To analyze their answers, all three authors went through participants' open-ended answers and, based on this survey, created general categories into which participants' answers fell. These categories, along with examples of participants' answers falling into these categories, are presented in Table 5.1 for definitions of good taste and Table 5.2 for definitions of bad taste.

Table 5.1 Participants' definitions of good taste. First column indicates the name of the category. Second column gives the category's definition, as used by coders. Third column gives an example of participants' answers corresponding to this category. Fourth column gives the % of participants' answers falling into this category (as well as the raw number of participants who gave this answer). Bold, italicized text indicates higher-order categories.

Category	Definition of good taste	Examples of participants' answers	% (N)
RELATIVISM	Participant stresses that the notions 'good' and 'bad' tastes are relative or that it depends on the person or that it's all 'subjective'.	"Good taste is a relative term. It means that a particular work of art appeals to an individual for one reason or another. It also means that the same work of art may not appeal to a different observer."	08.5% (19)
Agreement			41.1% (92)
SUBJECTIVISM	A person who has good taste is a person who likes the kinds of things the participant likes.	"Normally when I describe things of being of good taste or bad taste, I really just mean to say that those who have good taste like the things that I like in a joking manner. Taste is subjective and judging whether or not someone has good or bad taste runs the risk of classism."	25.0% (56)
CONSENSUS	A person who has good taste is a person whose preferences are shared or approved by most people or a person who likes things that have stood the test of time.	"Someone with good taste is someone with a culturally and societally good taste. Means that if you say *The Office* is good, most people would agree. Since it is expected from a lot of people."	14.7% (33)
EXPERTS	A person who has good taste is a person whose preferences are in accordance with the verdict of experts.	"They like something that is usually critically acclaimed. It may be seen as intelligent or very insightful."	01.3% (3)
CHOOSER	A person who has good taste is able to choose and guess what will please other people.	"Someone that can appreciate the things that can bring happiness to other people that people without good taste cannot see."	06.7% (15)
TREND-SETTERS	A person who has good taste is a person whose taste sets trends or is imitated by others.	"When I think of someone who has good taste, I think of someone who is trendy, and most people would admire them for their good taste. I think they would take pride in their appearance and their surroundings. They just look good overall. Trendsetters."	00.8% (2)

(*Continued*)

Table 5.1 (Continued)

Category	Definition of good taste	Examples of participants' answers	% (N)
Taster's nonaesthetic dispositions and virtues			19.6% (44)
REASONABLENESS	A person who has good taste is a person whose tastes are reasonable, understandable.	"When I say someone has good taste I mean that generally the person is not overly brash or overly timid. Someone with good taste values things on a logical and emotional level. People with good taste don't try to show off or simply follow trends."	04.5% (10)
JUSTIFICATION	A person who has good taste is able to explain and justify their taste OR is a person whose taste is the product of reflection on their own tastes, and not a passively acquired disposition.	"If someone has good tastes, they can explain why they like something and be able to defend their position."	06.7% (15)
OPENNESS	A person who has good taste is a person who is able to appreciate a wide variety of things or who has been exposed to a wide variety of things.	"Someone who has an eye for different arts, music, and elements of life. Those who choose to try new arts out, and branch their tastes into new places."	04.5% (10)
BACKGROUND KNOWLEDGE	A person who has good taste is a person who has enough background knowledge (e.g., academic or historical knowledge) about the works of art and their creators.	"This person has a sense of high culture, a refined aesthetic sensibility, an acquired taste. Good taste is typically something that has to be earned through study at a university or college. There is usually depth and intelligence in good taste."	04.0% (9)
INDEPENDENT MIND	The taste of a person with good taste is really *their own* and not the result of mere conformism.	"It means that their taste is distinguished and different from the masses. They think and express themselves outside of the box."	04.5% (10)

			29.9% (67)
Detection of aesthetic or aesthetically relevant properties			
DISTINCTION	A person who has good taste is able to distinguish good art from bad art, what is appealing from what is not, quality over quantity. This is a person who likes works that have positive aesthetic values.	"People who have good taste have more refined senses. Their sense of aesthetic is more mature. They pick up on the more subtler beauty in the world."	25.9% (58)
DEPTH	A person who has good taste is able to perceive properties of works of art that are not perceptible at first sight. They are able to pay attention to small details. They do not stop at the *surface* of works of art but are able to perceive their *depth*.	"Good taste is being able to take in multiple aspects of a work, including history as well as aesthetic and appreciate something as a whole even if it's not immediately beautiful."	05.8% (13)
Nonaesthetic properties of works of art			13.4% (30)
GENTLE	A person who has good taste does not like things that are harmful, immoral, or offensive.	"I think it means that people chose to do or see or say or dress or participate in a way that is morally good and not offensive to other people. They don't like things that are garish. They respect other people and interact with them as they would want others to interact with them. They are not exhibitionists."	05.4% (12)
INTELLECTUAL	A person who has good taste likes educational works of art, or works of art with high intellectual value, rather than dumb, non-intellectual stuff.	"Liking shows that have an involved plot to them or are dispensing educational information. Murder mysteries, detective shows, and some superhero shows are good examples of the former. Documentaries about geology, history, and animals are examples of the latter."	04.9% (11)
EXPENSIVE	A person who has good taste likes expensive things, luxury goods.	"A person who has a good taste is a person who likes nice and expensive stuff. For example, he/she likes "Rolex" watch, that's mean he/she has a good taste in watch particularly. Another example, he/she likes expensive painting like "Picasso" for art."	03.1% (7)

(*Continued*)

Table 5.1 (Continued)

Category	Definition of good taste	Examples of participants' answers	% (N)
Others (agent-based)			18.3% (41)
DESIGNER	A person who has good taste is a person able to compose beautiful things or to match things together (clothes, decoration, etc.).	"Obviously having 'good taste' is subjective to a certain degree. But for example, to me having good taste when referring to clothing means that an individual knows how to properly mix and match articles of clothing in a way that is visually appealing."	10.7% (24)
PLEASANT	A person who has good taste is pleasant to be around, either because they are not rude, immodest, loud, or wear kitsch or garish clothes.	"I tend to assume someone has good taste if they present themselves in a pleasant and coherent manner, if they speak with good vocabulary, if their jokes are clever, if they are pleasant to look at and to listen to."	07.6% (17)

De Gustibus Est Disputandum   89

5.1. Participants' Definitions of Good Taste

After categories for participants' definitions of good taste were created, two coders (FC and SHD) independently went through participants' answers and indicated for each answer into which categories the answer fell. The same answer could fall into several categories. Interrater agreement was good (Cohen's kappa = 0.64 [0.59, 0.68]). Remaining disagreements were settled by a third coder (CB). Final results are presented in Table 5.1 (rightmost column) and Figure 5.1.

5.2. Participants' Definitions of Bad Taste

Participants' definitions of bad taste were analyzed following the same method as their definitions of good taste. After categories were created (see Table 5.2), two coders (FC and CB) independently went through participants' answers and indicated for each answer into which categories this answer fell. Inter-rater agreement was good (Cohen's kappa = 0.70 [0.67, 0.74]). Remaining disagreements were settled by a third coder (SHD). Final results are presented in Table 5.2 (rightmost column).

5.3. Demographic Variations in Participants' Definitions of Taste

Additionally, we looked at whether participants' definitions of good and bad aesthetic tastes varied along with certain demographic variables: age, gender (coded as: 1 = man, 2 = woman), socioeconomic status (measured through education levels for nonstudent participants and education level of their parent with the highest education level for student participants), political orientation (from left to right), and frequency of engagement in art-related activities. For each category of definition presented in Tables 5.3 and 5.4, we performed logistic regression with endorsement of category as dependent variable, and all five demographic variables as predictors. As can be seen, socioeconomic status or engagement with art did not seem to impact participants' choices significantly.

5.4. Discussion

What lesson can be drawn from these results regarding the folk concept of taste? Most of our participants (93%) agreed to say that they considered that certain people had *better* aesthetic taste than others. This confirms that the notions of good and bad aesthetic taste are part of our everyday aesthetic lives. But what exactly do people mean by 'good' and 'bad' aesthetic tastes?

(i) A first finding, which came as a surprise, was that, contrary to what is usually discussed in the philosophical literature (see Schellekens, 2009),

Table 5.2 Participants' definitions of bad taste. The indications for the columns are the same as for Table 5.1.

Category	Definition of bad taste	Example	% (N)
RELATIVISM	Participant stresses the fact that 'good' and 'bad' tastes are relative notions or that it depends on the person or that it's all 'subjective'.	"Nowadays is only a joke to people who likes things that I personally don't like or dislike. In the past I would mean it, but after time and experience, I have learned taste is a subjective aspect in the human nature."	06.3% (14)
Agreement			34.8% (78)
SUBJECTIVISM	A person who has bad taste is a person who likes things the participant doesn't like.	"When I say someone has bad taste I usually am just referring to when we disagree on something or they don't value something the same amount as I do."	20.1% (45)
DISSENSUS	A person who has bad taste is either a person who has preferences that are not shared by most people or a person who has preferences of which most people disapprove.	"If majority of people think what they think is good is bad then it usually means they have bad taste compared to everyone."	15.2% (34)
OUT-OF-FASHION	A person who has bad taste is a person whose taste is outdated or is not in line with current trends.	"A person has bad taste when they don't follow current trends. They are unable to think outside the box and refuse to see things from different points of view. They get stuck in one thing and end up getting left behind."	02.7% (6)
Taster's nonaesthetic dispositions and virtues			17.4% (39)
ALIEN	A person who has bad taste is a person whose tastes are weird, hard to understand, unreasonable.	"It would make me think about what is going on in their head. I would think less of them because apparently, we think differently."	03.6% (8)

LACK OF JUSTIFICATION	A person who has bad taste is unable to explain or justify their tastes OR is a person whose tastes are not the product of active reflection on their behalf but are rather the product of a passively acquired disposition.	"If someone has bad tastes they are unable to explain why they like something and can not defend their position."	03.6% (8)
NARROW-MINDED	A person who has bad taste is a person who never tries new things, who prefers to stick to the same kinds and genres of works of art.	"When someone has bad taste this person has yet to try many things in life. They solely stick to a couple of choices in their food, clothing etc. For example a person eats McDonalds shows he/she hasn't tried something better."	04.0% (9)
NO BACKGROUND KNOWLEDGE	A person who has bad taste is a person who has not enough background knowledge (e.g., academic or historical knowledge) about the works of art and their creators.	"They do not understand the creation. They are not educated enough to appreciate what it is or means."	02.2% (5)
FOLLOWER	A person who has bad taste is a person whose taste is not really *their own* but the mere result of blind conformism.	"I'd say someone with a 'bad taste' doesn't really like things on their own, they tend to be a follower for what's popular so they don't end up with much of a taste at all. I'd also say it's when they like a lot of things that other people tend to dislike, so they'd have a 'bad taste' compared. Again though, really depends on cultures and areas they grew up, what may be bad tastes where they are, could be good tastes elsewhere."	05.8% (13)
Detection of aesthetic and aesthetically relevant properties			39.7% (87)
NO VALUE	A person who has bad taste is a person who likes things that have *no aesthetic values* or *negative aesthetic values* OR is unable to make the distinction between things that have aesthetic values and those that don't.	"They don't or can't appreciate the beauty and quality of fine art or food, etc. Bad taste usually means that the person enjoys something of a lesser quality."	29.0% (65)

Table 5.2 (Continued)

Category	Definition of bad taste	Example	% (N)
GAUDY (subcategory of NO VALUE)	A person who has bad taste is a person who likes things that are gaudy, flashy, attention-getting, pompous, ostentatious, tacky (or has similar properties).	"It means they do not have a clue about what looks good, what is quality, what is in style, is desirable. Usually they like gaudy and tacky things that may be expensive but horrible looking."	09.8% (22)
SHALLOW/EASY	A person who has bad taste is a person unable to make an effort to perceive and appreciate properties of works of art that are not immediately obvious OR is a person who stops at the surface of works of art and thus only likes superficial things that are easy to appreciate.	"Attracted to things that have no depth."	12.1% (27)
Nonaesthetic properties of works of art			20.1% (45)
HARMFUL	A person who has bad taste is a person who likes things that are harmful, immoral, or offensive.	"If someone finds humor by making fun of someone. If there is violence, or abuse."	15.6% (35)
DUMB	A person who has bad taste is a person who likes things or people that are dumb or lack any epistemic value.	"Generally something dumb that can be appreciated by the lowest common denominator, is my best way of summing it up. This can also change depending on who is saying it."	04.0% (9)
CHEAP	A person who has bad taste is a person who likes things that are not expensive, or cheap.	"A person who has a bad taste is a person who likes ugly and cheap stuff. He/she likes to collect junk or dress ugly. For example, he wears jean and t-shirt to a wedding. Another example, she collects junk jewelry like fake ugly bracelet."	02.2% (5)

Others (agent-based)			22.8% (51)
BAD DESIGNER	A person who has bad taste is a person who designs things or chooses compositions that are aesthetically unpleasant (clothes, decoration, etc.).	"Specific examples come to mind right away, of bad taste. In clothing, for example, a blouse, that combines plaid and stripes, anything with a leopard or snake print, or any clothing that lacks modesty for the wearer. A person with bad taste, in my opinion, lacks the ability to create something of beauty."	12.1% (27)
UNPLEASANT	A person who has bad taste is a person who is annoying to be around, either because they are rude, immodest, or loud or wear kitsch or garish clothes.	"bad taste to me is being unkempt in yourself. A lack of positivity which shows in almost everything a person does."	11.6% (26)

94 C. Bonard, F. Cova, and S. Humbert-Droz

Table 5.3 Demographic predictors of participants' definitions of good taste. For each category presented (DISTINCTION, SUBJECTIVISM, CONSENSUS, and GENTLE), we performed a logistic regression with Age, Gender (1 = Man, 2 = Woman), Socioeconomic status, Engagement in art-related practices, and Political orientation as predictors. Each cell presents the regression coefficient and the standard error on the first line and the standardized regression coefficient (β) on the second line.

	Distinction	Subjectivism	Consensus	Gentle
Age	0.04 (0.01)	−0.04 (0.01)	−0.01 (0.01)	0.03 (0.02)
	β = 1.40***	β = −1.34**	β = -0.40	β = 1.87
Gender	−0.15 (0.33)	0.67 (0.34)	−0.40 (0.39)	0.00 (0.61)
	β = −0.17	β = 0.78*	β = −0.56	β = 0.00
Socioeconomic	−0.17 (0.17)	−0.28 (0.17)	0.17 (0.20)	0.12 (0.32)
	β = −0.38	β = −0.64	β = 0.48	β = 0.52
Art-related practices	0.11 (0.37)	−0.70 (0.44)	−0.48 (0.48)	−1.02 (0.84)
	β = 0.11	β = −0.70	β = −0.57	β = −1.95
Political	0.05 (0.08)	0.02 (0.09)	0.05 (0.10)	0.19 (0.16)
	β = 0.27	β = 0.08	β = 0.24	β = 1.55

Table 5.4 Demographic predictors of participants' definitions of bad taste. The indications for the columns are the same as for Table 5.3.

	Relativism	Dissensus	No Value	Shallow/ Easy	Harmful
Age	−0.01 (0.02)	−0.02 (0.01)	0.01 (0.01)	−0.01 (0.01)	0.02 (0.01)
	β = −0.77	β = −0.71	β = 0.31	β = −0.72	β = 0.78
Gender	0.21 (0.57)	−0.25 (0.39)	0.30 (0.31)	−0.81 (0.45)	0.37 (0.39)
	β = 0.43	β = −0.35	β = 0.33	β = −1.23°	β = 0.51
Socio-economic	−0.26 (0.29)	−0.16 (0.19)	−0.04 (0.16)	0.15 (0.22)	0.08 (0.20)
	β = −1.03	β = −0.43	β = −0.09	β = 0.46	β = 0.23
Art engagement	−0.39 (0.72)	−0.61 (0.49)	−0.26 (0.37)	0.86 (0.48)	−0.28 (0.46)
	β = −0.69	β = −0.73	β = −0.24	β = 1.14°	β = −0.33
Political	0.10 (0.15)	0.02 (0.10)	−0.13 (0.08)	−0.32 (0.14)	−0.16 (0.11)
	β = 0.79	β = 0.11	β = −0.52	β = −1.84*	β = −0.83

good taste is not only associated with judgment, perception, or enjoyment but also with an ability to create, compose, and design. About 1 in 10 participants gave an answer falling into the DESIGNER (10.7%) or BAD DESIGNER (12.1%) category and considered that good taste comes with creative abilities such as selecting clothing items that fit together, arranging a living room harmoniously, etc.

De Gustibus Est *Disputandum* 95

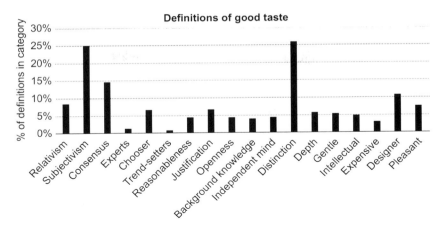

Figure 5.1 Percentage of participants' definitions of *good taste* falling into each category.

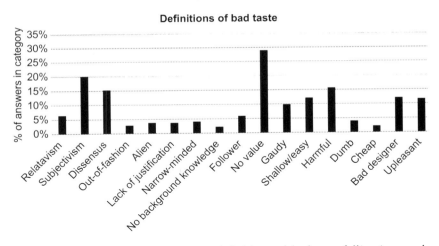

Figure 5.2 Percentage of participants' definitions of *bad taste* falling into each category.

(ii) Beyond this unexpected observation, a second finding was that participants' definitions of good and bad aesthetic taste mirrored the kind of tension highlighted by Hume, illustrating the paradox of taste. On the subjective side, 25% of good taste definitions and 20.1% of bad taste definitions fell into the SUBJECTIVISM category, in which participants defined good and bad taste in reference to their own taste. At the same time, 25.9% of good taste definitions and 29% of bad taste definitions fell respectively into the DISTINCTION and NO VALUE categories, according to which having good taste is liking good art and/or being able to distinguish good from bad works of art, and having bad taste is liking things that lack positive aesthetic values. Among participants whose definition of bad taste fell into the NO VALUE category, a third also fell into the GAUDY category, meaning that they considered that people of bad taste enjoy objects that instantiate negative properties that form a specific cluster—including being gaudy, kitsch, or tacky.

It is worth noting that SUBJECTIVIST answers are not *absolutely* incompatible with answers that fall into the DISTINCTION and NO VALUE categories, as shown by a participant who answered:

> *When I say someone has bad taste I usually mean someone who thinks fast food is delicious, or someone who doesn't appreciate great dialog in a movie. I think bad taste is liking clothes that aren't classic-looking. But it appears my perception of "bad taste" is solely my own opinion.*[3]

However, it is clear that answers in the DISTINCTION and NO VALUE categories easily lend themselves to an objectivist reading, according to which good taste is the ability to discriminate the *true* aesthetic value of objects. Thus, the fact that participants' answers are split between these categories and the SUBJECTIVISM one seems to speak in favor of the dichotomy Hume pointed out three centuries ago. The following answer perfectly illustrates this:

> *Their taste aligns closely to mine, or is similar but "better" than mine. By "better," I mean like disliking something I know (sort of objectively) is not that good (like laughing at a joke that's so unfunny that it comes back around into being funny again).*

Interestingly, while roughly the same percentage of good taste definitions fell into the DISTINCTION and SUBJECTIVISM categories (25.9 vs. 25%), there was a 9% gap between the NO VALUE and SUBJECTIVISM categories for bad taste definitions (29.0 vs. 20.1%). This might reflect a tendency in participants to become more objectivist when focusing on the bad (rather than the good). Such a tendency has been observed in the past for moral objectivism (Beebe, 2014; Goodwin & Darley, 2010), though not for aesthetic objectivism (Cova & Pain, 2012).

(iii) Hume's solution to this paradox of taste was to keep both subjectivity and objectivity by grounding the standard of taste in the opinion of experts. As one can see, this solution wasn't favored by our participants: only 1.3% of participants considered that good taste is determined by the taste of EXPERTS. A much more popular position was that good taste is to be found in what is widely appreciated: 14.7% of good taste definitions fell into the CONSENSUS category,[4] and 15.2% of bad taste definitions fell into the DISSENSUS category. This inclusive stance is in stark contrast with Hume's elitist hypothesis, but it can be seen as another way to combine the mind-dependence of aesthetic properties with the existence of an objective standard of taste.[5]

(iv) Burke's contention that good taste is an active ability was well reflected by the proportion of bad taste definitions falling into the SHALLOW/EASY (12.1%) and FOLLOWERS (5.8%) categories. Indeed, the definitions in both of these categories rely on the idea that people of bad taste indulge in effortless consumption and fail to put in the effort required by good taste. For example, when explaining how taste could be improved (see Section 7), one participant even claimed that having a better taste is not a question of changing preferences but a question of having experiences grounded in better experiences and judgment:

> *Having new experiences in food, racing or sports exposes the individual to other possibilities. Once they can distinguish differences, their taste has been improved. A change in taste may not reflect a change in preference.*

The definitions provided by these participants also fit well with the thesis that good taste is an Aristotelian virtue since the latter requires continuous training (see notably Lopes, 2008; Goldie, 2008).

(v) Finally, participants also appealed to moral considerations (e.g., whether one likes offensive works of art) to define good and bad taste. This was clearer for definitions of bad taste (HARMFUL: 15.6%) than for definitions of good taste (GENTLE: 5.4%). The difference between the two conditions is statistically significant: $\chi^2(1) = 11.51$, $p < 0.001$. This might reflect the fact that offensive works of art can be talked about as being in "bad taste", while "good taste" doesn't seem to have clear moral connotations. For example, in everyday life, we say that a morally dubious remark is in 'bad taste', but we wouldn't say that a morally virtuous remark is in 'good taste'. This also suggests that liking what is morally bad can be a defeater for good taste, although liking what is morally good isn't sufficient for having good taste. Hume formulates a similar idea:

> Where vicious manners are described without being marked with the proper characters of blame and disapprobation this must be allowed to disfigure the poem and to be a real deformity. [H]owever I may excuse the poet, on account of the manners of his age, I never can relish the composition.
>
> (1757/1987, p. 153)

Participants with higher education (which we used as a proxy for socioeconomic level) were not less likely to ground their definition of good and bad taste in moral considerations (in fact, they were even nonsignificantly

98   *C. Bonard, F. Cova, and S. Humbert-Droz*

more likely). Thus, our results seem to conflict with Bourdieu's claim that "popular classes" are more likely to blend aesthetic and moral judgments, in opposition with the 'disinterested' Kantian view that morality and aesthetics are orthogonal (1979/1984, p. 41). However, it should be stressed that Bourdieu focused on the (moral) *content* of the work, while our participants more frequently referred to the works' *impact* on real-life individuals (and how they could be offended). This difference should be kept in mind while interpreting our results.

6.   Good and Bad Taste Across Domains

We have seen that most people think that there can be good and bad aesthetic taste, even if they do not all seem to mean the same things by these expressions. However, our initial question (Taste_Possibility) was restricted to works of art (even if participants didn't necessarily take this restriction into account). This raises a question: Do people think that the distinction between good and bad taste is specific to the artistic domain, or do they think that it can be found in other domains as well? To find out, we presented participants with 19 domains (beer, car races, clothing, comic books, food, graphic design, interior design, jewelry, literature, marijuana, movies, music, paintings, sculpture, sports, TV shows, video games, wine, and wrestling) and asked them for each domain:

1.   To which extent it *makes sense* to *say* that someone has good or bad taste in this domain (for one half of participants) or to *distinguish* between good and bad tastes in this domain (for the other half) (on a scale from -3 = "No sense at all" to 3 = "Completely sense").
2.   To which extent it is *important* to have good taste in this domain (on a scale from 0 = "Not important at all" to 6 = "Extremely important").
3.   To which extent they were *knowledgeable* in this domain (on a scale from 0 = "Not knowledgeable at all" to 6 = "Very knowledgeable").

6.1.   *Participants' Answers on Good and Bad Taste Across Domains*

Participants' answers to these questions are organized by domain in Table 5.5 (standard deviation in parentheses). The rightmost column presents the result of an additional survey on 42 French-speaking participants presented with the same list of domains and asked to rate to which extent each domain is generally considered "highbrow" (on a scale from 0 = "Completely disagree" to 6 = "completely agree"). This survey was conducted to determine to what extent participants' conceptions of taste track what counts as "highbrow".

Table 5.5 Means and SDs for participants to our four questions about domains (*say, distinguish, important, knowledgeable*). The rightmost column presents the results of an additional survey in which participants were asked to rate to what extent each domain is generally considered "highbrow".

Domain	Say	Distinguish	Important	Knowledgeable	Highbrow
Beer	0.81 (1.89)	0.91 (1.76)	2.22 (2.05)	2.12 (1.89)	1.98 (1.32)
Car races	−0.95 (1.85)	−1.00 (1.65)	0.85 (1.32)	0.77 (1.23)	1.26 (1.42)
Clothing	2.05 (1.41)	2.07 (1.31)	4.23 (1.60)	3.24 (1.57)	3.12 (1.50)
Comic books	0.59 (1.80)	0.43 (1.85)	1.82 (1.78)	1.51 (1.64)	1.90 (1.21)
Food	1.75 (1.60)	1.76 (1.43)	4.15 (1.82)	4.05 (1.49)	3.48 (1.42)
Graphic Design	1.70 (1.57)	1.58 (1.44)	3.46 (1.88)	2.19 (1.86)	3.79 (1.12)
Interior Design	2.03 (1.45)	2.01 (1.18)	3.94 (1.79)	2.36 (1.73)	3.95 (1.43)
Jewelry	1.61 (1.60)	1.61 (1.31)	3.12 (2.00)	2.15 (1.76)	4.00 (1.48)
Literature	1.86 (1.57)	1.93 (1.34)	3.92 (1.81)	3.29 (1.73)	4.98 (1.07)
Marijuana	−0.25 (2.09)	−0.28 (2.04)	1.51 (1.95)	1.53 (1.93)	0.90 (1.14)
Movies	1.70 (1.62)	1.96 (1.21)	3.85 (1.70)	3.85 (1.50)	3.17 (1.21)
Music	1.96 (1.49)	2.14 (1.11)	4.27 (1.72)	3.98 (1.57)	3.83 (1.50)
Paintings	1.74 (1.80)	1.86 (1.37)	3.68 (1.88)	2.47 (1.77)	4.64 (1.43)
Sculpture	1.49 (1.63)	1.59 (1.39)	3.05 (2.06)	1.69 (1.59)	5.07 (1.22)
Sports	−0.37 (1.94)	−0.26 (1.82)	1.59 (1.80)	2.04 (1.88)	1.88 (1.38)
TV shows	1.38 (1.64)	1.73 (1.37)	3.49 (1.79)	3.63 (1.59)	1.38 (1.13)
Video games	0.35 (1.99)	0.55 (2.00)	2.26 (2.08)	2.47 (2.09)	1.57 (1.17)
Wine	1.48 (1.82)	1.46 (1.61)	2.91 (2.12)	1.89 (1.76)	4.48 (1.21)
Wrestling	−0.94 (1.96)	−1.03 (1.78)	0.88 (1.52)	0.92 (1.56)	0.81 (1.06)

Because participants' answers to the *Say* and *Distinguish* question were closely aligned across domains: $r(17) = 0.99$, we merged them into a single score (*Taste*). Participants' *Taste* answers were significantly correlated with their answers to the *Important* and *Knowledgeable* questions: $r(4577) = 0.64$, $r(4577) = 0.44$. Participants' answers to the *Important* and *Knowledgeable* questions were also correlated: $r(4577) = 0.59$.

Using domains rather than participants as data points, we also found a significant correlation between *Taste* and *Highbrow* answers: $r(17) = 0.79$. Partial correlations suggested that being knowledgeable in a domain and considering it highbrow made independent contributions to the idea that there are good and bad tastes within this domain: $r(17) = 0.80$, $r(17) = 0.83$.

6.2. Discussion

(i) A first remark is that these participants thought that it makes sense to distinguish between good and bad taste in domains other than the artistic. This clashes with an interpretation of Kant, according to which aesthetic judgments and judgments of the agreeable are restricted to specific domains. Kant gave food and wine as examples of domains in which we make judgments of the agreeable rather than aesthetic judgments (1790/1914, p. 57 & p. 158; see also Ginsborg, 2019, §2.1)—because such judgments usually involve a desire for the object, often don't purport to be universal judgments about which everyone ought to agree, and involve sense modalities (smell and taste) that don't "permit contemplation" (Scruton, 2001, p. 103), in contrast to hearing and sight. Contrary to this Kantian view, food and wine scored highly on the *Say*, *Distinguish*, and *Important* questions.

We may interpret this as suggesting that contrary to what Kant claimed, common sense doesn't treat judgments about beauty and art differently from judgments of the agreeable. Alternatively, it may be interpreted as suggesting that there are more domains, e.g., food and wine, in which aesthetic judgments are relevant than were indicated by Kant and some of his interpreters (however, see our next point).

(ii) Because participants considered that it doesn't make sense to distinguish between good and bad taste in certain domains, these results seem to conflict with the appealing conjunction of two plausible ideas: (1) that domains in which it makes sense to distinguish between good and bad taste are domains in which we can adopt an aesthetic attitude, and (2) that we can adopt an aesthetic attitude toward any kind of object (Irvin, 2008). If it doesn't make sense to distinguish good and bad taste concerning, say, marijuana—as participants, on average, seem to think—either (1) or (2) should be rejected.

(iii) As predicted by a popular hypothesis, participants' conceptions of taste seemed driven by their knowledge of a given field. For example, the more people knew about comic books, video games, or marijuana, the more they found it made sense to distinguish between good and bad taste in these domains (respectively: $r = 0.41, 0.51, 0.43$). However, knowledge didn't explain everything: for example, participants were way more knowledgeable in Food than in Interior Design and still answered that it made a bit more sense to distinguish between good and bad taste for Interior Design.

(iv) Another factor might then be whether domains are considered 'highbrow' or not. Indeed, the categories for which the *Say* and *Distinguish* scores are negative are considered "lowbrow" (*Highbrow* average score below 2): wrestling, sports, marijuana, and car races. Furthermore, among the 13 domains in which participants usually didn't consider themselves knowledgeable (those for which the average score for *Knowledgeable* is below 3), the only five in which they tended to consider it important to distinguish between good and bad taste (average score for *Important* above 3) are domains that are considered highbrow: sculpture, painting, jewelry, interior design, and graphic design (average score for *Highbrow* above 3).

This result fits well with the Bourdieusian idea that it is more valuable to have good taste in domains that are associated with the dominant classes (highbrow domains) because taste is often used to signal one's social status.

7. Can Taste Be Improved? And How?

Finally, we asked our participants whether people could improve their taste relative to fine arts; 92.5% of participants answered positively. We then asked participants who answered positively to explain how people could improve their taste.

After categories were created, all three coders independently went through participants' answers and indicated for each answer into which categories this answer fell. FC coded all answers and CB and SHD coded one half each. Interrater agreement was good (Cohen's kappa = 0.68 [0.64, 0.73]). Remaining disagreements were settled by a third coder (CB or SHD, depending on the second coder's identity). Final results are presented in Table 5.6 (rightmost column).

7.1. Participants' Answers to How Taste Can Be Improved

7.2. Discussion

As we saw, most participants answered that people can improve their taste, which is in line with the fact that most participants admitted making a distinction between good and bad taste.

(i) 55.6% of those who thought that people cannot improve their taste (7.5% of all participants) considered that this is not possible because

Table 5.6 Participants' methods to improve taste. The indications for the columns are the same as for Table 5.1.

Category	Method to improve	Example	%
Exposure			66.4% (148)
VARIETY	Expose oneself to a wide variety of works of art (by travelling, etc.).	"They can improve their tastes by starting to value new things. I haven't always liked the same things but over time my taste has become more refined. Anyone can do that. It's not something you are born with."	40.4% (90)
AGAINST	Go against oneself by trying things one does not like or by going out of one's comfort zone and trying unusual things (e.g., things that are not mainstream).	"People can improve their taste by giving chances to art that is not their go-to piece. For instance, listen to a genre of music you are not familiar with or ordinarily do not like but instead try to find the beauty/harmony in it."	10.8% (24)
QUALITY	Expose oneself to or acquaint oneself with things that are high-quality OR are considered high-quality by most people and/ or critics.	"By choosing specific topics within a given subject that are considered good. For example, one can improve their taste in music by listening to bands and artists that are considered good. Not forcing themselves to like it, however."	17.5% (39)
CONFORMITY	Try to imitate the taste of the majority or of one's in-groups.	"People should know what is accepted as good by most of the people and try to stick with such good things to improve their taste."	06.3% (14)
EMULATION	Try to imitate the taste of experts and role models.	"By educating themselves and mirroring behaviors of those with good taste."	08.5% (19)
Knowledge			41.7% (93)
BACKGROUND KNOWLEDGE	Acquire factual knowledge about works of art and their creator (by reading, getting an education, etc.).	"Finding out more about a subject will improve a person's taste. Like reading a book about movies or taking a class will help a person to understand what makes a movie good or bad."	36.8% (82)

DISCUSS	Discuss taste with others, try to understand others' taste, ask others to explain their taste.	"Consumption is very important, it helps people gain perspective, discussing with others the strong and weak points of a given work is also very important."	06.3% (14)
EXPLAIN	Learn to explain and/or justify one's preferences and tastes.	"People can improve their taste by being reflective on something they enjoyed. It is easy to think 'wow that was good' but to think back and pick apart why you liked or did not like something is the path to refining your taste."	02.7% (6)
Skills (Know-how)			04.5% (10)
PERCEPTION	Learn to pay attention to and perceive more details, learn to adopt new perspectives on works of art.	"I think just being able to pay more attention to the subtle details in those areas can actually elevate a person's perception of things."	04.5% (10)
Others			07.6% (17)
AGE	Taste changes during one's life.	"As people age, their preferences and choices changes and it leads to betterment most of the time."	02.7% (6)
RELATIVISM	Someone's taste becomes 'good' when it coincides with the participant's taste.	"If someone begins to have similar opinions to me on a form of entertainment then I would say that they can improve their taste."	02.2% (5)
DESIGN	Learn to compose aesthetically pleasant things (e.g., coordinating clothes, colors, or sounds).	"Often people are unaware that certain qualities of an object enhance or detract from the surrounding objects. Once they have a few examples of how objects and colors can work with or against each other, they are freer to experiment and find combinations that are more pleasing to them and others. This is sometimes seen when people are given a course in choosing clothes."	02.7% (6)

taste is relative and/or is akin to subjective preferences—due to space constraints, we do not produce the table; all materials and data can be found at osf.io/ckx2z/.[6] Another common answer as to why people cannot improve their taste is that it is somehow too hard to change one's taste (NO CHANGE, 27.8%) due to a lack of motivation (NO MOTIVA-TION, 16.7%) or to habits or difficulties in modifying preferences and beliefs:

> *I believe people already have in them what they like and what they are accustomed to. It's very hard to change adults for their beliefs and training.*

(ii) 40.4% of participants considered that we can improve our taste by being exposed to a wide variety of objects, genres, experiences, etc. This intuition was shared by Hume and Burke. Quite often (17.5%), participants explicitly specify that one needs to be exposed to high-quality objects and experiences, such as high art, masterpieces, or just beauty (as in the following Kantian-ish example):

> *People could improve their taste in fine art by being exposed to more of the beauty of God's creation . . . mountains, sunrises and sunsets, trees, etc.*

Additionally, it is interesting to note that our participants' emphasis on diversity is in line with the results of a recent sociological study that highlights the fact that, nowadays, high-status tastes are characterized by a greater diversity and inclusivity at the level of genres (while still being characterized by a narrower focus on "high-quality" items within each genre) (Childress et al., 2021). Thus, it might be that participants' conceptions of the best ways to improve one's aesthetic taste are driven by the models offered by contemporary high-status tastes.

(iii) 41.7% of participants gave an answer that we categorized as involving the acquisition of some kind of knowledge (see the BACKGROUND KNOWLEDGE, DISCUSS, and EXPLAIN categories). According to these participants, we can improve our taste by improving our cognitive capacities and by learning from books and discussions with others. These answers are in line with Burke's contention that taste is akin to judgment, in contrast to mere passive perception.

Nevertheless, as we saw in Section 5, only 4% of participants' definitions of good taste were classified as BACKGROUND KNOWLEDGE and 4.9% as INTELLECTUAL. Aesthetic taste is rarely defined in cognitive terms. This seems to be in tension with a strict reading of Burke's view that taste is a kind of judgment, but it is not incompatible with a more moderate interpretation of his ideas, e.g., Carroll's (1984) Burkian hypothesis that cognition plays a central role in aesthetic enjoyment and taste.

8. Conclusion

In this chapter, our goal was to explore the everyday concept of aesthetic taste with the aim of improving our grasp of what people mean when they distinguish between 'good' and 'bad' aesthetic taste. A first result was that most of our participants (drawn from a stratified US sample) indeed made such a distinction and considered that people could improve their aesthetic taste.

However, this apparent uniformity hides a wide variety of definitions of good and bad aesthetic taste. Though a variety in expression (i.e., definitions given) does not necessarily reflect variety in the underlying construct (i.e., the folk concept of aesthetic taste), participants' answers seem torn between the idea that taste is merely a matter of personal preference and the idea that taste is an ability to discriminate the true value of aesthetic objects. Between 20% and 25% of participants gave a subjectivist answer according to which taste is a mere preference that differs from one person to another, while 25% to 29% of participants defined good and bad taste as the ability or inability to appreciate what is really aesthetically valuable. This tension reflects Hume's paradox of taste, which we described in the introduction.

Our results suggest that our participants see good taste as something that is actively developed, while bad taste is passively absorbed. While our participants do not necessarily think that having good taste requires going against the consensus—quite the contrary, as many answers fell into the CONSENSUS or DISSENSUS categories—various participants stressed that good taste has to be autonomously and consciously developed, making the person with good taste able to explain and justify their preferences. This is in line with Burke and Carroll's claims that taste, like judgment, has to be actively exercised to be improved.

Most participants answered that improving one's taste required exposing oneself to a wide and diverse array of works of art and/or acquiring factual knowledge about works of art. This might reflect that even if taste is simply a preference, some preferences are better because they are more informed and the product of better judgment. To come back to the metaphor of gustatory taste (*pace* Kant), one could say that taste as preference is subjective but that it is better when it is grounded in an accurate ability to distinguish between the ingredients of a dish. This might also explain why people tend to think that it makes more sense to distinguish between good and bad taste for domains about which they have more knowledge: their knowledge makes them more conscious of the quantity of knowledge required to fully appreciate an object. Nevertheless, people also seemed to attribute importance to mastering good taste in domains about which they are not knowledgeable but that considered socially highbrow—which is close to Bourdieu's hypothesis.

Going back to our initial question of whether people are implicitly aesthetic objectivists, what can be learned from our results? First, it is indeed hard to deny that people do distinguish between good and bad taste. However, as we saw, this is not always incompatible with subjectivism about aesthetic properties: many participants simply defined good taste as taste similar to theirs or as taste in line with the consensus of the majority. Still, the high proportion of definitions assimilating good taste to the ability to discriminate and/or appreciate the true aesthetic values of works of art and the fact that most people accept the idea that taste can be improved might reveal an objectivist strain in laypeople's views about aesthetic properties. This is a question that might need to be tackled more directly in future work.

Among other questions that might need to be addressed in the future, one is whether people who think of good taste as an ability to recognize what has true aesthetic value think that good judgment has to be accompanied by enjoyment to count as good taste. What about someone who is able to recognize good art after a lot of training but is unable to enjoy and appreciate it? Does this person have good taste? Does good taste necessarily include an affective component?

Such are the questions we plan to address in future work. Meanwhile, we would like to conclude by pointing out the striking relevance of empiricists' analyses of aesthetic taste. It is heartening to note that aesthetic intuitions that are more than 260 years old have not drastically shifted. Hence, classical philosophers are not merely confined to history classes but can participate actively in contemporary debates. While the question of good taste is little discussed in philosophy (if not reduced to being merely subjective), both Hume and common sense show us that on taste, there is much to debate.

Notes

1. Authors are listed in alphabetical order.
2. Throughout the study, we use scales ranging from -3 to 3 when answers can be interpreted as representing the participant's attitudes toward a certain proposition (against/in between/in favor), and scales ranging from 0 to 6 when participants are asked to estimate a certain quantity for which negative values would not make sense (e.g., importance or knowledge).
3. The last sentence does not necessarily contradict the first because the participant may consider that expressions such as 'delicious' or 'great dialogue' mean something like 'delicious for me' or 'great dialogue according to me'.
4. Among the 33 participants who gave an answer in the CONSENSUS category, only 4 gave an answer that mentioned what philosophers call the 'test of time'.
5. We classified as 'experts' people's reference to professionals of artistic domains. Hume was rather referring to ideal judges (see Levinson, 2002 for an enlightening discussion). Since nearly nobody referred to judges, the difference between ideal or professional judges is not of great importance here.

6. Note however that some who think that taste is subjective believe that we can nevertheless improve our taste, as the following example shows: "*People can continue to expose themselves to arts and design. Over time the person should develop what they think is a pleasing style. This should improve their taste.*"

References

Beebe, J. R. (2014). How different kinds of disagreement impact folk metaethical judgments. In J. C. Wright & H. Sarkissian (Eds.), *Advances in experimental moral psychology: Affect, character, and commitments* (pp. 167–178). Bloomsbury.

Beebe, J. R., Qiaoan, R., Wysocki, T., & Endara, M. A. (2015). Moral objectivism in cross-cultural perspective. *Journal of Cognition and Culture, 15*(3–4), 386–401.

Beebe, J. R., & Sackris, D. (2016). Moral objectivism across the lifespan. *Philosophical Psychology, 29*(6), 912–929.

Bourdieu, P. (1979/1984). *Distinction: A social critique of the judgement of taste* (R. Nice, Trans.). Harvard University Press.

Burke, E. (1757/1998). *A philosophical enquiry into the origin of our ideas of the sublime and beautiful* (A. Phillips, Ed.; Reiss). Oxford University Press.

Carroll, N. (1984). Hume's standard of taste. *The Journal of Aesthetics and Art Criticism, 43*(2), 181–194.

Childress, C., Baumann, S., Rawlings, C. M., & Nault, J. F. (2021). Genres, objects, and the contemporary expression of higher-status tastes. *Sociological Science, 8*, 230–264.

Cova, F. (2018). Beyond intersubjective validity: Recent empirical investigations into the nature of aesthetic judgment. In F. Cova & S. Réhault (Eds.), *Advances in experimental philosophy of aesthetics* (pp. 13–32). Bloomsbury Publishing.

Cova, F., Garcia, A., & Liao, S. Y. (2015). Experimental philosophy of aesthetics. *Philosophy Compass, 10*(12), 927–939.

Cova, F., Olivola, C. Y., Machery, E., Stich, S., Rose, D., Alai, M., . . . & Zhu, J. (2019). *De Pulchritudine non est Disputandum?* A cross-cultural investigation of the alleged intersubjective validity of aesthetic judgment. *Mind & Language, 34*(3), 317–338.

Cova, F., & Pain, N. (2012). Can folk aesthetics ground aesthetic realism? *The Monist, 95*(2), 241–263.

Cova, F., & Réhault, S. (2018). *Advances in experimental philosophy of aesthetics*. Bloomsbury Publishing.

Ginsborg, H. (2019). Kant's aesthetics and teleology. In E. N. Zalta (Ed.), *The Stanford encyclopedia of philosophy* (Winter 2019). Metaphysics Research Lab, Stanford University. https://plato.stanford.edu/archives/win2019/entries/kant-aesthetics/

Goffin, K., & Cova, F. (2019). An empirical investigation of guilty pleasures. *Philosophical Psychology, 32*(7), 1129–1155.

Goldie, P. (2008). Virtues of art and human well-being. *Aristotelian Society Supplementary Volume, 82*(1), 179–195.

Goodwin, G. P., & Darley, J. M. (2008). The psychology of meta-ethics: Exploring objectivism. *Cognition, 106*(3), 1339–1366.

Goodwin, G. P., & Darley, J. M. (2010). The perceived objectivity of ethical beliefs: Psychological findings and implications for public policy. *Review of Philosophy and Psychology, 1*(2), 161–188.

Goodwin, G. P., & Darley, J. M. (2012). Why are some moral beliefs perceived to be more objective than others? *Journal of Experimental Social Psychology, 48*(1), 250–256.

Hume, D. (1757/1987). *Essays, moral, political, and literary* (E. F. Miller, Ed.; Rev. ed.). Liberty Classics.

Hutcheson, F. (1727/2008). *An inquiry into the original of our ideas of beauty and virtue: In two treatises* (W. Leidhold, Ed.; Rev. ed.). Liberty Fund.

Irvin, S. (2008). The pervasiveness of the aesthetic in ordinary experience. *The British Journal of Aesthetics, 48*(1), 29–44.

Kant, I. (1790/1914). *The critique of the power judgement* (Bernard, Trans). Macmillan.

Korsmeyer, C. (2013). Taste. In B. Gaut & D. M. Lopes (Eds.), *The Routledge companion to aesthetics* (pp. 193–202). Routledge.

Levinson, J. (2002). Hume's standard of taste: The real problem. *The Journal of Aesthetics and Art Criticism, 60*(3), 227–238.

Lizardo, O. (2014). Taste and the logic of practice in distinction. *Czech Sociological Review, 50*(3), 335–364.

Lopes, D. M. (2008). Virtues of art: Good taste. *Proceedings of the Aristotelian Society, Supplementary Volumes, 82*, 197–211.

Moss, D., & Bush, L. S. (2021). Measuring metaaesthetics: Challenges and ways forward. *New Ideas in Psychology, 62*, 100866.

Mothersill, M. (1989). Hume and the paradox of taste. In G. Dickie (Ed.), *Aesthetics: A critical anthology* (pp. 269–286). St. Martin's.

Murray, D. (2020). Maggots Are delicious, sunsets hideous: False, or do you just disagree? Data on truth relativism about judgments of personal taste and aesthetics. In T. Lombrozo, J. Knobe, & S. Nichols (Eds.), *Oxford studies in experimental philosophy* (Vol. 3, pp. 64–96). Oxford University Press.

Rabb, N., Han, A., Nebeker, L., & Winner, E. (2020). Expressivist to the core: Metaaesthetic subjectivism is stable and robust. *New Ideas in Psychology, 57*, 100760.

Schellekens, E. (2009). Taste and objectivity: The emergence of the concept of the aesthetic. *Philosophy Compass, 4*(5), 734–743.

Scruton, R. (2001). *Kant: A very short introduction* (Revised). Oxford University Press.

Zangwill, N. (2018). Beauty and the agreeable: A critique of experimental aesthetics. In F. Cova & S. Réhault (Eds.), *Advances in experimental philosophy of aesthetics* (pp. 289–308). Bloomsbury Publishing.

6 Contextualism Versus Relativism
More Empirical Data

Markus Kneer

1. Introduction

Let me not waste your time: There are three major truth-conditional accounts that purport to explain the semantics of perspectival claims regarding e.g. personal taste,[1] epistemic modality,[2] or aesthetic evaluation.[3] They differ with respect to two orthogonal dimensions, namely (i) whether the perspectival element (e.g. a standard of taste or an epistemic perspective) is conceived as part of the *content* of the proposition uttered or as a *parameter* in the circumstance of evaluation and (ii) whether the extension of such claims is sensitive to the *context of utterance* or whether it can, at times, be sensitive to a *context of assessment*. (For recent reviews of the literature, see e.g. Stojanovic, 2017 and Glanzberg, 2021.)

According to indexical contextualism (e.g. Glanzberg, 2007; Stojanovic, 2007, 2017; Cappelen & Hawthorne, 2009; Schaffer, 2011) an utterance of "Salmon is delicious" features a tacit, quasi-indexical perspectival element in the proposition's *content* which is drawn from the context of utterance. Nonindexical contextualists (e.g. Kölbel, 2002, 2004, 2009; Recanati, 2007) argue that a position of this sort cannot accommodate the phenomenon of faultless disagreement. The proposition itself, they suggest, is taste-neutral, and the standard of taste is, like worlds or times, part of the Kaplanian circumstance of evaluation (or a Lewisian index).

Relativists (e.g. MacFarlane, 2014; Egan, 2007, 2010) agree with nonindexical contextualists that perspectival features are best located in the circumstance and not the propositional content. However, and in contrast to both kinds of contextualism, relativists look beyond the context of utterance and make room for dynamic updating: people's tastes, aesthetic standards, and epistemic situations can change, and if they do, a perspectival claim true at the context of utterance might be false as evaluated from a later context of assessment. Here's MacFarlane:

> When our own tastes change, so that a food we used to find pleasant to the taste now tastes bad, we may say that we were mistaken in saying that the food was "tasty." When I was a kid, I once told my

DOI: 10.4324/9781003184225-8

110 *Markus Kneer*

mother, "Fish sticks are tasty." Now that I have exposed my palate to a broader range of tastes, I think I was wrong about that; I've changed my mind about the tastiness of fish sticks. So, if someone said, "But you said years ago that fish sticks were tasty," I would retract the earlier assertion. I wouldn't say, "They were tasty then, but they aren't tasty any more," since that would imply that their taste changed. Nor would I say, "When I said that, I only meant that they were tasty to me then." I *didn't* mean that. At the time I took myself to be disagreeing with adults who claimed that fish sticks weren't tasty.

(2014, pp. 13–14)

What the passage highlights is that the dynamic nature of the relativist view entails *two* norms of assertion. One, labelled the "Reflexive Truth Rule," specifies the conditions under which one is warranted to *make* an assertion.

> **Reflexive Truth Rule:** An agent is permitted to assert that p at context c_1 only if p is true as used at c_1 and assessed from c_2.

(2014, p. 103)

Given that the only context that matters for the making of assertions is the context of utterance (or "use"), this might leave "contexts of assessment without any *essential* role to play" (2014, p. 104). However, on the dynamic account of assertion proposed by relativists, there's a second rule in place—a rule which specifies under which conditions one must *retract* an assertion:

> **Retraction Rule:** An agent in context c_2 is required to retract an (unretracted) assertion of p made at c_1 if p is not true as used at c_1 and assessed from c_2.

(2014, p. 108)

Naturally, a retraction cannot simply wipe the retracted assertion from the conversational record. However, that's not the point. Instead, in taking back an assertion we attempt "to 'undo' the normative changes effected by the original speech act" (MacFarlane, 2014, p. 108; for discussion about retraction in particular, see e.g. Ferrari (2016), Marques (2014a, 2018), Kneer (2015, 2021a), Zakkou (2019a), Caponetto (2020), and Dinges (this volume)).

Truth relativism about perspectival expressions is a descriptive theory, which makes hypotheses about norms of assertion in ordinary English. The norms in question are conventional, non-codified, behaviour-dependent rules, which govern our linguistic practice (at least in certain domains). Norms of this kind are social facts, and as such, they are suited to empirical investigation: we can test whether ordinary language speakers are

Contextualism Versus Relativism 111

inclined to act in conformity with the proposed linguistic conventions and whether their normative assessments of pertinent perspective-dependent assertions track the Truth and Retraction Rules. If this were the case, then the core tenets of relativism are in place (though they could possibly be spelled out in terms of competing theories with similar explanatory power). If people's linguistic behaviour (and assessment thereof) proves inconsistent with the proposed norms of assertion, both the force of the relativist critique of contextualism as well as the central pillars of the relativist view itself collapse.

This chapter surveys some recent experiments concerning the norms of assertion proposed by relativism (Section 2). Amongst ordinary English speakers, there is evidence against the Truth Rule (Knobe & Yalcin, 2014; Kneer, 2015, 2021a) and the Retraction Rule (Kneer, 2015, 2021a; Marques, ms). Moreover, the empirical literature on norms of assertion is increasingly converging on the position that such a norm is not factive in the first place. Consequently, there's little reason to assume that the norms of *perspectival* assertions differed in this regard.

However, there are some interesting diverging findings. Dinges and Zakkou (2020) present conflicting results regarding the Truth Rule, reporting a distinct lack of agreement with *both* contextualist and relativist predictions concerning the truth assessment of taste claims. Furthermore, according to Knobe and Yalcin (2014), the folk seem to agree with some sort of retraction rule for epistemic modal claims (despite disagreeing with MacFarlane's Truth Rule). Both in Dinges and Zakkou's and in Knobe and Yalcin's experiments, I would like to suggest, the tested target statements might not adequately mirror what is at stake in the contextualism/relativism debate.

To anticipate the findings: in Dinges and Zakkou's study, the lack of agreement with the contextualist predictions might be due to an inadequate formulation of the response claim. Three experiments that attempt to remedy this potential shortcoming lend support to contextualist truth assessment (Sections 3 to 5). Knobe and Yalcin's study concerning a norm of retraction, by contrast, asks participants whether it is "appropriate" for a speaker to take back an epistemic modal claim whose prejacent is false at the context of assessment. What is appropriate, however, need not be required. Relativists like MacFarlane (see quotation earlier), just like most theorists in the debate concerning norms of assertion, however, tend to state their hypothesized rules in terms of what is *required* or *mandatory*, or what *must*, *ought* and *should* be done. What they are concerned with are *core* or potentially *constitutive* rules of assertion, and these can be expected to invoke strict normative force. Such rules contrast with *peripheral rules* that help regulate our assertive practices, characterized inter alia by a more lenient normative force, of which there surely are many. It is, for instance, *appropriate* or *commendable* to express oneself with *clarity* and *precision*. However, neither of these two norms have

112 *Markus Kneer*

witnessed much attention in the literature about *the* (central or constitutive) norms of assertion, let alone the contextualism/relativism debate. Section 6 thus reports a replication of Knobe and Yalcin's study, both with their original formulation of the retraction question as well as a version that tracks MacFarlane's Retraction Rule. Whereas people—in line with Knobe and Yalcin's results—find it appropriate to take back epistemic modal claims whose prejacent turns out false at the context of assessment, they *disagree* with the assessment that retraction is *required*.

Overall, the findings of the three experiments question the adequacy of the relativist Truth Rule and the Retraction Rule. The extension of perspectival claims depends on the context of utterance, and there is no requirement of any sort to retract them at a later context of assessment (although one may sometimes do so).

2. Empirical Data

2.1. *Utterance Sensitivity and Retraction for Perspectival Claims*

Let's begin with the story MacFarlane uses to motivate relativism with respect to predicates of personal taste. In several experiments (Kneer, 2015, ch. 7; 2021a), participants were presented with a scenario based on said fish sticks scenario, quoted earlier. The vignette came in two versions, either containing a claim about the truth assessment of a previous taste claim [A] or else the requirement for retraction [B]:

FISH STICKS

John is five years old and loves fish sticks. One day he says to his sister Sally: "Fish sticks are delicious." Twenty years later his taste regarding fish sticks has changed. Sally asks him whether he still likes fish sticks and John says he doesn't anymore.

[A] Sally says: "So what you said back when you were five was false."
[B] Sally says: "So you are required to take back what you said about fish sticks when you were five."
Q. To what extent do you agree or disagree with Sally's claim?

Participants responded to the questions on a seven-point Likert scale anchored at 1 with "completely disagree" and at 7 with "completely agree." Advocates of a contextualist semantics would hypothesize agreement with both claims of Sally to be low. After all, what, on this theory, matters for truth-assessment is the context of utterance, at which John's claim was true. A relativist semantics, however, would predict agreement

Contextualism Versus Relativism 113

with Sally's assertion that John's original claim was false, since it is false at the context of assessment. Given that it *is* false at the context of assessment, relativists would further hypothesize, and given that Sally challenges John, he must retract his original claim. Relativists would predict mean agreement with the proposed truth assessment and required retraction to be significantly above the midpoint of the scale. Contextualists, by contrast, would predict the means to lie significantly below the midpoint of the scale.

Consistent with contextualism and inconsistent with relativism, people strongly disagreed with the claim that John's original assertion was false or that he should retract it. Similar results were found for another predicate of personal taste, namely "fun" (the "Sandcastle scenario"). Although it is the relativist's paradigm example, reasonable concerns might be voiced concerning the time lag between a childhood claim as to fish sticks' tastiness and a challenge in adult life. Reducing the time span between the context of utterance and the context of assessment, however, does not make a difference (Kneer, 2021a, Exp. 2, "Salmon scenario"). Figure 6.1 visually represents the findings. All means are significantly below the midpoint of the scale (one-sample *t*-tests, all *p*s < .001).

For a different type of perspectival expression (epistemic modals), Knobe and Yalcin (2014) also report evidence for truth-assessment along contextualist lines. Kneer (2015, ch. 6; ms) further finds that assertions such as "John might be in China" are judged truth-conditionally on a par with "For all I know, John is in China," the contextualist's preferred interpretation of "might" claims. Marques (ms) reports results favouring

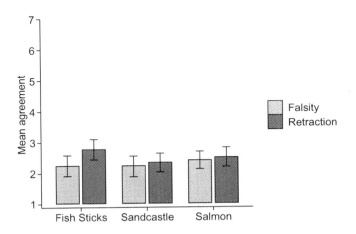

Figure 6.1 Mean agreement with the statement that an original taste claim was false at the context of utterance and that it must be retracted given preference reversals across different scenarios. Error bars denote standard error of the mean.

114 *Markus Kneer*

a contextualist semantics for epistemic modals for native Spanish speakers. Despite considerable convergence, there are some findings that call contextualism into question. To these we will turn in Sections 2.3 and 2.4 after a brief look at the literature on norms of assertion that is not directly concerned with perspectival claims.

2.2. *Norms of Assertion*

Much of the contextualism/relativism debate centers on the validity of the norms of assertion and retraction proposed by relativists. It is thus surprising that the extensive literature about norms of assertion in general is hardly discussed in this context. However, as I will briefly argue, the latter also casts doubt on the hypotheses that our assertions—perspectival or not—are governed by (something like) MacFarlane's Truth Rule or the Retraction Rule.

For several decades, philosophers have explored the question of what, if anything, is required of a speaker to be in a position to assert a certain proposition x (for an excellent review, see Pagin, 2014). On the most demanding (and most widely defended) account, in order to assert x, the speaker must *know that x* (the *knowledge account*, see e.g. Williamson, 1996, 2000; Hawthorne, 2004; Turri, 2011). According to an alternative view, for a speaker to assert x, x must simply be *true*—though it need not be known (the *truth account*, see e.g. Weiner, 2005). Both views are *factivist* in so far as they require the asserted proposition to be true. *Nonfactivists* argue that if it were only ever appropriate to assert true propositions, the number of warranted assertions we make would be rather limited. This either suggests that the alleged (factive) norm of assertion doesn't really do much to regulate our communicative behaviour (the force and importance of such a norm is limited), or else the norm of assertion simply is not factive. The position that the central rule of assertion is not tied to propositional truth, it should be noted, still allows for the possibility that assertion *aims* at (the conveying of) truth (see Marsili, 2018, 2020, 2021). Some nonfactivists thus propose that in order to assert x, it suffices to have a justified belief as to x, even if x is false (the *justified belief account*, e.g. Douven, 2006; Lackey, 2007). Other nonfactivists are more lenient still and advocate a view according to which one can say whatever one believes (the *belief account*, e.g. Bach, 2008; Hindriks, 2007; Mandelkern & Dorst, ms).

What the debate about norms of assertion can contribute to the debate about norms of retraction is this: only if assertability depends on propositional truth in general does it make sense to postulate norms of assertion and retraction for perspectival claims that do. If, for instance, the justification account were correct and it were acceptable to assert a justified yet false proposition, then it is obscure why perspectival claims should be governed by something like MacFarlane's Truth and Retraction Rules.

Contextualism Versus Relativism 115

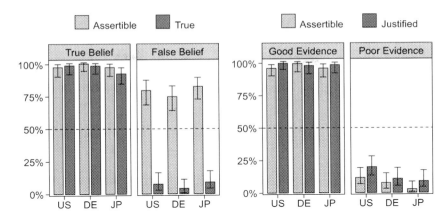

Figure 6.2 Left—Proportions of participants who judged a justified claim *x* assertible and true across conditions (true v. false); *Right*—Proportions of participants who judged a claim assertible and justified across conditions (good v. poor evidence).
Source: Kneer (2021b, p. 2).

Whether human communication is indeed regulated by norms of assertion and what these might be is, of course, an empirical question (Douven, 2006; Turri, 2013; Pagin, 2016). There is some evidence that points towards a factive norm of assertion (Turri, 2011, 2015; for an overview see Turri, 2017). However, studies from other researchers have increasingly converged on the position that the norm of assertion is most likely justified belief (Kneer, 2018; Reuter & Brössel, 2019; Marsili & Wiegmann, 2021). In a large cross-cultural study with more than 1,000 native speakers from the US, Germany, and Japan, for instance, it perspired that people think that a speaker should assert that *x* in cases where *x* is false yet justified (Figure 6.2, left), though should not assert that *x* when he has poor evidence for his claim (Figure 6.2, right).

In short, given that assertion, in general, does not seem to be governed by a norm tied to propositional truth, it is unclear why perspectival claims should.

2.3. Knobe and Yalcin

Knobe and Yalcin (2014) presented their participants with the following vignette, which is closely modelled on an example by MacFarlane (2011):

> Sally and George are talking about whether Joe is in Boston. Sally carefully considers all the information she has available and concludes that there is no way to know for sure.

SALLY SAYS: "Joe might be in Boston."
Just then, George gets an email from Joe. The email says that Joe is in Berkeley. So George says: "No, he isn't in Boston. He is in Berkeley."

On a seven-point Likert-scale, participants were asked to report to what extent they agreed or disagreed with one of the following two claims:

[Truth assessment] What Sally said is false.
[Retraction] It would be appropriate for Sally to take back what she said.

As a control condition, there was an alternative scenario in which Sally does not say that Joe *might be* in Boston but simply asserts that he *is* in Boston. The experiment thus took a 2 *claim type* (indicative v. modal) × 2 *question type* (truth assessment v. retraction) between-subjects design. Figure 6.3 graphically represents the results.

The truth assessment of epistemic modal claims, the results suggest, is sensitive to the context of utterance and not the context of assessment. It thus confirms a contextualist view of epistemic modals and challenges relativism. What is astonishing is this: although the modal claim is *not* considered false, it is nonetheless judged appropriate to retract it. Beddor and Egan (2018, p. 9) thus wonder whether the data really support contextualism. There are thus three questions that arise: (i) Why do they differ from other retraction findings for both epistemic modals and taste claims that uniformly suggest there is no norm of retraction, (ii) what could explain them, and (iii) does the data cast doubt on contextualism as, e.g., Beddor and Egan (2018, p. 9) wonder? We will come back to these questions in section 6.

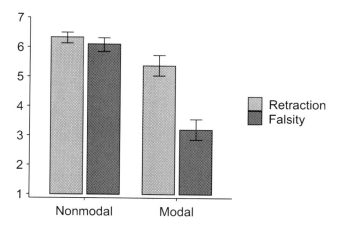

Figure 6.3 Mean ratings for the nonmodal and modal condition. Error bars designate standard error of the mean.
Source: (Knobe & Yalcin, 2014, p. 15)

2.4. Dinges and Zakkou

In a rich and interesting paper, Dinges and Zakkou report experiments concerning the expression "tasty." Here's one of their vignettes (2020, p. 8) and the questions they asked participants:

> Yumble is a new brand of bubblegum. You have never had a Yumble. One day you decide to try one. You don't like the taste. You tell your friend Paul:
> "Yumble isn't tasty."
> A few weeks later, you and Paul meet at the check-out in the supermarket. Yumble hasn't changed its taste, but you have now come to like it. You take a pack from the shelf. Paul says:
> "That's funny, I have a clear recollection of you saying 'Yumble isn't tasty' last time we met!"
> For each of the following responses, please tell us how likely you would be to give this response to Paul's remark in the given context.
> "What I said was false. Yumble is tasty." [Scale from 0–100]
> "What I said was true. Still, Yumble is tasty." [Scale from 0–100]

The key idea of the experiment was to have people rate *both* a relativist response ("What I said was false. Yumble is tasty") *and* a contextualist response ("What I said was true. Still, Yumble is tasty"). In the scenario, Paul starts out disliking Yumble and comes to like it. This type of preference reversal, labelled "not liking to liking" or "NLtoL" by Dinges and Zakkou, is complemented by one in the opposite direction, labelled "liking to not liking" or "LtoNL" for short. Participants were presented with either the NLtoL or the LtoNL condition. Figure 6.4 graphically presents the results.

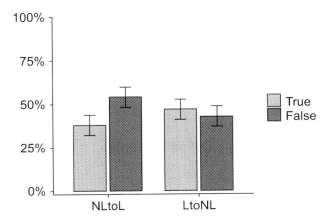

Figure 6.4 Mean ratings by condition. Error bars show 95% CI.
Source: (Dinges & Zakkou, 2020, p. 10).

118 *Markus Kneer*

A mixed ANOVA with *truth assessment* (true v. false) as the within-subjects variable and taste reversal *direction* (NLtoL v. LtoNL) as the between-subjects variable revealed no significant main effect for truth assessment ($p = .11$) or direction ($p = .50$). The interaction, however, was significant ($p = .007$, $\eta_p^2 = .025$ a small effect). The data thus suggests two main findings: First, neither of the two responses—one relativist, one contextualist—finds particular favour or disfavour with participants. The reported likelihood of asserting either sit roughly at the midpoint of the scale. Dinges and Zakkou call this finding the *Even Split*. Second, the direction of preference reversal—liking to not liking versus not liking to liking—does have an impact on the results (the *Direction Effect*).

What should give us pause is the *Even Split*.[4] Contextualists and relativists would predict mean endorsement of the response corresponding to their position to be not only significantly but substantially above the midpoint (perhaps around 70%, though what counts as "substantially above" is of course debatable). However, mean endorsement for all four values hovers around the midpoint (and for most does not differ substantially from it), suggesting that on average, people report it neither likely nor unlikely that they'd make either of the two suggested utterances in response to their interlocutor's challenge. These results are at odds with most previous studies—for both predicates of personal taste and epistemic modals—which found robust support for contextualist and against relativist truth-assessment. What explains the difference in results and how come—overall—there is no significant, let alone substantive endorsement of either claim in Dinges and Zakkou's studies?

2.5. *Summary and Outlook*

Let's take stock: Some results suggest that the truth of perspectival claims is sensitive to the context of utterance and that there is no retraction requirement. Findings of this sort exist for both taste claims (Kneer, 2015, 2021a) and epistemic modals (Kneer, 2015, ms; Marques, ms). Knobe and Yalcin's (2014) data are consistent with these results as regards the truth assessment of epistemic modal claims, whose truth is shown to depend on the context of utterance, not the context of assessment in several studies. Curiously, however, Knobe and Yalcin nonetheless find evidence in favour of a retraction rule, even for claims that are deemed true at the relevant context of assessment. Dinges and Zakkou's findings challenge the results of all other studies that converge on contextualist truth assessment: people are neither particularly willing nor particularly unwilling to answer in line with the predictions of contextualism or relativism. Given that the Truth Rule is more fundamental than the Retraction Rule, I will first explore Dinges and Zakkou's findings in more detail.

Contextualism Versus Relativism   119

3.   The Even Split—Experiment 1

In Dinges and Zakkou's scenario, the reader is in the role of someone whose tastes regarding a particular bubble gum changes either from liking to not liking or vice versa. The reader is then prompted to rate how likely they are to give one of the following two responses (here in the case of liking to not liking) upon being challenged by another character:

> [Relativist] "What I said was false. Yumble is tasty." [Scale from 0–100]
>
> [Contextualist] "What I said was true. Still, Yumble is tasty." [Scale from 0–100]

As discussed, participants' likelihood ratings were roughly at the midpoint of the scale for either response (see Figure 6.4). What could explain these results? Perhaps the evident place to look is the formulation of the contextualist claim: "What I said was true. Still, Yumble is tasty." Contextualists might object that this is an adequate way of testing their predictions. Dinges and Zakkou address precisely this worry:

> Contextualists might still complain that we are artificially downgrading the "true" response. A more natural way of putting it, they might say, would be something like "What I said was true. Still, Yumble is tasty *to me now*." Contextualists would presumably explain the difference in naturalness between this response and the one we offer by assuming some kind of communicative ideal to make tacit arguments explicit whenever there is a threat of misunderstanding. Note, however, that our primary concern is whether people prefer the "true" to the "false" response or *vice versa*. Even if our "true" response fails to live up to the indicated ideal, it should still be preferable to the "false" response according to contextualism. After all, even as stated, the "false" response is false according to contextualism and the "true" response true. One would normally not prefer to say something outright false to saying something true just because the true claim is not ideal in terms of a possible misunderstanding. This is not to say, of course, that it would be uninteresting to modify the "true" response in the suggested way and to see how this affects results.
>
> (p. 9, FN. 21)

As a card-carrying contextualist, my worry about the formulation of the contextualist claim is not quite put to rest by this. According to contextualist semantics, the context of assessment simply doesn't play a meaningful role for truth-assessment. In the experiment, following up one's insistence "What I said was true" with "Still, Yumble is tasty" sounds confusing, if not confused, and the expression "still" can trigger a sense

120 *Markus Kneer*

of contradiction. Dinges and Zakkou argue that "[e]ven if our "true" [i.e. the contextualist] response fails to live up to the indicated ideal, it should still be preferable to the "false" response according to contextualism." But this is not evident. If, as suggested, the "true" response sounds confused, it remains unclear why it should do any better than the "false" response (i.e. the relativist response), for which previous experiments, like Dinges and Zakkou's itself, do not find much support. These complications could have been avoided by employing the standard design for experiments of this sort, in which people are simply asked to what extent they agree with the claim that a previous perspectival assertion is true or false.[5]

If these thoughts are on the right track, then the reason why the proposed contextualist response does little better than the relativist response is simply because there is something amiss in this particular formulation. To explore this possibility, I ran an experiment similar to the one reported by Dinges and Zakkou. The relativist response was left unchanged; the contextualist one was modified. Take the *dislike-to-like* situation, where Yumble is not deemed tasty at the context of utterance, yet considered tasty at the context of assessment. Instead of following up "What I said was true" with a potentially confusing second sentence ("Still, Yumble is tasty"), it was followed with what a contextualist would provide as the rationale of their truth-assessment: "At the time, I didn't find Yumble tasty." The revised formulation thus mirrors the structure of the relativist statement ("What I said was false. Yumble is tasty."), in so far as here, too, the second sentence supports and explains the truth-assessment expressed by the first sentence of the response. In a nutshell, the revised design establishes parity between the two responses. Each of the responses points to the context that is deemed relevant for truth-evaluation according to the respective semantic view. The relativist response highlights the context of assessment, the contextualist one the context of utterance—and not something that simply does not play a role on that account.

3.1. Participants

A total of 294 participants were recruited via Amazon Mechanical Turk. The IP address was restricted to participants from the US. In line with the preregistered criteria,[6] 55 participants who failed an attention check, took less than 20 seconds to answer the main questions or whose native tongue was not English were excluded, leaving a sample of 239 participants (female: 51%; age M = 43 years, SD = 13 years, range: 20–76 years).

3.2. Methods and Materials

Participants read Dinges and Zakkou's Bubble Gum scenario (see Appendix). They were randomly assigned to either the *dislike-to-like* condition or to the *like-to-dislike* condition. Following the original methodology, participants were asked how likely they were to respond with one of the following two claims (here reproduced for the *like-to-dislike* condition, the order was counterbalanced) on a scale of 0–100:

(i) [Relativist (unchanged)] "What I said was false. Yumble is tasty."
(ii) [Contextualist (revised)] "What I said was true. At the time I didn't find Yumble tasty."

3.3. Results

A mixed-design three-way ANOVA (Table 6.1) with *order of presentation* (relativist claim first v. second) and *direction of preference reversal* (dislike to like v. like to dislike) as between-subjects factors, and *assessment* (relativist v. contextualist) as within-subject factor revealed a significant effect of *assessment* ($F(1, 235) = 500.760$, $p < .001$, $\eta_p^2 = .681$, a large effect). All other factors, as well as all interactions were non-significant (all $ps > .05$). Figure 6.5 presents the results.

Given that the *direction of preference reversal* and the *direction*assessment* interaction were nonsignificant, there is no evidence for a direction effect of any sort. As is clearly visible from Figure 6.5, the results also testify against an *Even Split* result. Whereas in either direction of preference reversal the likelihood of giving the contextualist response exceeded 80% (and was significantly above the midpoint, one-sample t-tests, $ps < .001$), the likelihood of giving the relativist response was below 25% (significantly below the midpoint, one-sample t-tests, $ps < .001$). For both scenarios, the effect size of the difference between contextualist and relativist response was again large (Cohen's $ds > 1.41$).

Table 6.1 Mixed ANOVA for the likelihood of uttering a contextualist or relativist response.

IV	DFn	DFd	F	p	η_p^2
Order	1	235	1.691	0.195	0.007
Direction	1	235	< 0.001	0.975	< 0.001
Assessment	1	235	500.76	< 0.001*	0.681
Order*Direction	1	235	0.847	0.358	0.004
Order*Assessment	1	235	0.31	0.578	0.001
Direction*Assessment	1	235	0.068	0.795	< 0.001
Order*Direction*Assessment	1	235	0.019	0.890	< 0.001

Note: Within factor = assessment, all other factors were manipulated between subjects.

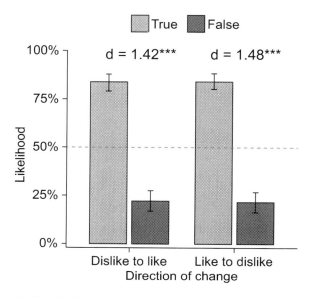

Figure 6.5 Likelihood of uttering a contextualist (true) response and a relativist (false) response across directions of preference reversal. Error bars denote 95% confidence intervals.

3.4. Discussion

Experiment 1 could not find support for the Even Split results reported by Dinges and Zakkou, according to which the likelihood of giving a contextualist and a relativist response sits somewhere around the midpoint. Instead, the findings indicate strong support for truth-assessment along contextualist lines, and they challenge truth-assessment along relativist lines. The effect size for the difference in likelihood across response types is very large (Cohen's ds > 1.42). What is more, truth assessment is unaffected by the direction of preference reversal. The nonsignificant direction*assessment interaction suggests that there is no direction effect.

One finding is particularly interesting: Although the relativist answer was *not* changed from Dinges and Zakkou's experiments, the reported mean likelihood of responding in that way dropped from about 50% in their experiments to less than 25% in the present experiment. As in every empirical experiment, this might just be an oddity in the data. However, it need not be: if it were true, as hypothesized, that the contextualist response sounds somewhat confusing or potentially contradictory in Dinges and Zakkou's experiments, it might be that the relativist response held more appeal *by comparison*.[7] Once the contextualist response is improved, the comparative appeal of the relativist response declines. To explore whether

Contextualism Versus Relativism 123

the distaste for the relativist response replicates, I ran another experiment. So as to increase external validity, I switched to a forced-choice response mechanism where participants could select between the relativist response, the contextualist response, or neither.

4. The Even Split—Experiment 2

4.1. Participants

A total of 158 participants were recruited online via Amazon Mechanical Turk. Following the preregistered criteria,[8] 13 participants who failed an attention check or took less than 15 seconds to answer the main questions were excluded, leaving a sample of 145 participants (female: 47%; age M = 43 years, SD = 14 years, range: 22–75 years).

4.2. Methods and Materials

The scenario and the conditions were the same as in Experiment 1. Participants were randomly assigned to either the *like-to-dislike* or the *dislike-to-like* condition of the Bubble Gum scenario. This time, however, participants had to choose amongst three options: the contextualist response, the relativist response, or neither. In the dislike-to-like vignette, where Paul doesn't like Yumble at the context of utterance yet comes to like it later, for instance, the question read (labels in square brackets omitted):

Please tell us which of the following responses you'd be more likely to give to Paul (if any) in the given context:

[Relativist] "What I said was false. Yumble is tasty."
[Contextualist] "What I said was true. I didn't find Yumble tasty at the time."
[Neither] "Neither."

4.3. Results

The results are graphically represented in Figure 6.6. As in the previous experiment, more than 3 in 4 participants opted for the contextualist response (as binomial tests show, significantly above chance—i.e. 33%, $ps < .001$, and significantly above the midpoint, $ps < .001$). Agreement with the relativist response was even less pronounced than in Experiment 1 and under 10% in either condition (significantly below chance and the midpoint, $ps < .001$).

The fact that hardly anyone opted for the option "neither response" (significantly below chance and the midpoint, $ps < .001$) suggests that people are happy with a contextualist response as proposed. Interestingly,

124 *Markus Kneer*

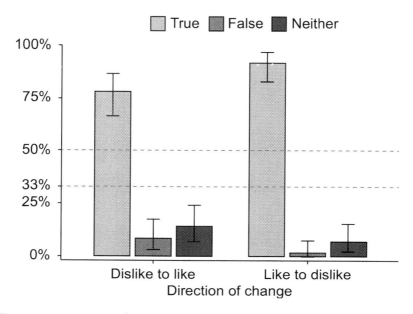

Figure 6.6 Proportion of responses (forced-choice) across direction of preference reversal. Error bars denote 95%-confidence intervals.

there is a bit of a direction effect this time: agreement with the contextualist response is somewhat more pronounced in the *like-to-dislike* condition than in the *dislike-to-like* condition, and vice versa for the relativist response; a Fisher's Exact Test revealed a significant effect for the direction of change ($p < .05$, Cramer's $V(2) = .21$). However, there is little reason to investigate this further: given that the effect size is once again small, yet this time goes in the *opposite* direction as in the original studies and is absent in Experiment 1, there simply does not seem much of a systematic phenomenon (and less of a pressing one given the absence of the Even Split effect).

4.4. Discussion

Consistent with the majority of results for taste predicates and epistemic modals in the empirical literature generally as well as the findings reported in Experiment 1, the second replication of Dinges and Zakkou's study also supports a contextualist semantics of perspectival claims. Note that, once again, we found strong evidence *against* relativism, although for the relativist response the *exact same formulation* was employed as in Dinges

Contextualism Versus Relativism   125

and Zakkou's original studies. But if support for the unchanged relativist response drops away once a plausible contextualist response is available, the external validity of Dinges and Zakkou's results is in doubt.

5.   The Even Split—Experiment 3

The majority of empirical findings concerning the truth assessment of perspectival claims support contextualist predictions and challenge relativist predictions. This pattern arises in experiments where the perspectival claim is simply specified as true or false without further details and participants are asked whether they agree or disagree with this evaluation. The previous two experiments have shown that the same pattern is found with likelihood-of-response judgements where the contextualist and relativist answers invoke those contexts that are of relevance for the respective positions—the context of utterance in the contextualist case and the context of assessment in the relativist case. The diverging findings of Dinges and Zakkou, I have argued, are explained by the fact that their contextualist response only makes mention of the context of assessment—a context that is irrelevant for contextualist truth assessment and thus triggers a sense of confusion. Once this is rectified, not only does the contextualist response receive pronounced support, but the unchanged relativist response is deemed inadequate.

In line with the suggestions of one of the editors—and in the hope of putting all remaining skepticism to rest—I have run a final experiment employing Dinges and Zakkou's methodology. In this version the contextualist and relativist response mention *both* the context of utterance *and* the context of assessment. To make the responses as intuitive as possible, the context deemed relevant by each of the two positions is mentioned first. So, in the *dislike-to-like* situation, where the speaker has said that Yumble is not tasty, the contextualist response is "What I said was true. At the time Yumble wasn't tasty to me [reference to C_u], although it's tasty to me now [reference to C_a]." The relativist response is "What I said was false. Yumble is tasty to me now [reference to C_a], although at the time it wasn't tasty to me [reference to C_u]."

5.1.   Participants

A total of 262 participants were recruited online via Amazon Mechanical Turk. In line with the preregistered criteria,[9] 80 participants who failed an attention test, were not native speakers of the English language, or took less than 20 seconds to answer the main questions were excluded, leaving a sample of 182 participants (female: 46%; age M = 41 years, SD = 13 years, range: 20–91 years).

126 *Markus Kneer*

5.2. *Methods and Materials*

The scenario and the conditions were the same as in Experiment 1. Participants were randomly assigned to either the *like-to-dislike* or the *dislike-to-like* condition of the Bubble Gum scenario. On a scale of 0–100, participants again had to report how likely they were to give either of the two responses. This time the responses read:

Dislike to like

[Relativist] "What I said was false. Yumble is tasty to me now, although at the time it wasn't tasty to me."
[Contextualist] "What I said was true. At the time Yumble wasn't tasty to me, although it's tasty to me now."

Like to dislike

[Relativist] "What I said was false. Yumble is not tasty to me now, although at the time it was tasty to me."
[Contextualist] "What I said was true. At the time Yumble was tasty to me, although it's not tasty to me now."

5.3. *Results*

A mixed-design ANOVA with *direction of preference reversal* (dislike to like v. like to dislike) as between-subjects factor and *assessment* (relativist v. contextualist) as within-subjects factor revealed a significant effect of *assessment* ($F(1, 180) = 241.64, p < .001, \eta_p^2 = .573$, a large effect). *Direction of preference reversal* was nonsignificant ($p = .484$); the interaction was significant though the effect size was once again small ($F(1, 180) = 5.92, p = .016, \eta_p^2 = .032$). Figure 6.7 presents the results.

Consistent with the two previous experiments, the findings support contextualism and challenge relativism. In either direction of preference reversal the mean likelihood of giving the contextualist response exceeded 75% (significantly above the midpoint, one-sample t-tests, $ps < .001$). Consistent with the findings from Experiment 1 and 2 and inconsistent with Dinges and Zakkou's findings, the mean likelihood of responding with a relativist response was again very low (significantly below the midpoint, one sample t-tests, $ps < .001$). For both scenarios, the effect size of the difference between contextualist and relativist response was large (Cohen's $ds > .97$).

5.4. *Discussion*

Experiment 3 replicates the findings from Experiments 1 and 2 with different formulations of the responses. Overall, then, the results of the three

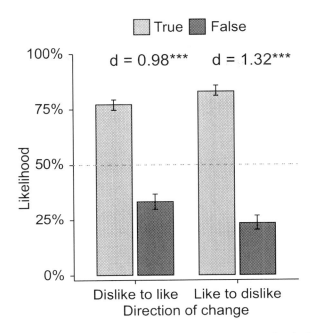

Figure 6.7 Likelihood of uttering a contextualist (true) and relativist (false) response across directions of preference reversal. Error bars denote standard error of the mean.

experiments with distinct formulations and designs constitute support for contextualist truth assessment. The results of all three experiments (two of which used the exact same prompt for the relativist response as Dinges and Zakkou's studies) cast doubt on the plausibility of relativist truth assessment. Given that, in total, about a dozen studies (differing with regards to scenario, type of perspectival claim, response mechanism, and language, cf. Knobe & Yalcin, 2014; Kneer, 2015, 2021a; Marques, ms) converge on the same pro-contextualist results, Dinges and Zakkou's diverging findings seem to be owed to an idiosyncrasy in design choices.

6. Retraction

Knobe and Yalcin (2014), we saw earlier (Section 2.4), report evidence supporting a retraction rule of sorts for epistemic modal claims whose prejacent is false at the context of assessment. Knobe (2021) has recently argued that similar behavior is to be expected in preference-reversal cases for taste claims. The evidence is surprising for two reasons: First, truth assessment of perspectival claims is near-uniformly sensitive to the context of utterance. Second (see Section 2.3), recent evidence suggests that

128   *Markus Kneer*

the norm of assertion (tout court) is *nonfactive*, so it would be odd in the extreme to find norms of retraction to be sensitive to propositional truth. In the following, I'd like to suggest that the astonishing findings are explained by the normative force invoked in the way Knobe and Yalcin formulated their retraction question.

6.1.   *Normative Force*

Norms come in different kinds and flavours. On the one end of the spectrum concerning normative force, we find prescriptive norms (one *ought* to do x) and proscriptive norms (one *ought* not to do x). Strong norms, concerned with what one *ought*, *should*, or *must* do, contrast with weaker ones regarding what it is *appropriate* or *permissible* to do or what one *may* do. Whereas strong norms entail their weaker equivalent—what one should do must at least be appropriate or permissible—the reverse is not the case: The fact that doing x might be permissible or appropriate does not entail that one should or ought to do x. If doing x is permissible, it can also be permissible to refrain from doing x. If, however, one must or ought to do x, it is standardly inacceptable to not do x.

Philosophical accounts concerning norms of assertion standardly invoke strong force: In order to be in a position to assert that x, one "must" (Williamson, 2000) or "should" (Douven, 2006; Turri, 2013) fulfil certain epistemic conditions (be it knowledge, justified belief, or something else). Norms of retraction tend to be formulated in similar fashion. Dummett (1978, p. 20), for instance, writes that "[t]here's a well-defined consequence of an assertion proving incorrect [false], namely that the speaker *must withdraw* it." As quoted earlier, MacFarlane's *Reflexive Retraction Rule* states that "[a]n agent in context c_2 is *required to retract* an (unretracted) assertion of p made at c1 if p is not true as used at c_1 and assessed from c_2."

A potential reason why Knobe and Yalcin's findings in the Boston experiment (quoted earlier) differ strongly from the majority of results (including their own Experiment 3) is presumably this: rather than testing a prescriptive norm as to whether Sally, the speaker, is *required to retract* her epistemic modal claim whose prejacent is false at the context of assessment, they ask people whether "[i]t *would be appropriate* for Sally to take back what she said." It is, however, entirely possible for a retraction to be appropriate or permissible, without there being any *requirement* to take it back. In order to explore whether people would also be willing to impose such a requirement on Sally, I reran Knobe and Yalcin's experiment manipulating the formulation (also previously done in Kneer, 2015, ch. 6). In one version, the retraction question was left exactly as phrased by Knobe and Yalcin; the other asked whether Sally is "required to take back what she said."

Contextualism Versus Relativism 129

6.2. Participants

A total of 196 participants were recruited online via Amazon Mechanical Turk. The IP address was restricted to the United States. Thirty-seven participants who failed an attention check or took less than 15 seconds to answer the main questions were excluded, leaving a sample of 159 participants (female: 44%; age M = 43 years, SD = 13 years, range: 23–76 years).

6.3. Methods and Materials

In a between-subjects experiment, participants were presented with Knobe and Yalcin's *Boston* vignette (see Section 2.2). There were two conditions: One used Knobe and Yalcin's original formulation of the retraction question invoking "appropriate . . . to take back" (Retraction[Weak]). The other formulation (Retraction[Strong]) followed MacFarlane's formulation of the reflexive retraction rule and asked whether Sally is "required to take back" what she said:

> [Retraction[Weak]] It would be appropriate for Sally to take back what she said.
> [Retraction[Strong]] Sally is required to take back what she said.

Participants were randomly assigned to one of the two conditions.

6.4. Results

The results are graphically represented in Figure 6.8. A one-way ANOVA (see Appendix) revealed a significant effect of formulation ("retraction appropriate" v. "retraction required"; $F(1, 157) = 56.11$, $p < .001$, $\eta_p^2 = .265$, a large effect). Agreement with the claims that it is *appropriate* for Sally to take back what she said was significantly above the midpoint (M = 5.75, $p < .001$), replicating the findings of Knobe and Yalcin. Agreement with the claim that Sally is *required* to take back what she said, however, was significantly *below* the midpoint (M = 3.41, $p = .020$),[10] replicating the findings from Kneer (2015, ms) and Marques (ms), who report similar findings for native Spanish speakers. The effect size of formulation was large (Cohen's $d = 1.19$).

6.5. Discussion

The results suggest that there is no requirement to retract an epistemic modal claim from a context of assessment at which its prejacent is known to be true. However, under certain circumstances (such as those of the

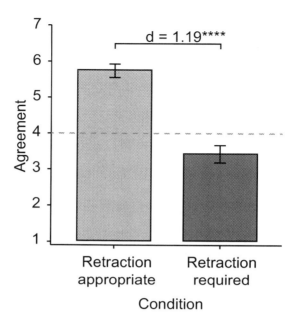

Figure 6.8 Agreement with proposed retraction across formulation ("retraction appropriate" v. "retraction required"). Error bars denote standard errors.

scenario) it is deemed nonetheless appropriate to do so. Knobe and Yalcin explain the latter finding thus:

> One possible approach would be to view retraction as a phenomenon whereby speakers are primarily indicating that they no longer want a conversational common ground incorporating the update associated with a sentence that they previously uttered. On this approach, *what is retracted* is a certain conversational update; retraction is in part a means of undoing or disowning the context change or update performed by a speech act.
>
> (2014, p. 17)

This conclusion dovetails nicely with some interesting observations by Khoo (2015), which served as inspiration for Knobe and Yalcin (for related discussion see also Khoo & Knobe, 2018). Much of the literature on disagreement, Khoo argues, makes the following assumption:

> Rejecting is contradicting: to reject an assertion just is to claim that what is asserted by it is false.
>
> (2015, p. 515)

This assumption, however, is misconceived. Although it's rather uncontroversial that, most times, in rejecting an assertion, one intends

Contextualism Versus Relativism 131

to flag it as false, this need not always be the case. Here are three examples:

A: Jim ate some of the cookies from last night.
B: No, he ate *all* of the cookies from last night.

(Khoo, 2015, p. 517)

A, B and C are sharing a flat and the kitchen tends to be a mess.
A: "I made B clean up the kitchen last night."
B: "No. You *asked* me to clean up the kitchen and I did it."

A and B are wondering whether the bank is open (it's a Saturday). A has just called a friend who told A that the bank was open last Saturday.

A: The bank is open today.
B: No, the bank *might* be open today. Banks are never open on national holidays, and we still don't know whether today is a national holiday.

(Khoo, 2015, p. 516)

As Grice (1989) observed, communication is not limited to *what is said* (the semantic content) but frequently revolves around *what is meant*, which includes conversational implicatures. In the first two examples, although *what is said* by A is true, B still has grounds to reject the assertions due to the fact that they carry certain objectionable implicature: That Jim ate *some but not all* of the cookies or that A had the *authority or power to force* B to clean up the kitchen. Concerning the third example and epistemic modals more generally, Khoo suggests what he calls the *Update Observation*:

> *The Update Observation*: generally, assertively uttering an epistemic possibility sentence involves proposing that it not be common ground that its prejacent is false. (Thus, generally, the communicative impact of assertively uttering an epistemic possibility sentence will involve the property of not having as a member the negation of its prejacent.)
>
> (2015, p. 528)

Whether we are, like Khoo or Knobe and Yalcin, inclined to invoke a Stalnakerian (1978, 1999, 2002) framework or else Grice's theory of implicature to explain rejections not aimed at the truth value of the proposition expressed doesn't matter much. What seems evident is that rejecting a claim can go beyond objecting to its alleged falsity. Instead, one might be objecting to certain implicatures it carries on its heels and/or to certain updates of the common ground it tends to engender.

I find the explanation of Khoo and Knobe and Yalcin deeply plausible. It sheds light on our communicative practices in general and the conversational move of retraction more particularly. Note, however, that data

132   *Markus Kneer*

as to what kinds of (nonrequired) moves in communication are appropriate, permissible, or commendable does not have any particular impact on the quest for a *constitutive* or *central* norm of assertion, and neither does it matter much for the contextualism/relativism debate. Assertion is governed by a plethora of peripheral rules (concerning clarity, precision, relevance, etc.), none of which can be expected to be core to the characterization of the practice itself. Moreover, the dispute between contextualists and relativists concerns the truth-conditional semantics of perspectival claims, and weak norms of retraction, just like other peripheral norms, simply do not matter for this debate. I would thus like to resist any suggestions that data of this sort, which is not predicted by any of the three main theories of perspectival claims, requires "amendments" of any kind (Khoo, 2015) or revive hope for (some version of) relativism (Beddor & Egan, 2018, § 4.1)—for the simple reason that said theories are justly mute on such questions.

7. Conclusion

The debate between contextualism and relativism revolves around two points of contention: *Truth assessment*, i.e. the question whether the extension of perspectival claims is assessment-sensitive on the one hand and whether such claims are governed by a *norm of retraction* on the other. The *content* of the contentious norm is to invoke propositional truth at the context of assessment, and its *force* is prescriptive (when appropriately challenged, one is *required* to retract a previous perspectival claim).

Consistent with the majority of findings from the empirical literature on perspectival claims, we have found that the truth assessment of taste claims is sensitive to features of the context of utterance and not to features of the context of assessment (Experiments 1–3). This invalidates the relativist position not only with regards to truth assessment itself but also with respect to a norm of retraction whose requirements allegedly track assessment-sensitive propositional truth. If the truth of perspectival claims is not assessment-sensitive, a situation in which MacFarlane's reflexive retraction rule takes grip can simply not arise. As argued, there are further, independent reasons to question said rule: Converging evidence from the empirical literature on the norm of assertion suggests that the latter is nonfactive and that one is warranted in asserting false beliefs for which one has good reasons. This suggests that norms of retraction are not tied to propositional truth of any sort. It would be odd if one were held to stricter normative standards for *retracting* a claim than for *asserting* it in the first place.

Given that the norm of assertion—and by extension the norm of retraction—is most likely not sensitive to propositional truth, and given that the truth of perspectival claims is not assessment-sensitive anyway,

Contextualism Versus Relativism 133

the findings reported by Knobe and Yalcin might come as a surprise. Experiment 4 has shown that for their scenario, too, there is no *prescriptive* norm according to which one is *required* to retract an epistemic modal claim, whose prejacent turns out false at the context of assessment. People do, however, deem it *appropriate* to retract such a claim, in line with Knobe and Yalcin's original findings.

The retraction findings lend support to an explanation of the sort proposed by Khoo (2015) and Knobe and Yalcin (2014), according to which updating of the common ground can be effected due to reasons that go beyond propositional truth. Importantly though, norms of this sort simply do not bear on the discussion concerning a plausible *truth-conditional semantics* of perspectival claims (see also Marques, 2018, on this point). The kinds of norms that let us draw inferences about semantics are unlikely to be loose principles of guidance as to what it is permissible, commendable, or appropriate to say and do—if one so fancies. Rather, rules of this sort can be expected to carry strong normative force—they regulate what one is *required* to do or must do—just like the kinds of norms proposed by MacFarlane, which we found invalidated by the data.[11]

Notes

1. See *inter alia* Kölbel (2002, 2004, 2009), Lasersohn (2005, 2008, 2009, 2016), Glanzberg (2007, 2021), MacFarlane (2007, 2014), López de Sa (2007, 2015, this volume), Recanati (2007), Stojanovic (2007, 2017), Stephenson (2007), Sæbø (2009), Cappelen and Hawthorne (2009), Moltmann (2010), Barker (2010), Egan (2010), Sundell (2011), Schaffer (2011), Huvenes (2012), Pearson (2013, this volume), Kennedy (2013), Snyder (2013), Collins (2013), Plunkett and Sundell (2013), Marques and García-Carpintero (2014), Marques (2014a, 2014b, 2018), Clapp (2015), Ferrari (2015, 2016), Hîncu (2015), Zakkou (2015, 2019a, 2019b), Kneer (2015, 2021a, 2021c), Kennedy and Willer (2016), Zeman (2016a, 2016b, 2017, 2020), Dinges (2017a, 2017b, this volume), Kneer et al. (2017), Wyatt (2018, 2021, this volume), Kindermann (2019), Kaiser and Rudin (2020), Dinges and Zakkou (2020), Hîncu and Zeman (2021), Kaiser & Stojanovic (this volume), Rudolph (this volume), Willer & Kennedy (this volume).
2. See *inter alia* Kratzer (1977, 2012), Egan (2007, 2011), Stephenson (2007), Hawthorne (2007), von Fintel and Gillies (2008, 2011), MacFarlane (2010, 2011, 2014), Schaffer (2011), Dowell (2011, 2017), Swanson (2011), Willer (2013), Knobe and Yalcin (2014), Yanovich (2014, 2020), Khoo (2015), Kneer (2015, ms), Beddor and Egan (2018), Marushak (2018), Marushak and Shaw (2020).
3. See *inter alia* Schafer (2011), Kölbel (2016), McNally and Stojanovic (2017), Stojanovic (2016, 2017, 2018), Marques (2016), Liao and Meskin (2017), Cova et al. (2019), Collins (2021), Bonard et al. (this volume), Martínez Marín & Schellekens (this volume), Wallbank & Robson (this volume).
4. Personally, I am not particularly worried about the *Direction Effect*. Note that there are no main effects (neither response is significantly more or less favoured across directions of preference reversal), and the effect sizes of the interaction are small (Experiment 1: $\eta_p^2 = .025$, Experiment 2: $\eta_p^2 = .020$). Furthermore,

134 *Markus Kneer*

the main reason why the Direction Effect could be interesting is that it arises in conjunction with the Even Split Effect. However, the Even Split will be challenged in the experiments that follow. What is more, in the experiments reported in what follows the Direction Effect is sometimes absent and sometimes it goes in the *opposite* direction of what Dinges and Zakkou report. Given that the effect's size is always at best small and its direction capricious, there simply does not seem to be a robust phenomenon that requires explanation.

5. Dinges and Zakkou's design is motivated by a critique of extant studies (2020, p. 7), which apparently run the risk of a normative confound by asking questions as to whether it is "appropriate" (Knobe & Yalcin, 2014) to retract a certain claim or whether the speaker is "required" to do so (Kneer, 2015, 2021a, Marques, ms). On Dinges and Zakkou's view, such "permissibility-related judgments" might be sensitive to normative factors that go beyond linguistic rules (e.g. norms of morality or etiquette). But even if there were reason to be concerned about a normative confound (I do not quite see how morality or etiquette could interfere in the short scenarios about the gustatory merits of bubble gum or fish sticks) this argument seems to miss the mark: the criticized questions test norms of *retraction*, not *truth assessment*, which is the topic of Dinges and Zakkou. As regards the latter, the cited papers simply test *agreement* with a proposed truth-evaluation. It is not evident what kind of normative confound could be lurking here or why this tried-and-tested methodology needs revision.

6. https://aspredicted.org/J9F_7WW

7. As detailed, the two responses were judged independently. But given that they were presented on the same screen, it is perfectly plausible that the merits of each response were assessed with an eye to the alternative.

8. https://aspredicted.org/GP2_HCK

9. https://aspredicted.org/HJC_RP7

10. Advocates of relativism might sense hope in light of the fact that the mean is not that much below the midpoint (for arguments of this sort, see e.g. Beddor & Egan, 2018, § 4.1). Two points: *First*, what the relativist predicts is significant agreement with a required retraction claim, i.e. a mean rating that is not only somewhat below or nonsignificantly different from the midpoint but *significantly above* the midpoint. Differently put, she predicts means of the magnitude we find for the "appropriate" formulation of the retraction claim, and the effect size of the difference between the two formulations here is instructive: it's very large ($d = 1.19$). *Second*, the means of this particular experiment—such is the nature of empirical research—simply seem to be a little higher than in related studies. In Kneer (2015, Exp. 5) the mean retraction results for Knobe and Yalcin's scenario is $M = 3.2$ (SD = 2.2); Marques (ms, Exp. 1) reports near-identical results for English speakers and even lower means ($M = 2.9$) for native Spanish speakers (ms, Exp. 2). For a similar yet slightly different scenario (*China*, Kneer, 2015, Exp. 3) mean agreement with required retraction is considerably lower ($M = 1.6$, SD = 1.2).

11. For comments and help, I would like to thank Joshua Knobe, Teresa Marques, Neri Marsili, Marc-André Zehnder, and the editors. I do not want to imply that any of them agree with me. This work was supported by a Swiss National Science Foundation Grant (PZ00P1_179912).

Bibliography

Bach, K. (2008). Applying pragmatics to epistemology. *Philosophical Issues, 18*, 68–88.

Contextualism Versus Relativism 135

Barker, S. (2010). Cognitive expressivism, faultless disagreement, and absolute but non-objective truth. *Proceedings of the Aristotelian Society, 110*, 183–199.

Beddor, B., & Egan, A. (2018). Might do better: Flexible relativism and the QUD. *Semantics and Pragmatics, 11*(7), 1–47.

Bonard, C., Cova, F., & Humbert-Droz, S. (This volume). De gustibus est disputandum—An empirical investigation of the folk concept of aesthetic taste.

Caponetto, L. (2020). Undoing things with words. *Synthese, 197*(6), 2399–2414.

Cappelen, H., & Hawthorne, J. (2009). *Relativism and monadic truth*. Oxford University Press.

Clapp, L. (2015). A non-alethic approach to faultless disagreement. *Dialectica, 69*(4), 517–550.

Collins, J. (2013). The syntax of personal taste. *Philosophical Perspectives, 27*(1), 51–103.

Collins, J. (2021). A norm of aesthetic assertion and its semantic (in)significance. *Inquiry, 64*(10), 973–1003.

Cova, F., Olivola, C. Y., Machery, E., Stich, S., Rose, D., Alai, M., . . . & Zhu, J. (2019). De Pulchritudine non est Disputandum? A cross-cultural investigation of the alleged intersubjective validity of aesthetic judgment. *Mind & Language, 34*(3), 317–338.

Dinges, A. (2017a). Relativism and assertion. *Australasian Journal of Philosophy, 95*(4), 730–740.

Dinges, A. (2017b). Relativism, disagreement and testimony. *Pacific Philosophical Quarterly, 98*, 497–519.

Dinges, A. (This volume). Non-indexical contextualism, relativism, and retraction.

Dinges, A., & Zakkou, J. (2020). A direction effect on taste predicates. *Philosophers' Imprint, 20*(27), 1–22.

Douven, I. (2006). Assertion, knowledge, and rational credibility. *Philosophical Review, 115*(4), 449–485.

Dowell, J. L. (2011). A flexible contextualist account of epistemic modals. *Philosophers' Imprint, 11*(14), 1–25.

Dowell, J. L. (2017). Contextualism about epistemic modals. In J. Jenkins Ichikawa (Ed.), *The Routledge handbook of epistemic contextualism* (pp. 388–399). Routledge.

Dummett, M. (1959/1978). Truth. In M. Dummett (Ed.), *Truth and other enigmas* (pp. 1–24). Harvard University Press.

Egan, A. (2007). Epistemic modals, relativism and assertion. *Philosophical Studies, 133*, 1–22.

Egan, A. (2010). Disputing about taste. In R. Feldman & T. A. Warfield (Eds.), *Disagreement* (pp. 247–286). Oxford University Press.

Egan, A. (2011). Relativism about epistemic modals. In S. D. Hales (Ed.), *A companion to relativism* (pp. 219–241). Wiley-Blackwell.

Ferrari, F. (2015). Disagreement about taste and alethic suberogation. *The Philosophical Quarterly, 66*(264), 516–535.

Ferrari, F. (2016). Assessment-sensitivity. *Analysis, 76*(4), 516–527.

Glanzberg, M. (2007). Context, content, and relativism. *Philosophical Studies, 136*, 1–29.

136 *Markus Kneer*

Glanzberg, M. (2021). *Judges, experiencers and taste* [Manuscript].

Grice, P. (1989). *Studies in the way of words*. Harvard University Press.

Hawthorne, J. (2004). *Knowledge and lotteries*. Oxford University Press.

Hawthorne, J. (2007). Eavesdroppers and epistemic modals. *Philosophical Issues*, *17*, 92–101.

Hîncu, M. (2015). Context, compositionality, and predicates of personal taste. In S. Costreie & M. Dumitru (Eds.), *Meaning and truth* (pp. 111–139). Pro Universitaria.

Hîncu, M., & Zeman, D. (2021). On Wyatt's absolutist account of faultless disagreement in matters of personal taste. *Theoria*, *87*(5), 1322–1341.

Hindriks, F. (2007). The status of the knowledge account of assertion. *Linguistics and Philosophy*, *30*, 393–406.

Huvenes, T. T. (2012). Varieties of disagreement and predicates of taste. *Australasian Journal of Philosophy*, *90*(1), 167–181.

Kaiser, E., & Rudin, D. (2020). When faultless disagreement is not so faultless: What widely-held opinions can tell us about subjective adjectives. *Proceedings of the Linguistic Society of America*, *5*(1), 698–707.

Kaiser, E., & Stojanovic, I. (This volume). Exploring valence in judgments of taste.

Kennedy, C. (2013). Two sources of subjectivity: Qualitative assessment and dimensional uncertainty. *Inquiry*, *56*(2–3), 258–277.

Kennedy, C., & Willer, M. (2016). Subjective attitudes and counterstance contingency. *Proceedings of Semantics and Linguistic Theory*, *26*, 913–933.

Khoo, J. (2015). Modal disagreements. *Inquiry*, *58*(5), 511–534.

Khoo, J., & Knobe, J. (2018). Moral disagreement and moral semantics. *Noûs*, *52*(1), 109–143.

Kindermann, D. (2019). Coordinating perspectives: De se and taste attitudes in communication. *Inquiry*, *62*(8), 912–955.

Kneer, M. (2015). *Perspective in language* [Unpublished doctoral dissertation]. EHESS/ENS Paris.

Kneer, M. (2018). The norm of assertion: Empirical data. *Cognition*, *177*, 165–171.

Kneer, M. (2021a). Predicates of personal taste: Empirical data. *Synthese*. https://doi.org/10.1007/s11229-021-03077-9

Kneer, M. (2021b). Norms of assertion in the United States, Germany, and Japan. *Proceedings of the National Academy of Sciences of the United States of America*, *118*(37). https://doi.org/10.1073/pnas.2105365118

Kneer, M. (2021c). Predicates of personal taste, semantic incompleteness, and necessitarianism. *Linguistics and Philosophy*, *44*, 981–1011.

Kneer, M. (ms). Epistemic modals: 'data' and data.

Kneer, M., Vicente, A., & Zeman, D. (2017). Relativism about predicates of personal taste and perspectival plurality. *Linguistics and Philosophy*, *40*(1), 37–60.

Knobe, J. (2021). *Proposition or update? Two accounts of retraction* [Conference presentation]. Theoretical and Empirical Challenges to Retraction, University of Warsaw, Warsaw. https://danzeman.weebly.com/retraction-workshop.html

Knobe, J., & Yalcin, S. (2014). Epistemic modals and context: Experimental data. *Semantics and Pragmatics*, *7*(10), 1–21. http://doi.org/10.3765/sp.7.10

Kölbel, M. (2002). *Truth without objectivity*. Routledge.

Kölbel, M. (2004). Faultless disagreement. *Proceedings of the Aristotelian Society*, *104*, 53–73.

Kölbel, M. (2009). The evidence for relativism. *Synthese*, *166*, 375–395.

Kölbel, M. (2016). Aesthetic judge-dependence and expertise. *Inquiry*, *59*(6), 589–617.

Kratzer, A. (1977). What "must" and "can" must and can mean. *Linguistics and Philosophy*, *1*(3), 337–355.

Kratzer, A. (2012). *Modals and conditionals: New and revised perspectives*. Oxford University Press.

Lackey, J. (2007). Norms of assertion. *Noûs*, *41*(4), 594–626.

Lasersohn, P. (2005). Context dependence, disagreement, and predicates of personal taste. *Linguistics and Philosophy*, *28*, 643–686.

Lasersohn, P. (2008). Quantification and perspective in relativist semantics. *Philosophical Perspectives*, *22*(1), 305–337.

Lasersohn, P. (2009). Relative truth, speaker commitment, and control of implicit arguments. *Synthese*, *166*, 359–374.

Lasersohn, P. (2016). *Subjectivity and perspective in truth-theoretic semantics*. Oxford University Press.

Liao, S. Y., & Meskin, A. (2017). Aesthetic adjectives: Experimental semantics and context-sensitivity. *Philosophy and Phenomenological Research*, *94*(2), 371–398.

López de Sa, D. (2007). The many relativisms and the question of disagreement. *International Journal of Philosophical Studies*, *15*(2), 269–279.

López de Sa, D. (2015). Expressing disagreement: A presuppositional indexical contextualist relativist account. *Erkenntnis*, *80*(1), 153–165.

López de Sa, D. (This volume). Disagreements and disputes about matters of taste.

MacFarlane, J. (2007). Relativism and disagreement. *Philosophical Studies*, *132*, 17–31.

MacFarlane, J. (2010). *Epistemic modals: Relativism vs. cloudy contextualism*. Chambers Philosophy Conference on Epistemic Modals.

MacFarlane, J. (2011). Epistemic modals are assessment sensitive. In A. Egan & B. Weatherson (Eds.), *Epistemic modality* (pp. 144–178). Oxford University Press.

MacFarlane, J. (2014). *Assessment sensitivity: Relative truth and its applications*. Oxford University Press.

Mandelkern, M., & Dorst, K. (ms). Assertion is weak.

Marques, T. (2014a). Relative correctness. *Philosophical Studies*, *167*(2), 361–373.

Marques, T. (2014b). Doxastic disagreement. *Erkenntnis*, *79*(1), 121–142.

Marques, T. (2016). Aesthetic predicates: A hybrid dispositional account. *Inquiry*, *59*(6), 723–751.

Marques, T. (2018). Retractions. *Synthese*, *195*(8), 3335–3359.

Marques, T. (ms). Falsity and retraction.

Marques, T., & García-Carpintero, M. (2014). Disagreement about taste: Commonality presuppositions and coordination. *Australasian Journal of Philosophy*, *92*(4), 701–723.

Marsili, N. (2018). Truth and assertion: Rules versus aims. *Analysis*, *78*(4), 638–648.

Marsili, N. (2020). The definition of assertion. *SSRN Papers*. https://papers.ssrn.com/sol3/papers.cfm?abstract_id = 3711804

138 *Markus Kneer*

Marsili, N. (2021). Truth: The rule or the aim of assertion? *Episteme*. https://doi. org/10.1017/epi.2021.28

Marsili, N., & Wiegmann, A. (2021). Should I say that? An experimental investigation of the norm of assertion. *Cognition*. 10.31234/osf.io/cs45j

Martínez Marín, I., & Schellekens, E. (This volume). Aesthetic taste: Perceptual discernment or emotional sensibility?

Marushak, A. (2018). *Reasons and modals* [PhD dissertation]. University of Pittsburgh.

Marushak, A., & Shaw, J. (2020). *Epistemics and emotives* [Ms]. University of Pittsburgh. https://bit.ly/3muP4K7.

McNally, L., & Stojanovic, I. (2017). Aesthetic adjectives. In J. O. Young (Ed.), *The semantics of aesthetic judgements* (pp. 17–37). Oxford University Press.

Moltmann, F. (2010). Relative truth and the first person. *Philosophical Studies, 150*, 187–220.

Pagin, P. (2014). Assertion. In E. Zalta (Ed.), S*tanford encyclopedia of philosophy*. https://plato.stanford. edu/entries/assertion/.

Pagin, P. (2016). Problems with norms of assertion. *Philosophy and Phenomenological Research, 93*(1), 178–207.

Pearson, H. (2013). A judge-free semantics for predicates of personal taste. *Journal of Semantics, 30*(1), 103–154.

Pearson, H. (This volume). Individual and stage-level predicates of personal taste: Another argument for genericity as the source of faultless disagreement.

Plunkett, D., & Sundell, T. (2013). Disagreement and the semantics of normative and evaluative terms. *Philosophers' Imprint, 13*(23), 1–37.

Recanati, F. (2007). *Perspectival thought: A plea for (moderate) relativism.* Oxford University Press.

Reuter, K., & Brössel, P. (2019). No knowledge required. *Episteme, 16*(3), 303–321.

Rudolph, R. E. (This volume). Differences of taste: Analyzing phenomenal and non-phenomenal appearance sentences.

Sæbø, K. J. (2009). Judgment ascriptions. *Linguistics and Philosophy, 32*, 327–352.

Schafer, K. (2011). Faultless disagreement and aesthetic realism. *Philosophy and Phenomenological Research, 82*(2), 265–286.

Schaffer, J. (2011). Perspective in taste predicates and epistemic modals. In A. Egan & B. Weatherson (Eds.), *Epistemic modality*. Oxford University Press.

Snyder, E. (2013). Binding, genericity, and predicates of personal taste. *Inquiry, 56*(2–3), 278–306.

Stalnaker, R. (1978). Assertion. In P. Cole (Ed.), *Syntax and semantics 9: Pragmatics*. Academic Press.

Stalnaker, R. (1999). *Context and content*. Oxford University Press.

Stalnaker, R. (2002). Common ground. *Linguistics and Philosophy, 25*, 701–721.

Stephenson, T. (2007). Judge dependence, epistemic modals, and predicates of personal taste. *Linguistics and Philosophy, 30*, 487–525.

Stojanovic, I. (2007). Talking about taste: Disagreement, implicit arguments, and relative truth. *Linguistics and Philosophy, 30*, 691–706.

Stojanovic, I. (2016). Expressing aesthetic judgments in context. *Inquiry, 59*(6), 663–685.

Stojanovic, I. (2017). Context and disagreement. *Cadernos de Estudos Linguísticos, 59*(1), 7–22.

Stojanovic, I. (2018). An empirical approach to aesthetic adjectives. In F. Cova & S. Réhault (Eds.), *Advances in experimental philosophy of aesthetics* (pp. 221–240). Bloomsbury.

Sundell, T. (2011). Disagreements about taste. *Philosophical Studies, 155,* 267–288.

Swanson, E. (2011). How not to theorize about the language of subjective uncertainty. In A. Egan & B. Weatherson (Eds.), *Epistemic modality* (pp. 249–269). Oxford University Press.

Turri, J. (2011). The express knowledge account of assertion. *Australasian Journal of Philosophy, 89*(1), 37–45.

Turri, J. (2013). The test of truth: An experimental investigation of the norm of assertion. *Cognition, 129*(2), 279–291.

Turri, J. (2015). Knowledge and the norm of assertion: A simple test. *Synthese, 192*(2), 385–392.

Turri, J. (2017). Experimental work on the norms of assertion. *Philosophy Compass, 12*(7), e12425.

von Fintel, K., & Gillies, A. S. (2008). CIA leaks. *The Philosophical Review, 117*(1), 77–98.

von Fintel, K., & Gillies, A. S. (2011). *Might* made right. In A. Egan & B. Weatherson (Eds.), *Epistemic modality* (pp. 108–130). Oxford University Press.

Wallbank, R., & Robson, J. (This volume). Over-appreciating appreciation.

Weiner, M. (2005). Must we know what we say? *The Philosophical Review, 114*(2), 227–251.

Willer, M. (2013). Dynamics of epistemic modality. *The Philosophical Review, 122*(1), 45–92.

Willer, M., & Kennedy, C. (This volume). Perspectival content and semantic composition.

Williamson, T. (1996). Knowing and asserting. *The Philosophical Review, 105*(4), 489–523.

Williamson, T. (2000). *Knowledge and its limits*. Oxford University Press.

Wyatt, J. (2018). Absolutely tasty: An examination of predicates of personal taste and faultless disagreement. *Inquiry, 61*(3), 252–280.

Wyatt, J. (2021). The nature of disagreement: Matters of taste and environs. *Synthese,* 1–29. https://doi.org/10.1007/s11229-021-03266-6

Wyatt, J. (This volume). How to Canberra-plan disagreement: Platitudes, taste, preferences.

Yanovich, I. (2014). Standard contextualism strikes back. *Journal of Semantics, 31*(1), 67–114. https://doi.org/10.1093/jos/ffs022

Yanovich, I. (2020). Epistemic modality. In D. Gutzmann, L. Matthewson, C. Meier, H. Rullmann, & T. E. Zimmerman (Eds.), *The Wiley Blackwell companion to semantics*. Wiley-Blackwell.

Zakkou, J. (2015). *Tasty contextualism* [Unpublished doctoral dissertation]. Humboldt University Berlin.

Zakkou, J. (2019a). Denial and retraction: A challenge for theories of taste predicates. *Synthese, 196*(4), 1555–1573.

Zakkou, J. (2019b). Embedded taste predicates. *Inquiry, 62*(6), 718–739.

Zeman, D. (2016a). Contextualism and disagreement about taste. In C. Meier & J. van Wijnbergen-Huitink (Eds.), *Subjective meaning: Alternatives to relativism* (pp. 91–104). Mouton de Gruyter.

Zeman, D. (2016b). The many uses of predicates of taste and the challenge from disagreement. *Studies in Logic, Grammar and Rhetoric, 46*(1), 79–101.

Zeman, D. (2017). Contextualist answers to the challenge from disagreement. *Phenomenology and Mind, 12,* 62–73.

Zeman, D. (2020). Minimal disagreement. *Philosophia, 48*(4), 1649–1670.

Part III
Metaphysics

7 Disagreements and Disputes About Matters of Taste

Dan López de Sa

Let's keep it simple. You find boiled spinach not only healthy but quite delicious. I disagree profoundly: flavor, texture, smell, I dislike them all—except, perhaps, for the various tones of green. We sometimes express disagreements like this in language, sometimes saying things like "Mmmm, tasty!" or "Not at all!" My aim in this chapter is to illustrate how it is crucial to differentiate questions and facts about the relations between mental states that constitute *disagreements* from questions and facts about how these disagreements are linguistically expressed in *disputes*. There is an element of stipulation here with respect to both 'disagreement' and 'dispute'—what is crucial is to keep issues of language and mind separate, whatever the labels. Proper attention to this, I'll argue, is essential to properly assessing the relevant metaphysical and semantic alternatives with respect to the realm of the tasty and our discourse about it.

The plan is as follows. I'll start with a fairly standard presentation of the *relativistic effects* that so-called predicates of personal taste like 'tasty' intuitively exhibit and of *contextualism* as a straightforward, semantically moderate view that accounts for them (Section 1). Many have thought, and still seem to believe, that there is nonetheless a severe problem with contextualism: the so-called problem of 'lost disagreement', to the effect that contextualism *loses* disagreement in cases where it is intuitively present (Section 2). Some of us have attempted on various occasions to dispel this worry. The alleged problem is spurious, we say, because it presupposes an unduly restrictive conception of what it is to *disagree*, intuitively speaking (see *inter alia* López de Sa, 2008, 2015; Sundell, 2011; Plunket & Sundell, 2013). The fact that this point hasn't come across and people still hold 'lost disagreement' to be the "Achilles' heel of contextualism" (MacFarlane, 2014, p. 118) suggests, at least, that the task of elaborating the point anew may worth be pursuing if the point is indeed well taken.[1] So here I'll try again, drawing on recent empirical results that were not previously available (Section 3). I'll also offer a more speculative, theoretical metaphysical framework to ground the relevant intuitions, which I think is particularly plausible in the domain of the tasty, appealing to the traditional notion of *disagreement in attitude*—although I'll emphasize

DOI: 10.4324/9781003184225-10

144 *Dan López de Sa*

how this goes beyond what contextualism as such is in the business of explaining (Section 4). I'll end by recalling how there is indeed a genuine difficulty in the vicinity for contextualism; but this is one that has to do with facts about how we *dispute* matters of taste, that is, facts about the possibilities and limitations of our ways of expressing in language the relevant disagreements. This difficulty is indeed genuine, but it is one for which (I hope) promising responses have already been made on behalf of contextualism in the literature (see again López de Sa, 2008, 2015; Sundell, 2011; Plunket & Sundell, 2013, 2021; as well as Silk, 2016; Khoo & Knobe, 2018; Zakkou, 2019, *inter alia*).

1. Relativistic Effects, Faultless Disagreement, and Contextualism

In an excellent recent paper, Rachel Etta Rudolph (2020) presents the phenomenon of apparent faultless disagreement via the *relativistic effects* to which the widely discussed domain of predicates of personal taste gives rise.

Consider the following contrasting dialogues:

(1) Aline and Bob have both tried the same cake. Aline enjoyed it, but Bob didn't.

> a. **Aline:** This cake is tasty.
> b. **Bob:** No, it's not tasty!

Thus they here license *linguistic denial* in as strong a form as they would with *factual* predicates, which seems to be a sufficiently good indication of their being in disagreement:

(2) a. **Aline:** This cake is vegan.

> b. **Bob:** No, it's not vegan!

But there also seems to be an intuitive contrast between these cases:

> [In the dispute about taste in (1)], it's tempting to say that so long as each speaker is basing their claim sincerely on how they experience the cake, there's a sense in which neither is mistaken. The contrast with the purely factual case is brought out in the following:

(3) a. As far as its taste suggests, this cake is vegan; but maybe it isn't (actually) vegan.

> b. ?? As far as its taste suggests, this cake is tasty; but maybe it isn't (actually) tasty.

> No matter one's evidence or experience, it is appropriate to express uncertainty about a purely factual matter, like the cake being vegan. By contrast, given a certain experience of the cake, it becomes very odd to express uncertainty about whether the cake is tasty. This is the intuition behind the faultlessness side of faultless disagreement.
>
> (Rudolph, 2020, p. 201)

Indeed. On the face of it, it seems possible for Aline and Bob to disagree on whether the cake is tasty without either of them being at fault. Likewise for our initial disagreement about spinach. And likewise for (by now) philosophically familiar disagreements as to whether Homer Simpson is funny, whether licorice is disgusting, and whether roller coasters are fun.[2]

I myself applaud Rudolph's choice to speak of *relativistic effects* in a way that is generally connected to intuitions concerning appearances of faultless disagreement exhibited in disputes about taste—and perhaps others too—as opposed to tying this label to one specific theory of how to vindicate such appearances.[3] Following the lead of Crispin Wright, I have previously suggested that *relativism*, in general, is best conceived as the general attempt to endorse vindicating the appearances of faultless disagreement (López de Sa, 2011, p. 104). So understood, *contextualism* is not an *alternative to* but rather a particularly straightforward, semantically moderate *version of* relativism. Here we can simplify our discussion by characterizing contextualism about a predicate such as 'tasty' via the contention that it contributes different properties in different contexts—typically, relative to the sense of taste of the speaker or whoever is appropriately salient in the conversation that takes place at the center of the context (for further details, see again López de Sa, 2011, based on Lewis, 1980, and references therein). To illustrate: 'tasty' in Aline's context may contribute a property relative to Aline's sense of taste, whereas in Bob's context it may contribute another property, relative to Bob's sense of taste. Given that Aline's and Bob's tastes may differ, the explanation of how there can be faultlessness with respect to 'tasty', in contrast with 'vegan', is straightforward. *Mutatis mutandis* for our original disagreement about spinach. In virtue of the different contributions the expression makes—e.g., being tasty for those with my sense of taste when I say it and being tasty for those like you when you say it—spinach can respectively have and lack those properties if our tastes diverge sufficiently, and we can make corresponding judgments to that effect which may be simultaneously true—and thus faultless.

Contextualism is a particularly straightforward, semantically moderate version of relativism and seems to be well positioned to account for intuitions about faultlessness. For a while, and partly due to the works of John MacFarlane (2014, *inter alia*), some thought that contextualism had difficulties with 'retraction', and this motivated an alternative form

146 *Dan López de Sa*

of relativism: *assessment relativism* (or *radical relativism*). Although this is not our topic here, let me say, for what it's worth, that I fear that conceptions of the notion of 'retraction' may be too elusive to provide any valuable data. As Diana Raffman suggests,

> our intuitions are sufficiently divergent, and/or simply anemic, that MacFarlane's constructed examples cannot always bear the weight he places on them.
>
> (Raffman, 2016, p. 172)[4]

And to the extent that the relevant scenarios are interpreted in specific ways, subjects' responses seem to align more closely with contextualism than with MacFarlane's radical conjectures (see Kneer, 2021, and references therein).

Contextualism, then, is a particularly straightforward semantically moderate version of relativism, which seems to be well positioned to account for intuitions about faultlessness and seems to face no difficulties regarding retraction. Yet, as I said, many have thought and still seem to believe that there is nonetheless a severe problem with contextualism: the problem of 'lost disagreement'.

2. The So-Called Problem of Lost Disagreement

The so-called problem of lost disagreement is the alleged problem that contextualism *loses* disagreement in cases where it is intuitively present.

Consider again our dispute over the taste of the cake in (1):

- This cake is tasty.
- No, it's not tasty!

According to contextualism, both of these assertions are true in the situation considered, since 'tasty' contributes different properties in the relevant contexts. (Hence, as we saw, the faultlessness of the judgments expressed.) Now, intuitively, the people are here *in disagreement*—as much as they are in factual cases—as is strongly indicated by the felicity of the linguistic denial "No!" *This* is the disagreement that, many worry, would be 'lost' if contextualism was correct. Here is an early formulation of the worry by Crispin Wright:

> If [contextualism] were right, there would be an analogy between disputes of inclinations and the 'dispute' between one who says "I am tired" and her companion who replies, "Well, I am not" (when what is at issue is one more museum visit). There are the materials here, perhaps, for a (further) disagreement but no disagreement has yet

Disagreements and Disputes   147

been expressed. But ordinary understanding already hears a disagreement between one who asserts that hurt-free infidelity is acceptable and one who asserts that it is not.

(Wright, 2001, p. 451)

And here is another example from Max Kölbel:

> Suppose you utter (B) ["Blair ought to go to war"] and I answer by uttering the negation of (B): "It is not the case that Blair ought to go to war". Suppose we are both sincere. According to [contextualism], we don't disagree any more than we do if you say "I have a guinea-pig" and I answer "I don't have a guinea-pig".
>
> (Kölbel, 2004, p. 304)

This often-made objection is, for many, the main problem that contextualism faces; serious enough for it to be decisive. The general form of the objection is as follows. There are certain disputes in which the speakers are intuitively in disagreement ("This cake is tasty"/"No"). According to contextualism, these disputes involve uttering sentences (expressing judgments) that are simultaneously true. These sentences are thus, according to contextualism, in this respect similar to other pairs of context-dependent sentences (expressing judgments) that are also simultaneously true ("I am tired"/"I am not"). The latter are not, intuitively, disputes in which people are in disagreement. *Therefore*, according to contextualism, the former aren't disputes in which people are in disagreement. But, intuitively, they are! That is to say, disagreement *would get lost* if contextualism was correct. Hence the (alleged) problem of 'lost disagreement'.

I'll now argue that this alleged problem of 'lost disagreement' is spurious in that it presupposes an *unduly restrictive* conception of what disagreement requires—to anticipate that disagreement requires exclusionary contents that cannot all be true. Before moving on to this, however, let me make a couple of further observations.

'Disagreement' and cognates in English (and in other languages) is sometimes used to describe the *mental states* that two or more people are in—as when we say that the ancient Greeks were in disagreement with the ancient Indians about whether the bodies of the dead should be burned or buried—and sometimes in connection with an *activity* that people can engage in—as when we say that the neighbors had a loud and tiring disagreement until late last night. How these senses are interrelated is indeed an interesting issue in itself.[5] For present purposes, however, and in accordance with (some of) the literature, I'll reserve the expression 'disagreement' for the contrasting states that are expressed in the kind of dialogue under consideration. Admittedly, this is partly *stipulative* in that, as just mentioned, English is not so restricted. But it is only *partly* stipulative, in that speakers would ordinarily describe the people in the

148   *Dan López de Sa*

dialogues as being in disagreement. It is in this sense that both the alleged problem and its deflation concern *ordinary* ideas about disagreement.[6] And for present purposes, and again in accordance with (some of) the literature, I'll continue to use the expression 'dispute' and cognates for linguistic exchanges such as the dialogues considered here, where—all parties agree—intuitively, people disagree.

The restrictive conception of what the ordinary notion of disagreement requires is the following. Let's revisit in more detail situations involving clearly context-dependent expressions, like the indexical 'I' in:

- I'm tired.
- I'm not.

Because 'I' may refer to different people in different contexts, these utterances (and the judgments they express) have contents that are not *exclusionary*, i.e., they can both be true. *And* this exchange does not seem to be a dispute; nor do the people involved seem to be in disagreement. According to the restrictive conception of disagreement that is operative in the problem of 'lost disagreement', instead of 'and' we could also have said 'therefore'. *Disagreement requires exclusionary contents. Because* the relevant contents in the relevant contexts—*that I am tired* and *that you are not tired*, say—can be all true, there is no disagreement. We can now see the role of this conception of disagreement in the (alleged) problem explicitly. The sentences

- This cake is tasty.
- No, this cake is not tasty.

are, according to contextualism, relevantly similar to the previous ones. Thus, according to contextualism, the relevant contents—*that this cake is tasty for A* and *that this cake is tasty for B*, say—are not exclusionary. Thus, if we conceive of disagreement as requiring exclusionary contents, then if contextualism is correct, this would not be a case in which people are in disagreement. But intuitively, they are. Hence, disagreement gets 'lost'—*assuming that disagreement requires exclusionary contents.*

This conception of disagreement, according to which disagreement requires exclusionary contents, is popular in some philosophical circles. It is arguably *unduly restrictive*, however. The ordinary notion of disagreement is much more flexible and need not involve exclusionary contents.

3.   The Flexibility of Disagreement

Disagreement, according to our ordinary ideas about it, need not involve exclusionary contents; it is much more flexible than that. That this is so has been defended on numerous occasions—by López de Sa (2008, 2015),

Sundell (2011), Huvenes (2012), Plunkett and Sundell (2013), MacFarlane (2014), Marques and García-Carpintero (2014), and by many others. As I said, this appeal to such flexibility was made in the context of deflating the so-called problem of lost disagreement. Besides attempting to clarify and straighten out this overall consideration, further attempts will be made here to strengthen the case on a couple of related counts.

On the one hand, the envisaged flexibility seems to be corroborated beyond the aforementioned claims of philosophers and linguists. In a recent paper, Justin Khoo and Joshua Knobe report:

> Across a series of experimental studies, we show that people's judgments about exclusionary content systematically come apart from their judgments about disagreement. Specifically, in cases very much like the dialogue between Jim and Yör ["What Dylan did is morally wrong"—"No, what Dylan did isn't morally wrong"] people show a tendency to say that the speakers do disagree but that their claims are not exclusionary.
>
> (Khoo & Knobe, 2018, p. 109)

This evidence suggests that, as was contended, disagreement, according to our ordinary ideas, is in effect much more flexible than the restrictive conception assumes, and, crucially, it suggests that it does *not require exclusionary contents*. Given this finding, contextualism's alleged problem of 'lost disagreement' immediately vanishes (which is not to deny that there is no genuine difficulty in the vicinity). The alleged problem presupposes a restrictive conception of what disagreement requires, which is simply *too* restrictive according to our ordinary ideas, which in fact allow for much more flexibility.[7]

In fact, contextualism may even be indirectly *supported* by this evidence, as contextualism may seem particularly well positioned to account for such flexibility. As Khoo & Knobe say,

> Not only is it *not* problematic for a theory if it fails to predict exclusionary content in all cases of [disagreement], but it *is* problematic for a theory if it *does* predict exclusionary content in all cases of [disagreement]. To accord with people's ordinary judgments, a theory should allow for the possibility of non-exclusionary [disagreements].
>
> (Khoo & Knobe, 2018, p. 110)

4. Disagreement in Attitude

The so-called problem of lost disagreement presupposes a conception of disagreement according to which it requires exclusionary contents. But our ordinary ideas about disagreement allow for much more flexibility. Hence this alleged problem for contextualism is just spurious.

150 *Dan López de Sa*

In my mind, this is enough to deflate the alleged problem of 'lost disagreement' for contextualism. But given that some of us have submitted the previous consideration without great success in the past, I now want to try to reinforce the case with the following additional consideration. In addition to the fact that ordinary ideas about disagreement seem at odds with the unduly restrictive conception that is presupposed by the alleged problem, there is a certain theoretical articulation of such flexibility, which contextualists, as much as anybody else, may find philosophically appealing. This, of course, is the Stevensonian idea of *disagreement in attitude* (other than belief). Here is one of Stevenson's classic formulations of this idea:

> Suppose that two people have decided to dine together. One suggests a restaurant where there is music; another expresses his disinclination to hear music and suggests some other restaurant . . . The disagreement springs more from divergent preferences than from divergent beliefs, and will end when they both wish to go to the same place . . . it will be a 'disagreement' in a wholly familiar sense . . .
>
> John's mother is concerned about the dangers of playing football, and doesn't want him to play. John, even though he agrees (in belief) about the dangers, wants to play anyhow. Again, they disagree.
>
> (Stevenson, 1944, p. 3)

More generally, he says:

> Two men [*sic*] will be said to disagree in attitude when they have opposed attitudes to the same object—one approving of it, for instance, and the other disapproving of it—and when at least one of them has a motive for altering or calling into question the attitude of the other.
>
> (1944, p. 3)

This, in full, particularly with the last clause about motives, is a plausible characterization of disagreement in attitude *in activity*—if the analogy with disagreement in belief is to be preserved. Thus I take the Stevensonian account of disagreement in attitude to concern only the first component about people and their attitudes (see also Ridge, 2013), and I leave the second component for inclusion in an account of the pragmatics of the relevant activity, in line with the infamous "Do so as well!" (Ridge, 2003).

The idea, then, is that according to our ordinary ideas, there is disagreement in cases in which people are in disagreement ultimately in virtue of holding *contrasting* or *opposing* attitudes (other than doxastic ones).

What does this mean, exactly? What is it, exactly, to disagree *in attitude*—or, if you prefer, *practically*? What specific kind of *contrast* or *opposition* is required among the attitudes for them to constitute a

Disagreements and Disputes 151

disagreement? These are indeed interesting and complex questions (for a recent survey, see Huvenes, 2017, and references therein). Some take quite a liberal view of this. Here is MacFarlane:

> Suppose that Jane likes Bob, but Sarah hates him. In a perfectly respectable sense, Jane disagrees with Sarah, even if she believes all the same things about Bob. . . . In the same sense, two kids might disagree about licorice, one wanting to eat it, the other being repulsed by it. There need not be any proposition they differ about for them to disagree about licorice. It is enough if they just have different attitudes towards licorice.
>
> (2014, p. 122)

For what it's worth, I am myself inclined to favor the maximally liberal account that is suggested by this last remark, which could perhaps be labeled the *mere divergence view*. As part of any full defense of this view, I would try to highlight the intuitive distinction between mere disagreement and actual *conflict*: the possibility of which may indeed be constitutive of disagreement but for which pressures for coordination, and ultimately the importance attached to the issue, have to be present (see López de Sa, 2015, 2017; Manne & Sobel, 2014).[8] A fuller articulation of this view would appeal to the dispositional and response-dependent nature of the relevant properties and contents, following the Lewisian general account of values (see López de Sa, 2017).[9]

It is important to observe that, interesting and complex as these issues are, they go beyond contextualism proper. Contextualism is a semantic claim to the effect that in matters of personal taste and the like, the relevant expressions make different contributions in different contexts. As a result of this, according to contextualism, some disputes involve people being in disagreement without exclusionary contents. There would be a genuine problem of 'lost disagreement' if disagreement required exclusionary contents. But it doesn't; our ordinary ideas about disagreement allow for much more flexibility. So it is in fact an advantage of contextualism that it allows (and predicts!) nonexclusionary disagreements. At least in the domain of the tasty, there is a theoretical articulation of such flexibility involving the Stevensonian idea of disagreement in attitude. This idea may come with its own interesting and complex issues. But still, it is an idea that contextualists, as much as anybody else, may find philosophically appealing. To this extent, I hope, it may provide further indirect support to the present point.

I want to end this section with the following consideration. I have been claiming that the so-called problem of lost disagreement presupposes an unduly restrictive conception of disagreement. This is true insofar as the alleged problem concerns *ordinary* ideas about the disagreement that is present in our disputes. And this is a fair characterization of how the

152   *Dan López de Sa*

often-made and quick objection to contextualism is usually expressed. Recall Wright:

> But *ordinary understanding already hears a disagreement* between one who asserts that hurt-free infidelity is acceptable and one who asserts that it is not.
>
> (2001, p. 451, my emphasis)

Still, one is certainly free to stipulate richer senses for specific theoretical purposes; for instance, *doxastic disagreement that requires exclusionary contents*, or *Disagreement*, with a capital D, if one is so inclined, to disambiguate. Quite obviously, contextualism is incompatible with people being in Disagreement in the relevant disputes. *Suppose*, then, that one could argue that there is reason to believe that there are Disagreements in a certain domain or in a certain kind of case; for instance, because this is how people regard those specific cases and/or because accounting for them in nondoxastic or, more generally, nonexclusionary ways is not promising. *Then* there would be a good objection to contextualism about that domain or about that kind of case.[10] But providing such an argument would go way beyond the quick general appeal to 'ordinary understanding' that we have been considering. And for what it's worth, I find it hard to imagine any such argument in the particular case of the tasty.

Some may be surprised by my conditional narrative in the last paragraph.[11] Can't one interpret some elements of the recent debate as attempting to provide such further arguments? I may be wrong, but my take on the literature is that what objectors have been pointing to is the existence of a genuine difficulty in the vicinity; but this is one that concerns the *linguistic expression* of disagreement in disputes, to which now I turn.

5.   Felicity of Linguistic Denial (and the Like)

The worry that disagreement would be 'lost' if contextualism was correct depends on an unduly restrictive conception, according to which disagreement requires exclusionary contents; thus this worry should carry no conviction.

That being said, just invoking the flexibility allowed by our ordinary ideas about disagreement, even with the further claim that relevantly contrasting nondoxastic attitudes may ultimately constitute such disagreements (however this is to be eventually articulated), despite sufficing to reject that spurious problem, does not suffice for a full defense of contextualism (*pace* Huvenes, 2012; Marques & García-Carpintero, 2014). And this is because there is indeed a genuine difficulty for contextualism in the vicinity, which calls for explanation. But as anticipated, this genuine

Disagreements and Disputes 153

difficulty does not concern any alleged 'lost disagreement' but rather concerns how to account for certain facts about how these disagreements are linguistically expressed in disputes.

Recall, from Rudolph's discussion of relativistic effects:

(1) Aline and Bob have both tried the same cake. Aline enjoyed it, but Bob didn't.

    a. **Aline:** This cake is tasty.
    b. **Bob:** No, it's not tasty!

According to contextualism, the property that 'tasty' contributes in A's context is relative to A's sense of taste. Suppose that A had chosen to express *this very same property* by other means; for instance, by making such relativization explicit. B would still be in disagreement with A, of course, but would no longer be in a position to *linguistically express it* in the same way:

(4) a. **Aline:** This cake is tasty *for me*.

    b. **Bob:** #No, it's not tasty *for me*!

Instead, B would have to say something like:

    c. **Bob:** Well, not for me. Too sweet.
    d. **Bob:** I disagree.

(As usual, I use '#' to mark the relevant sort of infelicity.)

To illustrate further, consider the following case, which is arguably ultimately constituted by contrasts in, say, senses of humor. Not all *linguistic expressions* of such disagreements in disputes allow for the same pattern. For instance, in response to:

•   I find Homer Simpson very amusing.

one might say:

•   Well, he doesn't amuse me *at all* . . .

or perhaps even:

•   I disagree: you have a terrible sense of humor!

But we wouldn't say:

•   #No, I don't.

154 *Dan López de Sa*

and even less:

- #That's false: he doesn't amuse me at all.

Yet the latter kind of response would have been perfectly appropriate in a different way of expressing the disagreement:

- Homer Simpson is so funny!
- No, he's not.
- False, not at all.

What is it in the semantics of predicates of personal taste like 'tasty' or 'funny' that, when they are used in this kind of linguistic environment, allows for the felicity of linguistic denials such as these? This is a genuine difficulty for contextualism, because contextualism contends that, in virtue of the potentially different contributions of the predicate, the two contrasting sentences could themselves have nonexclusionary contents; that is, both be true.[12] And this is a genuine difficulty in the vicinity: not one about any alleged 'lost disagreement' but instead concerning how disagreements are linguistically expressed in disputes.

However, this is a difficulty to which there are already proposed solutions in the literature. For what it's worth, the view that I myself have defended elsewhere (see *inter alia* López de Sa, 2008, 2015) again finds inspiration in Lewis's account of values. If contextualism (i.e., contextualist relativism) is correct, he wonders:

> Wouldn't you hear them saying "value for me and my mates" or "value for the likes of you"? Wouldn't you think they'd stop arguing after one speaker says X is a value and the other says it isn't?—Not necessarily. They might always presuppose, with more or less confidence (well-founded or otherwise), that whatever relativity there is won't matter in *this* conversation.
>
> (Lewis, 1989, p. 84)

I contend that the relevant predicates trigger a *presupposition of commonality*, to the effect that the addressees are relevantly like the speaker or, more generally, that they are relevantly in keeping with the way of valuing that is salient in the conversation that is taking place at the center of the context.

The notion of *presupposition* that I presuppose here is basically Stalnakerian (for a not-so-recent statement of this, see Stalnaker, 2002, pp. 716–717). In terms of this basic notion of 'pragmatic' presupposition,

Disagreements and Disputes 155

one can characterize the 'semantic' presupposition that an expression triggers along the following lines:

> A given *expression* triggers a certain presupposition if an utterance of it would be infelicitous when the presupposition is not part of the common ground of the conversation—unless participants accommodate it by coming to presuppose it on the basis of the fact that the utterance has been produced.

It is in this way that the presupposition-of-commonality approach is to be understood. And it is this presuppositional component that, I claim, puts contextualism in a position to account for the felicity of linguistic denial.

For suppose that 'tasty' does trigger such a presupposition of commonality. Then an utterance of "This cake is tasty" would be infelicitous when the presupposition is not part of the common ground of the conversation (unless people accommodate it). In any ordinary, nondefective conversation, all of the parties to the conversation presuppose the same things. So, in particular, if A says "This cake is tasty", the participants would presuppose that they have the same commonality, i.e., share the relevant sense of taste. But then B can felicitously express disagreement with "No!"

What if a presupposition of commonality in the conversation is, in fact, false? Well, then the participants' presumption that the utterances contradict each other is also, in fact, false. Which might be OK for the purpose of the conversation: *accepting* is not *believing*. What if the participants actually presuppose otherwise? The prediction is then that the participants would refrain from using the relevant unconditionalized predicates. Instead, they might cancel the presupposition by conditionalizing; which seems to me to be precisely what happens: "Come here and try this cake! This is so tasty!"—"Tasty *for you*, darling. You keep forgetting how much I hate spinach all the time! (And in a cake!?)" (although see what follows for further discussion). What if you reach the relevant point of the original conversation by other means? Then, in those specific contexts, you can indeed say "No!"

That was a very brief statement of my favorite view, for what it's worth. But it is not the only extant solution. There is a family of somehow similar proposals. Egan (2014) defends a view that arguably turns out to be the 'nonindexical' counterpart of this; although, he contends, it is somehow more organic than mine in that it does not posit a presuppositional element as a separate component of the semantics of the relevant lexical items.[13] Dinges (2017) contends that instead of a presupposition of commonality, the proper taste claims require the absence of a presupposition of noncommonality,[14] whereas Zakkou (2019) posits a presupposition of *superiority*.[15] Meanwhile, Silk (2016) has submitted his "discourse contextualism", which, according to him, supersedes

156 *Dan López de Sa*

my proposal, in that instead of having presuppositions of commonality triggered as separate components of meaning associated with individual lexical items, on his account, the relevant presuppositions are assimilated to "the presuppositions associated with variables more generally" (2016, pp. 64–65).[16]

Furthermore, there are views which I'm inclined to see as complementary rather than as rivals, most notably the *metalinguistic* account of David Plunkett and Tim Sundell (see *inter alia* Sundell, 2011; Plunkett & Sundell, 2013, 2021), in which linguistic behavior similar to that involved in the presumption of contradiction is accounted for in terms of the metalinguistic negotiation that may occur in specific contexts.[17] Clearly, such a phenomenon also exists. The reason our respective proposals nicely complement each other is, in brief, because the most serious objection to each of them is just one of partiality. Their explanation is partial in that it is not available in some relevant cases, where (as context makes clear) people agree in their relevant semantic standards and yet still felicitously express their disagreement with plain predications that license denials. In turn, some people have also denied the basic prediction of the presupposition of commonality: to repeat, that people will refrain from using the relevant unconditionalized predicates when participants actually presuppose *un*commonality—and they may instead conditionalize etc. (see also Egan, 2014). MacFarlane, for instance, claims to disagree:

> Let it be mutually known by Yum and Yuk that their tastes in foods tend to be very different. The dialogue with which we began
>
> [Yum: This is tasty!
> Yuk: No, it is not tasty.]
> still sounds natural.
>
> (2014, p. 131)

This would of course require much further discussion that is not pertinent here and, indeed, is in my view ultimately to be resolved partly by appeal to the kind of empirical result that has started to be obtained in recent years. But for what it's worth, and in order to illustrate how, in my view, presuppositions of commonality are also just partial: MacFarlane's straightforward dialogue assuming *un*commonality does *not* sound natural to me at all *unless* we think of the kind of context in which the right standard is being negotiated.

Be that as it may, the aim of this chapter has not been to defend any specific contextualist account. Rather, it has been to show how it is crucial to differentiate questions and facts about the relations between mental states that constitute *disagreements* from questions and facts about how these disagreements are linguistically expressed in *disputes*—in order to

Disagreements and Disputes 157

distinguish genuine difficulties concerning the felicity of linguistic denials and the like from spurious problems like the one of so-called lost disagreement.[18]

Notes

1. See (Khoo, 2017) and (Beddor, 2019) for a couple of recent handbook articles and references therein.
2. In this paper, Rudolph argues that nonevaluative expressions that exhibit such relativistic effects are what she labels "appearance predicates", such as 'tastes vegan' and 'looks blue', thus allowing a generalization to *experiential* predicates. Interestingly, this allows her to conjecture that the relativistic effects of experiential values are due to variation in subjective experiences across perspectives (2020, p. 207). She then notes:

   > This possibility is significant for determining the scope of relativist effects in natural language. If it's right, theorists shouldn't jump from the recognition of relativist effects with predicates of personal taste to the view that all evaluative language must behave relativistically; nor need they worry, if they opt for a relativist analysis of experiential language, that they will need to abandon objectivism for weighty evaluative language, for instance about morality.
   >
   > *(ibid.)*

   This would depend on the further issue concerning whether moral, or more generally, evaluative predicates can all be conceived as experiential. This is not the topic, however, of the quoted paper; nor, unfortunately, of this one. Thanks to Rachel Etta Rudolph for discussion.
3. "What I say about relativist effects in this paper will not settle whether they in fact call for a relativist analysis, or whether they can instead be accounted for adequately within other approaches" (Rudolph, 2020, p. 200).
4. MacFarlane himself is somewhat sympathetic to this kind of skepticism: "It is hard to get at retraction empirically . . . I prefer 'Do you stand by your earlier assertion?' but Raffman's remarks make me worry that a negative answer needn't mean retraction" (MacFarlane, 2016, p. 198).
5. It would be quite surprising for there to be no connection. With MacFarlane, I conjecture that "any account of the activity will make reference to the state" (2014, p. 120). Very plausibly, one component of disagreement in the activity sense is that it *expresses* disagreement in the state sense (that is, such activities count as *disputes* in the sense of this chapter); although this may not suffice to account for the interactive component in full. If this component of expression of the state is required nonetheless, then cases of apparently disagreeing in the activity sense without disagreeing in the state sense should be assimilated to related cases of apparently asserting without genuinely asserting, on the one hand, and also to cases of conventional, noncommunicative speech acts, like testifying in a courtroom. Both of these analogies strike me as independently plausible and offer defenses against the arguments to the contrary given by Cappelen and Hawthorne (2009, pp. 60–61) and MacFarlane (2014, p. 120). For further discussion of these issues, to which I am very much indebted, although it is ultimately in defense of a different view, see Pietroiusti (forthcoming).
6. A further complication: strictly speaking, the assumption is that speakers would describe people in the dialogues as being in disagreement *in those dialogues*. These people could be in those states even without interacting,

158   *Dan López de Sa*

but it doesn't *strictly speaking* follow that speakers would still be described as being in disagreement in those other situations. Plausible as it may be, this further contention about the English expression 'disagreement' vis-à-vis inter-actionless scenarios would require additional argumentation. Note, however, that appealing to our *ordinary* ideas about disagreement in our discussions, both in this chapter and elsewhere, doesn't require this further contention, plausible as it may be. Thanks to Giulio Pietroiusti for discussion.

7. This is not to say that there could not be *further* responses on behalf of contextualism which do not challenge this unduly restrictive conception of disagreement. Just to mention one: people can be in disagreement in the kind of case under consideration in virtue of having judgments with exclusion-ary contents that are less immediately linked to the literal contents of the utterances involved in the dialogues under consideration. Thanks to David Plunkett and Tim Sundell for discussion.

8. So if Jack prefers the lean and his wife prefers the fat, then they differ psycho-logically: they do not desire alike. So, I say, they disagree. Lewis may seem to disagree: "But they do agree, because if he eats no fat and she eats no lean, that would satisfy them both . . . Agreement in desire makes for harmony; desiring alike may well make for strife" (Lewis, 1989, p. 75). To my mind, however, this is clearly just a (legitimate) local stipulation, in order to mark a certain distinction, important as it may be—rather than a point about our intuitive, ordinary ideas about agreement and disagreement. For according to the latter, I take it, it is indeed clearly the case that in this scenario, Jack and his wife can also be said to be *in disagreement*—as to whether fat meat is preferable, say, if one of them prefers it and the other does not, in a perfectly ordinary sense of disagreement. As I said, what I think this shows is that not every case of disagreement (intuitively conceived) need give rise to a case of conflict (intuitively conceived).

9. A recent proposal that also appeals to this is (Zouhar, 2021).

10. As I said, this is not to say that there cannot be further responses on behalf of contextualism even in this case; see earlier, footnote 6.

11. Thanks to Dan Zeman for discussion.

12. On the face of it, some contextualists may seem to dispute the datum; in particular, Huvenes (2012, p. 177), and Marques and García-Carpintero (2014, p. 721). Hence their defense of contextualism in effect reduces to the previous point that disagreement in attitude can be nonexclusionary. Given that the contrast seems to be quite robust (and otherwise accepted and exploited in the literature), the best I can make of this is the following. What they are in fact observing is that, *in the appropriate specific supple-mented contexts*, linguistic denial may be licensed and felicitously express disagreement, even with "I like it". So reinterpreted, the observation would be correct. Indeed, as we are about to see, this is part of what some of the extant solutions of the genuine linguistic difficulty, offered on behalf of contextualism, do in fact elaborate.

13. See Egan (2014), p. 82 and fn. 21. For the contemporary rendering of the distinction between indexical and non-indexical versions of contextualism, see *inter alia* MacFarlane (2014); López de Sa (2011). And for skepticism about its substance, to which I am myself very much sympathetic, see Lewis (1980). In Egan's footnote he mentions a second reason for preferring his version to mine: "on the present account, the disagreement doesn't hinge on the presupposition's being in place. Even in cases where presupposition's absent, we still get disagreement on this picture". But, as should be clear, my presuppositions of commonality are posited in order to account for facts about the *expression* of disagreement, such as the felicity of linguistic denial.

Disagreements and Disputes 159

The *existence* of disagreement itself, of course, does not depend on this. I covered this point explicitly in earlier work (López de Sa, 2008), although perhaps without stressing it appropriately:

> Hannah and Sarah might disagree as to whether Homer is funny, and their respective distinctive senses of humor be perfectly apparent to them . . . Intuitively, I submit, *the disagreement in our case is constituted by the contrastive features of Hannah's and Sarah's senses of humor* (say). In non-defective conversations where they presuppose they are alike, this disagreement would be naturally expressible by the relevant pair of (unqualified) contrasting utterances . . . But in equally non-defective conversations where they do not presuppose they are alike, but may indeed presuppose they are not, *their disagreement exists all the same*, but it need not be so expressible.
>
> (López de Sa, 2008, pp. 307–308, underlines added)

For a similarly confused objection, see Marques and García-Carpintero (2014, p. 715); although in an even more peculiar setting, as they describe it to be "precisely what we take to be the main objection to López de Sa's proposal", before immediately adding "of which he is well aware" and quoting exactly the same previous paragraph of mine, where I explicitly assert, as underlined, what presuppositions of commonality are *not* expected to do. Oh well!

14. I find his rationale dubious: "if tastiness assertions did require a presupposition of commonality, they should be problematic . . . where someone rejects my assertion of 'This is delicious' at the dinner table. For, in this case, there is no such presupposition" (Dinges, 2017, p. 734, fn. 6). This doesn't follow: the presupposition may very well be in place, and one may express one's disagreement with that assumption with the rejection. Alternatively, one can refuse to accommodate the presupposition, which is what I take to happen in the *correction* that Dinges quotes: "'Come here and watch this! *King of the Hill* is so funny!'—'Funny *for you*, darling. You should remember that it doesn't amuse me at all.'" Thanks to Alexander Dinges for discussion.

15. Besides issues about disagreement, she appeals to what she labels *retraction data*. Although Zakkou refers to MacFarlane (2014), which, as we saw, may be problematic in the light of recent findings (see Kneer, 2021), her statement of them is weaker, and much more plausible, given that she contends that the relevant retraction responses, of the form "I take that back", are *permissible*, not required—against which, as she points out, no empirical evidence has been provided (Zakkou, 2019, p. 1558). The broad notion of *retraction* that "I take that back" tracks is, however, too indiscriminating. It arguably aims to remove the relevant (illocutionary) effects (see Caponetto, 2018) but without *criticizing* the original speech act. Compare: I say something, Giulio starts being difficult, and I'm just too tired to start a discussion again: "You know what? I take it back. Forget it!" (It is not clear to me yet what the results are with respect to the other component of the data, concerning "What I said was false"; see Dinges & Zakkou, 2020; Kneer, 2021.) With respect to Zakkou's own superiority proposal, what about felicitous assertions like: "I know full well that others know better about this. But this wine is just delicious!" Further discussion of the basic empirical predictions of the view in connection with cases like this would be welcome. Thanks to Julia Zakkou for discussion.

16. He in fact offers another pair of considerations (Silk, 2016, p. 65). The first of these rejects the basic prediction of the view; see the discussion that follows. The second is yet another instance of the confused pseudo-objection discussed above; see footnote 11.

160   *Dan López de Sa*

17. Interestingly, they also suffer from the pseudo-objection that their metalinguistic story fails to account "for disagreement" (see Egan, 2014, p. 84; Finlay, 2017, pp. 192–193). And interestingly, they had also explicitly asserted that this was *not* what their story was in the business of explaining: "Recall that [the metalinguistic proposal] was called into explain, not the intuition that Bettie and Alphie disagreed with each other, but rather *the fact that in their conversation, linguistic denial was a felicitous move* . . . That leaves to be explained . . . the intuition of conflict. . . . But as we've seen, that kind of intuition does not require that inconsistent propositions be expressed. . . . [The metalinguistic story] was never required to explain the intuition of conflict. So long as there is a conflict of attitudes, speakers can perceive themselves to be at odds" (Sundell, 2011, p. 284, my emphasis).

18. My research was funded by the project Social Metaphysics (PGC2018-094563-B-I00 MCIU/AEI/FEDER UE), and the group Law & Philosophy (AGAUR 2017 SGR 823). Earlier versions of this material were presented at the Josh Parsons Memorial Conference, St Andrews, 2018, and the 1st BIAP Workshop, Barcelona, 2019. Thanks to my audiences on those occasions and to Alexander Dinges, Manuel García-Carpintero, John Horden, Josep Macià, Teresa Marques, JJ Moreso, Michele Palmira, Giulio Pietroiusti, Miguel A. Sebastián, Crispin Wright, Julia Zakkou, Elia Zardini, and Dan Zeman. My biggest debt, of course, is to David Plunkett and Tim Sundell: this work can be seen as part of an ongoing collaboration in which we explore and further compare our views.

References

Beddor, B. (2019). Relativism and expressivism. In M. Kusch (Ed.), *The Routledge handbook of philosophy of relativism* (pp. 529–539). Routledge.

Caponetto, L. (2018). Undoing things with words. *Synthèse, 197*(6), 2399–2414. https://doi.org/10.1007/s11229-018-1805-9

Cappelen, H., & Hawthorne, J. (2009). *Relativism and monadic truth.* Oxford University Press.

Dinges, A. (2017). Relativism and assertion. *Australasian Journal of Philosophy, 95*(4), 730–740. https://doi.org/10.1080/00048402.2017.1284248

Dinges, A., & Zakkou, J. (2020). A direction effect on taste predicates. *Philosophers' Imprint, 20*(27), 1–22. http://hdl.handle.net/2027/spo.3521354.0020.027

Egan, A. (2014). There's something funny about comedy: A case study in faultless disagreement. *Erkenntnis, 79,* 73–100. https://doi.org/10.1007/s10670-013-9446-3

Finlay, S. (2017). Disagreement lost and found. In R. Shafer-Landau (Ed.), *Oxford studies in metaethics* (Vol. 12, pp. 187–205). Oxford University Press.

Huvenes, T. (2012). Varieties of disagreement and predicates of taste. *Australasian Journal of Philosophy, 90*(1), 167–181. https://doi.org/10.1080/00048402.2010.550305

Huvenes, T. (2017). On disagreement. In J. J. Ichikawa (Ed.), *The Routledge handbook of epistemic contextualism* (pp. 272–281). Routledge.

Khoo, J. (2017). The disagreement challenge to contextualism. In J. J. Ichikawa (Ed.), *The Routledge handbook of epistemic contextualism* (pp. 257–271). Routledge.

Khoo, J., & Knobe, J. (2018). Moral disagreement and moral semantics. *Noûs, 52,* 109–143. https://doi.org/10.1111/nous.12151

Kneer, M. (2021). Predicates of personal taste: Empirical data. *Synthese*, online first. https://doi.org/10.1007/s11229-021-03077-9

Kölbel, M. (2004). Indexical relativism versus genuine relativism. *International Journal of Philosophical Studies*, 12(3), 297–313. https://doi.org/10.1080/0967255042000243966

Lewis, D. (1980). Index, context, and content. In S. Kanger & S. Öhman (Eds.), *Philosophy and grammar*. Reidel. Reprinted in D. Lewis (1998), *Papers in philosophical logic* (pp. 21–44). Cambridge University Press.

Lewis, D. (1989). Dispositional theories of value. *Proceeding of the Aristotelian Society*, 63, 113–138. Reprinted in D. Lewis (2000), *Papers in ethics and social philosophy* (pp. 68–94). Cambridge: Cambridge University Press.

López de Sa, D. (2008). Presuppositions of commonality. In M. García-Carpintero & M. Kölbel (Eds.), *Relative truth* (pp. 297–310). Oxford University Press.

López de Sa, D. (2011). The many relativisms: Index, context, and beyond. In S. D. Hales (Ed.), *A companion to relativism* (pp. 102–117). Blackwell.

López de Sa, D. (2015). Expressing disagreement: A presuppositional indexical contextualist relativist account. *Erkenntnis*, 80, 153–165. https://doi.org/10.1007/s10670-014-9664-3

López de Sa, D. (2017). Making beautiful truths. In J. O. Young (Ed.), *Semantics of aesthetic judgements* (pp. 38–60). Oxford University Press.

MacFarlane, J. (2014). *Assessment sensitivity: Relative truth and its applications*. Oxford University Press.

MacFarlane, J. (2016). Replies to Raffman, Stanley, and Wright. *Philosophical and Phenomenological Research*, 92(1), 197–202. https://doi.org/10.1111/phpr.12265

Manne, K., & Sobel, D. (2014). Disagreeing about how to disagree. *Philosophical Studies*, 168, 823–834. https://doi.org/10.1007/s11098-013-0217-4

Marques, T., & García-Carpintero, M. (2014). Disagreement about taste: Commonality presuppositions and coordination. *Australasian Journal of Philosophy*, 92(4), 701–723. https://doi.org/10.1080/00048402.2014.922592

Pietroiusti, G. (forthcoming). Having a disagreement: Expression, persuasion and demand. *Synthese*.

Plunkett, D., & Sundell, T. (2013). Disagreement and the semantics of normative and evaluative terms. *Philosophers' Imprint*, 13(23), 1–37. http://hdl.handle.net/2027/spo.3521354.0013.023

Plunkett, D., & Sundell, T. (2021). Metalinguistic negotiation and speaker error. *Inquiry*, 64(1–2), 142–167. https://doi.org/10.1080/0020174X.2019.1610055

Raffman, D. (2016). Relativism, retraction, and evidence. *Philosophical and Phenomenological Research*, 92(1), 171–178. https://doi.org/10.1111/phpr.12264

Ridge, M. (2003). Non-cognitivist pragmatics and Stevenson's "do so as well!" *Canadian Journal of Philosophy*, 33(4), 563–574. https://doi.org/10.1080/00455091.2003.10716555

Ridge, M. (2013). Disagreement. *Philosophy and Phenomenological Research*, 86(1), 41–63. https://doi.org/10.1111/j.1933-1592.2011.00551.x

Rudolph, R. E. (2020). Talking about appearances: The roles of evaluation and experience in disagreement. *Philosophical Studies*, 177, 197–217. https://doi.org/10.1007/s11098-018-1185-5

Silk, A. (2016). *Discourse contextualism: A framework for contextualist semantics and pragmatics*. Oxford University Press.

162 *Dan López de Sa*

Stalnaker, R. (2002). Common ground. *Linguistics and Philosophy, 25*, 701–721. https://doi.org/10.1023/A:1020867916902

Stevenson, C. L. (1944). *Ethics and language*. Yale University Press.

Sundell, T. (2011). Disagreements about taste. *Philosophical Studies, 155*, 267–288. https://doi.org/10.1007/s11098-010-9572-6

Wright, C. (2001). On being in a quandary. *Mind, 110*, 45–98. Reprinted in C. Wright (2003). *Saving the Differences* (pp. 443–509). Cambridge, MA: Harvard University Press.

Zakkou, J. (2019). Denial and retraction: A challenge for theories of taste predicates. *Synthese, 196*, 1555–1573. https://doi.org/10.1007/s11229-017-1520-y

Zouhar, M. (2021). On the nature of non-doxastic disagreement about taste. In T. Ciecierski & P. Grabarczyk (Eds.), *Context dependence in language, action, and cognition* (pp. 41–62). De Gruyter.

8 How to Canberra-Plan Disagreement
Platitudes, Taste, Preferences

Jeremy Wyatt

1. Introductory Remarks

Disagreement is a pervasive phenomenon in our everyday lives. One of the most familiar sorts of disagreement in which we engage is disagreement concerning matters of gustatory taste, which I'll simply call *taste disagreement* in what follows.[1] The main question that I'll take up in this chapter is 'What is taste disagreement?' Given that taste disagreement is so utterly familiar, considering this question may cause us to experience a sense of complacency. I relish the flavour of espresso, while you find it oppressively bitter. You are enchanted by the unique, slippery mouthfeel of natto, while I can't stand to take one bite. We might express our incompatible views about these comestibles in conversation or we might not, but still, we are in disagreement about the flavours of espresso and natto. Moreover, the nature of our disagreement might seem rather obvious—I like the flavour of a particular food or drink and you don't, or vice versa. So why engage in a lengthy discussion of the nature of taste disagreement?

The main reason is that the apparent simplicity of taste disagreement is misleading. Going forward, we'll see that in fact, taste disagreement is a wonderfully complex phenomenon. This is just the sort of thing that we've come to expect from philosophical reflection—a revelation that what we thought was too simple to discuss is far more subtle than we could have imagined. Moreover, given that taste disagreement is so pervasive in our lives, the significance of its striking complexity is more than academic.

Another reason to think carefully about taste disagreement is that questions about its nature have been at the heart of contemporary debates about *taste discourse* for the past twenty years. Theorists interested in the semantics and pragmatics of taste discourse have appealed to considerations regarding taste disagreement to motivate their theories and to challenge rival theories. Accordingly, a proper understanding of the nature of taste disagreement will considerably improve our understanding of how these debates ought to play out.[2]

A third reason to concentrate on taste disagreement is that an appreciation of its nature will help to set up an informed comparison between

DOI: 10.4324/9781003184225-11

164 *Jeremy Wyatt*

taste disagreement and *other kinds* of disagreement, including aesthetic, moral, religious, scientific, and political disagreement. Comparing these kinds of disagreement will put us in a position to better understand how they arise in our lives, whether/why it is valuable to engage in them, and whether/how they ought to be resolved when they do arise. This is a project that promises not only intellectual satisfaction but practically significant knowledge about ourselves and how we do and ought to relate to others in our overlapping communities.[3]

In the remainder of the chapter, I'll be focusing on the following questions, which remain unsettled in the contemporary debates about taste disagreement:

- What *methods* should we use when thinking about the nature of taste disagreement?
- What are the *relata* of the relation of taste disagreement?
- What is the nature of the *relation* of taste disagreement itself?

Prior work on these questions has, I think, systematically overlooked a key point. This is that the second and third questions are *metaphysical* rather than linguistic questions. This point has a clear implication regarding the first question. Even if the second and third questions prove to have linguistic relevance, we should see whether we can use the methods of metaphysics to make headway on them.

I'll be addressing these three questions using a framework, the Canberra Plan, that has been influentially applied in other metaphysical contexts. This framework underscores certain platitudes about disagreement that enable us to determine what sort of relation we're hunting for when we aim to determine what taste disagreement is. Jumping ahead a bit, my contention will be that this relation is *preferential type-noncotenability*, where the preferences at issue concern matters of gustatory taste. After motivating and elaborating this account of taste disagreement, I'll close by saying a few words about how it can inform the existing debates about taste discourse, taste disagreement, and disagreement in general.

2. Canberra-Planning Disagreement

2.1. *Platitudes about Disagreement*

We want to know what taste disagreement is. To acquire this knowledge, we first need to identify what we already know about disagreement, and we can then determine what more we can say about the particular nature of taste disagreement. More exactly, we can start by examining how our ordinary concept DISAGREEMENT—the concept that we deploy when identifying cases like those mentioned already as cases of disagreement— behaves.[4] The way to really get going with this project is to *empirically*

How to Canberra-Plan Disagreement   165

examine the behaviour of this concept using the methods of e.g. psychology and experimental philosophy.[5] But before we do this empirical work, we need reasonable hypotheses to test, and this is where armchair conceptual analysis can earn its keep.

In generating these hypotheses, we should begin by asking ourselves: what are the *platitudes* about disagreement? Once we amass a body of platitudes about disagreement, we will be in a position to identify the functional role that the ordinary concept DISAGREEMENT plays in our cognitive lives. This functional role tells us what the world would be like if it contained disagreement. We will then be able to draw on our current evidence to determine whether disagreement in fact exists and if so, what it is like. This sort of approach was pioneered by advocates of the *Canberra Plan* such as Frank Jackson (1998) and David Lewis (1966, 1970, 1972, 1994).

What is a platitude about disagreement? As we're using the term, a platitude needn't be an old saw. Rather, a platitude about x is a proposition that is constitutive of the ordinary concept of x. In more detail, this is what it takes for a proposition to be a platitude about disagreement:[6]

> (Platitude) Proposition p is a platitude about disagreement iff p is a member of a set D of propositions such that: person A possesses the ordinary concept DISAGREEMENT iff A is disposed to accept each of the members p' of D (i) in the absence of supporting argumentation for p' and (ii) in the presence of a suitable prompt (e.g. a well-constructed vignette) that causes A to consider p'.

So which propositions are platitudes about disagreement? In light of my own experiences with disagreement as well as the knowledge that I have about academic work on the subject, I assign a reasonably high prior probability to the hypothesis that the propositions expressed by the following are among the platitudes about disagreement:[7]

> *Irreflexivity:* For all persons A, matters m, and times t: it is not the case that A is in disagreement with A over m at t
>
> *Symmetry:* For all persons A and B, matters m, and times t: if A is in disagreement with B over m at t, then B is in disagreement with A over m at t
>
> *Non-transitivity:* It is not the case that (for all persons A, B, and C, matters m, and times t: if A is in disagreement with B over m at t and B is in disagreement with C over m at t, then A is in disagreement with C over m at t) and it is not the case that (for all persons A, B, and C, matters m, and times t: if A is in disagreement with B over m at t and B is in disagreement with C over m at t, then A is not in disagreement with C over m at t)

166   *Jeremy Wyatt*

> *Disagreement Principle:* For all persons A and B, matters m, and times t: A and B are in disagreement over m at t iff at t, A has a (doxastic or non-doxastic) attitude y about m and B has a (doxastic or non-doxastic) attitude z about m, and y and z are incompatible$_{y,z}$ with one another
>
> *Mistake Principle:* For all persons A and B and propositions p: if A believes p, then if A also believes that they are in disagreement with B as to whether p is true, then A believes that B has made a judgement about p that is mistaken.

Let me say a few words about how these platitudes are supposed to work. First of all, I've formulated them in terms of *persons* because I would hypothesise that in the first instance, we take persons to be the relata of the relation of disagreement. When we acquire the ordinary concept DISAGREEMENT, we presumably do so after observing or being told about cases in which two or more persons (e.g. family members or children in the schoolyard) are in disagreement with one another. As a result, we are led to think of *personal disagreement* as being the paradigm sort of disagreement. Later on, the concept becomes more abstract (and perhaps metaphorical) in that we also sometimes think of ourselves simply as disagreeing with what someone believes, what they said or assumed, or decisions that they made. Then, especially if we study some philosophy, we may come to think about disagreement even more abstractly, taking e.g. assertions, theories, plans, or propositions to disagree with one another.[8]

Additionally, I have formulated the platitudes so that they pertain not to the bare relation of disagreement but to the relation of disagreement over matter m. This is because I would conjecture that even when we use the construction 'A disagrees with B,' what we have in mind is that there is some matter over which A and B are in disagreement, e.g. whether espresso is delicious, whether the effects of climate change will be disastrous, or whether Michael Jordan is the most talented basketball player of all time. We don't think of persons as simply being in disagreement— rather, we think of them as being in disagreement about some issue/matter/subject/topic. This is so even if, given the information that we have, we can't specify which matter that is (consider 'Susan, who knows both of them well, said that A and B are in disagreement. I'm not sure what they would disagree about, but she must be right').

Irreflexivity says that no person disagrees with themselves at a given time t. The hypothesis, then, is that if a possessor of the ordinary concept DISAGREEMENT were presented with a suitable prompt (e.g. a well-constructed vignette), they would probably be disinclined to say that a given person A disagrees with themselves at a particular time. We are all too familiar, of course, with cases in which someone has, at a particular time, incompatible desires about a certain course of action, e.g. proposing

How to Canberra-Plan Disagreement   167

marriage to a wealthy but emotionally exhausting person or consuming a delicious but rather unhealthy food or drink. Yet we presumably wouldn't be inclined to say that in cases such as these, a person disagrees with themselves. Rather, we would simply say that they are conflicted, that they have incompatible desires.[9]

What about someone with dissociative identity disorder, one of whose personalities believes that p and another of whose personalities believes that not-p? Here, we might be more inclined to say that the person disagrees with themselves. However, I suspect that most of us would favour the verdict that while such a person doesn't disagree with themselves, one of their personalities disagrees with another of their personalities.[10]

With regard to Symmetry, perhaps the most important thing to say is that we may feel some initial resistance to Symmetry if we're not careful to distinguish disagreement as a *state* from disagreement as an *activity*.[11] If Henry believes that the earth is 6,000 years old and Stephen believes that the earth is 4.5 billion years old, then Henry is in a state of disagreement with Stephen, and likewise, Stephen is in a state of disagreement with Henry. This is so even if neither Henry nor Stephen has ever discussed the other's views about the age of the earth. This and many other familiar cases speak in favour of Symmetry being a platitude about the state of disagreement.

It is, on the other hand, implausible to regard Symmetry as a platitude about the activity of *disagreeing*. If Henry is in the US and Stephen is in England, then Stephen might sit for an interview on the age of the earth during which the interviewer informs him about Henry's views. Stephen might then go on to explain at length why he takes Henry's views to be false, in which case he is engaged in the activity of disagreeing with Henry. However, if Henry is fast asleep while the interview is taking place, then he isn't simultaneously disagreeing with Stephen. Since they hold incompatible views about the age of the earth, they are simultaneously in disagreement about this issue, but they aren't simultaneously disagreeing about it. Thus, when we consider Symmetry, we must be sure to consider it as a platitude about disagreement rather than disagreeing.

Non-Transitivity tells us that disagreement is neither transitive nor anti-transitive. This is very easy to see. Suppose that there is a disagreement in the kingdom as to who is the rightful successor to the throne. A believes that it is Elisabeth, B believes that it is Victoria, and C believes that it is Elisabeth. In this case, A is in disagreement with B as to who is the rightful successor, B is in disagreement with C as to who is the rightful successor, but A isn't in disagreement with C as to who is the rightful successor. This shows that disagreement isn't transitive. It might also be that A believes that Elisabeth is the rightful successor, B believes that Victoria is, and C believes that George is. In this case, A is in disagreement with B as to who is the rightful successor, B is in disagreement with C as to who is the

168 *Jeremy Wyatt*

rightful successor, and A is in disagreement with C as to who is the rightful successor. This shows that disagreement isn't anti-transitive.

Turning to the Disagreement Principle, this principle is meant to capture in highly general terms what we ordinarily take disagreement to be. In essence, it says that disagreement between A and B consists in an incompatibility between two attitudes that A and B respectively hold. Potential examples of these attitudes include beliefs, doubts, hopes, wishes, desires, and preferences.[12]

The reason that I've subscripted 'incompatible' in this principle is that I suspect that we are disposed to regard attitudes y and z as generating disagreement between A and B iff y and z are incompatible in a sense that is specific to those attitudes. For instance, if y and z are preferences held by A and B, then I conjecture that we are disposed to regard y and z as generating disagreement between A and B iff y and z stand in an incompatibility relation R_1. By contrast, if y and z are beliefs held by A and B, then I suspect that we are disposed to regard y and z as generating disagreement between A and B iff y and z stand in a distinct incompatibility relation R_2. It may even be that there are *mixed cases*, e.g. a case in which I hope that the Texas Rangers will win the World Series and you believe that they won't, in which we take attitudes of *different kinds* to generate disagreement between their possessors. Anticipating that the relevant incompatibility relation might differ across these mixed cases, I've simply subscripted 'incompatible' with 'y, z'. We'll briefly return to these issues in §5.

Lastly, I think that the plausibility of the Mistake Principle is nicely articulated by Mark Richard in these probing reflections on disagreement:

> [W]hen one is willing to ascribe truth or falsity to a particular claim p, one treats p and the claim that p is true as equivalent . . . Suppose I think that Beaufort is a better cheese than Tome, and you think the reverse . . . Then not only can I . . . say that Beaufort is better than Tome, I can . . . say that it's true that Beaufort is better than Tome. And of course if you think Tome is better than Beaufort and not vice versa I can also . . . say that you think that it's not the case that Beaufort is better than Tome. So I can . . . say that it's true that Beaufort is better than Tome though you think Beaufort isn't better than Tome. From which it surely follows that you're mistaken—after all, if you have a false belief, you are mistaken about something. *This line of reasoning is sound no matter what the object of dispute.*
>
> (2008, p. 132, italics added)

As Richard points out, it seems quite clear that no matter which subject matter the proposition p is about, one will take another person to have made a mistaken judgement (e.g. formed a false belief or credal state) about this matter if one believes p and believes that one is in disagreement with that person as to whether p is true. The Mistake Principle, then, looks to mark out important connections between the ordinary concepts DISAGREEMENT, BELIEF, and MISTAKE.[13]

2.2. Ramsification

Now that we've identified at least some of the platitudes about disagreement, the next step is to use those platitudes to generate a *Ramsey sentence* for disagreement, which tells us what a world containing disagreement must be like. In essence, the Ramsey sentence for disagreement says that there is a relation x which has the features that are described in the platitudes about disagreement. In more detail, the semi-formal version of the Ramsey sentence for disagreement looks like this:

> (Ramsey$_D$) There is an x such that: (x is a relation) and (for all persons A and all times t: it is not the case that A stands in x to A at t) and (for all persons A and B and all times t: if A stands in x to B at t, then B stands in x to A at t) and [it is not the case that (for all persons A, B, and C, matters m, and times t: if A stands in x to B over m at t and B stands in x to C over m at t, then A stands in x to C over m at t) and it is not the case that (for all persons A, B, and C, matters m, and times t: if A stands in x to B over m at t and B stands in x to C over m at t, then A does not stand in x to C over m at t)] and (for all persons A and B, matters m, and times t: A and B stand in x over matter m at t iff there is a y such that y is an attitude about m and A possesses y at t and there is a z such that z is an attitude about m and B possesses z at t and y and z are incompatible with one another) and (for all persons A and B and propositions p: if A believes p, then if A also believes that they stand in x to B as to whether p is true, then A believes that B has made a judgement about p that is mistaken).

If we were pursuing the metaphysics of disagreement as such, we would now turn to ask whether our current evidence indicates that there is in fact such a relation in the world that we inhabit. However, as we're primarily interested in the metaphysics of taste disagreement, our main questions in §§3 and 4 will be these:

- Is there a relation that makes (Ramsey$_D$) true whose relata pertain to matters of gustatory taste?
- If so, then when this relation obtains, does it obtain in virtue of any other, more fundamental relations, or is it the most fundamental relation of taste disagreement?

3. The Nature of Taste Disagreement

3.1. Why Taste Disagreement Is Probably Not Doxastic

Over the past twenty years, philosophers of language and linguists have offered a massive and highly diverse array of hypotheses regarding the nature of taste disagreement.[14] To make this set of hypotheses more

170 *Jeremy Wyatt*

manageable, we can sort it into two categories. On the one hand, we have hypotheses according to which taste disagreement involves a relation between *doxastic attitudes* such as beliefs. On the other hand, we have hypotheses according to which taste disagreement involves a relation between *conative attitudes* such as preferences. A representative example of the former sort of hypothesis runs as follows:[15]

> (TD$_B$) Persons A and B are in disagreement about a matter of gustatory taste m iff (i) A has a belief b_1 whose content is the proposition p_1, which is about m; (ii) B has a belief b_2 whose content is the proposition p_2, which is also about m; and (iii) it would be incoherent for A to adopt b_2 while retaining b_1 and *mutatis mutandis* for B.

(TD$_B$) is a very natural account of taste disagreement. Many paradigmatic cases of disagreement, such as the disagreement between Henry and Stephen that we considered in §2.1, involve incompatible beliefs. It is natural to generalise from these paradigm cases, inferring that disagreement *as such* involves incompatible beliefs, and to then propose that taste disagreement must turn on the disputants' possession of incompatible gustatory beliefs.

Consider, for instance, how (TD$_B$) will represent the case involving natto that we described in §1. You find natto delicious, but I find it disgusting. Accordingly, (TD$_B$) will represent you as believing the proposition that natto is delicious and it will represent me as believing the proposition that it is disgusting. It would seem to be incoherent for you to retain your belief while adopting mine, and the same goes for me, so (TD$_B$) entails that we disagree about whether natto is delicious or, on the other hand, disgusting. This entailment coincides with what will surely be a common intuition—that we do disagree in this case—so in this respect, (TD$_B$) looks to be in good shape.[16] It also seems easy enough to adapt (TD$_B$) so that it identifies a relation whose relata pertain to matters of gustatory taste that makes (Ramsey$_D$) true. Thus, (TD$_B$) initially seems to be a promising account of the nature of taste disagreement.

(TD$_B$) runs into trouble, though, when we consider how it squares with a body of evidence from experimental philosophy and psychology that encompasses nine independent studies. A representative study was conducted by Florian Cova and Nicolas Pain (2012).[17] Cova and Pain's main aim was to determine the extent to which their participants were *normativists* in their application of the aesthetic predicates 'is beautiful' and 'is ugly.' As Cova and Pain use the term, one is a normativist about a matter m to the extent that one believes that if one disagrees with another person B about m, then the judgement about m that B has made is mistaken. By way of comparison, they also examined the extent

How to Canberra-Plan Disagreement 171

to which their participants were normativists about matters of gustatory taste, e.g. whether Brussels sprouts are disgusting or whether pasta with ketchup is delicious.

Using a 0–3 scale, they assigned a 'normativism score' to their participants. They found (ibid., Figures 8.2 and 8.3) that the average normativism score with regard to matters of gustatory taste was below 0.5 (and hence well below 1.5). Accordingly, Cova and Pain's findings indicate that when it comes to these matters, we don't tend to be normativists.[18]

To see the problem that these findings pose for (TD_B), we must consider them in conjunction with the Mistake Principle. As can be easily seen by reviewing Cova and Pain's definition of 'normativism,' the Mistake Principle entails that if we tended to believe *absolute, gustatory propositions* such as the proposition that natto is delicious or the proposition that natto is disgusting, then we would tend to be normativists about the matters of gustatory taste that these propositions are about. For instance, it entails that if you and I tended to believe absolute, gustatory propositions, then we would probably be normativists about whether natto is delicious and also about whether it is disgusting. Cova and Pain's findings indicate, however, that we *don't* tend to be normativists about matters of gustatory taste. This, together with the conditional that is delivered by the Mistake Principle, sets up a *modus tollens*, the conclusion of which is that we don't tend to believe absolute gustatory propositions.

In short, Cova and Pain's findings (as well as all of the corroborating findings), when combined with the Mistake Principle, provide empirical evidence that (TD_B) misrepresents the nature of taste disagreement. This shortcoming of (TD_B) is psychological—(TD_B) represents us as having mental states about matters of gustatory taste which, according to our current body of evidence, we just don't tend to have. So while it seems clear that (TD_B) identifies a relation that makes $(Ramsey_D)$ true, that relation doesn't seem to be the relation in which taste disagreement—or at least the taste disagreement in which we actually tend to engage—consists.[19] Moreover, given that (TD_B) is a representative doxastic account of taste disagreement, we have good reason to consider whether taste disagreement might involve a relation between conative rather than doxastic attitudes.

3.2. Taste Disagreement as Preferential Noncotenability

It is easy to see that conative attitudes play significant roles in our gustatory behaviour. To take a simple example, suppose that you are eating at an Asian fusion restaurant and you are offered either natto or kimchi as a side dish. You quite like the flavour of natto, insofar as experiencing natto's flavour brings you a good deal of pleasure, whereas you don't much like the flavour of kimchi, insofar as experiencing kimchi's flavour brings you a good deal of displeasure. Accordingly, you have a stable

172 *Jeremy Wyatt*

preference to experience natto's flavour, all else being equal, rather than kimchi's flavour. Given that you have this preference and that as far as you know, all else (e.g. the price and freshness of the dishes and how well they will pair with your main dish) is equal, you choose the natto rather than the kimchi. This case and countless other structurally similar cases are utterly familiar. Accordingly, it would be wise to consider whether taste disagreement may consist in a relation between preferences.

The $64,000 question, though, is 'which relation?' One relation that is worth considering is the preferential analogue of the relation that is described in (TD_B). Say that A's preference p_A is *noncotenable* with B's preference p_B iff A could not coherently adopt p_B while retaining p_A, and *mutatis mutandis* for B. We might try to analyse taste disagreement as follows:

> (TD_{NC}) Persons A and B are in disagreement about a matter of gustatory taste m iff A and B respectively have preferences about m that are noncotenable.

(TD_{NC}) is certainly an improvement over (TD_B), insofar as it isn't disconfirmed by Cova and Pain's findings. Moreover, it initially seems to capture what is going on in typical cases of taste disagreement. Return to the Asian fusion restaurant and suppose that I am also offered either natto or kimchi. I like the flavour of kimchi much more than the flavour of natto. As a result, I have a stable preference to experience kimchi's flavour rather than natto's flavour, all else being equal. This leads me to order the kimchi rather than the natto.[20]

Given our respective preferences, it is natural to say that you and I are in disagreement with respect to whether natto or kimchi is gustatorily superior. We might be in agreement when it comes to all sorts of other issues regarding natto and kimchi—which has a slipperier mouthfeel, which tends to be saltier, which is more widely consumed in Japan, and which is better for digestive health. However, we are certainly in disagreement as to which of them has more gustatory value. It initially seems that (TD_{NC}) is able to explain why we are in taste disagreement about this matter insofar as it would seem incoherent for you to adopt my preference while retaining yours, and *mutatis mutandis* for me.

This initial impression, however, is misleading. In fact, (TD_{NC}) entails that we *aren't* in taste disagreement in this case. To see this, we need to reflect a bit more carefully on the contents of our respective preferences. We said that you have the preference to experience natto's flavour rather than kimchi's flavour and that I have the preference to experience kimchi's flavour rather than natto's flavour. But to describe our preferences in this way is to *underdescribe* them. More carefully, you prefer that *you* experience natto's flavour rather than kimchi's flavour, whereas I prefer that *I* experience kimchi's flavour rather than natto's flavour.

How to Canberra-Plan Disagreement 173

After all, the reason that you have your preference is that you like natto's flavour and dislike kimchi's flavour, and the reason that I have my preference is that I like kimchi's flavour and dislike natto's flavour. These individual affective experiences are what cause us to form our respective preferences. Moreover, as we've described this case, which is perfectly ordinary, I'm asked to decide what to order for myself and you're asked to decide what to order for yourself. It's natural to hypothesise, then, that the preference which causes you to place your order is a preference which pertains to your gustatory experiences, and likewise for me. For these reasons, we should regard our preferences as having what we might call *individualised contents*.[21]

Now that we've fully fleshed out the contents of our preferences, it is easy to see that they are actually *cotenable*: you could coherently adopt my preference while retaining yours, and *mutatis mutandis* for me. If you adopted my preference while retaining yours, then you would have the following two preferences:[22]

p_{you}: the preference that, all else being equal, you experience natto's flavour rather than kimchi's flavour

p_{me}: the preference that all else being equal, I experience kimchi's flavour rather than natto's flavour.

It seems entirely coherent for you to have both p_{you} and p_{me}. After all, you can order natto at the restaurant while I order kimchi, and we can then happily dine together. More generally, you can go on choosing natto over kimchi while I go on choosing kimchi over natto.[23]

But couldn't you encounter a problem if we're forced to *coordinate*? We might choose to dine out together and find that only two nearby restaurants are open—the Japanese restaurant where they serve natto and the Korean restaurant where they serve kimchi. Would your recognition of the fact that we can only dine out together at one of the restaurants force you to give up one of p_{you} or p_{me}, thereby revealing a tension between these preferences in at least some cases that require coordination?

Not at all. The reason is that in this situation, it *isn't* the case that all else is equal. You believe (indeed, you know) that we've chosen to dine out together, and you also believe (indeed, you know) that we can only dine together at either the Japanese or the Korean restaurant. Call the former belief b_d and call the latter belief b_{JK}. Moreover, call the set of preferences and beliefs that an individual has at a given time their *cognitive set*. Here is a way for you to coherently update your initial cognitive set $\{p_{you}, p_{me}, b_d, b_{JK}\}$:

(i) Retain p_{you}, p_{me}, b_d, and b_{JK}
(ii) Acquire the belief b_n that it is not the case that in the present context, all else is equal

174 *Jeremy Wyatt*

(iii) Acquire the preference p_{coor} that all things considered, we dine at the Japanese restaurant rather than the Korean restaurant.

You might update your cognitive set in this way because you remember that we encountered this situation not so long ago and that we agreed to dine at the Korean restaurant. This, you think, means that the fairest course of action would be for us to now dine at the Japanese restaurant instead. Of course, if you remembered that we decided back then to dine at the Japanese restaurant, then instead of acquiring p_{coor}, you might instead acquire the preference p_{coor*} that all things considered, we dine at the Korean restaurant rather than the Japanese restaurant. Either way of updating your cognitive set looks coherent, which shows that even in cases requiring coordination, it can be coherent for you to have both p_{you} and p_{me}.

The upshot, then, is that while (TD_{NC}) is more attractive than (TD_B), it doesn't give us a workable account of taste disagreement. If we're going to analyse taste disagreement in terms of conative attitudes, we'll have to do better than (TD_{NC}).

3.3. *Taste Disagreement as Preferential Type-Noncotenability*

To improve upon (TD_{NC}), we should develop a way of understanding taste disagreement that reflects (TD_{NC})'s initial plausibility while also avoiding the pitfall into which it leads. We can do this by analysing taste disagreement in terms of a relation that is a close cousin of preferential noncotenability. First, where p_A is A's preference that they do act a_1 rather than act a_2, let the *anonymised variant* $p_A{}^N$ of p_A be the preference for doing a_1 rather than a_2. As the name suggests, the key difference between p_A and $p_A{}^N$ is that p_A is a preference about what a particular person A does, whereas $p_A{}^N$ isn't about any particular person. It is useful to think of $p_A{}^N$ as telling us what *type* of preference p_A is: p_A is a preference for doing act a_1 rather than act a_2.[24]

With the notion of an anonymised variant in hand, we can say that an arbitrary person C *has* $p_A{}^N$ *with respect to themselves* iff C prefers that they do a_1 rather than a_2. For instance, suppose that $p_A{}^N$ is the preference for earning an academic's salary while being happy rather than earning a CEO's salary while being miserable. I have $p_A{}^N$ with respect to myself, since I prefer that I earn an academic's salary while being happy rather than earning a CEO's salary while being miserable.

Lastly, say that preferences p_A and p_B are *type-noncotenable* iff an arbitrary person C couldn't coherently have both $p_A{}^N$ and $p_B{}^N$ with respect to themselves. We now have an attractive analysis of taste disagreement that runs as follows:

> (TD_{TNC}) Persons A and B are in disagreement about a matter of gustatory taste m iff A and B respectively have preferences about m that are type-noncotenable.

How to Canberra-Plan Disagreement 175

Like (TD_{NC}), (TD_{TNC}) avoids the empirical problem that besets (TD_B). But unlike (TD_{NC}), (TD_{TNC}) has the desirable consequence that you and I disagree about the comparative gustatory values of natto and kimchi in the case that we've been imagining. You have the preference p_{you}, whereas I have the preference p_{me}. The anonymised variant p_{you}^{N} of p_{you} is the preference to experience natto's flavour rather than kimchi's flavour, all else being equal. The anonymised variant p_{me}^{N} of p_{me} is the preference to experience kimchi's flavour rather than natto's flavour, all else being equal. If an arbitrary person C had both p_{you}^{N} and p_{me}^{N} with respect to themselves, then C would prefer:

(i) That all else being equal, they experience natto's flavour rather than kimchi's flavour and
(ii) That all else being equal, they experience kimchi's flavour rather than natto's flavour.

It seems right to say that this preference set (which would, of course, be a part of C's overall cognitive set) is incoherent, which means that p_{you} and p_{me} are type-noncotenable. This means that according to (TD_{TNC}), we disagree about the comparative gustatory values of natto and kimchi, which is precisely the result that we want.

3.4. (TD_{TNC}) and the Platitudes

Despite its advantages over (TD_B) and (TD_{NC}), a potential worry about (TD_{TNC}) still lingers.[25] (TD_{TNC}) represents a perfectly ordinary phenomenon, taste disagreement, as being rather complicated, insofar as it involves unfamiliar things like the anonymised variants of preferences and the relation of having such an anonymised variant with respect to oneself. This may cause us to wonder whether (TD_{TNC}) might suffer from the flaw of overintellectualisation.

However, as I mentioned at the start of this discussion, we shouldn't let the fact that taste disagreement is an ordinary phenomenon mislead us into thinking that its nature must be simple. Of course, we should begin by considering the simplest analyses of taste disagreement that we can devise, but if those analyses don't pass muster—as looks to be the case with (TD_B) and (TD_{NC})—then we should be willing to entertain more complex analyses.

Another way of assuaging this worry is to appreciate that the relation of having type-noncotenable preferences, where the preferences at issue are gustatory, is (with one caveat to be discussed in what follows) a disagreement relation according to our ordinary concept DISAGREEMENT. That is, where the relevant preferences are gustatory, the relation of having type-noncotenable preferences makes $(Ramsey_D)$ true. To see this, we can

176 *Jeremy Wyatt*

consider how this relation fares with respect to each of the platitudes about disagreement.[26]

It's easy to see that (TD_{TNC}) secures the symmetry of taste disagreement by considering the natto case, or any other clear case of taste disagreement, as an arbitrary case.

Similarly, it's easy to see that (TD_{TNC}) secures the non-transitivity of taste disagreement. Consider the following case:

- You have the preference p_{you} that, all else being equal, you experience natto's flavour rather than kimchi's flavour
- I have the preference p_{me} that all else being equal, I experience kimchi's flavour rather than natto's flavour
- Susan has the preference p_{Susan} that all else being equal, she experiences natto's flavour rather than kimchi's flavour.

(TD_{TNC}) entails that you and I are in disagreement about the comparative gustatory values of natto and kimchi and that I am in disagreement with Susan about the same. However, it's clear that you and Susan have *type-cotenable* preferences, which means that you aren't in disagreement with Susan about this matter. This shows that (TD_{TNC}) entails that taste disagreement isn't transitive.

Additionally, consider this case:

- You have the preference p_{you} that, all else being equal, you experience natto's flavour rather than experiencing kimchi's flavour or experiencing the flavour of neither natto nor kimchi
- I have the preference p_{me} that all else being equal, I experience kimchi's flavour rather than experiencing natto's flavour or experiencing the flavour of neither natto nor kimchi
- Susan has the preference p_{Susan} that all else being equal, she experiences neither natto's flavour nor kimchi's flavour rather than experiencing the flavour of either.

(TD_{TNC}) entails that you and I are in disagreement about the comparative gustatory values of natto and kimchi and that I am in disagreement with Susan about the same. I take kimchi to have more gustatory value than natto, whereas Susan doesn't take either to have more gustatory value than the other—she dislikes the flavour of both of them. (TD_{TNC}) also entails that you are in disagreement with Susan about the comparative gustatory values of natto and kimchi for a similar reason. This shows that (TD_{TNC}) entails that taste disagreement isn't anti-transitive, which means that (TD_{TNC}) entails that taste disagreement is non-transitive.

It's also straightforward to see that (TD_{TNC}) makes the Disagreement Principle true, when that principle is regarded as concerning taste disagreement. The relevant attitudes will of course be gustatory preferences,

How to Canberra-Plan Disagreement   177

and the incompatibility relation that is indexed to pairs of such preferences will be type-noncotenability.

In thinking about the Mistake Principle in this context, we should consider a formulation of this principle that pertains specifically to taste disagreement:

> *Mistake Principle*$_{TD}$: For all persons A and B and propositions p concerning matters of gustatory taste: if A believes p, then if A also believes that they are in taste disagreement with B as to whether p is true, then A believes that B has made a judgement (e.g. formed a belief or a credal state) about p that is mistaken.

(TD_{TNC}) is meant to specify the nature of the taste disagreement in which we actually tend to stand, and it tells us that this disagreement is preferential rather than doxastic. Accordingly, (TD_{TNC}) tells us that this sort of disagreement isn't disagreement about whether certain believed propositions are true or untrue. For this reason, (TD_{TNC}) delivers the result that the second embedded antecedent in Mistake Principle$_{TD}$ ('A also believes that they are in taste disagreement with B as to whether p is true') comes out *false* in all actual, typical cases. This suffices to show that in all such cases, Mistake Principle$_{TD}$ comes out true.[27]

Turning lastly to Irreflexivity, we encounter a complication. This is simply that (TD_{TNC}) doesn't entail that taste disagreement is irreflexive. As I see it, there are three potential responses to this complication.

One strategy would be to argue that it is *impossible* for a person A at time t to have type-noncotenable preferences p_1 and p_2 pertaining to a matter of gustatory taste m. This strategy may work, but it doesn't look especially promising in light of what psychologists call *framing effects*.[28]

Suppose that a diner A is presented with two menus that each contain descriptions of two dishes that are equally priced along with descriptions of several other dishes that are priced arbitrarily. Call the target dishes from Menu #1 d_1 and d_2 and call the target dishes from Menu #2 d_3 and d_4. A is told to first make a choice between d_1 and d_2 and to then make a choice between d_3 and d_4. Unbeknownst to A, $d_1 = d_4$ and $d_2 = d_3$. However, on Menu #1, d_1/d_4 is described in a vivid, engaging manner that is intended to elicit a high degree of attraction, whereas on Menu #2, d_1/d_4's ingredients are listed out one by one in a matter-of-fact way, and the converse is true of d_2/d_3. In effect, d_1/d_4 is framed positively on Menu #1 and neutrally on Menu #2, and the converse is true of d_2/d_3. It's plausible that because of this variable framing, A might have the following type-noncotenable preferences when she is selecting a dish from Menu #2 at time t:

(i) That all else being equal, she experience the flavour of d_1 rather than d_2
(ii) That all else being equal, she experience the flavour of d_3 rather than d_4.

178 *Jeremy Wyatt*

This suggests that it is actually possible for a person A at time t to have type-noncotenable preferences p_1 and p_2 pertaining to a matter of gustatory taste m. As a result, the strategy of securing irreflexivity by denying this possibility is questionable.

This sort of case might lead us to wonder about a second possible strategy: why shouldn't we say that it is actually possible for a person to be in taste disagreement with themselves at a particular time t, thereby *denying* Irreflexivity? Perhaps the best reason to not go this way is that we *can't* unless we want to change the subject. I've hypothesised that according to our ordinary concept DISAGREEMENT, disagreement—including taste disagreement—is irreflexive. So if we say instead that taste disagreement is non-reflexive, then it would seem that we've opted, in effect, to discard our ordinary concept DISAGREEMENT in favour of an alternative concept DISAGREEMENT*. In doing so, we will have shifted from trying to identify the nature of disagreement to recommending that we change how we think about the structural features of disagreement. This recommendation may ultimately prove to have merit. However, changing the subject is a theoretical cost, and it seems unnecessary to bear it in this context.[29]

To secure the irreflexivity of taste disagreement, thereby preserving Irreflexivity, I propose that we should build the irreflexivity of taste disagreement into (TD_{TNC}) as follows:

> $(TD_{TNC}{}^*)$ Persons A and B are in disagreement about a matter of gustatory taste m at t iff (i) $A \neq B$ and (ii) A and B respectively have preferences about m at t that are type-noncotenable

$(TD_{TNC}{}^*)$'s structure differs slightly from that of prior accounts of taste disagreement such as (TD_B) and (TD_{NC}), but this just seems to be a fact about, not a problem with, $(TD_{TNC}{}^*)$. Moreover, if we endorse $(TD_{TNC}{}^*)$, then we avoid changing the subject, which is a significant benefit. We should also bear in mind that an advocate of (TD_B) or (TD_{NC}) will confront the very same dilemma that we're considering here: preserve Irreflexivity by modifying the initial structure of their account of taste disagreement or retain that initial structure at the cost of changing the subject. Accordingly, it's fair to predict that this dilemma arises for theories of taste disagreement generally, which means that it doesn't present a special challenge for (TD_{TNC}).

4. Digging Deeper: Paralysis Inducement

We've seen thus far that (TD_{TNC}), which we might call the *type-noncotenability model* of taste disagreement, looks to fare rather well. However, we shouldn't be entirely satisfied with the model as it stands. This is because it involves a critical notion that we have yet to say much about: the notion of *coherence*. (TD_{TNC}) tells us that taste disagreement consists in the possession of type-noncotenable gustatory preferences. Preferences are type-noncotenable iff an arbitrary person C couldn't coherently have the preferences' anonymised variants with respect to themselves. But if C couldn't coherently have the relevant preferences' anonymised variants with respect to themselves, what would *explain* this fact?

One way to proceed here would be to regard this fact as *primitive*. Of course, it seems that explanations must bottom out somewhere. However, when offering explanations of the phenomena that we encounter, we should also try to push these explanations as deep as they can go. When it comes to taste disagreement, we can push the explanation that is offered in (TD_{TNC}) at least one level deeper.

To see how, return to the Asian fusion restaurant. It would be incoherent for an arbitrary person C to have the anonymised variants p_{you}^N and p_{me}^N of p_{you} and p_{me} with respect to themselves. Why would this be incoherent? A plausible explanation is that having p_{you}^N and p_{me}^N with respect to themselves would dispose C to pursue two courses of action both of which they cannot successfully pursue. If C were in a situation in which all else is equal and they are asked to choose between natto and kimchi, they would be stuck. C would be disposed to choose an experience of natto's flavour over an experience of kimchi's flavour, all else being equal. They would also be disposed to choose an experience of kimchi's flavour over an experience of natto's flavour, all else being equal. Accordingly, C would experience a kind of *practical paralysis*, being unable to choose one of these courses of action rather than the other. In short, we can say that if p_A and p_B are type-noncotenable, then this is because their anonymised variants p_A^N and p_B^N are *paralysis-inducing*.[30]

Our overall picture of taste disagreement, then, is this. Taste disagreement is preferential rather than doxastic in nature. Specifically, taste disagreement consists in the disputants' possession of type-noncotenable gustatory

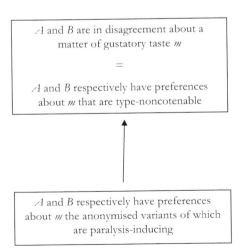

Figure 8.1 The nature of taste disagreement.

180 *Jeremy Wyatt*

preferences. Moreover, if their preferences are type-noncotenable, then this type-noncotenability is grounded in a fact about those preferences' anonymised variants—namely, that they are paralysis-inducing.[31]

5. Going Forward: Taste Discourse and the Nature of Disagreement

To wrap up, I want to briefly indicate how the debates about taste discourse, taste disagreement, and disagreement in general might fruitfully proceed in light of what I've done here. The main takeaways from my discussion, I think, are these:

- Taste disagreement is a species of *disagreement*, so any account of taste disagreement must be sensitive to the features that disagreement has, according to our ordinary concept DISAGREEMENT
- The investigation of disagreement must ultimately be empirical, not purely *a priori*
- Taste disagreement is, as far as we know, preferential rather than doxastic in nature
- The nature of taste disagreement is surprisingly complex, so we should be wary of naïve assumptions when developing theories of this (or any other sort of) disagreement.

Regarding the linguistic debates about taste discourse, my main suggestion would be that we reassess the role that considerations about taste disagreement have played in these debates. Any argument that is premised on a doxastic account of taste disagreement like (TD_B) is bound to be problematic, so we should be on guard against such arguments.[32] Additionally, we should seriously consider whether a preferential account of taste disagreement such as (TD_{TNC}) might be naturally combined with an *expressivist* account of taste discourse. Expressivism has been a relatively unpopular option thus far, but it may be time for its day in the sun.[33]

Regarding broader discussions of disagreement, I would highlight one issue in particular. I've argued that taste disagreement is preferential in nature. But it seems obvious that some disagreement, e.g. scientific disagreement, does involve doxastic attitudes such as beliefs and credences. This should lead us to seriously consider going *pluralist* about disagreement. I think that the machinery of the Canberra Plan will enable us to precisely articulate this sort of pluralism, much as it has done in debates about truth, but the details will have to be worked out.[34]

We have a long way to go in attempting to understand the nature of disagreement and the roles that it plays in our cognitive and social lives. My view is that the intricacy and cross-disciplinary relevance of this topic should be invigorating, motivating us to carry out the delicate empirical and conceptual work that remains to be done.[35]

Notes

1. While I'll focus here on disagreement about matters of gustatory taste, it should be straightforward to generalise the results of the discussion so that they also cover e.g. disagreement about which of two video games is more fun and disagreement about which of two post-rock bands is cooler.
2. For helpful overviews of these debates, see Baghramian and Carter (2020, §5), Cappelen and Huvenes (2018), Kölbel (2008, 2015a, 2015b), López de Sa (2011), MacFarlane (2012), and Zeman (2020a).
3. For stimulating comparisons between various kinds of disagreement, see Eriksson (2016), Ferrari (2016, 2018), Kivy (2015, esp. chs. 6 and 7), Stojanovic (2019), Pedersen (2020), and Pietroiusti (2020) and the sources cited therein.
4. I make no commitments about the nature of DISAGREEMENT, or concepts in general, beyond the commitment described in what follows, that DISAGREEMENT is constituted by certain platitudes.
5. Cp. Wyatt (2018b) on the ordinary concept TRUTH. See also Jackson (1998, pp. 36–37), and cf. Wright (2021) on the "folk view" of faultless disagreement.
6. For discussion of how platitudes should be understood in the Canberra Plan, see Nolan (2009). If a platitude is fairly complex, such as Non-Transitivity in what follows, then it may be necessary to use separate vignettes for each of its truth-functional components.

   Knowing of no evidence to the contrary, I hypothesise here that there is a single ordinary concept DISAGREEMENT and that we can identify the platitudes that constitute it. It may be that there is actually more than one ordinary disagreement concept, but this is something that would have to be investigated empirically.

   Also, for present purposes, we don't need to commit to any particular view about the nature of propositions. They can be regarded as Fregean, Russellian, pleonastic, act-theoretic, or what have you.
7. We could also consider diachronic versions of Irreflexivity, Symmetry, and Transitivity, but I'll stick with the synchronic versions here. For an interesting discussion of whether, upon reflection, we should accept Symmetry, see Rast (2016, §3.3, 2018, §§3–5). For a discussion of the non-transitivity of both 'narrow' and 'wide' disagreement, see Rast (2016, p. 857).

   I offer a schematic variant of the Mistake Principle in Wyatt (2021), whereas the Mistake Principle, as formulated here, is quantified. As far as I can see, these principles differ only formally. Of course, the reason for using a quantified principle here is that I've defined platitudes as being propositions, and schemas don't express propositions.

   Lastly, note that as I formulate it here, Symmetry bears on different issues than does Bondy's (2020, §3) discussion of the 'symmetry' of diachronic intrapersonal disagreement.
8. This developmental story should be evaluated empirically, and I know of no extant studies which aim to do so. However, it seems like a reasonable starting point. Moreover, it is clear that we do regularly speak of two or more persons being in disagreement with one another. Accordingly, even if it isn't the case that our initial concept of disagreement applies only to persons, it is clearly worthwhile to amass a list of platitudes about personal disagreement.
9. Some evidence in favour of this hypothesis is that a search of COCA (the Corpus of Contemporary American English) on 7 January 2021 yielded 13 entries for '[disagree] with myself/himself/herself/oneself' and 17,727 entries for '[disagree] with.' Similarly, a COCA search on 14 May 2021 yielded

182 *Jeremy Wyatt*

12 entries for 'at odds with myself/himself/herself/oneself' and 3,210 entries for 'at odds with.' Search results from the iWeb and GloWbE corpora were similar. Thanks to Charles Pigden for prompting the 'at odds with' searches.

10. For discussion of other cases related to synchronic intrapersonal disagreement, which bear directly on Irreflexivity, see Bondy (2020, §§4–9) and Coliva (2019, §§2–6).

11. See Cappelen and Hawthorne (2009, pp. 60–61). See also Balcerak Jackson (2014, p. 33), Chalmers (2011, p. 518), Jenkins (2014, p. 13), Kinzel and Kusch (2018), MacFarlane (2014, §6.1), Rott (2015), and Rowbottom (2018, §5). For an importantly different contrast between 'disagreements' and 'disputes,' see Belleri (2014).

12. For similar glosses on disagreement, see Baker (2014, p. 41), Dugas (2018, pp. 138, 146), Huvenes (2012, p. 178), Ridge (2013, pp. 55–56, 59–60, 2014, pp. 187, 189–190), Wright (2001, p. 53, 2006, p. 38), and Zeman (2020b).

13. The Mistake Principle raises important questions about two phenomena that have been discussed in contemporary debates about disagreement. The first is whether any disagreements, e.g. disagreements about matters of taste, can be *faultless*. At the end of the quoted paragraph, Richard draws the conclusion that 'Faultless disagreement is possible—but such disagreement is not one to be evaluated in terms of truth.' This conclusion is meant to be at odds with contemporary relativists' accounts of faultless disagreement (e.g. that of Kölbel (2004a)). Boghossian (2011, §2.1) develops this line of argument, concurring with Richard's conclusion. My own view, which I can't go into here, is that the considerations advanced by Richard, and thus the Mistake Principle, are fully compatible with the existence of doxastic disagreements that are faultless in the sense that is standardly associated with relativism.

    The other phenomenon at issue here is what Crispin Wright (2012, p. 439) calls *parity*. In effect, this is the phenomenon wherein A recognises that their disagreement with B is faultless. The Mistake Principle does rule out parity in cases in which A both believes that p and believes that they disagree with B as to whether p is true. However, it allows for parity in other cases, e.g. ones in which A (implicitly) recognises that the nature of their disagreement with B is non-doxastic (given the arguments in §§3–4, taste disagreement is probably a case of this sort).

14. See Baker and Robson (2017), Barker (2010), Barker (2013), Beall (2006), Beddor (2019, §4), Belleri (2010), Buekens (2009a, 2009b, 2011), Clapp (2015), Davis (2015), Díaz-Legaspe (2015, 2016), Egan (2014), Eriksson (2016), Gutzmann (2016), Hirvonen (2016), Hu (2020), Huvenes (2012, 2014), Kinzel and Kusch (2018), Kölbel (2002, ch. 4, 2004a), Lasersohn (2005, 2017), López de Sa (2007, 2008, 2010, 2015, §§2–3), MacFarlane (2014, pp. 134–135), Marques (2015), Marques and García-Carpintero (2014), Moltmann (2010, §5.3), Parsons (2013), Pearson (2013, §4.1), Plunkett and Sundell (2013), Richard (2008, ch. 5), Schafer (2011), Schaffer (2011, p. 219, cf. pp. 218–219, 219–220), Silk (2016, ch. 7), Smith (2010), Sundell (2011, 2016, 2017), Wyatt (2018a), Zakkou (2019 a, 2019b), and Zouhar (2018).

    My discussion in this section is adapted from the discussion in Wyatt (2021).

15. For discussions of the notion expressed in clause (iii), see Kölbel (2004b), MacFarlane (2014, p. 121), and Plunkett and Sundell (2013, p. 11). Cp. also Bondy (2020, §2), Coliva (2019, §6), Dreier (2009, p. 106), Verdejo and Donato-Rodríguez (2021), and Zouhar (2018, §4). For some illuminating suggestions regarding the notion of coherence at work here, see Worsnip (2018, 2019, 2021).

How to Canberra-Plan Disagreement 183

In considering (TD$_B$) and other accounts of the nature of taste disagreement in what follows, I will regard these as accounts of *autocentric* taste disagreement, i.e. taste disagreement in which the disputants have only their respective tastes in mind. As I explain in Wyatt (2021, §5.4), insofar as I am inclined to endorse a pluralist account of disagreement, I am happy to say that different kinds of taste disagreement, including autocentric and *exocentric* taste disagreement, have somewhat different natures. Thanks to Dan Zeman for prompting this note.

16. For evidence that this would be a common intuition, see Beebe (2014, Figure 1, pp. 172–176), Beebe et al. (2015, Table 3, Figure 2), Beebe and Sackris (2016, Figure 1), Cova and Pain (2012), Foushee and Srinivasan (2017, Figure 2, pp. 383–384), Goodwin and Darley (2008, Tables 1 and 2, Figure 1, 2012, p. 252), Kuhn et al. (2000, p. 318, Table 4), and Solt (2018, Figure 1). Regarding young children, cf. Foushee and Srinivasan (2017, Figures 4 and 5).

17. I also discuss Cova and Pain's findings in Wyatt (2018a, 2021), though the scope of my discussion here is broader.

18. Cova and Pain's findings are corroborated by numerous additional studies. These include Beebe (2014, Figure 1, pp. 172–176), Beebe et al. (2015, Table 3, Figure 2), Beebe and Sackris (2016, Figure 1), Cohen and Nichols (2010, Figures 1 and 2), Foushee and Srinivasan (2017, Figure 2, pp. 383–384), Goodwin and Darley (2008, Tables 1 and 2, Figure 1, 2012, p. 252), Kuhn et al. (2000, p. 318, Table 4), and Solt (2018, Figure 1). See also Cova et al. (2015, p. 930), Kuhn et al. (2000, p. 323), and Nichols and Folds-Bennett (2003, Table 1, p. B28 and Table 2, p. B30). Regarding young children, cf. Foushee and Srinivasan (2017, Figures 4 and 5). For some suggestive remarks to the contrary, see Hirvonen (2016, §3.1); for some interesting wrinkles, see Kaiser and Rudin (2020) and Rudin and Kaiser (2022); and for critical responses to Cova's work, see Andow (2021) and Zangwill (2019).

19. This conclusion is a claim about the nature of the taste disagreement in which we *typically* engage. As such, it's compatible with the claim that it's *possible* to engage in taste disagreement of the sort that is identified by (TD$_B$). It's also compatible with the claim that we do *sometimes* engage in such doxastic taste disagreement (e.g. perhaps committed wine critics sometimes engage in this sort of taste disagreement). If it turns out that we do sometimes engage in such doxastic taste disagreement, then that is just grist for my mill, insofar as I am ultimately inclined to take a *pluralist* attitude towards taste disagreement (see my brief remarks in §5).

20. In what follows, I'll mostly drop the 'all else being equal' qualifier when describing preferences, but it should still be mentally inserted.

21. It seems helpful to classify these contents as *de se*, though I lack the space to go into the implications of this classification.

22. Of course, if you were to describe these preferences, you would uniformly replace 'you' with 'me/I' and vice versa.

23. Cp. the problem for another sort of conative account of taste disagreement that is developed by both Beddor (2019, p. 5) and Marques (2015, p. 6, 2016, p. 310).

24. It would also be suitable to describe p_A^N as having the *generic content* that one do a$_1$ rather than a$_2$.

    As I argued in §3.2, my sense is that if we want to properly understand human gustatory psychology, then we'll need to do so in terms of non-anonymised preferences like p_A rather than their anonymised variants. Nevertheless, p_A^N is a theoretical entity that can earn its keep elsewhere, in a promising theory of the nature of taste disagreement.

25. I defend (TD$_{INC}$) against a range of additional objections in Wyatt (2021).

184　*Jeremy Wyatt*

26. If you're already happy with (TD_{INC}), then feel free to skip to the next section.
27. What about possible, if atypical, cases, e.g. a case in which two committed wine critics are in *doxastic* taste disagreement about whether a 1997 Beaucastel Chateauneuf du Pape is gustatorily superior to a 1996 Leroy Chambertin? (I owe this example to Barry Smith (2005, p. 86).) Here, Mistake Principle$_{\text{TD}}$ presumably comes out true, though we would need a full account of doxastic taste disagreement to confirm this.
28. See the sources discussed in Shafir (2016, §28.1).
29. There may be good reasons to use an alternative, non-reflexive concept of disagreement in other theoretical contexts. See Bondy (2020, §§6–8) and Coliva (2019, §§2–6).
30. The notion of paralysis inducement is clearly connected to the notion of preclusion of joint satisfaction that is discussed by MacFarlane (2014, §6.3) and has its origins in Stevenson (1963).
31. In Wyatt (2021), I discuss some further wrinkles that can be straightforwardly incorporated into this picture.
32. The core argument of Kölbel (2004a) is a particularly influential argument of this sort. Cp. the critical remarks in Huvenes (2012).
33. On this issue, see also Murray (2020), and see Zouhar (2019) for a recent critique of expressivism.
34. I discuss disagreement pluralism at greater length in Wyatt (2021). For other useful discussions, see Baker (2014), Diaz-Legaspe (2015, 2016), Egan (2012, pp. 575–576, 2014, pp. 95–97), Eriksson (2016, §8), Huvenes (2012, §7), López de Sa (2015, §2), MacFarlane (2014, ch. 6), Marques (2014), Marques and García-Carpintero (2014), Moruzzi (ms), Osorio and Villanueva (2019), Palmira (2017), Ridge (2013), and Sundell (2011, §§2 and 3). See also Davis (2015, n. 6), Stojanovic (2019, §5), as well as Baker and Woods (2015, §III)'s helpful remarks on 'A-type' and 'B-type discordance.' For an overview of the relevant debates about truth, see Pedersen and Wright (2018).
35. Thanks to Dan Zeman and to the members of the philosophy programme at the University of Otago for helpful feedback on this chapter.

References

Andow, J. (2021). Further exploration of anti-realist intuitions about aesthetics judgment. *Philosophical Psychology*, doi:10.1080/09515089.2021.2014440.

Baghramian, M., & Carter, J. A. (2020). Relativism. In *Stanford encyclopedia of philosophy*. https://plato.stanford.edu/entries/relativism/.

Baker, C. (2014). The role of disagreement in semantic theory. *Australasian Journal of Philosophy*, 92(1), 37–54.

Baker, C., & Robson, J. (2017). An absolutist theory of faultless disagreement in aesthetics. *Pacific Philosophical Quarterly*, 98(3), 429–448.

Baker, D., & Woods, J. (2015). How expressivists can and should explain inconsistency. *Ethics*, 125(2), 391–424.

Balcerak Jackson, B. (2014). Verbal disputes and substantiveness. *Erkenntnis*, 79(S1), 31–54.

Barker, C. (2013). Negotiating taste. *Inquiry*, 56(2–3), 240–257.

Barker, S. (2010). Cognitive expressivism, faultless disagreement, and absolute but non-objective truth. *Proceedings of the Aristotelian Society*, 110, 183–199.

Beall, J. (2006). Modelling the "ordinary view". In P. Greenough & M. Lynch (Eds.), *Truth and realism* (pp. 61–74). Oxford University Press.

Beddor, B. (2019). Subjective disagreement. *Noûs*, 53(4), 819–851.

Beebe, J. (2014). How different kinds of disagreement impact folk metaethical judgments. In H. Sarkissian & J. Wright (Eds.), *Advances in experimental moral psychology* (pp. 167–187). Bloomsbury.

Beebe, J., Qiaoan, R., Wysocki, T., & Endara, M. (2015). Moral objectivism in cross-cultural perspective. *Journal of Cognition and Culture*, 15(3–4), 386–401.

Beebe, J., & Sackris, D. (2016). Moral objectivism across the lifespan. *Philosophical Psychology*, 29(6), 912–929.

Belleri, D. (2010). Relative truth, lost disagreement, and invariantism on predicates of personal taste. In M. I. Crespo, D. Gakis, & G. Sassoon (Eds.), *Proceedings of the Amsterdam graduate philosophy conference 'truth, meaning, and normativity'* (pp. 19–30). ILLC Publications X-2011-01.

Belleri, D. (2014). Disagreement and dispute. *Philosophia*, 42(2), 289–307.

Boghossian, P. (2011). Three kinds of relativism. In S. Hales (Ed.), *A companion to relativism* (pp. 53–69). Blackwell.

Bondy, P. (2020). Deeply disagreeing with myself: Synchronic intrapersonal deep disagreements. *Topoi*. https://doi.org/10.1007/s11245-020-09707-0

Buekens, F. (2009a). Relativism, assertion, and disagreement in matters of taste. *Logique et Analyse*, 58(208), 389–405.

Buekens, F. (2009b). Faultless disagreement and self-expression. In J. M. Larrazabal & L. Zubeldia (Eds.), *Meaning, content and argument: Proceedings of the ILCCI international workshop on semantics, pragmatics and rhetoric* (pp. 249–267). Esukal Herrikeko Press.

Buekens, F. (2011). Faultless disagreement, assertions, and the affective-expressive dimension of judgments of taste. *Philosophia*, 39, 637–655.

Cappelen, H., & Hawthorne, J. (2009). *Relativism and monadic truth*. Oxford: Oxford University Press.

Cappelen, H., & Huvenes, T. (2018). Relative truth. In M. Glanzberg (Ed.), *The Oxford handbook of truth* (pp. 517–542). Oxford University Press.

Chalmers, D. (2011). Verbal disputes. *Philosophical Review*, 120(4), 515–566.

Clapp, L. (2015). A non-alethic approach to faultless disagreement. *Dialectica*, 69(4), 517–550.

Cohen, J., & Nichols, S. (2010). Colours, colour relationalism, and the deliverances of introspection. *Analysis*, 70(2), 218–228.

Coliva, A. (2019). Disagreeing with myself: Doxastic commitments and intrapersonal disagreement. *American Philosophical Quarterly*, 56(1), 1–13.

Cova, F., Garcia, A., & Liao, S. (2015). Experimental philosophy of aesthetics. *Philosophy Compass*, 10(12), 927–939.

Cova, F., & Pain, N. (2012). Can folk aesthetics ground aesthetic realism? *The Monist*, 95(2), 241–263.

Davis, J. (2015). Faultless disagreement, cognitive command, and epistemic peers. *Synthese*, 192(1), 1–24.

Díaz-Legaspe, J. (2015). Disagreeing over evaluatives: Preference, normative and moral discourse. *Manuscrito*, 38(2), 39–63.

Díaz-Legaspe, J. (2016). Evaluative disagreements. *Teorema*, 1, 67–87.

Dreier, J. (2009). Relativism (and expressivism) and the problem of disagreement. *Philosophical Perspectives*, 23(1), 79–110.

186 *Jeremy Wyatt*

Dugas, M. (2018). Relativism, faultlessness, and the epistemology of disagreement. *Logos & Episteme*, 9(2), 137–150.

Egan, A. (2012). Relativist dispositional theories of value. *Southern Journal of Philosophy*, 50(4), 557–582.

Egan, A. (2014). There's something funny about comedy: A case study in faultless disagreement. *Erkenntnis*, 79(S1), 73–100.

Eriksson, J. (2016). Expressivism, attitudinal complexity, and two senses of disagreement in attitude. *Erkenntnis*, 81(4), 775–794.

Ferrari, F. (2016). Disagreement about taste and alethic suberogation. *Philosophical Quarterly*, 66(264), 516–535.

Ferrari, F. (2018). Normative alethic pluralism. In J. Wyatt, N. Pedersen, & N. Kellen (Eds.), *Pluralisms in truth and logic* (pp. 145–168). Palgrave Macmillan.

Foushee, R., & Srinivasan, M. (2017). Could both be right? Children and adults' sensitivity to subjectivity in language. In *Proceedings of the 39th annual conference of the cognitive science society* (pp. 379–384).

Goodwin, G., & Darley, J. (2008). The psychology of meta-ethics: Exploring objectivism. *Cognition*, 106(3), 1339–1366.

Goodwin, G., & Darley, J. (2012). Why are some moral beliefs perceived to be more objective than others? *Journal of Experimental Social Psychology*, 48(1), 250–256.

Gutzmann, D. (2016). If expressivism is fun, go for it! Towards an expressive account of predicates of personal taste. In C. Meier & J. van-Wijnbergen-Huitnik (Eds.), *Subjective meaning: Alternatives to relativism* (pp. 21–46). de Gruyter.

Hirvonen, S. (2016). Doing without judge dependence. In C. Meier & J. van Wijnbergen-Huitink (Eds.), *Subjective meaning: Alternatives to relativism* (pp. 47–68). de Gruyter.

Hu, X. (2020). The epistemic account of faultless disagreement. *Synthese*, 197(6), 2613–2630.

Huvenes, T. (2012). Varieties of disagreement and predicates of taste. *Australasian Journal of Philosophy*, 90(1), 167–181.

Huvenes, T. (2014). Disagreement without error. *Erkenntnis*, 79, 143–154.

Jackson, F. (1998). *From metaphysics to ethics: A defence of conceptual analysis.* Oxford University Press.

Jenkins, C. (2014). Merely verbal disputes. *Erkenntnis*, 79(S1), 11–30.

Kaiser, E., & Rudin, D. (2020). When faultless disagreement is not so faultless: What widely-held opinions can tell us about subjective adjectives. *Proceedings of the Linguistic Society of America*, 5(1), 698–707.

Kinzel, K., & Kusch, M. (2018). De-idealizing disagreement, rethinking relativism. *International Journal of Philosophical Studies*, 26(1), 40–71.

Kivy, P. (2015). *De Gustibus: Arguing about taste and why we do it.* Oxford University Press.

Kölbel, M. (2002). *Truth without objectivity.* Routledge.

Kölbel, M. (2004a). Faultless disagreement. *Proceedings of the Aristotelian Society*, 104(1), 53–73.

Kölbel, M. (2004b). Indexical relativism vs. genuine relativism. *International Journal of Philosophical Studies*, 12(3), 297–313.

Kölbel, M. (2008). Introduction: Motivations for relativism. In M. García-Carpintero & M. Kölbel (Eds.), *Relative truth* (pp. 1–38). Oxford University Press.

How to Canberra-Plan Disagreement 187

Kölbel, M. (2015a). Relativism 1: Representational content. *Philosophy Compass*, *10*(1), 38–51.

Kölbel, M. (2015b). Relativism 2: Semantic content. *Philosophy Compass*, *10*(1), 52–67.

Kuhn, D., Cheney, R., & Weinstock, M. (2000). The development of epistemological understanding. *Cognitive Development*, *15*(3), 309–328.

Lasersohn, P. (2005). Context-dependence, disagreement, and predicates of personal taste. *Linguistics and Philosophy*, *28*(6), 643–686.

Lasersohn, P. (2017). *Subjectivity and perspective in truth-theoretic semantics*. Oxford University Press.

Lewis, D. (1966). An argument for the identity theory. *The Journal of Philosophy*, *63*(1), 17–25.

Lewis, D. (1970). How to define theoretical terms. *The Journal of Philosophy*, *67*(13), 427–446.

Lewis, D. (1972). Psychophysical and theoretical identifications. *Australasian Journal of Philosophy*, *50*(3), 249–258.

Lewis, D. (1994). Reduction of mind. In S. Guttenplan (Ed.), *Companion to the philosophy of mind* (pp. 412–431). Blackwell.

López de Sa, D. (2007). The many relativisms and the question of disagreement. *International Journal of Philosophical Studies*, *15*(2), 269–279.

López de Sa, D. (2008). Presuppositions of commonality. In M. García-Carpintero & M. Kölbel (Eds.), *Relative truth* (pp. 297–310). Oxford University Press.

López de Sa, D. (2010). The makings of truth: Realism, response-dependence, and relativism. In C. D. Wright & N. Pedersen (Eds.) *New waves in truth* (pp. 191–204). Palgrave Macmillan.

López de Sa, D. (2011). The many relativisms: Index, context, and beyond. In S. Hales (Ed.), *A companion to relativism* (pp. 102–117). Blackwell.

López de Sa, D. (2015). Expressing disagreement: A presuppositional indexical contextualist relativist account. *Erkenntnis*, *80*(1), 153–165.

MacFarlane, J. (2012). Relativism. In G. Russell & D. Graff Fara (Eds.), *The Routledge companion to philosophy of language* (pp. 132–142). Routledge.

MacFarlane, J. (2014). *Assessment sensitivity: Relative truth and its applications*. Oxford University Press.

Marques, T. (2014). Doxastic disagreement. *Erkenntnis*, *79*(S1), 121–142.

Marques, T. (2015). Disagreeing in context. *Frontiers in Psychology*, *6*, 1–12.

Marques, T. (2016). We can't have no satisfaction. *Filosofia Unisinos*, *17*(3), 308–314.

Marques, T., & García-Carpintero, M. (2014). Disagreement about taste: Commonality presuppositions and coordination. *Australasian Journal of Philosophy*, *92*(4), 701–723.

Moltmann, F. (2010). Relative truth and the first person. *Philosophical Studies*, *150*(2), 187–220.

Murray, D. (2020). Maggots are delicious, sunsets hideous. False, or do you just disagree? Data on truth relativism about judgments of personal taste and aesthetics. In T. Lombrozo, J. Knobe, & S. Nichols (Eds.), *Oxford studies in experimental philosophy* (Vol. 3, pp. 64–96). Oxford University Press.

Nichols, S., & Folds-Bennett, T. (2003). Are children moral objectivists? Children's judgments about moral and response-dependent properties. *Cognition*, *90*(2), B23–B32.

188   Jeremy Wyatt

Nolan, D. (2009). Platitudes and metaphysics. In D. Braddon-Mitchell & R. Nola (Eds.), *Conceptual analysis and philosophical naturalism* (pp. 267–300). MIT Press.

Osorio, J., & Villanueva, N. (2019). Expressivism and crossed disagreements. *Royal Institute of Philosophy Supplement, 86,* 111–132.

Palmira, M. (2017). How to be a pluralist about disagreement. In A. Coliva & N. Pedersen (Eds.), *Epistemic pluralism* (pp. 285–316). Palgrave Macmillan.

Parsons, J. (2013). Presupposition, disagreement, and predicates of taste. *Proceedings of the Aristotelian Society, 113*(Part 2), 163–173.

Pearson, H. (2013). A judge-free semantics of predicates of personal taste. *Journal of Semantics, 30,* 103–154.

Pedersen, N. (2020). On the normative variability of truth and logic. *Inquiry, 63*(3–4), 236–257.

Pedersen, N., & Wright, C. D. (2018). Pluralist theories of truth. In *Stanford encyclopedia of philosophy.* https://plato.stanford.edu/entries/truth-pluralist/

Pietroiusti, G. (2020). Disagreement and conflict: How moral and taste judgments do *not* differ. *Theoria.* https://doi.org/10.1111/theo.12296

Plunkett, D., & Sundell, T. (2013). Disagreement and the semantics of normative and evaluative terms. *Philosophers' Imprint, 13*(23), 1–37.

Rast, E. (2016). Modeling value disagreement. *Erkenntnis, 81*(4), 853–880.

Rast, E. (2018). Perspectival disagreement. *Theoria, 84*(2), 120–139.

Richard, M. (2008). *When truth gives out.* Oxford University Press.

Ridge, T. (2013). Disagreement. *Philosophy and Phenomenological Research, 86*(1), 41–63.

Ridge, T. (2014). *Impassioned belief.* Oxford University Press.

Rott, H. (2015). A puzzle about disputes and disagreements. *Erkenntnis, 80*(1), 167–189.

Rowbottom, D. (2018). What is (dis)agreement? *Philosophy and Phenomenological Research, 97*(1), 223–236.

Rudin, D., & Kaiser, E. (2022). Connoisseurial contradictions: Expertise modulates faultless disagreement. In N. Dreier, C. Kwon, T. Darnell, & J. Starr (Eds.), *Proceedings of SALT 31.* Linguistic Society of America. https://doi.org/10.3765/salt.v31i0.5099

Schafer, K. (2011). Faultless disagreement and aesthetic realism. *Philosophy and Phenomenological Research, 82*(2), 265–286.

Schaffer, J. (2011). Perspective in taste predicates and epistemic modals. In A. Egan & B. Weatherson (Eds.), *Epistemic modality* (pp. 179–226). Oxford University Press.

Shafir, E. (2016). Preference inconsistency: A psychological perspective. In M. Adler & M. Fleurbaey (Eds.), *The Oxford handbook of well-being and public policy* (pp. 844–870). Oxford University Press.

Silk, A. (2016). *Discourse contextualism: A framework for contextualist semantics and pragmatics.* Oxford University Press.

Smith, B. (2005). True relativism, interpretation, and our reasons for action. In *Lectures on relativism* (pp. 85–99). Göteborg.

Smith, B. (2010). Relativism, disagreement, and predicates of personal taste. In F. Recanati, I. Stojanovic, & N. Villanueva (Eds.), *Context-dependence, perspective, and relativity* (pp. 195–223). de Gruyter.

Solt, S. (2018). Multidimensionality, subjectivity and scales: Experimental evidence. In E. Castroviejo, L. McNally, & G. Sassoon (Eds.), *The semantics of gradability, vagueness, and scale structure: Experimental perspectives* (pp. 59–92). Springer.

How to Canberra-Plan Disagreement   189

Stevenson, C. L. (1963). *Facts and values: Studies in ethical analysis*. Yale University Press.

Stojanovic, I. (2019). Disagreements about taste vs. disagreements about moral issues. *American Philosophical Quarterly*, 56(1), 29–42.

Sundell, T. (2011). Disagreements about taste. *Philosophical Studies*, 155(2), 267–288.

Sundell, T. (2016). The tasty, the bold, and the beautiful. *Inquiry*, 59(6), 793–818.

Sundell, T. (2017). Aesthetic negotiation. In J. Young (Ed.), *Semantics of aesthetic judgements* (pp. 82–105). Oxford University Press.

Verdejo, V., & Donato-Rodríguez, X. (2021). Thinking disagreement. *Theoria*, https://doi.org/10.1111/theo.12364.

Worsnip, A. (2018). What is (in)coherence? *Oxford Studies in Metaethics*, 13, 184–206.

Worsnip, A. (2019). Disagreement as interpersonal incoherence. *Res Philosophica*, 96(2), 245–268.

Worsnip, A. (2021). *Fitting things together: Coherence and the demands of structural rationality*. Oxford University Press.

Wright, C. (2001). On being in a quandary: Relativism, vagueness, logical revisionism. *Mind*, 110(437), 45–98.

Wright, C. (2006). Intuitionism, realism, relativism, and rhubarb. In P. Greenough & M. Lynch (Eds.), *Truth and realism* (pp. 38–60). Oxford University Press.

Wright, C. (2012). Replies III: Truth, objectivity, realism, and relativism. In A. Coliva (Ed.), *Mind, meaning, and knowledge: Themes from the philosophy of Crispin Wright* (pp. 418–450). Oxford University Press.

Wright, C. (2021). Alethic pluralism, deflationism, and faultless disagreement. *Metaphilosophy*, https://doi.org/10.1111/meta.12491

Wyatt, J. (2018a). Absolutely tasty: An examination of predicates of personal taste and faultless disagreement. *Inquiry*, 61(3), 252–280.

Wyatt, J. (2018b). Truth in English and elsewhere: An empirically-informed functionalism. In J. Wyatt, N. Pedersen, & N. Kellen (Eds.), *Pluralisms in truth and logic* (pp. 169–196). Palgrave Macmillan.

Wyatt, J. (2021). The nature of disagreement: Matters of taste and environs. *Synthese*, 199(3–4), 10739–10767.

Zangwill, N. (2019). Beauty and the agreeable: A critique of experimental aesthetics. In F. Cova & S. Réhault (Eds.), *Advances in experimental philosophy of aesthetics* (pp. 289–307). Bloomsbury.

Zakkou, J. (2019a). Denial and retraction: A challenge for theories of taste predicates. *Synthese*, 196(4), 1555–1573.

Zakkou, J. (2019b). *Faultless disagreement: A defense of contextualism in the realm of personal taste*. Klostermann.

Zeman, D. (2020a). Faultless disagreement. In M. Kusch (Ed.), *The Routledge handbook of philosophy of relativism* (pp. 486–495). Routledge.

Zeman, D. (2020b). Minimal disagreement. *Philosophia*, 48(4), 1649–1670.

Zouhar, M. (2018). Conversations about taste, contextualism, and non-doxastic attitudes. *Philosophical Papers*, 47(3), 429–460.

Zouhar, M. (2019). On the insufficiency of taste expressivism. *Filozofia Nauki*, 27(3), 5–27.

Part IV

Philosophy of Language and Linguistics

9 Non-Indexical Contextualism, Relativism, and Retraction

Alexander Dinges

1. Introduction

It is commonly held that retraction data, if they exist, show that assessment relativism is preferable to non-indexical contextualism.[1] I argue that this is not the case. Whether retraction data have the suggested probative force depends on substantive questions about the proper treatment of tense and location. One's preferred account in these domains should determine whether one accepts assessment relativism or non-indexical contextualism.

I begin by briefly characterizing non-indexical contextualism and assessment relativism (§2). I present the standard argument for assessment relativism based on retraction data (§3). I present what I take to be the most promising response to this argument on behalf of non-indexical contextualism (§4). I show that this response essentially relies on certain views about tense and location (§5). Then I conclude (§6).

2. Non-Indexical Contextualism and Assessment Relativism

Non-indexical contextualism and assessment relativism have been proposed as semantics for a number of expressions including deontic and epistemic modals, predicates of personal taste, "knows," and more (see, e.g., MacFarlane, 2014). The structural points I make in this chapter apply equally in all domains. For concreteness, I focus on predicates of personal taste, more specifically, on the expression "tasty."

Non-indexical contextualists and assessment relativists agree that a proper semantics for "tasty" requires a notion of truth that is relative to a circumstance of evaluation and applies to propositions. A circumstance of evaluation, for them, is a tuple comprising at least a possible world, w, and (something like) a standard of taste, s. Let us use *fish sticks are tasty* to refer to the proposition we assert when we literally use "Fish sticks are tasty." Leaving aside other potential parameters of the circumstance of

DOI: 10.4324/9781003184225-13

194 *Alexander Dinges*

evaluation, assessment relativists and non-indexical contextualists agree on the following principle.

> *Fish sticks are tasty* is true relative to a circumstance of evaluation <w, s> iff, at w, fish sticks are tasty by the lights of s.

Non-indexical contextualists distinctively hold that we further need a notion of proposition truth that is relativized to a context of use. This notion can be defined as follows in terms of the suggested notion of truth relative to a circumstance of evaluation (see, e.g., MacFarlane, 2014, pp. 89–90; Ninan, 2016, pp. 441–442).

> A proposition p is true at a context of use C iff p is true relative to <w(C), s(C)>.

Here, w(C) is the world of C, and s(C) is the taste standard of C. For simplicity, I will equate the taste standard of C with the taste standard that the speaker of C has at the time of C.[2] Returning to our proposition *fish sticks are tasty*, we thus get the following principle.

> *Fish sticks are tasty* is true at a context of use C iff, at the possible world of C, fish sticks are tasty by the lights of the taste standard that the speaker of C has at the time of C.[3]

These abstract principles by themselves do not make testable predictions about language use. One way to derive such predictions is via norms of speech acts along the following lines (see, e.g., MacFarlane, 2014, p. 101; Ninan, 2016, p. 442 for these norms and, e.g., Dinges & Zakkou, 2020, pp. 7–8 on how to derive predictions about language use from such norms).

> **NIC-A** One is permitted to assert p in a context C only if p is true at C.
>
> **NIC-R** One is obligated in a context C2 to retract an assertion of p made in a context C1 if p is not true at C1.

To illustrate, consider an assertion of *fish sticks are tasty* in a context C. By the norm of assertion NIC-A, this assertion is permissible only if *fish sticks are tasty* is true at C, that is, only if fish sticks are tasty by the lights of the taste standard that the speaker of C has at the time of C (at the possible world of C—I take the possible world parameter to be tacitly understood in what follows). In brief, the assertion is permissible if the speaker currently likes fish sticks. By the retraction norm NIC-R, the assertion has to be retracted if this condition fails to be satisfied.

Contextualism, Relativism, and Retraction 195

Assessment relativists distinctively hold that we need a notion of proposition truth that is not just relativized to a context of use but also to a context of assessment. This notion can be defined as follows in terms of the suggested notion of truth relative to a circumstance of evaluation (see, e.g., MacFarlane, 2014, p. 90; Ninan, 2016, pp. 443–444).

> A proposition p is true at a context of use C1 and a context of assessment C2 iff p is true relative to <w(C1), s(C2)>.

Here, w(C1) is the world of C1, and s(C2) is the taste standard relevant in C2. As before, I will equate this taste standard with the taste standard that the speaker of C2 has at the time of C2 for simplicity. We now get the following principle.

> *Fish sticks are tasty* is true at a context of use C1 and a context of assessment C2 iff, at the possible world of C1, fish sticks are tasty by the lights of the taste the speaker of C2 has at the time of C2.

Again, these principles can be combined with norms of assertion and retraction to derive testable predictions about language use. Assessment relativists typically endorse norms along the following lines (see, e.g., MacFarlane, 2014, pp. 103–104, 108–110; Ninan, 2016, p. 444).

> **AR-A** One is permitted to assert p in a context C only if p is true at C and C.
>
> **AR-R** One is obligated in a context C2 to retract an assertion of p made in a context C1 if p is not true at C1 and C2.

In the assertion norm AR-A, the original context of assertion does double duty as both the context of use and the context of assessment. By this norm, an assertion of *fish sticks are tasty*, for instance, is permitted only if this proposition is true at the context of assertion (context of use) and the context of assertion (context of assessment). An assertion of *fish sticks are tasty* is thus permitted only if fish sticks are tasty by the lights of the taste the speaker has at the context of assertion. This prediction aligns with the non-indexical contextualist prediction given. Assessment relativism and non-indexical contextualism come apart when it comes to the norm of retraction. According to the assessment relativist norm of retraction AR-R, an assertion of *fish sticks are tasty* has to be retracted in a later context if fish sticks are not tasty by the lights of the taste the speaker has in this later context. In contrast, and as we have seen, the non-indexical contextualist norm of retraction NIC-R requires retraction depending on the speaker's taste in the original context of assertion. AR-R and NIC-R thus make different predictions when a speaker's taste changes over time

196 *Alexander Dinges*

from the original context of assertion to the context in which this assertion is assessed.

How do we determine which of the theories described is correct? Given the outlined predictions, retraction data are a natural place to look, and indeed, retraction data are normally offered as the main motivation for assessment relativism (see, e.g., MacFarlane, 2014, p. 108; Kölbel, 2015; Ninan, 2016, p. 445). I present retraction data and explain why they may seem to favour assessment relativism in the next section.

3. Retraction Data for Assessment Relativism

Suppose I liked fish sticks and correspondingly said, "Fish sticks are tasty." Later, I come to dislike fish sticks. Someone reminds me, "Didn't you say that fish sticks were tasty?" Now consider the following responses on my behalf.

> "I stand by that, but fish sticks aren't tasty."
> "I take that back. Fish sticks aren't tasty."

Assuming that fish sticks have not changed their taste, the second response seems intuitively much better than the first. Following, e.g., MacFarlane (2014, pp. 13–14), I assume that this is because the norms governing our communicative practice require retraction of previous "tasty" claims after a relevant change in taste. When I speak of retraction data in what follows, I will have these requirements to retract in mind.[4]

Retraction data support assessment relativism as follows. Assessment relativism, with its norm of retraction AR-R, predicts the indicated requirement to retract. Let's refer to the context in which I originally said "Fish sticks are tasty" as U and to the later context in which I assess this claim as A, and let's continue to use *fish sticks are tasty* as a name for the proposition I assert by means of my utterance in U. Given the previous characterization of assessment relativism, *fish sticks are tasty* is true at U and A iff fish sticks are tasty according to the taste standard I have at the time of A. So since I do not like fish sticks anymore at the time of A, *fish sticks are tasty* comes out untrue at U and A. Given AR-R, this means that my assertion in U should be retracted in A, as desired. Meanwhile, non-indexical contextualism, with its retraction norm NIC-R, fails to predict retraction data. According to NIC-R, the original assertion of *fish sticks are tasty* has to be retracted if *fish sticks are tasty* is not true at U. However, at U, this proposition is true because, by stipulation, I liked fish sticks initially. Thus, there is no obligation to retract, contrary to our data.

It is essential here that we focus on responses like "I stand by that/I take that back" rather than, e.g., "what I said is true/false" or "my assertion is permissible/impermissible." For non-indexical contextualism and assessment relativism make the same predictions about the latter responses, or

Contextualism, Relativism, and Retraction 197

at least they can be implemented such that they make the same predictions. Consider "what I said is true," and let us say for concreteness that what I said was *fish sticks are tasty*. Both non-indexical contextualists and assessment relativists can assume disquotation principles for the monadic truth-predicate involved in this sentence. A non-indexical contextualist can say that the proposition expressed by "what I said is true" is true at a context of use U iff *fish sticks are tasty* is true at U. An assessment relativist can say that the proposition expressed by "what I said is true" is true at a context of use U and a context of assessment A iff *fish sticks are tasty* is true at U and A.[5] By the reflexive norms of assertion NIC-A and AR-A, assertions of the proposition expressed by "what I said is true" thus come out as permissible under the same conditions, namely, when the speaker likes fish sticks (mutatis mutandis for "what I said is false"). Consider "my assertion is permissible." Non-indexical contextualists can say that the proposition expressed by this sentence is true at U iff the speaker's assertion is permissible (setting aside tense and modality). Assessment relativists can likewise say that the proposition expressed by this sentence is true at U and A iff the speaker's assertion is permissible (again setting aside tense and modality). Now, as indicated, non-indexical contextualists and assessment relativists agree on when taste assertions are permissible. So asserting "my assertion is permissible" comes out as permissible under the same conditions (mutatis mutandis for "my assertion is impermissible").[6]

4.   Non-Indexical Contextualism and Retraction Data

In this section, I propose and defend what I take to be the most promising account of retraction data on behalf of non-indexical contextualism. If this account withstands scrutiny, then retraction data do not motivate assessment relativism, contrary to the argument in the previous section. Given that retraction data seem to be the only reason to prefer assessment relativism to non-indexical contextualism, it even follows that we should stick with non-indexical contextualism. After all, non-indexical contextualism and assessment relativism come out as explanatorily equally powerful, while non-indexical contextualism is the simpler theory.

Here is my preferred non-indexical contextualist account of retraction data. Non-indexical contextualists should replace the previous retraction norm NIC-R with the following norm.

> NIC-R* One is obligated in a context C2 to retract an assertion of p made in a context C1 if p is not true at C2.

The only difference between this norm and the previous norm NIC-R is that requirements to retract now depend on the later context C2 rather than the original context C1. This modification allows non-indexical

198 *Alexander Dinges*

contextualists to explain the retraction data. According to our definition of non-indexical contextualism, *fish sticks are tasty* is true at A iff fish sticks are tasty according to the taste standard I have at the time of A. This condition does not hold in the envisaged cases. Hence, *fish sticks are tasty* is not true at A, and my original assertion in U has to be retracted in A given NIC-R*.

In the remainder of this section, I defend NIC-R* against three concerns that might naturally arise. First, one might worry that NIC-R* is problematic because it is incompatible with non-indexical contextualism. In particular, one might think that NIC-R* entails assessment relativism. Following MacFarlane (2014, p. 60), for instance, we cross the "philosophically interesting line" to assessment relativism if "we relativize truth not just to a context of use and an index, but also to a *context of assessment*." MacFarlane (2014, p. 60) describes a context of use as "a possible situation in which a sentence might be used" and a context of assessment as "a possible situation in which a use of a sentence might be *assessed*." Now in NIC-R*, we evaluate the truth of p relative to C2, and C2 is a context of assessment in the given sense. So it may seem that we have crossed the line to assessment relativism.

But this misinterprets MacFarlane's criterion. We do not get assessment relativism just by relativizing truth to contexts that happen to be contexts of assessment. Otherwise, the non-indexical norm of assertion NIC-A would already entail assessment relativism. Take an assertion of "Fish sticks are tasty" as made in a context of assessment, i.e., a context "in which a use of a sentence might be *assessed*." NIC-A tells us that this assertion is permissible if the asserted proposition is true at that context. Thus, NIC-A, just like NIC-R*, requires a truth-predicate that can take contexts of assessment as a relatum. This cannot suffice for assessment relativism. According to MacFarlane, I take it, we cross the line to assessment relativism only if we relativize truth to *two* contexts, a context of use and a context of assessment.[7] Neither NIC-A nor NIC-R* requires this type of double-relativization.

One might still worry that NIC-R* entails assessment relativism, because one might object to MacFarlane's characterization of assessment relativism (or my interpretation of it). Unlike MacFarlane, Kölbel (2015), for instance, suggests that "the important dividing line" between assessment relativism and non-indexical contextualism "is the one beyond which the normative status (i.e. as permissible or obligatory) of the use of a sentence is not absolute but depends on the situation in which its status is assessed." But even on this understanding of assessment relativism, NIC-R* does not cross the line to assessment relativism. NIC-R* only governs the use of sentences like "I take that back." And according to NIC-R*, the permissibility of using these sentences depends solely on their context of use. Moreover, NIC-R* is perfectly compatible with a norm of assertion like NIC-A for sentences like "Fish sticks are tasty," according

Contextualism, Relativism, and Retraction 199

to which the permissibility of using these sentences also depends solely on their context of use.

Unlike MacFarlane and Kölbel, Ninan (2016, p. 444) and Marques (2018, p. 3342) seem to construe assessment relativism as entailing the conjunction of the previously described assessment relative semantic framework with the retraction norm AR-R. On this interpretation, NIC-R* fails to cross the line to assessment relativism simply because NIC-R* differs from AR-R.

One might suggest that we cross the line to assessment relativism once the context of assessment partially determines whether a previous assertion must be retracted. Both AR-R and NIC-R* entail assessment relativism in this sense. But this definition of assessment relativism is untenable because it is too wide. Suppose I hold that assertions are permissible when the underlying belief is epistemically justified but that they have to be retracted when new evidence defeats this justification. This view does not entail relativism in any sense, and yet it would count as assessment relativism on the given definition because it would mandate retraction depending on the evidence available in the context of assessment (see, relatedly, MacFarlane, 2014, p. 110).

In sum, there is no plausible conception of assessment relativism on which NIC-R* entails assessment relativism.

Second, one might worry that NIC-R* clashes with plausible general principles about retraction. As indicated, non-indexical contextualists typically assume norms of assertion according to which an assertion of p is permissible only if p is true at the context of the assertion. NIC-R* thus entails that we sometimes have to retract permissible assertions; namely, when our taste standard has relevantly shifted so that the asserted proposition is no longer true at our present context. This result clashes with the initially plausible principle that one should not retract permissible assertions.

To respond, note that the very same problem arises for AR-R. As indicated, assessment relativists also tend to favour norms of assertion where an assertion of p is permissible only if p is true as used and assessed from the context of the assertion. As before in the case of NIC-R*, the satisfaction of this condition does not rule out a requirement to retract in a later context. So once more, we arrive at the conclusion that permissible assertions have to be retracted sometimes.

Maybe this means that we have to abandon both NIC-R* and AR-R and that neither non-indexical contextualism nor assessment relativism properly accommodates retraction data. This is unproblematic in the present context. My goal here is to elucidate how we can decide between non-indexical contextualism and assessment relativism *if* we want to subscribe to one or the other position. I do not want to argue that we should, or plausibly can, subscribe to such a view at all. Let me flag though that, on my view, we lack independent evidence for the claim that we should not

200   *Alexander Dinges*

retract permissible assertions, and so I think that both non-indexical contextualists and assessment relativists should respond to the above worry by just rejecting this principle.[8]

Third, one might worry that NIC-R* implausibly requires us to retract assertions made in relevantly different possible worlds. Assume that I assert that the earth is flat in a possible world w, where the earth in fact is flat. This proposition is not actually true, and thus it is not true at my actual context. Thus, it has to be retracted by NIC-R*; which is implausible. Once more, AR-R already has this consequence. Just assume that I assert that the earth is flat in a possible world w*, where the earth is not flat. This proposition is not true as used in the original context and assessed from the actual context. After all, the earth is not flat in w*. By AR-R, the assertion has to be retracted. We can easily avoid these problems if we stipulate that C1 and C2 in NIC-R* and AR-R must belong to the same possible world.

In sum, NIC-R* seems like a plausible alternative to AR-R, and if this principle withstands scrutiny, we should abandon assessment relativism. After all, non-indexical contextualism is the simpler theory while having equal explanatory power. As we will see in the next section, however, this conclusion is not quite warranted. If we accept certain views about tense and location, then NIC-R* is untenable, retraction data turn out to be a severe challenge for non-indexical contextualism, and we should opt for assessment relativism after all.

5. Temporalism and Locationism

Consider the sentence "It is raining," and let us use *it is raining* to refer to the proposition we assert when we literally use this sentence. Let us now define *temporalism* as a view that entails the following. A circumstance of evaluation comprises a time t in addition to the already established components w and s such that

> *It is raining* is true relative to <w, s, t> iff, at w, it is raining at t.

In maybe more familiar terms, temporalism says that *it is raining* is a temporally neutral proposition, one that changes its truth-value depending on the time of evaluation (see, e.g., Richard, 1981, p. 1).[9] If we adopt temporalism, so understood, the non-indexical contextualist has to adapt her notion of truth relative to a context of use, which so far assumes that circumstances of evaluation just comprise a world and a taste standard. In particular, we now get the following principle.

> A proposition p is true at a context of use C iff p is true relative to <w(C), s(C), t(C)>.

Contextualism, Relativism, and Retraction 201

Here, t(C) is the time of C, and everything else is as before. Applying this principle to our proposition *it is raining*, we get that

> *It is raining* is true at a context of use C iff, at the possible world of C, it is raining at the time of C.

Assume temporalism so understood. Assume further that it is raining at a given point in time and that I concurrently assert "It is raining." It stops raining, and someone reminds me that I said it was raining. Unlike in the case of "tasty," it would be odd to respond,

> *"I take that back. It isn't raining."*

The appropriate response rather seems to be,

> *"I stand by that. But it isn't raining (anymore)."*

According to NIC-R*, however, it should be the other way around. Let us use A to refer to the context in which it has stopped raining and U to refer to the context of my original assertion. Let us further continue to use *it is raining* for the proposition I assert by my use of "It is raining." The proposition *it is raining* is untrue at A because it is not raining at the time of A. Given NIC-R*, this means that, in A, I have to retract my assertion of *it is raining* in U.

No similar problem arises for the assessment relativist. Even granting temporalism, the assessment relativist can adopt the following definition of truth relative to a context of use and assessment.

> A proposition p is true at a context of use C1 and a context of assessment C2 iff p is true relative to <w(C1), s(C2), t(C1)>.

In other words, assessment relativists can assume that, while the taste standard is initialized by the context of assessment, world and time are set by the context of use. We thus get that

> *It is raining* is true at a context of use C1 and a context of assessment C2 iff, at the possible world of C1, it is raining at the time of C1.

Given that, an assertion of *it is raining* is true at U and A iff it is raining at the time of U. This condition is satisfied in the envisaged case described, so even given AR-R, no retraction is required when I find myself in A.

Similar points can be made with respect to location. Let us say that *locationism* is the view that adds a location to the circumstance of evaluation in the same way in which temporalists add a point in time (see, e.g., Kaplan, 1989, p. 504). Given locationism, NIC-R* makes the problematic prediction that we may have to retract assertions of *it is raining* just

202 *Alexander Dinges*

because we have moved to a different location where it is not raining. As before, the assessment relativist can avoid this commitment if she takes locations to be provided by the context of use rather than the context of assessment.[10]

I have assumed that, when we evaluate a previous utterance, then the time and the location of the context of evaluation are the time and the location at which the evaluation takes place. This assumption was essential for deriving the indicated problematic predictions, according to which assertions of *it is raining* must be retracted when it has stopped raining or when you have moved to a different location where it is not raining. One might suggest that non-indexical contextualists could be more flexible here. In particular, couldn't they say that the time and location of such contexts of evaluation are the time and location of the original utterance? This would avoid the previous problems.[11]

To make this plausible, one would need a suitable meta-semantic story of how contexts determine a time and a location, and I do not see what this story should be. For instance, suppose we say that the time of a context is the point in time that is most salient in the context. It might be that, typically, when I assess a previous utterance, the most salient point in time is the time of the original utterance. But this need not be the case. In principle, at least, it should be possible to consider a previous utterance while focusing on the present point in time. So there should be at least *some* contexts in which you have to retract an assertion of *it is raining* after a change in the weather, but there do not seem to be *any* such contexts. More generally, there seems to be a tension between the idea of adopting a *flexible* approach towards the question of how contexts determine points in time and locations and the entirely *stable* phenomenon that you are *never* required to retract assertions of *it is raining* just because of a change in the weather. So far, I do not see how this tension can be resolved.

As things stand, then, NIC-R* is untenable if we accept temporalism or locationism. A non-indexical contextualist who subscribes to either of these positions thus has to abandon NIC-R* in favour of some other plausible principle that predicts retraction data. It is far from obvious what this principle would be. Let me briefly address two options that might naturally come to mind.

First, some indexical contextualists offer pragmatic accounts of disagreement data (see, e.g., López de Sa, 2008; Plunkett & Sundell, 2013; Zakkou, 2019), and these accounts may be extendable to retraction data. Non-indexical contextualists might try to co-opt these pragmatic accounts. Following Zakkou (2019), for instance, they might argue that assertions of "Fish sticks are tasty" presuppose (or conventionally implicate) that one's own taste is superior to the others and that retraction is required after a change in taste, because after a change in taste, one can no longer accept this presupposition. But once we accept the presence

Contextualism, Relativism, and Retraction   203

of such a presupposition of superiority, it is unclear why we would still need non-indexical contextualism. According to Zakkou (2019), at least, such a presupposition explains, e.g., disagreement and retraction data even within an indexical contextualist framework (see likewise López de Sa, 2008; Plunkett & Sundell, 2013). Thus, appeals to, e.g., presuppositions of superiority on behalf of non-indexical contextualism are self-defeating.

Second, non-indexical contextualists could propose domain-specific norms of retraction, e.g., one for tensed propositions tied to the original utterance context and one for taste propositions tied to the context of assessment. They could specifically assume that an assertion of a tensed proposition must be retracted if the asserted proposition is false at the context of use, while an assertion of a taste proposition must be retracted if the asserted proposition is false at the context of assessment. However, take an assertion of the proposition *it is raining and fish sticks are tasty*, which is both a tensed proposition and a taste proposition. Now assume that the speaker likes fish sticks throughout, while it has stopped raining after the assertion. Retraction is intuitively not required. According to the given norms, however, retraction is required because *it is raining and fish sticks are tasty* is not true at the context of assessment where it is no longer raining and because, by the retraction norm for taste propositions, the respective assertion must be retracted under these conditions.

In sum, if we accept temporalism or locationism, retraction data raise a serious concern for non-indexical contextualism. My previous account in terms of NIC-R* comes out as untenable, and no alternative account seems forthcoming.

6.   Conclusion

We have seen that retraction data by themselves do not show that assessment relativism is preferable to non-indexical contextualism. If we reject temporalism and locationism, we should stick with non-indexical contextualism even in the face of retraction data. For NIC-R* makes perfect sense of retraction data, and there is thus no need to adopt the more complicated assessment relativist framework. Meanwhile, if we accept temporalism or locationism, then we should go for assessment relativism. For NIC-R* becomes untenable, and non-indexical contextualists have no alternative account of retraction data to offer. In sum, one's take on temporalism and locationism should determine one's preference for assessment relativism or non-indexical contextualism.

Which view should we adopt if we are still undecided whether temporalism or locationism holds? There is a methodological choice to be made. Either we go for assessment relativism in order to be safe. Assessment relativism properly accounts for retraction data even if temporalism and

204 Alexander Dinges

locationism turn out to be true. Or we go for non-indexical contextualism because we do not want to complicate our theory unless we are forced to. We can have it either safe or simple. I tend to side with the latter approach, but both strategies seem acceptable.

Notes

1. When I speak of assessment relativism, I have in mind what MacFarlane also calls truth-value relativism. Thus, I leave so-called content-relativism aside (see, e.g., Cappelen, 2008a, 2008b; MacFarlane, 2014, pp. 72–76).
2. So-called "exocentric uses" (Lasersohn, 2005) put pressure on this simple conception of the taste standard relevant in a given context. See also, e.g., Beddor and Egan (2018) for a more flexible form of relativism.
3. MacFarlane's own definition of truth at a context is slightly more complicated than mine because he wants to avoid talk of *the* world of a context of use (see, e.g., MacFarlane, 2014, p. 77). I ignore this for simplicity.
4. While I find it clear that "I take it back" sounds better than "I stand by it" in the earlier case, the indicated requirement to retract is controversial. For armchair challenges, see, e.g., von Fintel and Gillies (2008, pp. 81–82), Marques (2014, 2018, pp. 3345–3347), and Raffman (2016, p. 172). For experimental challenges, see, e.g., Marques (2018, p. 3353n10) and Kneer (2021), who criticize more favourable results from Knobe and Yalcin (2014, pp. 13–15). For responses to these concerns, see, e.g., MacFarlane (2014, pp. 258–260) and MacFarlane (2016, p. 198). For methodological concerns with the respective experimental studies, see, e.g., Dinges and Zakkou (2020, pp. 7–8). This debate has to be assessed separately in each domain in which relativism is proposed, and this goes beyond the scope of this chapter. I only want to address the question of whether assessment relativism can be motivated *if* we grant retraction data of the indicated kind.
5. See, e.g., MacFarlane (2014, p. 93) for further discussion of these disquotation principles.
6. See, e.g., Kölbel (2015) for further helpful discussion of these issues.
7. One should presumably add that both the context of use and the context of assessment must play some theoretical role in generating the predictions of one's overall semantic theory. See also MacFarlane (2014, p. 89n24) for helpful discussion on how one can accept this double relativization without making it "notationally salient."
8. See, e.g., MacFarlane (2014, p. 110) and Marques (2014, 2018, pp. 3347–3350) for further discussion of worries along the above lines. See also Dinges (2017). See Ross and Schroeder (2013), MacFarlane (2014, pp. 305–319), Ninan (2016, pp. 445–446), and Marques (2019) on the "rationality" of having a practice of assertion governed by norms like NIC-R* and AR-R.
9. To qualify as a temporalist in the envisaged sense, it does not suffice to posit temporally neutral compositional sentential semantic values. One must assume further that these semantic values are the objects of assertion. See, e.g., Rabern (2012) for pertinent discussion. The same goes for locationism in what follows.
10. One might think that a further problem arises for NIC-R* if we assume that, e.g., "My pants are on fire" can be used to assert a *de se* proposition that varies in truth-value with the speaker (see, e.g., Lewis, 1979). This is not the case, however. AR-R and NIC-R* impose retraction requirements only on one's own assertions. Thus, the speaker cannot relevantly vary. There is an

additional problem for NIC-R*, though, if the proposition asserted with, e.g., "Your pants are on fire" varies in truth-value with the addressee. This position should be added to the list of positions that make trouble for non-indexical contextualism to the extent that it is deemed defensible.

11. Thanks to Dan Zeman for pressing me on this point.

Bibliography

Beddor, B., & Egan, A. (2018). Might do better. Flexible relativism and the QUD. *Semantics and Pragmatics*, 11(7), 1–41. http://doi.org/10.3765/sp.11.7

Cappelen, H. (2008a). Content relativism and semantic blindness. In M. García-Carpintero & M. Kölbel (Eds.), *Relative truth* (pp. 265–286). Oxford University Press.

Cappelen, H. (2008b). The creative interpreter. Content relativism and assertion. *Philosophical Perspectives*, 22(1), 23–46.

Dinges, A. (2017). Relativism and assertion. *Australasian Journal of Philosophy*, 95(4), 730–740.

Dinges, A., & Zakkou, J. (2020). A direction effect on taste predicates. *Philosophers' Imprint*, 20(27), 1–22.

Kaplan, D. (1989), Demonstratives. In J. Almog, J. Perry, & H. Wettstein (Eds.), *Themes from Kaplan* (pp. 481–563). Oxford University Press.

Kneer, M. (2021). Predicates of personal taste: Empirical data. *Synthese*. https://doi.org/10.1007/s11229-021-03077-9

Knobe, J., & Yalcin, S. (2014). Epistemic modals and context. Experimental data. *Semantics and Pragmatics*, 7(10), 1–21.

Kölbel, M. (2015). Review of *Assessment Sensitivity*. *Notre Dame Philosophical Reviews*, 8(32).

Lasersohn, P. (2005). Context dependence, disagreement, and predicates of personal taste. *Linguistics and Philosophy*, 28(6), 643–686.

Lewis, D. (1979). Attitudes *De Dicto* and *De Se*. *The Philosophical Review*, 88(4), 513–543.

López de Sa, D. (2008). Presuppositions of commonality. An indexical relativist account of disagreement. In M. García-Carpintero & M. Kölbel (Eds.), *Relative truth* (pp. 297–310). Oxford University Press.

MacFarlane, J. (2014). *Assessment sensitivity: Relative truth and its applications*. Oxford University Press.

MacFarlane, J. (2016). Replies to Raffman, Stanley, and Wright. *Philosophy and Phenomenological Research*, 92(1), 197–202.

Marques, T. (2014). Relative correctness. *Philosophical Studies*, 167(2), 361–373.

Marques, T. (2018). Retractions. *Synthese*, 195(4), 3335–3359.

Marques, T. (2019). The case against semantic relativism. In M. Kusch (Ed.), *The Routledge handbook of philosophy of relativism* (pp. 507–517). Routledge.

Ninan, D. (2016). Review of *Assessment Sensitivity*. *The Philosophical Review*, 125(3), 439–447.

Plunkett, D., & Sundell, T. (2013). Disagreement and the semantics of normative and evaluative terms. *Philosophers' Imprint*, 13(23), 1–37.

Rabern, B. (2012). Against the identification of assertoric content with compositional value. *Synthese*, 189(1), 75–96.

Raffman, D. (2016). Relativism, retraction, and evidence. *Philosophy and Phenomenological Research*, *92*(1), 171–178.

Richard, M. (1981). Temporalism and eternalism. *Philosophical Studies*, *39*(1), 1–13.

Ross, J., & Schroeder, M. (2013). Reversibility or disagreement. *Mind*, *122*(485), 43–84.

von Fintel, K., & Gillies, A. S. (2008). CIA leaks. *The Philosophical Review*, *117*(1), 77–98.

Zakkou, J. (2019). Denial and retraction. A challenge for theories of taste predicates. *Synthese*, *196*(4), 1555–1573.

10 Perspectival Content and Semantic Composition

Malte Willer and Christopher Kennedy

1. Sæbø's Challenge

It is by now well established that there is a class of SUBJECTIVE ATTITUDE verbs which require their complements to encode (a certain type of) perspectival meaning. For example, English *find* can embed a small clause complement headed by the predicate *attractive* but not one headed by *unmarried* (see, e.g., Bouchard, 2012; Bylinina, 2017; Fleisher, 2013; Kennedy, 2013; Hirvonen, 2014; Reis, 2013; Sæbø, 2009; Stephenson, 2007; Umbach, 2016; Vardomskaya, 2018):

(1) a. Kim finds Lee attractive.

    b. # Kim finds Lee unmarried.

Sæbø (2009) uses subjective attitude verbs to explore different hypotheses about how the perspectival nature of predicates of personal taste in particular is grammatically encoded. His central comparison is between accounts in which the locus of perspectival meaning is reflected in the syntax (or logical type), such as typical contextualist approaches (e.g., Stojanovic, 2007) and those in which it is not, which include standard relativist accounts (e.g., Lasersohn, 2005).[1] Both classes of analysis provide a means of capturing the basic contrast between examples like those in (1): on a syntactic account, *find* expects the perspectival argument slot of its complement to be unsaturated and links this position with its subject; in non-syntactic accounts, *find* effectively presupposes the perspectival aspect of its complement's meaning to be "unfixed" in a way that differs according to the nature of the analysis.

In a bit more detail, according to the syntactic or type-theoretic approach, what makes a predicate perspectival is that it selects for an e-type internal argument, e.g., given some index of evaluation s and context c, *attractive* denotes a set of item-judge pairs—the set of $\langle x, y \rangle$ such that x is attractive to y at s—while a non-perspectival predicate such as *unmarried* simply denotes a set of objects—those that are not married at s, period. The role of *find* is to feed its subject to the internal judge argument

DOI: 10.4324/9781003184225-14

208 *Malte Willer and Christopher Kennedy*

slot of its complement; this, of course, can only be done if there is an open such slot to begin with.

(2) a. $[[\textit{find } \phi]]^{c,s} = \lambda x.[[\phi]]^{c,s}(x)$

   b. $[[\textit{attractive}]]^{c,s} = \lambda x \lambda y.\ x$ is attractive to y at s

   c. $[[\textit{unmarried}]]^{c,s} = \lambda x.\ x$ is not married at s

On this analysis, (1b) is marked due to a type mismatch: the attitude verb *find* supplies Kim as argument to the complement, yet the denotation of *Lee (is) unmarried* has no argument slot left to be filled. In contrast, due to the semantics of *attractive*, the complement in (1a) happily accepts Kim as the still-missing judge argument, and the sentence then evaluates to true just in case Lee is attractive to Kim (at the relevant index of evaluation).

A non-syntactic approach à la Lasersohn (2005) treats (1b) as marked because the attitude verb *find* makes no semantic contribution. Points of evaluation consist of a world, time of evaluation, and judge; all that *find* does is to fix its subject as the judge that matters when evaluating its complement for truth or falsity. That semantic contribution is vacuous if the proposition expressed by the complement is not sensitive to who the judge is.

(3) a. $[[\textit{find } \phi]]^{c,\langle w,t,j\rangle} = \lambda x.[[\phi]]^{c,\langle w,t,x\rangle}$

   b. A proposition p is JUDGE INVARIANT just in case for all worlds w, times t, and judges j, k: p is true at $\langle w,t,j\rangle$ just in case p is true at $\langle w,t,k\rangle$.

What makes the use of *find* in (1b) odd, then, is that it shifts the judge when the choice of who the judge is does not matter for the truth of the complement in the first place: whether or not Lee is married depends on the world and time of evaluation but not on the judge. Whether Lee is attractive, in contrast, is a judge-sensitive affair, and so of course the use of *find* in (1a) makes perfect sense.

Following Sæbø (2009), we have illustrated the non-syntactic approach against the background of a relativist setting, but it is important to note that its underlying intuition is not tied to such formal particulars. The basic intuition here is that *find* requires its complement to be perspectival in a distinct way and that this requirement is best understood as a kind of CONTINGENCY REQUIREMENT (Bouchard, 2012). In a relativist setting, this requirement happens to manifest in the form of a sensitivity to how a certain parameter of evaluation—the judge index—is chosen. But this is not the only way to go: Coppock (2018), for instance, replaces possible worlds with "outlooks," which are refinements of worlds that settle not only matters of fact but also matters of opinion, and then lets all

Perspectival Content, Semantic Composition 209

predicates—including predicates of personal taste—have ordinary extensions relative to these refined points of evaluation. Since opinions differ, a world will allow for different refinements and thus correspond to multiple outlooks. A proposition is DISCRETIONARY just in case its truth-value varies across the outlooks corresponding to a single world. Coppock's proposal for Swedish *tycka*—which patterns with English *find* in many ways—is that it presupposes its complement to be discretionary, i.e., to vary in truth-value across the outlooks corresponding to a single world. Similarly, Kennedy and Willer (2016, forthcoming) propose that subjective attitude verbs presuppose the contingency of their complement across a set of contextually salient doxastic alternatives, which agree on matters of fact but differ in resolutions of semantic and pragmatic indeterminacy.

The account that Sæbø (2009) introduces under a "relativist" heading is thus representative of a diverse class of proposals that emphasize perspectival content and thus embeddability under *find* as a matter of contingency rather than as one of semantic type.[2] It is thus very significant when Sæbø maintains that such non-syntactic, contingency-centric approaches flounder when it comes to explaining contrasts like those in (4) and (5), in which the complements of *find* show a greater degree of syntactic complexity than what we saw earlier in (1).

(4) a.   Kim finds Lee attractive and pleasant.
    b.   # Kim finds Lee attractive and unmarried.

(5) a.   Kim finds everyone who is unmarried pleasant.
    b.   # Kim finds everyone who is pleasant unmarried.

In short, the problem for non-syntactic accounts is that if a particular expression has a perspective-sensitive meaning—i.e., is judge-dependent in the way proposed by Lasersohn and other relativists or more generally contingent in a way that is tied to interpretation rather than semantic composition—then unless that content is fixed by some other expression, any larger constituent containing that expression (if consistent) should be perspective-sensitive in the same way. Thus given that *attractive* is perspective-sensitive, *attractive and unmarried* should be as well, and (4b) should be fine. Similarly, given that *pleasant* is perspective-sensitive (as shown by (5a)), *everyone who is pleasant* should be as well, as should the clausal constituent *everyone who is pleasant (is) unmarried*, and so (5b) should be fine.

In contrast, a syntactic or type-theoretic account provides a simple and straightforward explanation of these contrasts: a perspectival predicate like *attractive* is type-wise distinct from a non-perspectival predicate such as *unmarried*, and so assuming that conjunction requires likeness of semantic type, the perspectival argument of the former must be saturated before it can conjoin with the latter. But this means that unlike *attractive and pleasant*—which can compose before their respective perspectival arguments are saturated—*attractive and unmarried* in (4b) is of the wrong semantic type to compose with *find*. Similarly in (5b), the perspectival argument of *pleasant* must be saturated by the time of relative clause formation in order to ensure that the entire relative clause is of the right semantic type to compose with the quantifier *everyone*.[3]

At a more general level, Sæbø's claim is that only a fundamentally syntactic account of perspectival meaning can explain how perspectival meaning composes: when a complex constituent containing a perspectival expression itself has a perspectival meaning and when it does not. If Sæbø is correct, then examples like (4) and (5) present a challenge for a wide variety of analyses, which, to our knowledge, has not been adequately addressed by proponents of such accounts.[4] (We will address another class of cases that Sæbø discusses at a later stage.) The goal of this chapter is to respond to this challenge, which we will do in two steps.

First, after some brief critical reflections on the very idea of tying embeddability under *find* to argument structure, we will expand our attention to a second subjective attitude verb, *consider*. We will demonstrate that *consider* also requires its complement to be perspective-sensitive (though in a way different from *find*) and that it shows a similar pattern of (un)acceptability in examples involving complex complements that are parallel in the relevant respects to (4) and (5). However, we will also argue that *consider* is crucially different from *find* in that there is no plausible "syntactic" account of the basic pattern of complement selection; instead, some version of a non-syntactic account is the only game in town.

Second, we will show that, in fact, it is possible to come up with a simple and intuitive compositional semantics for at least one non-syntactic approach to perspectival meaning—the pragmatic theory articulated in Kennedy and Willer (2016, forthcoming)—which flows naturally from a general view of how perspective-sensitive meaning updates a context. We will provide a brief overview of the basic theory of perspectival meaning and will then lay out the compositional details, demonstrating that it accurately predicts when perspectival meaning "projects" and when it does not and that it captures contrasts like those in (4) and (5).

2. Against a Syntactic Account

For current purposes, we set aside specific technical concerns one might have about how Sæbø proposes to handle the crucial examples in (4) and (5). Instead, let us begin by highlighting a general worry about the proposal that a predicate is embeddable under *find* in virtue of the presence of an open argument position that *find* is designed to fill with its subject. In the case of predicates of personal taste, it is for sure not unreasonable to hypothesize such an argument, since a judge (or experiencer; see Muñoz, 2019) can be expressed overtly:

Perspectival Content, Semantic Composition 211

(6) a. Lee is attractive to Kim.
  b. Downhill skiing is fun for Kim.

Bylinina (2017) argues that such overt judge phrases are true arguments of a predicate of personal taste rather than mere adjuncts, pointing, for example, to the fact that the predicates often select for particular prepositions: switching *to* and *for* in (6a–b) leads to unacceptability. (See also Stephenson, 2007, 2008.)

But the class of expressions that embed felicitously under *find* goes beyond those that uncontroversially pertain to matters of personal taste, including character trait predicates, aesthetic predicates, and moral predicates (cf. Vardomskaya, 2018), as the following naturally occurring examples demonstrate.

(7) a. Kevin is somebody [with whom] I probably share as much of a world view as any world leader out there. I find him smart but humble.
  b. Yet the [SsangYong] Rodius is so freakishly ugly that someone is bound to find it kitsch.
  c. I'd also like to add that while I don't find cheating wrong, I'd rather not cheat in a game unless I've already completed it once without cheating.

There is an evaluative component to the meanings of predicates such as *smart*, *kitsch*, and *wrong*, and it makes sense to say that speakers assign extensions to them in ways that vary according to their own evaluations. It does not follow, however, that these expressions select for a distinct judge argument that could be filled by the subject of a *find*-construction. In particular, unlike *attractive* and *fun*, expressions such as *smart*, *kitsch*, and *wrong* do not seem to take judge PPs, as the following marginal cases suggest:

(8) a. # Lee is smart to/for Kim.
  b. # The car is kitsch to/for Kim.
  c. # Cheating is wrong to/for Kim.

If one wants to communicate that the judgments in question are from Kim's perspective in examples like these, one must resort to periphrastic constructions of the sort shown in (9a–c).[5]

(9) a. Lee is smart according to Kim.
  b. The car is kitsch in Kim's opinion.
  c. Cheating is wrong in Kim's view.

It is of course possible to maintain that the expressions under consideration here have a syntactic argument that, for some reason or another, cannot be overtly expressed. But a more plausible suggestion would be that perspectival content may manifest in a variety of ways. In some cases, the extension of the predicate in question may indeed be sensitive to a lexically designated judge argument. But this is not the *only* way for a predicate to be perspectival. MULTIDIMENSIONALITY, to give just one example, is another potential source (see Bylinina, 2017; Kennedy, 2013). Whether someone is smart, for instance, depends on a variety of factors—quick-wittedness, sound judgment, flexibility of mind, and so on. Even if these dimensions were to allow for objective measurement, how they factor in the application conditions of the predicate may vary from speaker to speaker, and it is in this sense that it can "depend on one's perspective" whether someone is smart, and even if the predicate *smart* lacks an internal judge argument.

Our first concern about a syntactic account, then, is that it rests on type-theoretic assumptions that we have good reason to resist, at least once the full variety of predicates that felicitously embed under *find* has come into view. Our second concern is that a syntactic account does not generalize to account for the full variety of subjective attitude verbs that a natural language such as English provides. The verb *consider* contrasts with *find* in that it can be used with predicates like *vegetarian* (as well as *attractive*):

(10) a. # Kim finds Lee vegetarian.
       b. Kim considers Lee vegetarian.

At the same time, *consider* shares with *find* a distinctly subjective flavor in that it rejects fully objective predicates:

(11) a. # Lee finds 37813 prime.
       b. # Lee considers 37813 prime.
       c. Lee believes 37813 to be prime.

What these facts show is that the attitude verb *consider*, like *find*, requires its complement to be subjective but in a less demanding way: a predicate such as *vegetarian*, for instance, is "subjective enough" to embed felicitously under *consider* but not under *find*. And crucially, *consider*-type subjective attitude verbs exhibit a pattern similar to their *find*-type cousins when it comes to more complex complements, as shown by the contrasts in (12) and (13).[6]

(12) a. Kim considers Lee vegetarian and intelligent.
       b. # Kim considers Lee vegetarian and in the cast of *Hamilton*.

(13) a. Kim considers someone who is in the cast of *Hamilton* vegetarian.
       b. # Kim considers someone who is vegetarian in the cast of *Hamilton*.

Perspectival Content, Semantic Composition 213

These types of contrasts are identical to the ones that motivated Sæbø's argument for a syntactic account of perspectival content in *find* complements, which would in turn suggest a syntactic account of perspectival content in the complement of *consider*. The problem is that it is difficult to see how a syntactic approach could generalize to capture the fine-grained differences in complement selection between *find* and *consider*. Such an analysis would, for example, need to assign to *vegetarian* a type such that this expression—unlike *prime*—embeds felicitously under *consider* but—unlike *attractive*—fails to embed felicitously under *find*. It is unclear what kind of semantic type that would be, but there are also independent reasons not to think that the differences in perspectival content between, say, *vegetarian* and *attractive* must correspond to a difference in semantic type.

Consider, for example, adjectives like *dense, heavy,* and *light*. These can have either a purely "quantitative" interpretation that characterizes the physical properties of a substance, as in (14a), or a more "qualitative" interpretation that can be used to describe objects which have no physical properties, as in (14b); when an object can be assessed from either a quantitative or qualitative perspective, as in (14c), both interpretations are possible (Kennedy, 2013).

(14) a. This metal is dense/heavy/light.
      b. This story is dense/heavy/light.
      c. This cake is dense/heavy/light.

When we turn to subjective attitude verbs, we see that these adjectives embed under *find* only when they are interpreted qualitatively. Thus (15a) is unacceptable under *find*, (15b) is fine under *find*, and (15c) is unambiguously qualitative under *find*; all examples/interpretations are acceptable under *consider*.

(15) a. # Kim finds this metal dense/heavy/light.
      b. Kim finds this story dense/heavy/light.
      c. Kim finds this cake dense/heavy/light.

(16) a. Kim considers this metal dense/heavy/light.
      b. Kim considers this story dense/heavy/light.
      c. Kim considers this cake dense/heavy/light.

While there is clearly some kind of meaning distinction between the quantitative and qualitative senses of adjectives like *dense, heavy,* and *light* (and indeed, this kind of polysemy appears to be quite productive), there is no obvious type-theoretic reflection of this difference: both senses are gradable, for example, and both have the same basic syntactic distribution, with the one exception of embeddability under *find*. So while *find* and *consider* are evidently sensitive to different ways that a predicate can be "perspectival" (or "subjective"), there is no independent evidence that this difference corresponds to a difference in semantic type.

In sum, a syntactic or type-theoretic account of perspectival content and embeddability under *find* fails to generalize twice over. First, it has trouble explaining why expressions that do not transparently select for an *e*-type internal judge argument—character trait predicates, aesthetic predicates, moral predicates, and so on—happily embed under *find*. And second, it fails to account for the more fine-grained differences between the subjective attitudes *find* and *consider* on pain of overgenerating type-theoretic differences.

We are thus left to conclude that the right account of perspectival content and embeddability under subjective attitude verbs must be a non-syntactic one, which leaves us with two challenges. First, such an account must provide a means of explaining the fine-grained distinctions between *find* and *consider* that we documented in this section. Second, such an account must support a general account of how perspectival content "projects" so that we can explain the contrasts observed in (4) and (5) and (12) and (13) and respond to Sæbø's challenge. Over the next two sections, we will provide such an account, starting with the basics from Kennedy and Willer (2016, forthcoming) and then presenting a proposal for handling complex complements.

3. Counterstance Contingency

The guiding idea behind Kennedy and Willer's (2016, forthcoming) proposal for *find* and *consider* is that subjective attitude verbs are like regular doxastic verbs such as *believe* in terms of their core at issue content but differ in their presuppositions. Specifically, subjective attitude verbs presuppose their complement to be contingent across a set of doxastic alternatives that they label COUNTERSTANCES. These alternatives arise from language users' sophisticated awareness that (what they take to be) matters of fact only partly determine what we say and think. Observe that in the following two examples, replacing *believe* with *consider* signals that the formation of the attitude under consideration must have involved a "leap from the facts":

(17) a. Kim believes this soup to be vegetarian
    b. Kim considers this soup vegetarian.

(18) a. Kim believes herself to be Russian.
    b. Kim considers herself Russian.

For example, (17b) signals that Kim's commitment to the soup being vegetarian is based not solely on knowledge of what is in it but also

Perspectival Content, Semantic Composition   215

on a pragmatic decision to treat certain ingredients (say, fish stock) as vegetarian. And (18b) would be appropriate in a context in which Kim identifies as Russian not because of her citizenship (she may be of French nationality or what have you) but because of her ancestry and fancy for all things Russian. Plain belief attributions, to be clear, do not exclude that adopting the commitment involves a distinct leap from the facts; but the use of *consider* explicitly signals the attitude to be perspectival in this specific way.

Whether an attitude is perspectival in the relevant way is not purely a matter of lexical semantics—context plays a crucial role as well. Consider, for instance, the contrast between (19a) and (19b):

(19)   a.   # Kim considers Burgundy part of France.
        b.   Kim considers Crimea part of Russia.

The intuitive explanation of the contrast is that, at the time of the writing of this article, the sovereignty over Crimea is disputed, hence the use of consider in (19b) seems appropriate, while Burgundy being part of France would count as uncontroversial, hence the use of *consider* in (19a) appears odd. This is not a purely semantic affair but crucially depends on specific features of the discourse context.

An ordinary agent's doxastic state thus has a pragmatic dimension to it, in the sense that some beliefs flow from the agent's pragmatic stance on how certain facts are to be interpreted. To capture this feature of everyday belief states, Kennedy and Willer suggest that context provides a function κ that tracks the contingency of the pragmatic decisions involved in achieving an information state. κ takes an information carrier i and derives a set $\kappa(i)$ of i's counterstances: alternative information states which agree on a contextually salient basis of matters of fact but take conflicting pragmatic stances on these matters. So for instance, a state i and its counterstances would agree on some food's ingredients but may disagree on what it takes for an ingredient to count as vegetarian. Kennedy and Willer's proposal for *consider* then is that it presupposes the COUNTERSTANCE CONTINGENCY of its complement with respect to the attributee's doxastic state: one of its counterstances is committed to p while another is committed to $\bar{p}$ (i.e., the negation of p).[7]

To capture the more fine-grained difference between *find* and *consider*, Kennedy and Willer suggest that the former presupposes a stronger kind of subjectivity that we label RADICAL counterstance contingency, which flows from a distinguished kind of pragmatic underdetermination. Sometimes it makes sense for speakers to propose to coordinate on a pragmatic stance by STIPULATION. This is what we see, for example, in (20), where "for present purposes" should be heard as referring to some salient task, action, or goal whose execution somehow requires categorization of objects according to whether they satisfy the predicate. For example,

216   *Malte Willer and Christopher Kennedy*

in (20), the relevant purpose might be mainly administrative; it may be to decide what kinds of meals to serve the guests at a party; or it may be to categorize a region using geographic, political, or ethnocultural criteria.[8]

(20)   For present purposes,

    a.   let's count farms with an annual gross cash farm income (GFCI) of \$1,000,000 or more as large, those with a GFCI between \$350,000 and \$999,999 as midsize, and those with a GFCI below \$350,000 as small.

    b.   let's count pescatarians as vegetarians.

    c.   let's count Mauretania as sub-Saharan.

Proposing to coordinate a stance by stipulation, however, does not make sense for all kinds of predicates. The following cases, for instance, seem odd.

(21)   For present purposes,

    a.   # let's count anyone with whom Obama shares a world view as smart.

    b.   # let's count Sean Connery as fascinating.

    c.   # let's count cheating as morally despicable.

The basic intuition here is that while one may try to make others adopt one's own perspective on a given subject matter, it is infelicitous to just stipulate some criterion as the basis for establishing a conversational convention for *smart*, *fascinating*, or *despicable*. Predicates that resist such stipulation give rise to radical counterstance contingency.

It is natural to ask in virtue of what a particular expression's application criteria in discourse are underdetermined in a way that allows or does not allow for coordination by stipulation. We address the question in more detail elsewhere (see Kennedy & Willer, forthcoming). What matters for current purposes is this: the previous observations suggest that each set of counterstances C may be partitioned into a set of sets of counterstances $\Pi(C)$: all elements of C, recall, agree on some salient matters of fact; counterstances within a single cell of $\Pi(C)$, in addition, share a pragmatic stance on those underdetermined issues that may be coordinated by stipulation. A proposition p is radically counterstance contingent with respect to some information state i just in case every cell of $\Pi\big(\kappa(i)\big)$ contains a counterstance that is committed to p and one that is committed to $\bar{p}$. The suggestion then is that *find* presupposes its complement to be radically counterstance contingent with respect to the attributee's doxastic state.

In a bit more detail, assume that agents are assigned belief states relative to indices of evaluation and that context fixes a counterstance selection function κ in addition to a partitioning of counterstance spaces.[9]

Perspectival Content, Semantic Composition   217

(22)   a.   A proposition p is *counterstance contingent* with respect to i in c iff $\exists i', i'' \in \kappa(i) : i' \subseteq p$ and $i'' \subseteq \bar{p}$.

b.   A proposition p is *radically counterstance contingent* with respect to i in c iff $\forall \pi \in \Pi(\kappa(i)). \exists i', i'' \in \pi : i' \subseteq p$ and $i'' \subseteq \bar{p}$.

The basic proposal for *find* and *consider*—basic in that the complement is assumed to be atomic for now—is then as follows:

(23)   a. $\llbracket consider\, p \rrbracket^{c,s}(x)$ is defined only if p is counterstance contingent with respect to $\mathrm{Dox}(x,s)$ in c.

b.   If defined, then $\llbracket consider\, p \rrbracket^{c,s}(x) = 1$ iff $\mathrm{Dox}(x,s) \subseteq p$.

(24)   a. $\llbracket find\, p \rrbracket^{c,s}(x)$ is defined only if p is radically counterstance contingent with respect to $\mathrm{Dox}(x,s)$ in c.

b.   If defined, then $\llbracket find\, p \rrbracket^{c,s}(x) = 1$ iff $\mathrm{Dox}(x,s) \subseteq p$.

Two specific predictions are worth highlighting here. First, whenever an expression embeds felicitously under *find*, it also embeds felicitously under *consider*; the reverse does not hold. Second, whenever an expression embeds felicitously under *find*, its criteria of application resist coordination by stipulation, at least in some respects that matter for deciding whether the expression truthfully applies to certain objects or not.

Summarizing, following Kennedy and Willer (2016, forthcoming), we have proposed that *find* and *consider* presuppose that their complements exhibit a distinguished kind of contingency that we have labeled "(radical) counterstance contingency." Insofar as subjective attitude verbs track content that is distinctly perspectival, this is just to say that content is perspectival insofar as it exhibits a distinct kind of contingency. This proposal is representative of a larger tradition in the philosophy of language that includes (but is not exhausted by) standard incarnations of the relativist paradigm.

4.   Counterstance and Composition

Content is perspectival, we said, insofar as it exhibits a distinct kind of contingency. This is an attractive proposal not least because it readily allows for content to be perspectival to varying "degrees": contingency, after all, comes in various degrees as well. Sæbø's original challenge to non-syntactic accounts, however, remains real. The problem, recall, is that without additional maneuvers, perspectival content does not seem to "project" in the right way to get the embeddability facts straight. Consider again the cases discussed earlier:

(4)   a.   Kim finds Lee attractive and pleasant.

b.   # Kim finds Lee attractive and unmarried.

218 *Malte Willer and Christopher Kennedy*

(5) a. Kim finds everyone who is unmarried pleasant.
     b. # Kim finds everyone who is pleasant unmarried.

(12) a. Kim considers Lee vegetarian and intelligent.
      b. # Kim considers Lee vegetarian and in the cast of *Hamilton*.

(13) a. Kim considers someone who is in the cast of *Hamilton* vegetarian.
      b. # Kim considers someone who is vegetarian in the cast of *Hamilton*.

The unacceptability of the (b) examples is unexpected given the basic proposal discussed in the previous section. This is straightforward to show when we look at the cases involving *consider*. Suppose that Kim considers Lee vegetarian and also believes him to be in the cast of *Hamilton*. Then the proposition that Lee is vegetarian and in the cast of *Hamilton* is counterstance contingent with respect to Kim's doxastic state—and yet (12b) is no good.[10] Relatedly, the complements of (13a) and (13b) are truth-conditionally equivalent, and so whenever the one expresses a counterstance contingent proposition, so does the other—yet only (13a) and not (13b) is felicitous. It is straightforward to verify, on parallel grounds, that the basic proposal from Section 3 does not predict a contrast in acceptability between (4a) and (4b) or between (5a) and (5b) either. In short, if we simply look at the (radical) counterstance contingency of the proposition expressed by the complement, we will not be able to explain the contrasts in acceptability between the (a) and (b) sentences in the examples.

Our response to the problem is that the proposition at play must not only exhibit the right kind of contingency but also do so for the right reasons. For a conjunction to embed felicitously under a subjective attitude verb, for instance, the (radical) counterstance contingency of the conjunction must flow from the (radical) counterstance contingency of both conjuncts: this is why (4a) and (12a) are fine while (4b) and (12b) are marked. For a quantified construction to embed under *find* and *consider*, in turn, the relevant contingency must flow from the at-issue content rather than the not-at-issue content and so from the contingency of the scope, not the restrictor. To say that Kim finds everyone who is unmarried pleasant is to say that Kim's attitude speaks to the question of who is pleasant—a question that allows for a radically counterstance contingent resolution. To say that Kim finds everyone who is pleasant unmarried is to say that Kim's attitude speaks to the question of which pleasant people are unmarried—a question that fails to allow for a radically counterstance contingent resolution. Hence the difference in acceptability between (5a) and (5b) and, inter alia, between (13a) and (13b). The basic observation, then, is that subjective attitude verbs not only

Perspectival Content, Semantic Composition 219

require that their complements exhibit a distinct kind of contingency: complex complements, in addition, impose distinct constraints on the set of doxastic alternatives that may witness the contingency at play. In the following, we will make a concrete proposal for how to spell out this picture in detail. As a preparation, and since our analysis includes quantifiers, let us assume explicitly that our language provides a set of variables $x, y, z, \ldots$ and that context fixes a variable assignment g_c. We say that $\mathrm{Alt}(c)$ is the set of contexts just like c except for their variable assignments.

We assume that every constant a and predicate expression F have their regular extensions at indices of evaluation $s(a)$ and $s(F)$, respectively. If α is a singular expression, then $d_c(\alpha)$—the *denotation* of α in c—is $s(\alpha)$ in case α is some constant, and is $g_c(\alpha)$ in case α is a variable. $c[x/a]$ is just like c except that $d_{c[x/a]}(x) = a$. Indices effectively map predicates to extensions: as usual, we say that $[[F\alpha_1 \ldots \alpha_n]]^{c,s} = 1$ just in case $< d_c(\alpha_1), \ldots, d_c(\alpha_n) > \in s(F)$, where $s(F)$ is the extension of F at s.

To get things going, we generalize the notion of a (radically) counterstance contingent proposition to the notion of a (radically) counterstance contingent *issue*. We associate with each sentence an issue by defining a question operator "?" as follows (cf. Groenendijk & Stokhof, 1984):

$$(25) \quad [[\phi?]]^{c,s} = \left\{ s' : [[\phi]]^{c',s} = [[\phi]]^{c',s'} \text{ for all } c' \in \mathrm{Alt}(c) \right\}$$

The semantic value of "$F\alpha_1 \ldots \alpha_n$?" at some index s is the set of indices at which the same n-tuples of individuals satisfy F as in s. If $\alpha_1 \ldots \alpha_n$ are all constants, then $[[F\alpha_1 \ldots \alpha_n?]]^{c,s}$ effectively partitions logical space into two sets of indices: those at which the sentence "$F\alpha_1 \ldots \alpha_n$" is true and those at which it is false. The open sentence "Fx?" denotes the set of true and complete answers to the question of who is F and so on.

It then makes sense to expand the notion of (radical) counterstance contingency to an issue I as follows (recall that we take context to provide a counterstance selection function κ as well as a partitioning of each counterstance space Π):

(26) Take any issue I and context c:

    a. I is *counterstance contingent* with respect to i in c iff for some $p \in I$, p is counterstance contingent with respect to i in context c.

    b. I is *radically counterstance contingent* with respect to i in c iff for some $p \in I$, p is radically counterstance contingent with respect to i in context c.

The simple intuition here is that an issue is (radically) counterstance contingent just in case one of its resolutions is (radically) counterstance contingent.

To make our refined analysis more precise, we will take some inspiration from the literature on dynamic semantics and state what it takes for an information state to be updated with some bit of information. A standard way of motivating a dynamic semantic perspective starts with Stalnaker's (1978) truism about assertion: assertions express propositions and are made in a context. Since language has context-sensitive expressions, which proposition the assertion expresses may very well depend on the context. On the other hand, context–content interaction is not a one-way street: assertions in turn affect the context, and they do so by adding the proposition expressed by that assertion to the context. This picture has all context change mediated by propositional content, but in principle, it does not have to be this way. Instead of being all about truth-conditions, a semantics may be all about how an utterance relates an input context (the context in which it is made) to an output context (the context posterior to the utterance). Semantic content then becomes relational: it is a relation between contexts.[11]

Here we will set aside the controversy between static and dynamic theories of meaning. In fact, we will continue to assign to attitude ascriptions truth-conditions relative to some context and index of evaluation. But we will enrich our framework with a dynamic update function to articulate a more fine-grained account of the constraints that subjective attitudes impose on their complements. Part of the inspiration here is that dynamic semantics has a proven track record of explaining how presuppositions project: we can articulate update rules that not only deliver intuitively adequate truth-conditions for complex sentences but also, if presuppositions are understood as definedness conditions on updating, make empirically adequate predictions about how such presuppositions project.[12] Likewise, then, we propose to think of content as perspectival insofar as it is an update operation satisfying certain definedness constraints that project in intuitive ways.

We start by distinguishing between ordinary, perspectival, and radically perspectival updates, and we do so on the basis of what it takes for a context to admit an update of each respective type.

(27) Consider arbitrary information carrier i, context c, and formula ϕ:

    i. the <u>o</u>rdinary update of i with ϕ in c, $i[\phi]_o^c$, is always admitted

    ii. the <u>p</u>erspectival update of i with ϕ in c, $i[\phi]_p^c$, is admitted iff $[[\phi?]]^c$ is counterstance contingent with respect to i in c

    iii. the <u>r</u>adically perspectival update of i with ϕ in c, $i[\phi]_r^c$ is admitted iff $[[\phi?]]^c$ is radically counterstance contingent with respect to i in c

In brief, to characterize some dynamic content as perspectival is to impose distinct constraints on what it takes for the update to be admissible: the

Perspectival Content, Semantic Composition 221

expression in question must give rise to a suitably counterstance contingent issue.

If perspectival content is content that comes with distinct admissibility criteria, then it makes good sense to say that admission failures result in an update being undefined. And if an update is admitted, we proceed in a fashion that is very familiar from the existing dynamic literature. Here is the proposal:

(28) Consider arbitrary information carrier i, context c, formula γ, and update type f. If $i[\gamma]_f^c$ is admitted, then updating with γ proceeds according to the following rules (here Q is any quantifier):

    a. $i\left[F\alpha_1 \dots \alpha_n\right]_f^c = \{s \in i : \; < d_c(\alpha_1), \dots, d_c(a_n) > \in s(F)\}$

    b. $i\left[\neg\phi\right]_f^c = i \setminus i\left[\phi\right]_f^c$

    c. $i\left[\phi \,\&\, \psi\right]_f^c = \left(i\left[\phi\right]_f^c\right)\left[\psi\right]_f^c$

    d. $i\left[Q_x(\phi)(\psi)\right]_f^c = \left\{ s \in i : \left\{ a \in D : s \in i\left[\phi\right]_{i_o}^{c[x/a]} \right\} \right.$

$$R_Q\{a \in D : s \in i\left[\phi\right]_{i_o}^{c[x/a]} \left[\psi\right]_f^{c[x/a]}\}\}$$

Else, $i[\gamma]_f^c$ is undefined and we write $i[\gamma]_f^c = \perp$, where $\perp$ is the *undefined state* such that $\perp\left[\phi\right]_f^c = \perp$ for all c, ϕ, and f.

An update with a closed atomic sentence simply adds the proposition expressed to the input state by eliminating all indices at which the proposition is false—assuming that the issue put into play by the sentence has the right kind of contingency for the update to be admitted in the first place. If not, the update is undefined.

Negation and conjunction work as expected in a dynamic system: an update with a negation just takes the complement of the result of updating with what is negated, and an update with a conjunction proceeds by updating with the first and then with the second conjunct. Note here that we immediately predict that a (radically) perspectival update with a conjunction is defined only if both conjuncts are (radically) perspectival.[13]

The generalized semantics for quantifiers in (28d) builds on the proposal from Chierchia (1992, 1995), where R_Q is the second-order relation appropriate to the determiner Q: the subset relation for *every*, the non-empty intersection for *some*, and so on. What is important here is that the update with the restrictor is ordinary and so effectively free of any perspectival presupposition. As such, the perspectival flavor of a quantified construction is fully determined by the perspectival flavor of its scope.

We can then wrap things up by refining our semantics of subjective attitude verbs as follows:

222 Malte Willer and Christopher Kennedy

(29) a. $[\![consider\,\phi]\!]^{c,s}(x)$ is defined only if $\text{Dox}(x,s)[\phi]^c_p$ is defined.

b. If defined, then $[\![consider\;\phi]\!]^{c,s}(x)=1$ iff $\text{Dox}(x,s)\subseteq[\![\phi]\!]^c$.

(30) a. $[\![find\,\phi]\!]^{c,s}(x)$ is defined only if $\text{Dox}(x,s)[\phi]^c_r$ is defined.

b. If defined, then $[\![find\,\phi]\!]^{c,s}(x)=1$ iff $\text{Dox}(x,s)\subseteq[\![\phi]\!]^c$.

The proposal continues to make good sense of subjective attitude verbs whose complements are atomic: [[Mary finds Lee fascinating]]^c, for instance, is defined only if Mary's commitment to Lee's being fascinating is radically counterstance contingent.[14] In addition, we now also make the right predictions when a subjective attitude verb has a complex complement. To see this, go back to the earlier observed contrasts involving *find*, repeated here:

(4) a. Kim finds Lee attractive and pleasant.
    b. # Kim finds Lee attractive and unmarried.

(5) a. Kim finds everyone who is unmarried pleasant.
    b. # Kim finds everyone who is pleasant unmarried.

A commitment to Lee being unmarried fails to be radically counterstance contingent, and so a radically perspectival update with "Lee is unmarried" will be undefined with respect to Kim's doxastic state—it follows immediately that a radically perspectival update with "Lee is attractive and unmarried" will be undefined with respect to Kim's doxastic state, and so (4b) is undefined, as required. (4a), in contrast, is fine due to the radical counterstance contingency of the issues raised by both conjuncts. This account also extends to data involving quantified constructions. The issue of who is (un)married does not allow for a radically counterstance contingent resolution, explaining why (5b) is unacceptable, while the radical counterstance contingency of the issue of who is pleasant licenses (5a).

The explanatory strategy outlined here extends directly to the corresponding data involving *consider* in (12) and (13) and, moreover, preserves the original idea that *find* and *consider* require their complement to express a (radically) counterstance contingent proposition to be defined. This leads to a number of additional subtle but correct predictions. For instance, given the standard definition of disjunction in terms of negation and conjunction, the sentence "Crimea is part of Russia or Ukraine" should fail to be perspectival in ordinary contexts, since every doxastic alternative agrees on the proposition expressed by that sentence (and even though the disjuncts taken in isolation are counterstance contingent). And indeed, (31) only has an interpretation in which disjunction is interpreted with matrix scope, indicating that a parse in which the disjunction is inside the complement is unacceptable.

Perspectival Content, Semantic Composition   223

(31)   Kim considers Crimea part of Russia or Ukraine.

Similarly, if some student is clearly tall while others are borderline, then the sentence "Some student is tall" fails to be perspectival (even though the issue of who is tall is counterstance contingent), whereas the sentence "Every student is tall" is perspectival.[15] And in such a context, (32a) is fine, and (32b) is acceptable only when *some student* is understood *de re*, such that Kim's attitude is about one of the borderline cases; crucially, (32b) lacks a *de dicto* reading that is available in (32c) (alongside the *de re* reading), which attributes to Kim the belief that there is a tall student.

(32)   a.   Kim considers every student tall.
       b.   Kim considers some student tall.
       c.   Kim believes some student to be tall.

In addition to accounting for subtle distinctions like these, the basic proposal can be further elaborated to handle a number of trickier examples. For example, Sæbø (2009) observes that in Norwegian, material that fails to be properly perspectival may nonetheless embed felicitously under the subjective attitude verb *synes* as long as it can be interpreted as presupposed (cf. Bouchard, 2012 on French *trouver*). For example, in a context in which it is common ground that the addressee is married to a man, (33) can be felicitously used to express a meaning that is equivalent to the English translation.

(33)   Jeg synes du er gift med en vakker man
       I SAV you are married with a beautiful man
       "I find the man you are married to beautiful." (*lit* "I find you married to a beautiful man.")

We can accommodate facts like these by adding the following update rule for presupposed material to the system (here we use "∂" to mark that some content is presupposed):

(34) $i[\partial\phi]_f^c = i$ if $i[\phi]_{io}^c = i$; otherwise $i[\partial\phi]_f^c = \perp$

In words: presupposed material imposes a definedness condition on updating (see Beaver, 2001; Heim, 1982, among others) but the presupposition operator neutralizes all existing perspectival constraints. As a result, only the at-issue content interacts with the definedness conditions imposed by the subjective attitude verb.

Summarizing, we propose to think of perspectival content as dynamic content that satisfies distinct recursively definable admissibility criteria, with counterstance contingency being the key grounding notion. A perspectival update is admitted only if the issue expressed is suitably

224 *Malte Willer and Christopher Kennedy*

counterstance contingent. In the atomic case, this is just in case the proposition expressed is counterstance contingent. If the complement is complex, local updates will impose additional admission criteria. In the case of a conjunction, for instance, both conjuncts must be suitably contingent for the update to be defined, and this just follows from our update rules. The fact that we can make also good sense of cases in which *find* and *consider* take quantifiers or presupposed content as their complement indicates that the proposal presented here is worth taking seriously.

5. Concluding Remarks

We have demonstrated that there is at least one instance of a non-syntactic, contingency-centered analysis of perspectival content—the one from Kennedy and Willer (2016, forthcoming)—that meets Sæbø's challenge from complex complements under the scope of *find*. This is good news, since we have also argued (in Section 2) that a syntactic, type-theoretic approach to perspectival content faces substantial difficulties when it comes to generalizing beyond the basic observations about predicates of personal taste under *find*. We conclude this discussion by asking whether the strategy we have proposed has something to offer for analyses of perspectival content other than Kennedy and Willer's (2016, forthcoming).

The key point is that the strategy we have pursued here—to offer a fine-grained conception of perspectival content using the tools and techniques provided by dynamic semantics—seems to be available to all non-syntactic accounts that are currently on the market, as nothing should prevent them in principle from appealing to update functions in articulating the subtle perspectival constraints that subjective attitude verbs impose on their complements (as we did in (28)). Indeed, the main challenge here is to articulate the key distinction between the kind of contingency that is required for a proposition to embed felicitously under *consider* and the one that licenses its embeddability under *find*. Once this is in place, any non-syntactic account may proceed as follows: first, lift this distinction so that it applies to issues, as in (26); then, adopt the update-based constraints for *find* and *consider* as spelt out in (27)–(30).

Let us begin with Coppock's (2018) proposal, which includes a set of possible worlds W and a set Ω of outlooks: $\propto$ is a one-to-one relation between elements of W and elements of a partition of Ω so that $O \propto w$ just in case each $o \in O$ is a refinement of w. Here, the obvious suggestion would be to distinguish between two kinds of refinements: "shallow" outlooks, let us say, are refinements of worlds; and then "deep" outlooks refine shallow ones. We may then say that given some contextually salient set of possible worlds, a proposition is shallowly discretionary just in case for each world in the set, the proposition is contingent across its outlooks; it is deeply discretionary just in case, for each such outlook, it is also contingent across that outlook's refinements.[16] So it looks as if an

Perspectival Content, Semantic Composition 225

outlook-based approach has the resources needed to draw a distinction between "shallow" (*consider*-licensing) and "deep" (*find*-licensing) perspectival content, in a way that is reminiscent of the distinction between plain and radical counterstance contingency.

Something similar is true when we consider the relativist paradigm. Here the perhaps most obvious path is to partition the space of judges. *Consider* requires simple judge sensitivity: keeping the world and time of evaluation constant, we can find some judge that makes the complement true and one that makes it false. And then we add the following requirement for *find*: in every partition we can, keeping the word and time of evaluation constant, identify some judge that makes the complement true and one that makes it false.[17]

Distinctions like the one we suggested for outlook-based semantics and relativism must be grounded in real distinctions that speakers draw in discourse. We have made a concrete proposal for what discursive practices could play this crucial role: belief formation involves acts of pragmatic enrichment beyond what is strictly licensed by the established facts on the ground, and some but not all pragmatic enrichments can be coordinated by stipulative discourse moves. Whether every contingency-centric account can adopt this grounding story is a question we cannot resolve here. For now, we conclude that a contingency-centric analysis (with a dynamic spin) is the way forward for a comprehensive understanding of what makes content perspectival and that the notion of counterstance contingency provides a fruitful conceptual framing for any such line of inquiry.[18]

Notes

1. The space of theoretical options in the controversy between relativists and contextualists is quite large (as Sæbø notes). In particular, contextualists need not assume that predicates of personal taste are context-sensitive in virtue of the presence of a syntactic argument whose value is fixed by context; relatedly, the value of such an argument may in principle be fixed along relativist lines, i.e., by the context of assessment rather than the context of production—see, e.g., Stephenson (2007), MacFarlane (2009), and Weatherson (2009) for discussion. The resulting complications need not detain us here: what matters for current purposes is the question of how the perspectival nature of certain natural-language expressions is grammatically encoded, not of how perspectives are fixed in discourse.
2. Other proposals in this spirit include the one from Bouchard (2012), who suggests that *find* carries a "subjective contingency presupposition": keeping all the non-subjective facts constant, it must be possible to judge the complement clause true, and it must be possible to judge it false (p. 10). Silk (2019), while avoiding reference to subjectivity or special kinds of content, also appeals to a contingency criterion when he suggests that "*find* is felicitous only if the use of the complement distinguishes among live representations of context, local or global" (p. 155). A different approach is taken by Stephenson (2007) and by Muñoz (2019), who tie acceptability under *find* to a requirement that its complement be sensitive to the subject's experiences in a particular way.

But insofar as such requirements project, these approaches are subject to the same criticisms Sæbø levels against relativist/contingency approaches that we outline in what follows.

3. If we assume that the subject DP undergoes Quantifier Raising in (5a) and (5b), then the judge argument of *pleasant* is still missing when the embedded clause meets the subjective attitude verb, as required, in (5a); but *unmarried* does not have such an argument slot to begin with, and hence (5b) is predicted to be marked.

4. Kennedy and Willer (2016) sketch a positive proposal that is also mentioned by Coppock (2018); our goal here is to substantially improve on this proposal in scope, empirical adequacy, and motivation.

5. Bylinina (2017) discusses similar contrasts between thematic and non-thematic "judges" in Russian. Predicates of personal taste like *interesnij* "interesting" can express the judge as a dative-marked noun phrase, but merely evaluative predicates like *krasivij* "beautiful" cannot:

> (i)   Mne interesen etot film.
>   me.dat interesting this film.
>   "This film is interesting to me."
>
> (ii) *Mne krasiv dom.
>   *me.dat beautiful house
>   "The house is beautiful to me" (*intended but unavailable reading*)

As in English, one must use a more periphrastic structure to convey this kind of meaning:

> (iii) Dlja menja/po-moemu krasiv dom.
>   For me.acc/in.my.opinion beautiful house
>   "The house is beautiful according to me/in my opinion."

6. (12b) and (13b) are fine if we can accommodate some discretion on behalf of the judge, e.g., if we are in a context in which the relevant theatrical practices do not settle whether understudies are cast members or not. For our purposes, it suffices to observe that as long as the cast of *Hamilton* is an objective affair, there is a clear contrast between (12a) and (12b) and between (13a) and (13b), respectively.

7. Here we depart (for reasons explained in Kennedy & Willer, forthcoming) from the proposal in Kennedy and Willer (2016), which works with a weaker counterstance contingency criterion: one of its counterstances is committed to p while another is not. Regardless of such matters of detail, we can note that if counterstance contingency is a presupposition, we fully expect there to be instances in which it fails to project due to a conflict with what is asserted or otherwise implied. For instance, a claim such as "Everyone considers the Burj Khalifa tall" may be read as suggesting that the truth of the opinion under consideration is not really up for debate; this reading cancels the presupposition triggered by the use of *consider*. (In contrast, the presupposition seems to project in "Everyone considers the Burj Khalifa tall, but it actually appears small once we reflect on what is technologically possible.") The claim that implicatures may cancel presuppositions is empirically well attested, though the former are not always given priority over the latter in case of a conflict. See Beaver (2010) and references therein for detailed discussion.

8. The farm classification (20a), in fact, has been developed by the USDA Economic Research Service for evaluation and reporting purposes. The United Nations, but not the African Union, counts Mauretania as sub-Saharan.

9. In Kennedy and Willer (forthcoming), the counterstance selection function is sensitive to an agent and a proposition, but such differences of detail need not

Perspectival Content, Semantic Composition 227

detain us here. We will omit writing subscripts as in "κ_c" and "Π_c" whenever this is harmless. Relatedly, "p" may stand for a sentence or the proposition it expresses; we let context disambiguate in most cases and explicitly distinguish between the sentence and $[[p]]^c$ whenever it does not.

10. In a bit <u>more</u> detail, suppose that $i \subseteq p \cap q$ and that $i' \subseteq \bar{p}$ for some $i' \in \kappa(i)$: then $i' \subseteq p \cap q$ and so the complement of (12b) is counterstance contingent with respect to Kim's beliefs whenever Lee being vegetarian is thus contingent and Kim believes the conjunction.

11. Some popular dynamic semantics: discourse representation theory (Kamp, 1981; Kamp & Reyle, 1993; Kamp et al., 2011), dynamic predicate logic (Groenendijk & Stokhof, 1991), file change semantics (Heim, 1982), update semantics (Veltman, 1985, 1996). There is a distinct sense in which our proposal will not be essentially dynamic, since updating will always amount to adding a proposition to the input state. What interests us here is how a system of update rules can capture the counterstance contingency of complex formulas. Crespo and Veltman (2019) also propose to use the tools and techniques provided by dynamic semantics to shed light on a number of issues surrounding predicates of personal taste, though their project is different from ours.

12. Heim's (1983) proposal is seminal (albeit not undisputed); the literature on the projection problem for presuppositions (the label goes back to Langendoen & Savin, 1971) is vast and cannot be efficiently reviewed here. Beaver (2001) offers a critical survey of the presupposition theory literature up to the turn of the twenty-first century; he also articulates a response to the projection problem for presuppositions in update semantics that will inform our upcoming proposal for counterstance contingency.

13. To see this, suppose that $[[\phi?]]^c$ fails to be, say, radically counterstance contingent with respect to i in c. Then $i[\phi]^c_r$ is not admitted and so $i[\phi]^c_r$ is undefined. Hence $i[\phi]^c_r = \bot$ and so $(i[\phi]^c_r)[\psi]^c_r = \bot$, and so $i[\phi \& \psi]^c_r$ is undefined. For parallel reasons, any radically perspectival update of i with $\ulcorner \phi \& \psi \urcorner$ is undefined in c. The fact that these results hold even if the proposition $[[\phi \& \psi]]^c$ is radically counterstance contingent is one respect in which the current framework improves upon the more basic proposal.

14. So here our proposal in fact exactly mirrors the basic proposal in Section 3. Note that a proposition is (radically) counterstance contingent just in case its negation is; hence if p is atomic, then $[[p]]^c$ is (radically) counterstance contingent just in case $[[p]]^c$ is. Since a perspectival update with p is admitted just in case $[[p?]]^c$ and hence $[[p]]^c$ are radically counterstance contingent, the two proposals make the same predictions when it comes to *find* and *consider* if the complement is atomic.

15. The crucial technical observation here is that $i[\phi]^c_f$ is admitted only if $[[\phi?]]^c$ is suitably contingent; otherwise, the question of whether ϕ is locally perspectival in the right way—has suitably perspectival disjuncts or suitably perspectival material in the scope of its quantifier, for instance—does not even come up.

16. One may wish to draw the distinction differently. Here is a proposal that immediately comes to mind: if some but not all worlds come with outlooks that render the proposition contingent, it is merely shallowly discretionary; if all worlds do, we have a deeply discretionary proposition. The proposal is technically straightforward, but it is not clear that it makes good sense for *consider*. Take Ludlow's case of the racehorse Secretariat: some consider Secretariat an athlete, while others do not. Is the question outlook-sensitive given some possible worlds but not others? It does not seem so. As Ludlow

(2014, p. 78) puts it: "[i]t is not as though the dispute would be resolved if Secretariat were a little bit faster or could throw a baseball."

17. While we have focused on outlook-based and relativist proposals, our account is, in principle, compatible with contextualist (Glanzberg, 2007; Zakkou, 2019) or even absolutist (see, e.g., Wyatt, 2018) frameworks. The key question is whether these proposals can leave room for perspectival content to be contingent in the way we have argued here, say, by appealing to an appropriate kind of context-sensitivity. We must leave a more detailed discussion of this question to another day.

18. Special thanks to Julia Zakkou for helpful comments on an earlier version of the manuscript.

References

Beaver, D. I. (2001). *Presupposition and assertion in dynamic semantics*. Stanford: CSLI Publications.

Beaver, D. I. (2010). Have you noticed that your belly button lint colour is related to the colour of your clothing? In R. Bäuerle, U. Reyle, & T. E. Zimmermann (Eds.), *Presuppositions and discourse: Essays offered to Hans Kamp* (pp. 65–99). Elsevier.

Bouchard, D.-E. (2012). *Long-distance degree quantification and the grammar of subjectivity* [PhD thesis]. McGill University, Montreal.

Bylinina, L. (2017). Judge-dependence in degree constructions. *Journal of Semantics*, *34*, 291–331.

Chierchia, G. (1992). Anaphora and dynamic binding. *Linguistics and Philosophy*, *15*, 111–183.

Chierchia, G. (1995). *Dynamics of meaning*. Chicago: University of Chicago Press.

Coppock, E. (2018). Outlook-based semantics. *Linguistics and Philosophy*, *41*, 125–164.

Crespo, I., & Veltman, F. (2019). Tasting and testing. *Linguistics and Philosophy*, *6*, 617–653.

Fleisher, N. (2013). The dynamics of subjectivity. In *Semantics and linguistic theory (SALT)* (Vol. 23, pp. 276–294). CLC.

Glanzberg, M. (2007). Context, content, and relativism. *Philosophical Studies*, *136*, 1–29.

Groenendijk, J., & Stokhof, M. (1984). *Studies on the semantics of questions and the pragmatics of answers* [PhD thesis]. University of Amsterdam, Amsterdam.

Groenendijk, J., & Stokhof, M. (1991). Dynamic predicate logic. *Linguistics and Philosophy*, *14*, 39–100.

Heim, I. (1982). *The semantics of definite and indefinite noun phrases* [PhD thesis]. University of Massachusetts, Amherst.

Heim, I. (1983). On the projection problem for presuppositions. In M. Barlow, D. Flickinger, & M. Westcoat (Eds.), *Proceedings of the second annual West Coast conference on formal linguistics* (pp. 114–126). CSLI Publications.

Hirvonen, S. (2014). *Predicates of personal taste and perspective dependence* [PhD thesis]. University College London, London.

Kamp, H. (1981). A theory of truth and representation. In J. Groenendijk, T. Janssen, & M. Stokhof (Eds.), *Formal methods in the study of language, part I* (pp. 277–320). Mathematisch Centrum.

Kamp, H., & Reyle, U. (1993). *From discourse to the logic: Introduction to modeltheoretic semantics of natural language, formal logic and discourse representation theory*. Kluwer Academic Press.

Kamp, H., van Genabith, J., & Reyle, U. (2011). Discourse representation theory. In D. M. Gabbay & F. Guenthner (Eds.), *Handbook of philosophical logic* (2nd ed., Vol. 15, pp. 125–394). Springer.

Kennedy, C. (2013). Two sources of subjectivity: Qualitative assessment and dimensional uncertainty. *Inquiry*, 56, 258–277.

Kennedy, C., & Willer, M. (2016). Subjective attitudes and counterstance contingency. In M. Moroney, C.-R. Little, J. Collard, & D. Burgdorf (Eds.), *Proceedings of SALT XXVI* (pp. 913–933). CLC Publications.

Kennedy, C., & Willer, M. (forthcoming). Familiarity inferences, subjective attitudes and counterstance contingency: Toward a pragmatic theory of subjective meaning. *Linguistics and Philosophy*.

Langendoen, D. T., & Savin, H. (1971). The projection problem for presuppositions. In C. Fillmore & D. T. Langendoen (Eds.), *Studies in linguistic semantics* (pp. 55–62). Holt, Rinehart and Winston.

Lasersohn, P. (2005). Context dependence, disagreement, and predicates of personal taste. *Linguistics and Philosophy*, 28, 643–686.

Ludlow, P. (2014). *Living words: Meaning underdetermination and the dynamic lexicon*. Oxford University Press.

MacFarlane, J. (2009). Nonindexical contextualism. *Synthese*, 166, 231–250.

Munõz, P. (2019). *On tongues: The grammar of experiential evaluation* [PhD thesis]. University of Chicago.

Reis, M. (2013). Dt. finden und "subjektive Bedeutung". *Linguistische Berichte*, 2013, 389–426.

Sæbø, K. J. (2009). Judgment ascriptions. *Linguistics and Philosophy*, 32, 327–352.

Silk, A. (2019). Evaluational adjectives. *Philosophy and Phenomenological Research*, 102, 127–161.

Stalnaker, R. C. (1978). Assertion. In P. Cole (Ed.), *Syntax and semantics* (Vol. 9, pp. 315–332). Academic Press.

Stephenson, T. (2007). *Towards a theory of subjective meaning* [PhD thesis]. MIT, Cambridge, MA.

Stephenson, T. (2008). Judge dependence, epistemic modals, and predicates of personal taste. *Linguistics and Philosophy*, 30, 487–525.

Stojanovic, I. (2007). Talking about taste: Disagreement, implicit arguments, and relative truth. *Linguistics and Philosophy*, 30, 691–706.

Umbach, C. (2016). Evaluative propositions and subjective judgments. In C. Meier & J. van Wijnbergen-Huitink (Eds.), *Subjective meaning: Alternatives to relativism* (pp. 127–168). De Gruyter.

Vardomskaya, T. (2018). *Sources of subjectivity* [PhD thesis]. University of Chicago.

Veltman, F. (1985). *Logics for conditionals* [PhD thesis]. University of Amsterdam.

Veltman, F. (1996). Defaults in update semantics. *Journal of Philosophical Logic*, 25, 221–261.

Weatherson, B. (2009). Conditionals and indexical relativism. *Synthese*, 166, 333–357.

Wyatt, J. (2018). Absolutely tasty: An examination of predicates of personal taste and faultless disagreement. *Inquiry*, *61*, 252–280.

Zakkou, J. (2019). *Faultless disagreement. A defense of contextualism in the realm of personal taste*. Klostermann.

11 Exploring Valence in Judgments of Taste

Isidora Stojanovic and Elsi Kaiser[1]

1. Introduction

In the literature on personal taste, it is often assumed that judgments of taste are evaluative; that is to say, that such judgments convey a positive or a negative assessment of the object under evaluation. The assumption is very prominent in the expressivist tradition, according to which to say/judge, for example, that the game of Monopoly is fun is analyzed in terms of recommending (approving, speaking in favor of) Monopoly, while to say that it is boring is analyzed in terms of rejecting (disapproving of, speaking against) it. Nevertheless, the evaluative character of predicates of personal taste (henceforth PPTs), in the sense of conveying something positive or negative, has received relatively little attention from a semantic point of view. This is somewhat surprising given that the notions of evaluativity and (positive and negative) valence have been central in psychology and certain fields of philosophy (value-theory and metaethics).

Our aim in this chapter is to fill out this lacuna. More precisely, we show that PPTs do not divide neatly into positively and negatively valenced terms. Instead, we argue that many PPTs, such as 'surprising', are *neutral*. That is to say, they are underspecified for their valence and, depending on the context, can give rise to a positive, a negative, or an ambivalent evaluation (and sometimes perhaps to no evaluation at all). Our primary aim in this paper is to investigate how such neutral PPTs differ from evaluative PPTs. We also investigate how they differ among themselves and how they differ from other terms (which we call *middling*) that are neither positive nor negative, such as 'average'.

We approach the topic of neutral PPTs using a two-pronged approach. On the one hand, we propose two novel linguistic tests that serve as diagnostics to distinguish the class of neutral PPTs from valenced PPTs. We use corpus examples to corroborate the tests. On the other, we use information from preexisting psychological norms of valence (Warriner et al., 2013) to further explore the class of adjectives that we hypothesize are neutral. This combination of linguistic tests, corpus examples, and large-scale data based on psychological norms opens up a novel research

DOI: 10.4324/9781003184225-15

perspective. What emerges is a rich and diverse class of neutral PPTs. We identify a set of subjective adjectives with features importantly different from the paradigmatic ones like 'fun' and 'boring' yet which have gone largely overlooked in the buoyant research on PPTs. We suggest that neutral PPTs come in at least three subtypes, which we call the *difficulty* class, the *excess* class, and the *surprise* class. We do not intend this to be an exhaustive classification. We also explore a fourth class, *middling* adjectives, whose status as PPTs is somewhat less clear.

We have purposefully cast a wide net in terms of the adjectives that we explore (and we do not claim that all of the adjectives that we discuss pattern uniformly in all respects), since one of our goals is to broaden the empirical basis of the kinds of adjectives that are discussed in relation to judgments of taste.

The chapter is structured as follows. Section 2 addresses the question of how to delineate PPTs in the first place. In a nutshell, PPTs are a subclass of a broader class of *subjective* terms, and those only partially overlap with *evaluative* terms. Three linguistic tests to distinguish PPTs commonly used in the literature are introduced and discussed. We also clarify what we mean by 'evaluative', in contrast to some other ways in which the term has been used in the literature. In Section 3, we present two new tests to identify *neutral* PPTs: (i) the Attitude Compatibility Test (AC Test), which probes the compatibility of attributing a PPT with both a positive and a negative attitude toward the object at stake, and (ii) the GOOD/BAD WAY test, which assesses the possibility of modifying the adjective with 'in a good/bad way'. We show that neutral PPTs pass these tests, in contrast to evaluative PPTs. In Section 4, we discuss data from psychological norms, which we propose can allow further insights into the class of neutral PPTs. Section 5 focuses on what we call *middling* adjectives, which we suggest need to be distinguished from the other neutral PPTs. Section 6 concludes.

2. What Are PPTs?

Our chapter focuses on predicates of personal taste that cannot be easily categorized as either positive or negative; that is to say, on neutral PPTs. But before we look more closely at such neutral PPTs, it will help to clarify what we take to be PPTs in the first place. Although the term has been firmly established in the literature, there is no consensus on how *predicates of personal taste* should be identified. Some authors see them as a very broad category that includes any kind of expression sensitive to a subjective point of view, including moral, epistemic, and gradable adjectives (Kölbel, 2002; Lasersohn, 2005; Sundell, 2011; Umbach, 2016, 2020, a.o.).[2] Other authors are more restrictive (Stephenson, 2007; Moltmann, 2010; Pearson, 2013; McNally & Stojanovic, 2017; Rudolph, 2020, a.o.). We belong among the latter. In this section, we present three linguistic criteria on which we rely to identify PPTs (2.1), and we clarify how we understand the relationship between PPTs, subjective, and evaluative predicates (2.2).

2.1. Three Tests for PPTs

In his seminal paper on PPTs, Lasersohn writes: "Exactly which predicates qualify as predicates of personal taste is an interesting question. (. . .) We will concentrate here on relatively mundane predicates such as *fun* and *tasty*, and leave open the status of more philosophically 'charged' predicates like *good* and *beautiful*. I do not offer here any firm diagnostic criteria for identifying predicates of personal taste, though I will return to this question briefly (. . .). Despite the absence of such criteria, I think the intuitive idea should be reasonably clear" (2005, pp. 644–645). And when he returns to the question after considering a possible criterion related to the modification by 'to/for' prepositional phrases and finding it problematic, Lasersohn concludes: "at present I see little reason to expect that subjective predicates may be identified by any straightforward linguistic test; it may be that the status of predicates must be argued for more on philosophical than linguistic grounds, on a case-by-case basis" (2005, pp. 682–683).

We are less optimistic than Lasersohn on the claim that "the intuitive idea should be reasonably clear" yet more optimistic than him on the prospects of using linguistic tests to distinguish PPTs. And while Lasersohn appears to use the terms 'PPT' and 'subjective predicates' interchangeably, we take the class of subjective predicates to be wider than that of PPTs.

To identify PPTs, we shall rely on the linguistic tests commonly used in the literature; see, e.g., Umbach, 2020 for a very recent overview.[3] Let us present the tests first and then briefly comment on their applicability.

(a) **The FIND Test:**

  PPTs embed felicitously under attitude verbs such as 'find', as illustrated by the following contrast:
  ✔ I find the game of Monopoly (to be) boring.
  # I find the game of Monopoly (to be) invented by an American.

(b) **The TO/FOR Test:**

  PPTs are felicitously modified by 'to-' and 'for-' phrases and dative-like constructions, as illustrated by the following contrast:[4]
  ✔ Monopoly is boring to me/to kids.
  #   Monopoly was invented by an American to me/to kids.

(c) **The Faultless Disagreement (FD) Test:**

  In contexts of disagreement, PPTs trigger the intuition that neither party need be wrong, as illustrated by the following contrast:

  (1a)
  Peter: "Monopoly is boring."
  Mary: "No, it isn't!"
  ✔ If Monopoly is boring to Peter but not to Mary, then neither of them speaks falsely.

234 *Isidora Stojanovic and Elsi Kaiser*

(1b)

Piotr: "Monopoly was invented by an American."

Maria: "No, it wasn't."

✖ If Piotr thinks that Monopoly was invented by an American and Maria thinks that it wasn't, then neither of them speaks falsely.[5]

All three tests are problematic. The FIND Test may be traced back to Sæbø (2009), who uses it not only to delineate PPTs but also to argue that they are sensitive to an experiencer argument. The test is further elaborated in Bylinina (2014). McNally and Stojanovic (2017) additionally use the FIND test to delineate PPTs from expressions that are evaluative but experiencer-insensitive, specifically certain aesthetic adjectives, while Stojanovic (2019) uses it to distinguish PPTs from moral adjectives. However, there is considerable disagreement on whether the verb 'find' selects for experiencer-sensitive adjectives rather than a broader class of subjective adjectives; for discussion, see, e.g., Coppock (2018), Kennedy and Willer (2016), Franzén (2018), Stojanovic (to appear), Willer (to appear). What is more, there is considerable cross-linguistic variation between the English 'find' and its equivalents (when there are such) in other languages, such as *'finden'* in German (see Umbach, 2017) or *'tycka'* in Swedish (see Coppock, 2018). In sum, then, paradigmatic PPTs are clearly felicitous under 'find', while factual expressions are clearly infelicitous, but there also appears to be a wide range of expressions whose behavior in these constructions is less well understood.

The problems with the TO/FOR Test stem from the highly polysemous character of these prepositions. With PPTs such as 'boring' and 'tasty', the preposition introduces an experiencer argument. But the same prepositions are also used to articulate other kinds of arguments, in particular *beneficiary* arguments: for example, 'Milk is good for kids' does not mean that kids are experiencing milk as good but rather that they are benefiting from it. Furthermore, especially when used at the beginning of a sentence, 'to-' and 'for-' constructions can be used to mean that the sentence reports someone's views or opinion, as in: 'To a kid who grew up as an altar boy, having the pope here was a big deal' (example found in COCA; Davies, 2008). (See also Stephenson, 2007, who notes that the choice of the preposition that introduces the experiencer appears to be idiosyncratic.) Hence, while it remains true that an expression that cannot be felicitously modified by a 'to' or a 'for' phrase is not a PPT, the fact that an expression can be so modified is not yet sufficient to make it qualify as a PPT.

When it comes to the Faultless Disagreement Test, several worries arise. First, people may have diverging intuitions on how faultless a given disagreement may be. Even in such simple cases like (1a), some people might insist that either Peter or Mary is right. This tends to happen even more when people are biased, in the sense that they have an opinion of their own as to whether Monopoly is boring or not. Additionally, further

Exploring Valence in Judgments of Taste 235

information on the context in which a dialogue like (1a) takes place can pull one's intuitions of faultlessness in one direction or another (see Stojanovic, 2007). Second, faultlessness appears to be a matter of degree. Thus Goodwin and Darley (2008) conducted a study in which they wanted to see whether disagreements over moral issues are perceived as subjective and compared them to disagreements over factual issues, disagreements over matters of taste, and disagreements over social conventions. What they found was that moral disagreements are perceived as significantly more subjective than both factual disagreements and disagreements over social conventions but, at the same time, significantly less subjective than disagreements over taste. In other words, the FD Test appears to require a yes–no answer, while there are disagreements for which participants prefer a graded answer: *faultless to a certain degree*. Results that go in the same direction have been presented in Solt (2016) and Soria Ruiz and Faroldi (2020). Thirdly, faultless disagreement can often result from a disagreement on how to understand certain terms and concepts; that is, a metalinguistic disagreement (see Barker, 2002; Sundell, 2011; Stojanovic, 2012). Fourthly, Kaiser and Rudin (2020, 2021) and Rudin and Kaiser (2021) present experimental data showing that the empirical profile of FD is more complex than often acknowledged and that people's judgments of FD are influenced by factors that go beyond the subjective predicate itself—including the object of predication, properties of the interlocutors, and even the judge's own attitudes. As a whole, these observations imply that the FD Test is too broad to track any specific lexical class, hence it is crucial to use it in combination with other diagnostics.[6]

Finally, a challenge that arises not just for these three tests but for the test methodology in general, including the two new tests that we present in Section 3, is that they rely on felicity judgments regarding sentences that are presented out of context. What one ordinarily does in such a case, presumably, is to generate some kind of default context. Thus, if an expression tends to sound felicitous in such a default context, it passes the test, and if it tends not to, it fails the test. We acknowledge that this leaves room for expressions for which, with enough creativity, one *could* come up with a particular context in which it may sound felicitous. However, in the discussion that follows, we focus on whether expressions sound felicitous without such special 'contextual contortions'. In other words, we do not focus on the possibility of coming up with a special context in which an expression seems to pass the test, even when it normally does not. Such a context is not sufficient to make the expression pass the test. What is relevant for us is that the corresponding felicity judgments should not rely on any special contextual features and that the expression passes the test consistently and systematically, even when presented out of context.

Despite these challenges, the linguistic tests still constitute an efficient methodology for investigating the typology of adjectives. Even if one can potentially come up with a context in which some expression that one would not want to include among PPTs appears to pass the tests, genuine PPTs pass the tests systematically. This is partly reflected in the frequency with which PPTs, as opposed to other adjectives, occur embedded under 'find' or modified by 'to-' or 'for-' phrases. Let us illustrate the point with the FIND Test. Consider the moral term 'wrong', as in 'I find lying wrong'. The combination does not sound infelicitous—at least, not to the same degree as it does with terms such as 'invented'. Nevertheless, this does not put the expression 'wrong' on a par with PPTs, for two reasons. First, even if such uses are possible, they are arguably statistically marginal. Some evidence to this effect is given in McNally and Stojanovic (2017), who report corpus data regarding the verb 'find' that show that most occurrences involve experiencer-sensitive adjectives such as 'difficult'. Second, as argued in Stojanovic (2019), even if the adjective itself is not sensitive to an experiencer argument, as in the case of 'wrong', embedding it under 'find' can coerce the whole embedded construction into one that is sensitive to an experiencer. In other words, 'I find lying wrong' would be tantamount to saying that the speaker's judgment that lying is wrong is based on their personal experience. In sum, although some non-PPT adjectives can sometimes pass some of the three linguistic tests, PPTs pass them more consistently and reliably.

What is more, the performance of these tests may be enhanced by applying them not only to the positive form of a predicate but also to the comparative form (see, i.a., Bylinina, 2014; Umbach, 2020). This will set apart adjectives such as 'expensive' from genuine PPTs:

(2a) ✔ I find Monopoly expensive.
(2b) ✔ I find Monopoly boring.
(2c) ?? I find Monopoly (to be) more expensive than Catan.
(2d) ✔ I find Monopoly (to be) more boring than Catan.

(3a) ✔ Monopoly is expensive for me.
(3b) ✔ Monopoly is boring to me.
(3c) ?? Monopoly is more expensive than Catan for me.
(3d) ✔ Monopoly is more boring than Catan to me.

(4a) Peter: "Monopoly is more expensive than Catan."
      Mary: "No, it isn't. Catan is more expensive."

(4b) Piotr: "Monopoly is more boring than Catan."
      Maria: "No, it isn't. Catan is more boring."

While the disagreement between Piotr and Maria (4b) appears to be faultless, Peter and Mary's (4a) clearly isn't.

2.2. PPTs, Subjectivity, and Evaluativity

Let us take stock. We have presented three tests that we take to jointly identify the class of PPTs, and at the same time, we have acknowledged that there are other adjectives that sometimes pass some of these tests, although less consistently and reliably than PPTs. Some adjectives, such as 'expensive', pass the three tests but only when used in the positive form, which sets them apart from PPTs. Other adjectives pass the FIND test—at least to a certain extent—and the FD test, both in the positive and in the comparative form, but fail the TO/FOR test. And, in fact, certain authors consider the FD test and, especially, the FIND test, as crucial (see, e.g., Franzén, 2020; Silk, 2021; Willer (to appear)).

Given this adjectival diversity, it is natural to wonder whether there is a broader class that consists of expressions that are not PPTs but have important features in common with them. We propose, indeed, that PPTs are a subtype of a broader category of *subjective* terms. We can potentially identify several other subtypes:

- *moral* and *deontic* terms, such as 'wrong', '(un)ethical', 'cruel', 'generous', 'important', and 'valuable' (see, e.g., Portner & Rubinstein, 2016; Stojanovic, 2019; Soria Ruiz & Faroldi, 2020)
- *epistemic terms*, such as 'likely', 'possible', 'credible', as well as epistemic modals (e.g., Kaiser, 2015; Umbach, 2020)
- *aesthetic* adjectives, such as 'beautiful', 'ugly', 'elegant', and 'garish' (e.g., McNally & Stojanovic, 2017)
- *psychological* adjectives, such as 'painful' (e.g., Korotkova, 2016) and *emotional* adjectives, such as 'sad' (e.g., Stojanovic, 2012)

We do not claim that this typology carves up the space neatly. To the contrary, we expect there to be substantive overlap among these subtypes. For example, 'surprising', which will be one of our core examples of PPTs discussed in later sections, can have an *epistemic* sense. Similarly, many PPTs and psychological predicates are often used to express *aesthetic* and *moral* properties: 'disturbing', 'disgusting', 'inspiring', and so on. Finally, given that PPTs are by their very nature closely tied to experience, the boundary between PPTs and psychological adjectives is bound to be blurry; for instance, 'pleasant' and its antonym, 'unpleasant', are often seen as paradigmatic examples of both PPTs and psychological adjectives. And again, 'surprising' is both a PPT and an *emotional* adjective, expressing the emotion of surprise.

Assuming that it makes sense to talk of such a broader phenomenon of subjectivity, the next question is how it relates to *evaluativity*. In other words, which subjective expressions are evaluative, and are there evaluative expressions that are not subjective? The answer depends, at least partly, on the choice of terminology. In fact, some of the literature uses the term 'evaluative' as an umbrella term for the broader category of expressions for which we are using here 'subjective' (e.g., Franzén, 2020; Umbach, 2021; Silk, 2021).[7] Let us, then, try to briefly explain how we understand evaluativity (for a more extended discussion, see Stojanovic (to appear)).

Pekka Väyrynen has proposed that "evaluation might (. . .) be understood as information to the effect that something has a positive or negative standing—merit or demerit, worth or unworth—relative to a certain kind of standard" (Väyrynen, 2013, p. 29).[8] This characterization of evaluativity brings together two important ideas: on the one hand, the idea of *valence*—positive versus negative—, and on the other, that of relativity to a standard. While standard-relativity is certainly central to the way in which, for instance, Bierwisch (1989) and Silk (2021) approach evaluative (or evaluational) adjectives, it is an aspect to which we will pay little attention here. Rather, we shall focus on the idea that 'evaluative' expressions are intimately tied to the notion of expressing something *positive* or *negative* about their subject. Now, it takes little to observe that pretty much any expression can be used, in a suitable context, to express something positive or negative. If Piotr tells Maria 'it is raining' in a context in which they are planning to go to the beach, his utterance will convey negative information, but if he announces it after a long heatwave in reply to Mary's worry that the plants may not survive, then it will convey positive information. We acknowledge that ordinary expressions can be used to convey evaluation, but we propose to call *evaluative* only those expressions that achieve this at least partly in virtue of their meaning. To drive the point home, then, a term is evaluative if it expresses, in virtue of its meaning, information to the effect that something has a positive or negative standing (relative to a certain kind of standard).

With this clarification in place, let us return to our question: are subjective terms, and PPTs in particular, evaluative? Many of them appear to be. To say that something is delicious, yummy, or fun is to express something positive about it; to say that it is disgusting, yucky, or boring is to express something negative. The idea that PPTs are, in general, evaluative is reflected in the way in which disagreements over taste are most often introduced. The idea of faultless disagreement is typically presented as a disagreement between speakers with clashing conative attitudes. In saying that Monopoly is boring, Peter expresses his dislike of Monopoly; in contradicting Peter by saying that it is fun, Mary expresses her positive appreciation of the game.[9] While many PPTs are evaluative, and while the ones typically discussed in the literature (*tasty, fun, boring*) are, we believe that there are also many PPTs that are not evaluative in this sense. However, deciding which ones are and which ones are not is far from trivial. The main goal of our chapter is, indeed, to delineate the class of neutral PPTs by using two distinct yet complementary routes: the linguistic test methodology (Section 3) and psychological norms of valence (Section 4).

3. Introducing Neutral PPTs

The topic of our inquiry is PPTs that are neither clearly positive nor negative, but that, depending on the context, can be used to express something positive or negative (as the case may be). Examples of such 'neutral' PPTs include adjectives such as *surprising, strange, intense, excessive*, as well as pairs of antonyms such as *simple/complex* and *easy/difficult*. What distinguishes neutral PPTs from evaluative PPTs? Our answer will be twofold. In this section, we put forward two novel linguistic tests that show that neutral and evaluative PPTs pattern differently in certain configurations; and in the next, we show that neutral and evaluative PPTs tend to score differently with respect to the valence ratings provided by psychological norms. By putting those two approaches together, we hope to set a precedent in the research on PPTs.

3.1. Two Linguistic Tests to Identify Neutral PPTs

In line with the methodology adopted in Section 2, we propose two tests that function as diagnostics to make a distinction that has been neglected in prior work—namely the distinction between evaluative and neutral PPTs. (The tests should be applicable to other adjectives as well, but we will confine our attention to PPTs.)

The Attitude Compatibility (AC) Test

A sentence that ascribes a neutral PPT to something in conjunction with a positive or a negative attitude toward it sounds felicitous; by contrast, a sentence that ascribes an evaluative PPT to something in conjunction with a mismatching attitude toward it tends to sound infelicitous.

(5a) ?? This game is fun and I don't like it.
(5b) ?? This game is boring and I like it.
(5c) ✔ This game is surprising and I (don't) like it.
(5d) ✔ This game is intense and I (don't) like it.

The GOOD/BAD WAY Test

Neutral PPTs sound felicitous when modified with the phrases 'in a good way' and 'in a bad way'; in contrast, evaluative PPTs tend to sound infelicitous in this configuration, as illustrated by the following examples:

(6a) ?? This game is fun in a good way.
(6b) ?? This game is fun in a bad way.
(6c) ?? This game is boring in a good way.
(6d) ?? This game is boring in a bad way.

240   *Isidora Stojanovic and Elsi Kaiser*

(6e)   ✔ This game is surprising in a good way.
(6f)   ✔ This game is surprising in a bad way.
(6g)   ✔ This game is intense in a good/bad way.

Like the tests proposed to identify PPTs, these tests that we propose to distinguish between evaluative and neutral PPTs are not without problems, so let us try to forestall some of the possible worries.

As previously noted, judging sentences for felicity out of context may seem problematic. Recall, however, that the tests do not mean that for a neutral predicate, the sentence is felicitous in any context whatsoever, while for an evaluative predicate, there is no context in which it is felicitous. Such an interpretation is too strong in both directions. In particular, with enough creativity, one can always come up with a context in which even predicates such as 'fun' and 'boring' may be felicitously modified with phrases 'in a good/bad way' and asserted in conjunction with an attitude of mismatching valence. Rather, the idea is that for a neutral predicate, contexts in which such sentences are felicitous come straightforwardly and naturally, but not so for evaluative predicates.

Let us look more closely at each test. For the AC Test, we have opted for a formulation with the verb 'like'.[10] The advantage of this choice is that 'liking' is a very natural way of expressing one's positive assessment of objects of taste; and indeed, this is how most of the literature on disagreement about taste does it. But there is a disadvantage, too. Note that one positive feature is not enough to make the overall assessment of an object positive and warrant that one shall like it. Similarly, one negative feature is not enough to warrant that one shall not like it either. What is more, a person may still like something that they recognize as deserving a negative assessment and, vice versa, dislike something that they recognize as positive.

Because of this subtle relationship between valence and likeability, we should expect that even in the case of evaluative PPTs, one can consistently apply a positive adjective to an object while denying that one likes the object or apply a negative adjective while affirming that one actually likes it. Nevertheless, in such cases, the speaker will indicate that there is an evaluative mismatch, for instance, by using the contrastive connective 'but' instead of 'and'. Here are two corpus-drawn examples. (In the corpus examples, the relevant adjective is underlined for ease of exposition.)

(7a)   My girlfriend is <u>boring</u>, but I truly do love her.[11]
(7b)   Jefferson is <u>fun</u>, but I don't like him.[12]

With neutral PPTs, we submit that no such contrastive particle is needed. In the next section, we will provide examples for half a dozen neutral PPTs.

Exploring Valence in Judgments of Taste 241

Turning to the GOOD/BAD WAY Test, our claim, once again, is a relative one: We claim that neutral PPTs can occur with 'in a good/bad way' more easily and naturally than evaluative PPTs. We do *not* claim that evaluative PPTs can never be modified with such phrases. Indeed, here are two corpus examples with the negative PPT 'boring' used with 'in a good/bad way':

(8a)   Ted was an accountant, and he acted like I expected an accountant to act, which doesn't mean that he was <u>boring</u>, but . . . Well, let's just say that he was more *adult* than any of my other friends. More *mature*. More . . . well, yes, *boring*, but *boring* in a good way. (The Night We Met, Rob Byrnes, p. 2; author's italics.)

(8b)   Not really exciting, <u>boring</u> in a bad way (yes, <u>boring</u> can sometimes be a good thing). Same effect, same location during the whole film.[13]

In the first example, we see that the author truly needs to build up a context in which 'boring in a good way' makes sense. In the second, the author is aware that 'boring in a bad way' sounds odd, since to say about something bad that it is so 'in a bad way' is redundant. This is why they explicitly deny the redundancy implicated by the adjective's meaning by adding that 'boring can sometimes be a good thing'. These examples thus fit with our claim that while neutral PPTs can easily occur with 'in a good/ bad way' (as discussed more in what follows), evaluative PPTs can only occur with these phrases when extra contextual support and explanation is provided.

Another potential worry with this test is that 'in a good/bad way' can be used to cancel an implicature, as the following corpus-drawn examples illustrate:

(9)   The meal was excellent (tapas plate and paella), the service was great, the wine was <u>cheap</u> (in a good way!), but forget all of that: try the dessert![14]

(10)   *Nisemonogatari* has proven itself to be a truly gripping and overly <u>satisfying</u> (in a good way) anime.[15]

To say of a wine that it is cheap invites the inference that it is not good; by adding 'in a good way', in parentheses and with an exclamation mark, the speaker of (9) successfully blocks this inference. Thus predicates that are not even PPTs, such as 'cheap/expensive', can felicitously combine with the phrase 'in a good/bad way' when it is used in this way. What is more, even evaluative predicates can do so, as (10) illustrates. To say of an object or an experience that it is 'satisfying' will often implicate that it is not particularly good—the implicature at stake can be seen as a *scalar* implicature: by placing an object at the level of 'satisfying', the speaker implicates that it

242 Isidora Stojanovic and Elsi Kaiser

does not reach any stronger level (such as 'good', 'very good', 'excellent', or 'outstanding'). Fortunately, implicature-cancelling uses of the phrase are often easy to detect: in writing, by typography (parentheses, exclamation marks, preceded by three dots or a hyphen), in speech, by prosody, and in general, when they are preceded by contrastive connectives such as 'but'.[16] Neutral PPTs, on the other hand, occur with the phrase 'in a good/bad way' *without* any kind of implicature-cancelling meaning. Thus, when applying the GOOD/BAD WAY Test as a diagnostic for neutral PPTs, we need to be careful to exclude implicature-cancelling uses.

Despite these and other worries,[17] we maintain that the GOOD/BAD WAY Test provides an efficient tool to categorize neutral PPTs. Once again, though, one needs to keep in mind that for an expression to pass the test, it is not enough to simply come up with a context in which it sounds good. Rather, what characterizes neutral PPTs is that they can be very easily and naturally modified by 'in a good/bad way.'

3.2. What Is in the Class of Neutral PPTs? Data From Linguistic Tests and Corpora

Now that the linguistic tests are in place, let us look at the PPTs themselves that, we think, qualify as neutral. Let us stress at the outset that the set of neutral adjectives considered here is not exhaustive. Rather, we will focus on some paradigmatic adjectives. What is more, we do not claim that the divide between neutral and evaluative PPTs is sharp. There may well be borderline cases; that is, adjectives for which it may be debated whether they are more like the (clearly) evaluative or the (clearly) neutral ones. The flexibility in deciding what to classify as evaluative rather than neutral follows from the nature of the tests and norms that we use in classification, and we take this to be a strength of our approach.[18]

We have grouped the neutral PPTs into three subclasses, as follows:

The difficulty class:

> basic, complex, complicated, easy, difficult, formidable, intricate, obvious, simple, sophisticated, straightforward, uncomplicated

The excess class:

> excessive, extraordinary, extravagant, flashy, grandiose, intense, lavish, ostentatious, provocative, remarkable

The surprise class:

> amazing, astonishing, bizarre, interesting, intriguing, odd, peculiar, strange, surprising, unexpected, unusual, weird

Exploring Valence in Judgments of Taste 243

We take this three-way classification to be rather intuitive, but nothing important hinges on it. We do not take these adjectives or subclasses to exhaust the class of neutral adjectives.[19] In fact, in Section 5, we will introduce and discuss yet another subclass: what we call *middling* adjectives. In the rest of this section, we describe each subclass, and in the next section, we apply the two new tests—the Attitude Compatibility Test and the GOOD/BAD WAY test—to some representative members of each class to show how the tests can be used to diagnose these adjectives as neutral.

In the **difficulty class**, we find PPTs related to the perceived difficulty or complexity of things. In the antonym pairs, such as difficult/easy and complex/simple, the first member often seems less positive than the second. Nevertheless, the reason we consider these adjectives to be neutral rather than evaluative is that their valence is highly context dependent: if we are talking, say, of one's personal situation, then difficult and complex are worse than easy and simple; but if we are talking about games and puzzles, then it is usually the other way round.[20]

In the **excess class**, as its name suggests, we find adjectives related to excess—or, to the extent that they are PPTs, to *perceived* excess and, more generally, deviation from a standard. Some deviations are good, some are bad. This intuitively explains why the adjectives in this class can be used with both a positive and a negative valence.[21]

In the **surprise class**, as the name suggests, we find adjectives that report surprise and other experiences of its ilk. Such experiences can be positive or negative. It is no coincidence that in the literature on emotions, surprise is a controversial topic. While all the other basic emotions are either clearly positive (e.g., happiness) or negative (e.g., fear, sadness, anger), surprise can be both.

In the remainder of this section, we will run a selection of these PPTs through the two tests from the previous section. More precisely, we will provide naturally occurring examples from corpora. In Section 4, we will return to these adjectives, and provide further evidence showing that they are importantly different from evaluative PPTs.

3.3.1. The Context Sensitive Class: Difficult and Easy

Our first example shows that 'difficult', despite having a *prima facie* negative connotation, patterns well in positive evaluation both with the AC Test (ex.11a) and with the GOOD/BAD WAY Test (ex.11b).:

(11a) The workshop was fun, challenging and <u>difficult</u> in a good way. We loved it.[22]

244   Isidora Stojanovic and Elsi Kaiser

There are thousands of similar corpus examples, most often related to games. But even with respect to games, difficult can be bad, as the following example illustrates:

(11b)   If you don't make it easy to get a reasonable selection of tiles out for the players to choose from, it becomes frustratingly dif-ficult (in a bad way) to build your ship.[23]

To complete the picture, here is 'difficult' passing the AC Test in the other direction (ex.11c), as well as examples displaying 'easy' with both tests (ex.12a,b,c).

(11c)   Mistakes happen. We f*ck up. It's not the end of the world. But it is difficult, and I don't like it.[24]
(12a)   It was very easy, in a good way.[25]
(12b)   Fun read, it was easy and I like it a lot![26]
(12c)   It was easy, agreed. But (. . .) I don't see the problem in giving our younger members something to look at, without putting them down by the 'it's easy, i don't like it' phrase I seem to hear so often.[27]

3.3.2.   The Excess Class: Excessive and Intense

'Excessive' with the AC Test:

(13a)   Her pout is excessive and I like it.[28]
(13b)   It's excessive and I hate it.[29]

'Excessive' with the GOOD/BAD WAY Test:

(13c)   The gastropub, widely known for their excessive (in a good way) beer list and perhaps not as widely known top notch service, opened its doors to bar goers on Friday, December 16th.[30]
(13d)   The games feel excessive in a bad way now. Over- or underde-signed, the dialogue is definitely not as great anymore . . .[31]

'Intense' with the AC Test:

(14a)   The Maddening is pretty intense and I like it.[32]
(14b)   His stare was intense and I didn't like it.[33]

'Intense' with the GOOD/BAD WAY Test:

(14c)   He was very bright, intense in a good way.[34]
(14d)   Being away from Diana at one part of the book hurt him so bad and made him super moody and blood-rushy—it was intense in a bad way.[37]

Exploring Valence in Judgments of Taste 245

3.3.3. The Surprise Class: Strange and Surprising

'Strange' with the AC Test:

(15a) Religious Overdose, from Northampton, were the first band to send me a tape. It was <u>strange</u> and I liked it.[36]
(15b) The way this book is written is very <u>strange</u> and I don't like it.[37]

'Strange' with the GOOD/BAD WAY Test:

(15c) Everything about this week's episode of *WWE SmackDown* was strange. The good parts were <u>strange</u> in a good way and the bad parts were <u>strange</u> in a bad way, in my opinion at least.[38]
(15d) Because you are <u>strange</u> in a good way, there is always room in this world for you.[39]

'Surprising' with the AC Test:

(16a) This book is interesting and a bit <u>surprising</u> and I like it![40]
(16b) The result is <u>surprising</u>: I don't like it.[41]

Turning to the GOOD/BAD WAY Test, the expressions 'surprising in a good way' and 'surprising in a bad way', as well as the related past participle forms, 'surpris*ed* in a good/bad way', abound on websites and platforms that provide reviews. Only on TripAdvisor, we find (at least) five reviews whose title is 'surprising in a good way', several more with 'bad', and many more occurrences of both phrases in the reviews themselves.

4. Neutral Predicates: Data From Psychological Norms

There is a long tradition of research in cognitive psychology regarding effects of valence on various aspects of human cognition and information processing, including attention and memory (e.g., Pratto & John, 1991; Ortony et al., 1983; Unkelbach et al., 2008; Alves et al., 2015). Thanks to the decades-long research interest in valence, there exist large-scale datasets (norms) that report people's valence judgments for large sets of words in different languages. In this section, we make use of one of the most recent and largest norms, collected by Warriner et al. (2013) for 13,915 English words, to explore the *valence ratings* given to the adjectives that we posit are neutral PPTs. Warriner et al. asked native English speakers to rate words on a nine-point scale ranging from *unhappy* (1) to *happy* (9)—thus, the higher the number, the more positively valenced the word.[42] Thus, the scale reflects the "valence (or pleasantness) of the emotions invoked by a word" (Warriner et al., 2013, p. 1192). This is, intuitively, a broad and emotion-based scale, in the sense that multiple factors/dimensions can contribute to whether something makes a person feel happy or unhappy. We view this as

246   *Isidora Stojanovic and Elsi Kaiser*

an advantage given that we are interested in the broad concept of valence. Indeed, the Attitude Compatibility Test and the GOOD/BAD WAY Test are also broad—in other words, they do not target a particular dimension (e.g., worth or unworth) but instead aim to tap into a broader notion of valence.[43]

The valence ratings are the main focus of this section, but we also report the *arousal ratings* for each of the neutral PPTs that we discuss in this chapter. Arousal is defined as "the intensity of emotion provoked by a stimulus" (Warriner et al., 2013, p. 1191). In addition to valence ratings, Warriner et al. also asked native English speakers to rate words on a nine-point scale ranging from *calm* (1) to *excited* (9) for arousal. (They also investigated a third dimension, which they term 'dominance', which is not relevant to the present discussion.)

To provide a sense of the ratings, here are some examples of valence and arousal ratings for some *nonneutral* PPTs: *tasty* valence 6.89, arousal 5.28; *fun* valence 8.37, arousal 6.32; *boring* valence 2.71, arousal 2.85; *frightening* valence 2.58, arousal 4.73.

It is worth pointing out that a word can have a high positive valence rating while also having a low arousal rating (e.g., *calm* is rated 6.89 out of 9 for valence and 1.67 out of 9 for arousal). Thus, a low arousal rating does not mean that a word does not elicit a valenced response; arousal simply reflects the emotional intensity of the response.

One of the reasons for investigating arousal ratings will become clear in Section 5: Arousal ratings play a key role in our comparison of neutral PPTs to what we call *middling* adjectives. We suggest that among the adjectives that are neither (clearly) positive nor negative, there is a difference between (i) what we call *neutral* PPTs, which we suggest are underspecified for their valence but can, depending on the context, be interpreted as expressing a clearly positive or a clearly negative evaluation and (ii) what we call *middling* adjectives, whose function is to place an object toward the middle of the scale (e.g., *average, mediocre*). In our view, therefore, middling adjectives are, crucially, not underspecified for valence. As we will show in Section 5, this distinction is reflected by the fact that middling adjectives score low(er) on 'arousal', which we think is because such adjectives typically, unlike the other neutral PPTs, do not convey a strong emotional response. We postpone a more detailed discussion of this class of middling adjectives and its relation to neutral PPTs until Section 5.

In addition to differentiating neutral PPTs and middling adjectives, arousal ratings provide another window into the semantics of the adjectives under discussion and, as we will see in the following sections, reveal some asymmetries between the three subtypes of neutral adjectives that we consider in this chapter.

4.1. *A Closer Look at Each Class*

Figures 11.1, 11.2, and 11.3 show the valence and arousal ratings for neutral PPTs that we suggest are in (i) the difficulty class, (ii) the excess

Exploring Valence in Judgments of Taste 247

class, and (iii) the surprise class, respectively. The adjectives are ordered on the x-axis with valence increasing from left to right. As we mentioned earlier, the adjectives that we suggest for each class are *not* intended to be an exhaustive list.

Recall that the higher the valence rating, the more positive the adjective was rated; the higher the arousal rating, the more intense the emotion elicited by the adjective. Because the scale goes from 1 to 9, the midpoint is 5.

The 12 adjectives that we grouped into the **difficulty class** (Figure 11.1) have an average valence rating of 5.56 out of 9 (range 3.78–7.47) and an average arousal rating of 4.09 out of 9 (range 2.71–5.75). Of the three classes, this is the only one that contains antonyms, such as *difficult/easy*, *complex/simple*, *complicated/uncomplicated*. Indeed, when we look at the valence ratings, it is clear that the highest (*easy, simple, uncomplicated*) and lowest (*difficult, complicated, complex*) valence ratings come from opposing members of these antonym pairs.

However, we note that even if these words may appear to be lexically valenced, their valence ratings are still near 5, the midpoint of the scale (see also Section 4.2). Thus, in our view, they still deserve to be considered as neutral PPTs given how they fare in terms of the Attitude Compatibility test and the GOOD/BAD WAY tests (see Sections 3.2 and 3.3).

The 10 adjectives that we grouped into the **excess class** (Figure 11.2) have an average valence rating of 5.84 out of 9 (range 4.37–7.45) and an average arousal rating of 5.07 out of 9 (range 3.73–6.6). The 12 adjectives that we grouped into the **surprise class** (Figure 11.3) have an average valence rating of 5.69 out of 9 (range 4.41–7.72) and an average arousal rating of 4.86 out of 9 (range 3.5–6.05). Thus, broadly speaking, all three

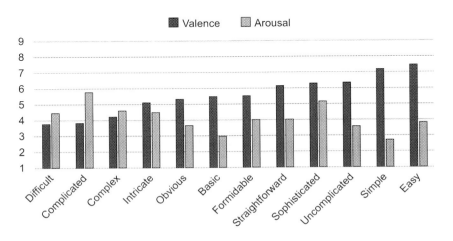

Figure 11.1 Difficulty class (Average valence: 5.56, average arousal: 4.09. Range for valence: 3.78–7.47, range for arousal: 2.71–5.75).

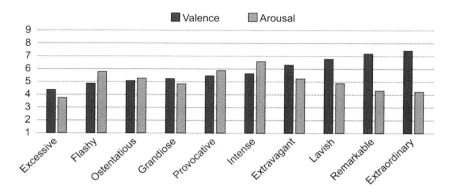

Figure 11.2 Excess class (Average valence: 5.84, average arousal: 5.07. Range for valence: 4.37–7.45, range for arousal: 3.73–6.6).

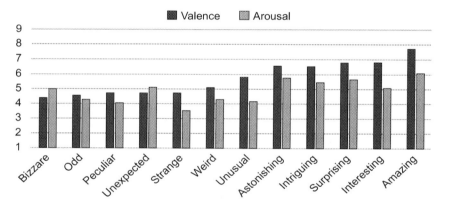

Figure 11.3 Surprise class (Average valence: 5.69, average arousal: 4.86. Range for valence: 4.41–7.72, range for arousal: 3.5–6.05).

classes have average valence and average arousal scores near the midpoint of the scale—in line with our characterization of them as *neutral* adjectives.

In all three classes, the average valence ratings are numerically higher than the average arousal ratings. Paired *t*-tests show that this difference is significant in the context-sensitive class and the surprise class but not in the excess class (Difficulty class: $t(11) = 2.576, p < 0.02$; Surprise class: $t(11) = 3.772, p < 0.01$; Excess class: $t(9) = 1.609, p = 0.142$). The lack of a clear valence-arousal difference in the excess class indicates that adjectives in this class tend to have more comparable levels of valence and arousal than those in the other two subclasses, which may be related to the emotional intensity (arousal) associated with exceeding a standard.

4.2. Comparing the Three Classes to Each Other

When we compare the *valence ratings* between the three classes of neutral adjectives, there are no statistically significant differences. In other words, the difficulty class, the excess class, and the surprise class have comparable valence ratings. This shows that there are no significant differences in the level of 'neutrality' of the three subclasses of neutral PPTs that we have been discussing.

In our view, this supports our classification of all three groupings as subclasses under the broader umbrella of neutral adjectives.

Once we turn to the arousal ratings, we find that arousal ratings for the difficulty class are significantly lower than the other two classes (unpaired t-tests: Difficulty vs. Excess: $t(20) = 2.652$, $p < 0.02$; Difficulty vs. Surprise $t(22) = 2.272$, $p < 0.05$; Excess vs. Surprise $t(20) = 0.592$, $p = 0.561$). This presumably stems from the fact that both 'exceeding a standard' and 'being surprised' involve more emotional intensity than—on average—the adjectives from the difficulty class.

5. 'Middling' Adjectives

In this section, we introduce yet another subclass of adjectives that are neither clearly positive nor clearly negative but that we think are interestingly different from the neutral PPTs that we have discussed so far. We call them *middling* adjectives, because their function is, in a nutshell, to place an object somewhere near the middle of a corresponding scale.[44]

The middling class:

> average, commonplace, habitual, humdrum, mediocre, moderate, mundane, normal, ordinary, plain, regular, routine, standard, typical

The neutral PPTs that we have previously discussed, be they in the difficulty class, the excess class, or the surprise class, are such that most often, they convey an evaluation—however, whether the evaluation is positive or negative depends on the context. Middling adjectives, on the other hand, may be said to systematically convey a 'neutral' evaluation—that is, to convey that a given object deserves neither a positive nor a negative evaluation.[45]

In light of this, we regard the two tests proposed, the Attitude Compatibility test and the GOOD/BAD WAY test, as not meaningful or well-suited for middling adjectives. This is because the function of middling adjectives—to place an object in the middle of a scale—clashes with the AC and GOOD/BAD WAY tests, which indicate a positive or negative evaluation. Thus, although the tests are well suited for neutral adjectives, which are *underspecified* for their valence and, depending on the context,

250 *Isidora Stojanovic and Elsi Kaiser*

can give rise to a positive, a negative, or an ambivalent evaluation (or maybe no evaluation at all), the tests are not suited for adjectives such as 'average', which we suggest *are specified* for a middling scale position. By definition, the aspects of meaning targeted by the tests are simply not present with the class of middling adjectives, so the tests do not apply to this class in a meaningful way. Thus, we do not use these tests as a tool to identify middling adjectives. Instead, in the following sections, we show that a comparison between middling adjectives and neutral PPTs from the standpoint of psychological norms reveals some intriguing differences that support the 'middling' status of this new class.

5.1. Data from Psychological Norms for Middling Adjectives

Figure 11.4 shows the valence and arousal scores for 14 adjectives that we propose are middling adjectives. Their average valence rating is 4.93 (range: 3.63–6.17), and their average arousal rating is 3.12 (range: 2.29–4). Similar to what we saw for the neutral PPTs, the valence ratings for these adjectives are higher than their arousal ratings (paired *t*-test: $t(13) = 8.407, p < 0.001$).

However, what is striking with middling adjectives is that this asymmetry is present for every adjective that we investigated, as can be seen in the heights of the darker and lighter bars in Figure 11.4. Earlier, for the three neutral subclasses, sometimes the arousal rating is numerically higher than the valence rating for a particular adjective, and sometimes it's lower. In contrast, with the middling adjectives shown in Figure 11.4, the arousal ratings (lighter bars) are consistently numerically lower than the valence ratings (darker bars) for every adjective. Indeed, in the next

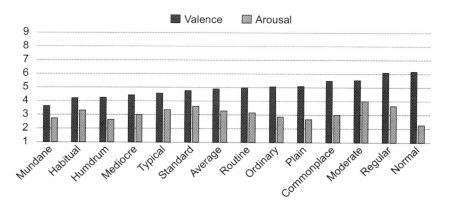

Figure 11.4 Middling adjectives (Average valence: 4.93, average arousal: 3.12. Range for valence: 3.63–6.17, range for arousal: 2.29–4).

Exploring Valence in Judgments of Taste 251

section, as we look statistically at how middling adjectives compare to the three neutral classes, it becomes clear that the arousal ratings, in particular, are much lower for middling adjectives.

5.2. Comparing Middling Adjectives to Neutral PPTs

In this section, we show how the arousal ratings distinguish neutral and middling adjectives. Figure 11.5 and Table 11.1 show the average valence and arousal ratings for adjectives in the neutral class (all three subclasses combined) and the middling class.

Statistical analyses confirm what can be seen visually in Figure 11.5: The valence ratings, and especially the arousal ratings, are lower for middling adjectives than neutral PPTs. First, when we compare the *valence ratings* between the middling adjectives and the others (using unpaired *t*-tests), we see that the valence ratings are significantly higher in the excess class than in the middling class ($t(22) = 2.52, p < 0.02$), marginally higher

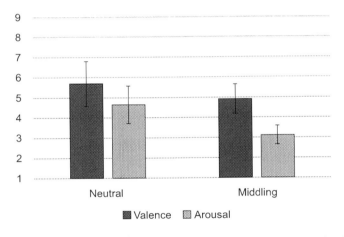

Figure 11.5 Average valence and arousal ratings for the 34 neutral adjectives (collapsing all three classes) and the 14 middling adjectives (error bars show +/-1 SD).

Table 11.1 Average valence and arousal ratings (standard deviation provided in parentheses).

	Valence	*Arousal*
Neutral	5.686 (1.106)	4.656 (0.921)
Middling	4.934 (0.716)	3.116 (0.461)

in the surprise class than in the middling class ($t(24) = 2.062, p = 0.0502$), and numerically (i.e., not significantly) higher in the difficulty class than in the middling class ($t(24) = 1.622, p = 0.116$). Thus, we see indications of a difference in valence between middling adjectives and neutral PPTs, but this is only significant with the excess subclass of neutral PPTs.

However, a much clearer asymmetry emerges between neutral PPTs and middling adjectives in the arousal ratings. When we compare the *arousal ratings* between the middling adjectives and the other three classes, we find that the arousal ratings are significantly higher in all three neutral PPT classes than in the middling PPT class (excess class vs. middling: $t(22) = 7.174, p < 0.0001$; surprise class vs. middling: $t(24) = 6.948, p < 0.001$; difficulty class vs. middling: $t(24) = 3.685, p < 0.01$).

In sum, adjectives in the middling class have significantly lower arousal ratings than each of the three neutral classes. This supports our suggestion that it is worth considering middling adjectives as a distinct group. More specifically, the finding that neutral PPTs have higher arousal ratings than middling adjectives fits with our view that (i) neutral PPTs are underspecified for their valence but can, depending on the context, be interpreted as expressing an evaluation, while (ii) middling adjectives simply place an object toward the middle of the scale (e.g., *average, mediocre*) without expressing a strong emotional response.

6.   Conclusions

In this chapter, we have challenged the widespread though often implicit assumption that predicates of personal taste are evaluative, i.e., that they convey either a positive or a negative assessment of the object of evaluation. We have suggested that some PPTs, e.g., 'surprising' and 'excessive', can be underspecified in terms of positive or negative valence and thus are not evaluative. We have explored how these kinds of *neutral PPTs* differ from evaluative PPTs and how different classes of neutral PPTs differ from each other, as well as how they relate to another class that we call *middling* adjectives, which are neither positive nor negative (e.g., 'average').

We have approached these issues from two perspectives: First, we have proposed two new linguistic tests that can act as diagnostics to identify neutral PPTs, and we have provided corpus evidence complementing the tests. Second, we have analyzed the valence and arousal ratings of the adjectives under consideration using preexisting psychological forms (Warriner et al., 2013).

This investigation yields a diverse and nuanced class of neutral PPTs, which we suggest can be broken down into at least three subclasses: the difficulty class (e.g., 'difficult', 'easy'), the excess class (e.g., 'ostentatious', 'intense'), and the surprise class (e.g., 'surprising', strange'). We have also explored a fourth class, middling adjectives, whose status as PPTs is less clear (e.g., 'mediocre', 'basic'). This is not intended to be an

Exploring Valence in Judgments of Taste   253

exhaustive classification, nor are the adjectives that we have analyzed intended to be regarded as exhaustive lists. Rather, we regard the adjectives simply as paradigmatic examples of the different types, and one of our aims is to broaden the kinds of adjectives that are included in the discussions of judgments of personal taste.

Broadly speaking, this work contributes to our understanding of subjective adjectives by separating the notion of evaluativity (conveying a positive or negative evaluation in virtue of the expression's meaning) from the broader notion of subjectivity and by identifying a rich class of neutral PPTs. In doing so, we also hope to have opened up new avenues for, on the one hand, linguistic research on underspecification and contextual effects on adjective interpretation, and, on the other, philosophical research on judgments of personal taste.

Acknowledgments

We are grateful to the Editors for the invitation to contribute to this volume, and, in particular, to Julia Zakkou for very helpful comments and suggestions. We would also like to thank Anouch Bourmayan, Malte Willer, Andrés Soria Ruiz, Victor Carranza, and Nils Franzén for comments on an earlier draft, as well as the audience at the LOGOS Colloquium in Barcelona, the PhiLang 2021 Conference, the Czech Society for Aesthetics, the Philosophy Colloquium at Texas Tech University, and the CCLAM Seminar at the University of Stockholm for discussion of this and related material. At an institutional level, Isidora Stojanovic acknowledges support from grant n. ANR-17-EURE-0017 FrontCog. Elsi Kaiser acknowledges support from the NSF, as this material is partially based upon work supported by the National Science Foundation under Grant No. 1749612 awarded to Elsi Kaiser.

Notes

1. We are co-first authors of this chapter.
2. Kölbel (2002) does not use the expression 'predicate of (personal) taste', introduced three years later in Lasersohn (2005). Nevertheless, he seems to group together into one and the same class all subjective predicates.
3. Umbach writes: "customary criteria are (a) the intuition of faultless disagreement, (b) grammaticality of experiencer arguments, (c) the acceptability of embedding under subjective attitude verbs like English find, and (d) the behavior of the comparative form with respect to (a)–(c)" (Umbach, 2020, p. 1). There are a few other tests to be found in the literature. One such test relies on the idea that PPTs typically trigger a so-called *acquaintance* inference (see Ninan, 2014). The idea is that a sentence such as 'Monopoly is boring, but I've never either played it or watched it' is infelicitous; but not so if 'boring' is replaced by a factual expression such as 'invented by an American' or even 'expensive' or 'popular'. Another test, proposed in McNally and Stojanovic (2017), looks at the implications of embedding an adjective under

'looks (to me)' and 'sounds (to me)' (2017, p. 27). Last but not least, Soria Ruiz and Stojanovic (2019) offer a series of criteria that are meant to identify not PPTs *per se* but expressive uses of all kinds of terms.

4. As we emphasize shortly, it is quite crucial that the modification should bear on the PPT directly rather than the entire sentence. For instance, 'To me, Monopoly is an American game' is felicitous as a way of expressing one's belief that Monopoly is an American game (or perhaps, more accurately, one's inclination to characterize it as an American game), even though '(to be) an American game' is clearly not a PPT. Hence, this kind of sentence-level modification is not relevant to our discussion.

5. We use the symbol # to denote infelicity and ✖ to denote falsity.

6. It bears mentioning that there is a rich literature on faultless disagreement in philosophy, with which we cannot engage in the present chapter. For recent surveys, see, e.g., Zakkou (2019) and Zeman (2020).

7. More precisely, Silk (2021) coins a new term, 'evaluational'. Our use of 'subjective', while in line with the literature (see Willer (to appear)), is not completely unproblematic either. In particular, it may be objected that whether moral and deontic judgments and (perhaps to a lesser extent) aesthetic judgments are 'subjective' has always been a matter of controversy. Let us stress that by choosing to call the broader category 'subjective', we do not mean to commit to any philosophical view regarding the status of such judgments.

8. Väyrynen attributes the idea to Williams (1985, p. 125) and notes that "mere reference to a degree that exceeds a contextually specified standard isn't sufficient for evaluation in this sense" (ibid.). The alternative sense corresponds, precisely, to how the term 'evaluative' is used in some of the linguistic literature; namely: "An adjectival construction is evaluative if and only if it conveys that the property associated with the adjective exceeds a relevant threshold" (Brasoveanu & Rett, 2017, p. 1). This somewhat technical sense of 'evaluative' will not be relevant to our discussion.

9. The idea that judgments of taste are inherently evaluative may be traced to a long-standing tradition of expressivism in philosophy (for a recent survey, see Soria Ruiz et al., 2021). While this tradition has been developed in metaethics and most forcefully applied to moral (but also aesthetic) judgments, its application to PPTs is straightforward. To judge a cake to be delicious or an activity to be fun is to express a PRO attitude; to judge a soup to be insipid or a game to be boring is to express a CON attitude. According to certain authors, it is precisely this clash of attitudes that drives the intuition of disagreement (e.g., Marques, 2015, López de Sa (this volume)). This being said, the expressivist literature also recognizes that not all such judgments need to be necessarily either positive or negative. That is to say, in addition to PRO attitude and CON attitude, there are attitudes of *indifference* (see Dreier, 2006).

10. It is worth noting that, in some contexts, in the phrase 'and I (don't) like it', 'it' can be interpreted as referring to an entire proposition. However, in the present discussion, we focus on the non-propositional reading in which the attitude is towards the object itself, e.g., the game in (5).

11. www.quora.com/My-girlfriend-is-boring-but-I-truly-do-love-her-How-do-I-bring-out-the-fun-in-our-relationship

12. https://discourse.disneyheroesgame.com/t/elimination-game/994504/835;

13. Review of the Oscar De La Renta 2011 fashion film; https://popseeculdotcom.wordpress.com/2011/07/16/fashion-films/

14. Review of Tres Leches Eatery; www.groupon.com/biz/jacksonville/tres-leches-1

Exploring Valence in Judgments of Taste 255

15. https://korabikka.wordpress.com/2012/03/21/nisemonogatari-11-review-final/
16. For information, in a corpus search performed on the COCA corpus, approximately 1 in every 6 occurrences of 'in a good way' is preceded by 'but'.
17. Yet another worry is that in English, the expression 'in a good/bad way' also has a metalinguistic use, meaning 'in the good/bad *sense* of the word'. An example is the English title of the Quebecois movie 'Charlotte a du fun', which is 'Slut in a good way' as a translation of the French phrase, used in the movie, '*salope dans le bon sens du terme*'. To detect such uses, one may run the test in a language free of such ambiguity.
18. For instance, 'entertaining' and 'intimidating' are such. 'Entertaining' has a positive valence but less strongly so than 'fun', and because of that, it patterns more easily with the two tests. 'Intimidating' has a negative valence, but because the negative experience that it reports is often based on positive features (e.g., a very smart person may be intimidating because of that), it can trigger a positive evaluation; at least, much more easily than 'boring' or 'disgusting'.
19. Although we do not focus on adjectives of gustatory taste, it seems that there may also be neutral PPTs used in the gustatory domain, for example *spicy* and *fruity* (though the adjective *tasty* is not neutral). Corpus examples show that *spicy* and *fruity* easily pass the Attitude Compatibility test and the GOOD/BAD WAY test. We include some examples here. We leave more detailed investigation of the neutrality of these gustatory expressions for future work.

    (i)   Oh, that is <u>fruity</u> and I like it [writing about beer] https://untappd.com/b/grand-river-brewery-blanc-stare/2462300
    (ii) Blue Oak's spicy chicken sandwich is only available on Tuesdays, so plan accordingly. The name doesn't lie: this one is so <u>spicy</u>! And I like it. https://antigravitymagazine.com/column/reality-bites-24/
    (iii) They are seasoned just perfectly and nothing was <u>spicy</u> in a bad. way www.tripadvisor.com/ShowUserReviews-g37209-d1094813-r679170047-Fogo_de_Chao_Brazilian_Steakhouse-Indianapolis_Indiana.html
    (iv) Our Belgian is super <u>fruity</u>, in a good way. We don't know why. [writing about beer] www.reddit.com/r/Homebrewing/comments/2z773h/our_belgian_is_super_fruity_in_a_good_way_we_dont/

20. In the present chapter, we leave aside the question of which mechanisms, semantic and pragmatic, determine the valence that a neutral PPT has on a specific occasion of use. This question was partly addressed in Stojanovic (2016) in relation to the adjective 'intense'.
21. There is a philosophical tradition, originating with Aristotle, that holds that excess is bad *per se*. On a linguistic level, the modifier 'too' (as in 'too easy'/'too difficult'), which indicates excess, appears indeed to always trigger a negative evaluation (see Bylinina, 2014; Väyrynen, 2013, ch. 7). Nevertheless, when we look at value scales that range from more negative to more positive, exceedance from mean value can clearly go in either direction.
22. www.sebright.hackney.sch.uk/maths/the-happy-puzzle-company
23. https://boardgamegeek.com/thread/939678/galaxy-trucker-tile-drafting-ship-construction-var
24. www.katetoon.com/is-speaking-at-international-events-worth-the-faff/
25. Said about a video game called *Wired*. www.engineering.com/story/wired-a-video-game-to-spark-interest-in-engineering
26. Said about a mystery teaser. www.braingle.com/brainteasers/teaser.php?id=29093&op=0&comm=1Note that the phrase 'it is easy and I like it' is very often found in relation to recipes, but there, the object arguably shifts—the preparation is easy, but the output is what is being liked.

27. www.braingle.com/brainteasers/teaser.php?op=2&id=15922&comm=1
28. https://bluefifthreview.wordpress.com/2012/09/19/the-blue-collection-2-music-12-19-summer-2012/
29. www.twixtmynethers.com/2018/06/22/the-don/
30. https://stepoutbuffalo.com/griffon-gastropub-opens-g3-in-east-aurora/
31. www.siliconera.com/tales-rays-shares-latest-key-visual-showing-original-characters-others/
32. https://echoesanddust.com/2020/03/bruxa-maria-the-maddening/
33. Lauren Nicolle Taylor, *The Woodlands Series Boxed Set*, ch. 39. Fantastic Fiction, 2017.
34. Ian Fisher, Do Threads of Five Lives Lead to One Serial Killer? *New York Times* 1993 (source: COCA).
37. https://blattzirkus.wordpress.com/2019/01/14/review-the-book-of-life-by-deborah-harkness-a-discovery-of-witches-3/
36. David Barker, cover of the album *Glass Hymnbook* (1980–82, released in 2017).
37. www.amazon.com/product-reviews/B00B63M468
38. www.sportskeeda.com/wwe/best-and-worst-of-wwe-smackdown-top-superstar-misses-the-show-extremely-strange-pairing
39. Lyrics of the song 'Strange in a good way' by Auna Sims, album *Evidence*, 2017.
40. www.goodreads.com/book/show/55200690-downeast
41. www.rig-talk.com/forum/threads/swapping-tubes-renegade.114859/
42. In the norming study, the words were presented in isolation, not in sentences or larger contexts. This allowed the researchers to ensure that participants' ratings were only based on the semantics of each individual word being tested rather than the semantic or pragmatic contribution of the rest of the sentence. In our view, the fact that the norms were collected on the basis of words in isolation is not incompatible with the possibility of a word's precise valence being potentially influenced by context (for related work on the distinction between negative words in isolation and in different contexts, see also Cepollaro et al., 2019).
43. Of course, we are aware that affective valence and (if we may call it so) axiological valence need not always align, especially in the moral and (to a lesser extent) aesthetic spheres. For instance, a person can feel very happy at the idea of leaving a restaurant without paying for their meal but at the same time recognize that such an action is morally bad. Similarly, a person can value a work of art very highly, such as Picasso's *Guernica* or Delacroix's *Massacre at Chios*, even if, because of their subject, such works are unlikely to elicit happiness. For a related discussion, see Stojanovic (to appear).
44. It is worth keeping in mind that middling adjectives may be felt, especially in some contexts, to be somewhat negative. For example, if a recommender describes an applicant as 'average' in a recommendation letter, this is perceived to be a negative recommendation. Even though, strictly speaking, 'average' picks out a value 'in the middle' of a scale, in many contexts, this is felt to be negative because a higher value is preferred. Thus, we suggest that the negative connotation may be a pragmatic, contextual inference due to Gricean reasoning about other adjectives that could have been used instead (e.g., 'outstanding' and so on). In the norms (without context), terms like 'mediocre' (valence 4.43) and 'average' (valence 4.89) receive ratings very close to 5, the scale midpoint.
45. If we help ourselves to the expressivist way of thinking (see footnote 9), we could say that just as judging something to be 'good' invites a PRO attitude and something to be 'bad' a CON attitude, judging something to be 'average'

Exploring Valence in Judgments of Taste 257

invites an attitude of indifference. Neutral PPTs, on the other hand, seldom invite indifference; rather, whether they invite a PRO or a CON attitude will depend on the context.

References

Alves, H., Unkelbach, C., Burghardt, J., Koch, A. S., Krüger, T., & Becker, V. D. (2015). A density explanation of valence asymmetries in recognition memory. *Memory & Cognition*, *43*, 896–909.

Barker, C. (2002). The dynamics of vagueness. *Linguistic and Philosophy*, *25*, 1–36.

Bierwisch, M. (1989). The semantics of gradation. In M. Bierwisch & L. Ewald (Eds.), *Dimensional adjectives* (pp. 71–261). Springer.

Brașoveanu, A., & Rett, J. (2017). Evaluativity across adjective and construction types: An experimental study. *Journal of Linguistics*, *54*, 263–329.

Bylinina, L. (2014). *The grammar of standards: Judge-dependence, purpose-relativity, and comparison classes in degree constructions.* LOT Dissertation Series 347. LOT.

Cepollaro, B., Sulpizio, S., & Bianchi, C. (2019). How bad is it to report a slur? An empirical investigation, *Journal of Pragmatics*, *146*, 32–42.

Coppock, E. (2018). Outlook-based semantics. *Linguistics and Philosophy*, *41*, 125–164.

Davies, M. (2008–). *The Corpus of Contemporary American English (COCA).* www.english-corpora.org/coca/

Dreier, J. (2006). Negation for expressivists: A collection of problems with a suggestion for their solution. In R. Safer-Landau (Ed.), *Oxford studies in metaethics* (pp. 217–233). Oxford University Press.

Franzén, N. (2018). Aesthetic evaluation and first-hand experience. *Australasian Journal of Philosophy*, *96*(4), 669–682.

Franzén, N. (2020). Evaluative discourse and affective states of mind. *Mind*, *129*, 1095–1126.

Goodwin, G., & Darley, J. (2008). The psychology of meta-ethics: Exploring objectivism. *Cognition*, *106*, 1339–1366.

Kaiser, E. (2015). Perspective-shifting and free indirect discourse. *Proceedings of SALT*, *25*, 346–372.

Kaiser, E., & Rudin, D. (2020). When faultless disagreement is not so faultless: What widely-held opinions can tell us about subjective adjectives. *Proceedings of the Linguistic Society of America*, *5*, 698–707.

Kaiser, E., & Rudin, D. (2021). Arguing with experts: Subjective disagreements on matters of taste. *Proceedings of the Annual Meeting of the Cognitive Science Society*, *43*.

Kennedy, C., & Willer, M. (2016). Subjective attitudes and counterstance contingency. *Proceedings of SALT*, *26*, 913–933.

Kölbel, M. (2002). *Truth without objectivity.* Routledge.

Korotkova, N. (2016). *Heterogeneity and uniformity in the evidential domain* [PhD dissertation]. UCLA.

Lasersohn, P. (2005). Context dependence, disagreement, and predicates of personal taste. *Linguistics and Philosophy*, *28*, 643–686.

López de Sa, D. (This volume). Disagreements and disputes about matters of taste.

Marques, T. (2015). Disagreeing in context. *Frontiers in Psychology*, 6, Article 257. https://doi.org/10.3389/fpsyg.2015.00257

McNally, L., & Stojanovic, I. (2017). Aesthetic adjectives. In J. Young (Ed.), *The semantics of aesthetic judgment* (pp. 17–37). Oxford University Press.

Moltmann, F. (2010). Relative truth and the first person, *Philosophical Studies*, 150, 187–220.

Ninan, D. (2014). Taste predicates and the acquaintance inference. *Proceedings of SALT*, 24, 290–309.

Ortony, A., Turner, T. J., & Antos, S. J. (1983). A puzzle about affect and recognition memory. *Journal of Experimental Psychology: Learning, Memory, & Cognition*, 9, 725–729.

Pearson, H. (2013). A judge-free semantics for predicates of personal taste. *Journal of Semantics*, 30, 103–154.

Portner, P., & Rubinstein, A. (2016). Extreme and non-extreme deontic modals. In N. Charlow & M. Chrisman (Eds.), *Deontic modality* (pp. 256–282). Oxford University Press.

Pratto, F., & John, O. P. (1991). Automatic vigilance: The attention grabbing power of negative social information. *Journal of Personality and Social Psychology*, 61, 380–391.

Rudin, D., & Kaiser, E. (2021). Connoisseurial contradictions: Expertise modulates faultless disagreement. In *Proceedings of SALT 31*, 385–404

Rudolph, R. (2020). Talking about appearances: The roles of evaluation and experience in disagreement. *Philosophical Studies*, 177, 197–217.

Sæbø, K. (2009). Judgement ascriptions. *Linguistics and Philosophy*, 32, 327–352.

Silk, A. (2021). Evaluational adjectives. *Philosophy and Phenomenological Research*, 102, 127–161.

Solt, S. (2016). Ordering subjectivity and the relative-absolute distinction. *Proceedings of Sinn und Bedeutung*, 20, 676–693.

Soria Ruiz, A., Cepollaro, B., & Stojanovic, I. (2021). The Semantics and pragmatics of value judgments. In P. Stalmaszczyk (Ed.), *The Cambridge handbook of the philosophy of language* (pp. 434–449). Cambridge University Press.

Soria Ruiz, A., & Faroldi, F. (2020). Moral adjectives, judge-dependency and holistic multidimensionality. *Inquiry*, 64, 1–30.

Soria Ruiz, A., & Stojanovic, I. (2019). On linguistic evidence for expressivism. *Royal Institute of Philosophy Supplement*, 86, 155–180.

Stephenson, T. (2007). Judge-dependence, epistemic modals, and predicates of personal taste. *Linguistics and Philosophy*, 30, 487–525.

Stojanovic, I. (2007). Talking about taste: Disagreement, implicit arguments, and relative truth. *Linguistics and Philosophy*, 30, 691–706.

Stojanovic, I. (2012). Emotional disagreement. *Dialogue*, 51(1), 99–117.

Stojanovic, I. (2016). Expressing aesthetic judgments in context. *Inquiry*, 59, 663–685.

Stojanovic, I. (2019). Disagreements about taste vs. disagreements about moral issues. *American Philosophical Quarterly*, 56, 29–42.

Stojanovic, I. (to appear). Evaluativity. In E. Lepore & U. Stojnic (Eds.), *The Oxford handbook of contemporary philosophy of language*. Oxford University Press.

Exploring Valence in Judgments of Taste 259

Sundell, T. (2011). Disagreements about taste. *Philosophical Studies*, 155, 267–288.

Umbach, C. (2016). Evaluative propositions and subjective judgments. In J. van Wijnbergen-Huitink & C. Meier (Eds.), *Subjective meaning. Alternatives to relativism*. De Guyter. https://www.degruyter.com/document/doi/10.1515/9783110402001-008/html

Umbach, C. (2020). Evaluative predicates beyond "fun" and "tasty". In D. Gutzmann, L. Matthewson, C. Meier, H. Rullmann, & T. E. Zimmermann (Eds.), *The Wiley Blackwell companion to semantics*. Wiley. https://onlinelibrary.wiley.com/doi/abs/10.1002/9781118788516.sem127, https://doi.org/10.1002/9781118788516.sem127

Unkelbach, C., Fiedler, K., Bayer, M., Stegmüller, M., & Danner, D. (2008). Why positive information is processed faster: The density hypothesis. *Journal of Personality and Social Psychology*, 95, 36–49.

Väyrynen, P. (2013). *The rude, the lewd and the nasty*. Oxford University Press.

Warriner, A. B., Kuperman, V., & Brysbaert, M. (2013). Norms of valence, arousal, and dominance for 13,915 English lemmas. *Behavior Research Methods*, 45(4), 1191–1207.

Willer, M. (to appear). Subjectivity. In E. Lepore & U. Stojnic (Eds.), *The Oxford handbook of contemporary philosophy of language*. Oxford University Press.

Williams, B. (1985). *Ethics and the limits of philosophy*. Harvard University Press.

Zakkou, J. (2019). *Faultless disagreement: A defense of contextualism in the realm of personal taste*. Klostermann.

Zeman, D. (2020). Faultless disagreement. In M. Kusch (Ed.), *The Routledge handbook of philosophy of relativism* (pp. 486–495). Routledge.

12 Differences of Taste
An Investigation of Phenomenal and Non-Phenomenal Appearance Sentences

Rachel Etta Rudolph

1. Introduction

Taste as it figures in philosophical and linguistic work about "personal taste" is different from yet related to taste as one of the five sensory modalities. For one, "personal taste" extends beyond gustatory taste. Matters of personal taste have to do not only with how things taste but also with more nebulously defined experiences of enjoyment, interest, boredom, and so on. It's a matter of personal taste not only that I like the taste of coconut but also that I find *The Lord of the Rings* movies dull.

In the other direction, there are matters of gustatory taste that are not intuitively matters of personal taste. Matters of personal taste are *evaluative*. To find coconut tasty or *The Lord of the Rings* movies boring is to give a thumbs-up or thumbs-down to something. Our personal tastes are a matter not solely of experiencing things but of experiencing them in a valenced way. When someone asks about your "tastes", they're asking about your likes and dislikes. If some dish tastes to you like it contains no salt, that has to do with how it tastes in the gustatory sense. But it seems not to be a "matter of personal taste".

There is, of course, an overlap. Key examples of matters of personal taste are what one finds tasty or disgusting—clearly also matters of gustatory taste. We have a variety of linguistic constructions for getting at this intersecting area. We can use canonical predicates of personal taste (PPTs) such as *tasty* and *disgusting*.[1] We can also use complex expressions that make the gustatory element more explicit, such as *taste good* and *taste gross*.

Note that matters of personal taste that aren't also matters of gustatory taste cannot be expressed with such complex predicates containing the verb *taste*: I can't express my boredom with *The Lord of the Rings* by saying that it *tastes dull* or anything similar. This observation seems so obvious that it's hardly worth stating. But it brings out the distinctiveness of talk about gustatory taste as compared with matters of personal taste of the broader evaluative kind. My starting point in the present chapter will be the language of gustatory taste (as well as the other sense

DOI: 10.4324/9781003184225-16

Differences of Taste 261

modalities) and challenges that arise from its combination with evaluative vocabulary. Throughout, I will also draw connections with discussion of appearance language, centering on *look*-sentences, from the literature in philosophy of perception.

There is a puzzle about complex gustatory-evaluative predicates, like *taste good*. As I'll show in Section 2, while *taste good* can be used synonymously with the simple PPT *tasty*, it need not be. How, then, should we analyze *taste good* so as to predict its possible interpretations? Similar questions also arise about the interpretation of sensory-evaluative predicates involving other appearance verbs, such as *look splendid*, *smell bad*, and so on. All of these constructions admit of apparently "phenomenal" as well as "non-phenomenal" readings.[2] To give a rough initial characterization of the distinction, in phenomenal uses, a quality is attributed to the appearance: that something *tastes good* means that its taste is good; by contrast, in non-phenomenal uses, a quality is attributed to the stimulus based on its appearance: that something *tastes good* means that its taste suggests *it* to be good.

There are two main options for predicting these different readings. The first, which I'll discuss in Section 3, is to posit an ambiguity in the appearance verb. I'll review how such a view has been motivated in previous literature, mostly by sentences with the verb *look* combined with non-evaluative adjectives, like *red* (e.g., Chisholm, 1957; Jackson, 1977; Brogaard, 2014, 2015; Glüer, 2017). Then I'll show that motivation for an ambiguity in appearance verbs is, if anything, stronger from the sensory-evaluative predicates that I am focusing on. Then I'll outline a verbal ambiguity analysis so that we can examine its workings more concretely.

In Section 4, I'll turn to the second strategy for predicting the different readings of sensory-evaluative constructions: namely, by appealing to flexibility in the complement adjective. These evaluative adjectives on their own, even without any appearance language, are very complex. For one, they are gradable adjectives, giving rise to all the subjectivity, vagueness, and context dependence that has been identified in that domain (Barker, 2002; Kennedy, 2007, among many others). Further, they are *multidimensional* gradable adjectives: Whether something is *good* depends on a variety of factors that may be combined and weighted in different ways, whereas whether something is *tall* (which is not multidimensional) simply depends on its height (e.g., Sassoon, 2013; Kennedy, 2013). Finally, these adjectives are *perspective-dependent* (Lasersohn, 2005), being used in different cases to express the assessments of different individuals. As I'll explain, these independently motivated factors in combination go a long way to predicting the availability of both phenomenal and non-phenomenal readings of sensory-evaluative predicates.

In Section 5, I'll conclude by taking stock of the prospects of the verbal ambiguity and adjectival approaches. I'll consider an important challenge that remains for the latter view, namely that the univocal analysis of appearance verbs has trouble explaining why certain other appearance constructions, like *taste like it's good*, don't seem to admit of phenomenal readings. While I'll consider a possible avenue of response, in the end, it may be that taking appearance verbs to be ambiguous best explains the range of possible readings of *taste good* and related appearance constructions. Still, carefully examining both approaches offers a clearer understanding of this complex area of language, showing in particular that motivation for appearance verb ambiguity is narrower than has often been assumed.

2. Two Uses of *Taste Good*

There is a puzzle for an analysis of complex sensory-evaluative predicates. Such predicates can be used in two notably different ways. To illustrate, observe the uses of *tastes good* in the two different contexts specified in (1).

(1) This cake tastes good.

> **Context A:** Speaker has just tasted a piece of cake and enjoyed it.
> **Context B:** Speaker is sampling cakes for a friend's wedding. The friend has instructed that the cake should be vanilla, which the speaker doesn't like; still, they're trying small bites of the cakes in order to determine which is likely to be a good choice. They taste a cake which they can tell is a good-quality vanilla one, though they don't enjoy it.

In context A, when the speaker says the cake tastes good, we take them to mean that they find the taste of the cake pleasing. In this case, they could have equivalently said the cake is *tasty*.[3] By contrast, in context B, the speaker's use of *tastes good* is not felt to be equivalent with the PPT *tasty*.[4] In context B, the claim that the cake tastes good is instead taken to mean that the cake tastes as if it would be good for the purposes at hand. The speaker can appropriately say this even if they do not enjoy the taste of the cake.

How should we characterize the meaning of *taste good* in these two contexts? And how is this predicted given the separate meanings of *taste* and *good*? It's undesirable just to say that *taste good*, as an unanalyzed unit, is ambiguous. For one thing, that would give up on the plausible idea that the meaning of *taste good* (on both uses) is a function of the meanings of its constituent expressions. But it would also make it mysterious why the exact same two-faced behavior arises with a whole range of similar sensory-evaluative predicates.

The puzzle arises not only with *taste good* and not only with predicates concerning gustatory tastes. It arises with all appearance verbs when combined with certain evaluative adjectives.

Differences of Taste   263

(2) The wine smells bad.

> **Context A:** Speaker has smelled the wine and its scent is rancid and unpleasant.
>
> **Context B:** Speaker has smelled the wine and can tell from the simplicity of the scent that it is of poor quality, but it doesn't smell unpleasant to them.

(3) The spread looks splendid.[5]

> **Context A:** Speaker sees the spread and finds its arrangement visually appealing; they have no judgment about the quality of the food.
>
> **Context B:** Speaker sees the spread and is impressed by the variety and quality of the food that it seems to contain; they may not judge the arrangement visually appealing.

(4) The singer sounds nice.

> **Context A:** Speaker is listening to a concert and enjoys the singer's voice performance.
>
> **Context B:** Speaker has heard a description of how friendly the singer is.

(5) The spaghetti feels gross.

> **Context A:** Speaker has put their hands into a bowl of spaghetti and doesn't enjoy its slimy feel.
>
> **Context B:** Speaker judges by touch that the spaghetti has been overcooked and wouldn't taste good; they may not find the feel of it unpleasant.

For each of these predicates, formed from an appearance verb and an evaluative adjective, we see that very different readings arise in the different contexts. In context A in the examples, the speaker is taken to be saying that the individual in question has an appearance with a certain quality, either positive or negative. While only *taste good* has the obvious PPT-correlate of *tasty*, *smell bad* perhaps corresponds roughly with *smelly*—a word that could be much more easily substituted in context A in (2) than in context B. In the other cases, there aren't simple PPTs we can use in the place of the complex predicates. Still, there are other ways of paraphrasing the sentences to bring out the intended readings. Let's consider some possible paraphrases for the example with *look* from (3).

(6) The spread looks splendid.

> a.   The spread is splendid-looking.
> b.   The look of the spread is splendid.

264 *Rachel Etta Rudolph*

The paraphrases in (6a–b) are appropriate in context A but not in context B. By contrast, the paraphrases in (7a–b) are appropriate in context B but not in A.

(7) The spread looks splendid.

    a. The spread looks like it's splendid.
    b. The spread looks to be splendid.

In context B, in other words, we hear the speaker to be saying that the appearance in question suggests the presence of some further property, which may be independent of that appearance.

To put some labels on this distinction, let us call the first reading—operative in context A—"phenomenal" and the second—operative in context B—"non-phenomenal".[6] At this point, I do not mean these labels to commit me to any particular approach to the distinction. They are simply supposed to latch onto two intuitively different uses of these complex sensory-evaluative predicates.

When it comes to giving an analysis of *look splendid*, *taste good*, and other sensory-evaluative predicates, there are two main options. The first is to posit an ambiguity in appearance verbs. On this view, the different readings arise due to different readings of *look* in *look splendid*, *taste* in *taste good*, and so on. I'll discuss this approach next, in Section 3. The second rejects any ambiguity in the verb and instead takes the different readings to arise due to flexibility in the interpretation of the complement adjective. On this view, the difference between phenomenal and non-phenomenal readings comes down to *splendid* in *look splendid*, *good* in *taste good*, and so on. I'll address this option later, in Section 4.

3. Are Appearance Verbs Ambiguous?

In this section, I consider the view that appearance verbs like *look* and *taste* are ambiguous, and that this is what explains the phenomenal and non-phenomenal readings observed in the previous section. I'll begin, in 3.1, by reviewing motivation for such an ambiguity view from the perception literature, focusing on Jackson's argument in chapter 2 of *Perception: A Representative Theory* (1977). This argument does not appeal to any evaluative language, nor does it consider appearance verbs beyond *look*.[7] Then, in 3.2, I'll consider how the motivation extends to the sensory-evaluative cases of interest here. We'll see that support for the verbal ambiguity view is, if anything, stronger from the evaluative cases than from Jackson's own examples. Finally, in 3.3, I'll sketch an implementation of the verbal ambiguity analysis.

3.1. *Jackson on* Looks

Jackson (1977, ch. 2) argues for an irreducibly phenomenal use of *look*. Consider (8).[8]

(8) The apple looks red.

Jackson argues that there is a use of (8) that cannot be accounted for by taking the predicate *red* to apply to red *things*. There are two options that he rules out here.[9] First, one might attempt to say that (8) means that the apple looks the way red things look in normal circumstances. However, Jackson holds, these claims come apart in both directions. First, something could look red even if there were no red things at all and so no way that red things normally look. Second, something can look the way red things normally look without looking red. Imagine we are totally color-blind and see the world in shades of gray. But we have extremely discerning gray vision; we are capable of making just as many distinctions among shades of gray as those with ordinary color vision can make among colors. Then something can look the way red things normally look—that very specific shade of gray—and yet it doesn't (phenomenally) look red.

This line of reasoning is also connected with Jackson's "knowledge argument" (1982, 1986). Mary, the color scientist who has never left her black-and-white room, can know that the apple looks red in the (non-phenomenal) sense of looking the way red things normally look. But it seems there's something else she does not know. And this "something else" is that the apple looks red in a further, phenomenal sense.

The second option that Jackson rules out regarding the interpretation of (8) is that it expresses the speaker's inclination to believe that the apple is red based on visual evidence. There are two problems with this. First, it's possible to felicitously assert (8) even with no inclination to believe that the apple is red (Jackson, 1977, p. 38). However, when Jackson himself first introduces the epistemic use of *look*, he cautions against taking it to imply that the speaker assents (even tentatively) to the claim that things are as they look. He writes:

> If this were the case, it would be *inconsistent* to say "They appear to be [F], but I happen to know that they are [not F]." . . . Our account handles such cases by describing them as cases where we take it that though a certain body of evidence supports that p, other (non-visual) evidence makes it certain that not-p.
>
> (p. 31)

In such a case, not only would the speaker not assent to the claim, say, that the apple is red, but they would also not be inclined to believe it.[10] Nevertheless, it won't work to take (8) to be about what the visual evidence supports, even if that evidence is recognized to be possibly misleading. After all, Mary in her black-and-white room has visual evidence that the apple is red. Still, it seems she can't appropriately say that the apple looks (phenomenally) red. Thus, Jackson's discussion leads to the conclusion that there is a sense of *look* that is irreducibly phenomenal.

266 *Rachel Etta Rudolph*

Before moving on, let me make a note about how these considerations relate to the acquaintance inference. Simple unembedded claims with experiential predicates have widely been observed to give rise to the inference that the speaker has some relevant firsthand acquaintance.[11] The presence of this inference is constant across all the different readings of appearance sentences that we've been considering so far. For instance, Mary can say *The apple looks red* because she has seen the apple and its visual appearance as manifested to her gives evidence that the apple is red. It's thus not only phenomenal readings that give rise to the acquaintance inference. What makes Mary unable to assert the phenomenal *look* claim is not that she isn't acquainted with the apple's visual appearance at all. Instead, the problem seems to be something else about the way that appearance is experienced by her. Because all appearance claims—both phenomenal and non-phenomenal—license the acquaintance inference, and because the acquaintance inference is tied with the speaker's experience, which is a kind of phenomenology, we must guard against the possible misunderstanding that all appearance statements are phenomenal in the sense of interest here, as defined in Section 2. They are not all phenomenal in that sense, in that they do not all seem to be directly characterizing the quality of the appearance. This is compatible with them all still placing some constraints on the speaker's perceptual experiences, as discussed under the header of the acquaintance inference.

3.2. *Sensory-Evaluative Predicates*

Although Jackson does not address appearance claims with evaluative adjectives, his reasons for recognizing a distinctively phenomenal reading of *look red* carry over to *look splendid* and the other sensory-evaluative predicates we saw in Section 2. In fact, as I'll discuss shortly, the reasons seem to be, if anything, more convincing when applied to the evaluative cases. Consider, again, the *look* claim in (9), in context A from earlier.

(9) **Context A:** Speaker sees the spread and finds its arrangement visually appealing; they have no judgment about the quality of the food.

The spread looks splendid.

As we saw with *look red*, there seems on the face of it to be a reading of this sentence that cannot be reduced to a claim about splendid *things* (or even splendid spreads). One possible non-phenomenal gloss would be that the spread looks the way splendid spreads look in normal circumstances. Jackson's first reason for rejecting the analogous option about *look red*—that it could be true that the spread looks splendid even if there are no splendid things—sits a bit oddly in this case. So I won't rely on it.[12] Instead, consider the possibility that splendid spreads, i.e., spreads with great quality and variety of food, normally look like messes. It's hard

Differences of Taste 267

to make a splendid spread look splendid. Whether or not this is true, it certainly seems possible. So there is a reading of (9) that is not equivalent to the non-phenomenal comparative claim.

The second possible non-phenomenal gloss that Jackson considers, appealing to visual evidence, is also clearly inadequate. In the given context, (9) does not mean that the visual appearance of the spread gives evidence that the spread is splendid. One can truthfully say that the spread looks splendid while not having visual evidence that the spread is splendid, given that one knows that splendid spreads tend to look awful.[13]

In fact, the case for phenomenal *look* is, if anything, more convincing based on the behavior of *look splendid* than *look red*. For instance, Martin (2010, sec. 5) offers a rehabilitation of a comparative (i.e., non-phenomenal) approach to *look red* that does not carry over to *look splendid*. The best case for phenomenal *look red* comes from the fact that there seems to be an available reading of (8) (*The apple looks red*) that is false in the scenario in which we all see the world in shades of gray. If this sentence has a false reading in the imagined scenario, it seems it must be on its phenomenal interpretation. However, Martin holds, it's not clear that this sentence does have a false reading instead of merely being unable to convey something we (thinking about the case from our position of full color vision) know but which is not part of the literal meaning of the sentence.

Martin offers an analogy with the following comparative claim, which contains no appearance language (2010, p. 193):

(10) John weighs as much as a sumo wrestler.

Most people have a rough idea about how much sumo wrestlers tend to weigh, and so upon being told (10), they learn something fairly specific about John's weight. And someone uttering (10) may intend to convey that specific information—reasonably so, given assumptions about common world knowledge. However, arguably, this more specific information is not part of the literal meaning of the sentence. If someone doesn't know anything about how much sumo wrestlers weigh, they can still learn (10) while remaining completely ignorant, say, about whether this means John is below or above average weight for an adult man.

Something similar, Martin suggests, is going on with the apparently phenomenal reading of (8). Literally, it just means that the apple looks the way red things look in normal circumstances. What we're missing, if we see the world in shades of gray, is further information about what this way is. That further information may be something that people, in our world in which most people have color vision, generally want to convey with (8). But this can be achieved without taking it to be part of the truth conditions of that statement.

This way of side-stepping the apparent motivation for a phenomenal reading of *look red* doesn't easily carry over to *look splendid*. Consider, again, a context in which the spread looks splendid (non-phenomenally) because it looks like it contains a great variety of high-quality food but doesn't look splendid (phenomenally) because it is a mess. Applying the comparative strategy we saw with *look red* to this case would involve saying that the spread really does look splendid (in every sense) but that the appearance of a false phenomenal reading is just due to the speaker not knowing more specifically what splendid spreads look like. But that seems wrong. What's missing here isn't any information about the appearance of splendid spreads. (And we can also assume the speaker has ample firsthand acquaintance with splendid-looking spreads.) These considerations point to an important difference between *red* and *splendid*. Although *being* red and *looking* red can clearly come apart in particular cases, there seems to be a deep connection between the two. However, *looking* splendid *being* splendid can simply come entirely apart.

3.3. *Verbal Ambiguity Analysis*

Given the different uses of appearance sentences discussed earlier, the idea has been proposed that appearance verbs are ambiguous. On this line, appearance verbs are ambiguous at least between a phenomenal and a non-phenomenal interpretation.[14] Note that I do not wish to rule out that there is some connection between the meaning of the verbs in both cases, so that this might be better thought of as *polysemy* than ambiguity. (It certainly isn't ambiguity of the *bank /bank* variety.)

I will now outline one way that a verbal ambiguity view could be implemented. I will apply it to cases involving sensory-evaluative predicates, given that, as just discussed, these provide the clearest motivation for a phenomenal/non-phenomenal ambiguity in appearance verbs. Let's work with the *look* sentence from before, repeated in (11), and let's consider, first, how to capture the non-phenomenal reading most natural in context B, where the speaker is impressed by the variety and quality of the food in the spread, but may not judge it to be visually appealing.

(11) The spread looks splendid.

An initial idea (which we will later revise) is that *look* is a raising verb (Brogaard, 2015, sec. 3). That is, although the surface structure does not suggest it, *splendid* is actually being predicated of the surface matrix subject, *the spread*. Thus the logical form of the non-phenomenal reading of (11) is something like the following:

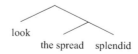

On this view, the appearance verb is a propositional operator, with a semantic value as in (12).

Differences of Taste 269

(12) **Non-phenomenal *look* (first pass)**

$$\left[\!\left[\text{look}_{np}\right]\!\right]^{c;w,j} = \lambda p. \text{ visual appearances at } w \text{ evidence to } j \text{ that } \left[\!\left[p\right]\!\right]^{c;w,j} = 1$$

(Note I include the judge as a parameter in the index primarily as a place-holder; I'll return to some issues connected to judge-dependence in 4.3.)

On the present proposal, (11) means that visual appearances provide evidence (to the judge) that the spread is splendid. An advantage of this analysis is that it makes good on the idea that the non-phenomenal statement is, in some way, about the spread *being* splendid. This comes out on the raising proposal in the fact that the proposition *that the spread is splendid* is a constituent in the logical form of the sentence in (11).

However, a simple raising analysis for non-phenomenal *look* sentences like (11) isn't quite right. Consider the sentence uttered in another context:

(13) **Context C:** Speaker knows that the boss at the catering company always looks happy when her employees set up a splendid spread; speaker sees her boss looking happy.

The spread looks splendid.

In this context, visual appearances suggest that the spread is splendid. And yet the *look* sentence—even on its non-phenomenal reading—is not felicitous. That sentence must mean that it is the visual appearance *of the spread* that suggests its splendid-ness.[15] One might claim that adequate visual evidence for the spread being splendid should come from the look of the spread itself. But this is not a satisfactory answer. For it is perfectly felicitous, in context C, to utter a different (also non-phenomenal) appearance sentence: *It looks like the spread is splendid.* Upon seeing her boss looking happy, we can imagine one catering employee appropriately saying this to another without even having seen the spread in question.

The problem with the raising analysis is that it is unable to recognize a semantic role for the matrix subject, *the spread*, in connection to the appearance verb, *look*.[16] This problem arises for an analysis of non-phenomenal appearance sentences with other appearance verbs as well. Return for a moment to *taste good*, in the non-phenomenal context B:

(14) **Context B:** Speaker is sampling cakes for a friend's wedding. The friend has instructed that the cake should be vanilla, which the speaker doesn't like. . . . They taste a cake which they can tell is a good-quality vanilla one, though they don't enjoy it.

This cake tastes good.

In this context, we explicitly specify that the speaker is basing her judgment on the taste of the cake. And this is essential for the appearance claim to be felicitous. It is perhaps not very common to get gustatory evidence about something from tasting something else, but it is clearly possible. Consider an alternative context for the *taste good* sentence:

(15) **Context C:** Speaker knows that the cake and the cupcake were made with the same recipe, by the same baker; she tastes the cupcake and judges it to be a good choice for the wedding.

The cake tastes good.

Surely, in context C, tasting the cupcake is good gustatory evidence about the quality of the cake. But still, the *taste* sentence in (15) is clearly unacceptable.

To account for this role of the matrix subject in the appearance sentences, we should replace the simple raising idea with something more complex. For instance, we could take the non-phenomenal appearance sentence to have a structure as follows:

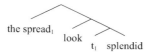

In this case, the semantic value for the verb is as in (16).

(16) **Non-phenomenal *look* (revised)**

$[\![\text{look}_{np}]\!]^{c;w,j} = \lambda p.\lambda x.VIS_w(x)$ evidences to j at w that $[\![p]\!]^{c;wj} = 1$

Here, $VIS_w(x)$ is the visual appearance of x at w; we can think of this as the denotation of the phrase, *the look of x*.[17] With this revision, the heart of the proposal about non-phenomenal appearance sentences is that they have as a constituent a proposition. And in the case of sentences as in (11) and (14), it is a proposition predicating the embedded adjective of the matrix subject.[18] It is on this point that the verbal ambiguity analysis will distinguish the non-phenomenal and phenomenal cases. As we saw, on the reading of (11) that is naturally heard in context A, where the speaker finds the look of the spread visually appealing (though perhaps thinking the food is awful), it does not seem that the proposition *that the spread is splendid* enters into the interpretation at all. And this is reflected in the following structure, which the ambiguity approach could offer for the phenomenal case:

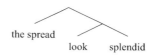

Here, the complement of *look* is not a full proposition but instead a property.

(17) **Phenomenal *look***

$$\left[\!\left[\text{look}_p\right]\!\right]^{c;w,j} = \lambda P.\lambda x.\left[\!\left[P\right]\!\right]^{c;w,j}(VIS_w(x)) = 1$$

The property of being splendid is predicated of the visual appearance of the spread and not the spread itself.

The same approach works well for the other cases of phenomenal appearance sentences with evaluative predicates. For example, that the cake tastes good (phenomenally) means that the gustatory appearance of the cake is itself good. Whether this means that the cake is good (for whatever purposes might be relevant) is another question.

Interestingly, applying this analysis to the original cases of interest to philosophers of perception like Jackson and Chisholm—with color predicates like *red*—seems more metaphysically loaded than applying it to the evaluative cases we've just been discussing. This is because, as Martin (2010) emphasizes, it would commit us to the view that looks have properties like being red. Ordinarily, we simply speak of objects in the world, not looks, having color properties. However, it's not nearly as controversial to hold that looks or other appearances can have evaluative qualities like being splendid, good, bad, and so on.

An ambiguity view along the lines spelled out here seems promising, empirically, for predicting the possible readings of appearance sentences with evaluative adjectives. But we might ask, is it really necessary to take the verb *look*, in a simple sentence like *The spread looks splendid*, to be ambiguous? While the considerations we've seen so far have led many theorists in that direction, there's another approach that is also worth exploring.

4. All in the Adjective

As we've seen, the appearance sentence repeated in (18) has two intuitively different readings, one phenomenal and one non-phenomenal.

(18) The spread looks splendid.

Earlier, we said that (18), on its phenomenal reading, does not seem to have the proposition *that the spread is splendid* as a constituent, whereas on its non-phenomenal reading, it does. In Section 3, this was then taken as support for the idea that while there is a version of *look* (the non-phenomenal) that takes a propositional complement, there also must be a version (the phenomenal) that does not.

However, that reasoning was a bit quick. What doesn't seem to be a constituent in the non-phenomenal sentence is the proposition that the spread is splendid in some *look-independent* way. But the adjective

272 *Rachel Etta Rudolph*

splendid has quite a flexible meaning. Indeed, depending on the context, one could seemingly utter (19) (with *no* appearance verb) to mean either that the spread is splendid in terms of the variety and quality of food it contains or that it's splendid in terms of its appearance.

(19) The spread is splendid.

Similarly, we observed that (20a), on its phenomenal reading, is equivalent with a sentence involving the PPT *tasty*, in (20b), whereas on its non-phenomenal reading, they are not interchangeable.

(20) a. The cake tastes good.
     b. The cake is tasty.

Only if the speaker enjoys the taste of the cake can they utter the phenomenal appearance sentence, or the PPT sentence, whereas if they judge the cake to be good for some purpose on the basis of its taste but don't enjoy it, they can still utter the non-phenomenal appearance sentence. This observation, however, is compatible with the proposition *that the cake is good* being a constituent in the phenomenal appearance sentence. The reason, again, is the great flexibility in the adjective *good*. Indeed, given a suitable context, *good* on its own can be used in a way that is felt to be equivalent with *tasty*. Upon tasting some cake, one could utter (21)—with no appearance verb and no PPT—to convey just the same thing as either (20a) (heard phenomenally) or (20b).

(21) The cake is good.

The adjective *good* can be used to talk of all sorts of varieties of goodness, including goodness in terms of taste, i.e., tastiness.[19]

The idea behind the "all in the adjective" approach, then, is to leverage this flexibility that is already present with adjectives like *splendid* and *good* to account for the felt difference between phenomenal and non-phenomenal appearance sentences. Doing this avoids the need to posit a structural ambiguity of the sort proposed in the previous section.

There are three key features of evaluative adjectives that may contribute to their two-faced behavior in sensory-evaluative constructions. First, they are gradable adjectives (4.1). Second, these gradable adjectives are multidimensional (4.2). And third, they are perspective dependent (4.3). I will discuss these features in turn and show how, together, they go a long way toward explaining the phenomena/non-phenomenal distinction.[20]

Before moving to that, note that I will here be developing the "all in the adjective" approach in a way that assimilates all appearance sentences

Differences of Taste 273

to the non-phenomenal analysis offered in 3.3. That is, I will take all of these sentences, at the level of logical form, to embed a full proposition, employing the semantic clause from (16). There is, however, another avenue one might want to pursue to avoid a verbal ambiguity view: namely, to assimilate all cases to the structure of the phenomenal sentences offered in 3.3, employing the semantics in (17). On this approach, all appearance sentences, both the intuitively phenomenal and non-phenomenal, would have the verb take a property-denoting complement that characterizes the look in question. Taking this approach, the phenomenal cases are easy, while the non-phenomenal ones are a challenge, whereas on the approach I will pursue, it is the reverse. One reason to prefer assimilation in the direction of the non-phenomenal analysis is that there are other forms of appearance sentences that almost certainly embed full propositions. These include, for instance, the constructions in (22).

(22) a. The spread looks to be splendid.
  b. The spread looks like it's splendid.
  c. It looks as if the spread is splendid.

It thus seems plausible that all appearance constructions include propositional constituents, while it's not plausible that none do. If we want an analysis that can extend to these further constructions, the non-phenomenal is most promising.[21]

4.1. Gradability

Evaluative adjectives are gradable. Things aren't just splendid or not, or good or not, but also splendid or good in varying degrees. One spread can be more splendid than another, for instance, even if neither is splendid, full stop. In this respect, evaluative adjectives are like adjectives such as *tall* and *wide*. In 3.3, I left the semantics of *splendid* unspecified, simply assuming that it denoted a function from individuals to truth values. To account for gradability, though, we should, as a first pass, take *splendid* to denote a measure function (a function from individuals to degrees), as in (23), where $splendid(x, w, j)$ is x's degree of splendidness for j at w.

(23) $[\![\text{splendid}]\!]^{c;w,j} = \lambda x.splendid(x, w, j)$

This measure function can then compose with various degree morphemes to form predicates. For instance, in our example, it would compose with the "positive form" POS morpheme, as in (24), where g is a variable over measure functions and $s_{g,c}$ is the standard for g in context c.

(24) $[\![\text{POS}]\!]^{c;w,j} = \lambda g.\lambda x.g(x) > s_{g,c}$ at w

274   *Rachel Etta Rudolph*

Gradability introduces a certain amount of subjectivity into discourse, given different possible contextually supplied standards for applying the positive form of the adjectives (e.g., Barker, 2002).

However, the role of a standard in applying the positive form isn't yet enough to capture the different uses of *splendid* in phenomenal and non-phenomenal appearance sentences. The difference between holding that the spread looks splendid in the phenomenal sense, of being splendid-looking and holding that it looks splendid, non-phenomenally, in the sense that it looks like it's splendid in a look-independent way, is not a difference in *how splendid* one thinks something had to be to count as splendid, full stop. Rather, the difference is in the *way* the spread is being evaluated as splendid or what *dimension* of splendidness is taken to be relevant.

4.2. Dimensions

Dimension-sensitivity is common with gradable adjectives and doesn't only show up with evaluative terms. That is, while some gradable adjectives, like *tall*, always denote the same measure function, others, like *splendid* (as well as *clever*, *healthy*, etc.) can denote different measure functions in different contexts.

Let us, then, revise our semantics for *splendid* so that it denotes a *context-sensitive measure function*, as follows:

(25) $[\![\text{splendid}]\!]^{c,w,j} = \lambda x.splendid_c(x,w,j)$

Here, $splendid_c(x, w, j)$ is x's degree of splendidness of the sort relevant at c for j at w. Adjectives that denote context-sensitive measure functions give rise to *ordering subjectivity* (e.g., Bylinina, 2017; Silk, 2021). That is to say, in different contexts, the ordering of objects by splendidness can differ (even without any change in the objects themselves). By contrast, the ordering of objects by height does not differ from context to context.

Simply taking *splendid* to denote a context-sensitive measure function still leaves unresolved several aspects of its interpretation. When an adjective has a denotation as in (25), at least two factors go into determining the output degree: (a) Which dimensions of the given property are relevant? (b) If there are multiple relevant dimensions, how are they to be combined to yield the ordering? Question (a) resolves *indeterminacy*, while question (b) resolves *multidimensionality*.

To see the difference between indeterminacy and multidimensionality, let us compare the adjectives *long* and *clever*. The adjective *long* can be used to talk of either temporal duration or physical length. But though the dimension of evaluation can change, only one is ever relevant for a given use of the adjective. Adjectives like this, that can be associated with different dimensions of evaluation in different cases, display indeterminacy.[22]

Differences of Taste 275

The adjective *clever* is arguably also indeterminate, capable of being used on different occasions to speak, as Klein (1980, p. 7) puts it, of "an ability to manipulate numbers, [or] an ability to manipulate people." But it seems that, in many contexts, multiple kinds of cleverness can all be relevant. They are combined and weighted in some way to yield an overall assessment of how clever someone is. Thus, *clever* is multidimensional in the sense of Sassoon (2013, p. 336): It can be "associated with many different dimensions simultaneously."[23]

The notions of indeterminacy and multidimensionality can be fruitfully applied to the evaluative adjectives involved in the sensory-evaluative constructions that we've been investigating. Earlier, we saw that (26a) (with no appearance verb) can, in a suitable context, be used equivalently to (26b) (with the appearance verb) and likewise with (27a–b).

(26) a. The spread is splendid.
     b. The spread looks splendid.

(27) a. The cake is good.
     b. The cake tastes good.

How are *splendid* and *good* in the non-appearance sentences to be interpreted so that we predict the possible equivalence of these sentences? I propose that we should view them (and other evaluative adjectives) as indeterminate between applying in terms of appearances and applying in terms of other respects. The spread can be splendid in way of looks, or *splendid-looking*, but not splendid in some other respect, just as Montana can be large in terms of its geographical extent but not large in terms of its population. That is, depending on the context, c, $splendid_c$ may be a function to degrees of splendidness in visual appearance or degrees of splendidness in other respects.

However, even settling on appearances versus other respects of evaluation, *splendid*, *good*, and so on are still multidimensional. We can both be talking about looks but still disagree about whether the spread is splendid(-looking), because we prioritize different aspects of the visual arrangement, say, color as opposed to balance. Multidimensionality persists with evaluative adjectives even once the indeterminacy between appearances and other respects is settled.

The result is that (26a) and (27a), with *no* appearance verbs, can in a sense be used "phenomenally" or not. The idea, then, is that when a sensory-evaluative predicate gets a phenomenal reading, this is because the relevant respect of evaluation for the embedded adjective is appearance and, more specifically, the modality of appearance specified by the verb. Thus, in effect, when used phenomenally, *look splendid* is heard as *look splendid-looking*.

The phenomenal reading could then, after all, be captured by taking the appearance verb to have a propositional argument; it just must not

276   *Rachel Etta Rudolph*

be a proposition about appearance-independent splendidness. But the adjective *splendid*, on its own, never had to be used that way anyway. In some cases, though, the sort of splendidness at issue is independent of the type of appearance specified by the verb. And in those cases, we get non-phenomenal readings of the sensory-evaluative construction.[24,25] Recognizing how dimensions enter into the interpretation of gradable adjectives—in ways motivated independently of anything about appearance language—takes us a long way toward being able to predict phenomenal and non-phenomenal readings of sensory-evaluative predicates. However, we need one more ingredient in order to capture all apparent phenomenal cases.

4.3. *Perspectives*

One might question: To get a phenomenal reading, is it enough to specify the dimension that is being used for evaluating the complement adjective? This might seem to be sufficient when considering the case of *look splendid*. However, recall the case with *taste good*, in the non-phenomenal context B, repeated here:

(28)   **Context B:** Speaker is sampling cakes for a friend's wedding. The friend has instructed that the cake should be vanilla, which the speaker doesn't like. . . . They taste a cake which they can tell is a good-quality vanilla one, though they don't enjoy it.

This cake tastes good.

The key thing to notice is that here, even on the non-phenomenal reading, the sentence with *taste good* is used to say that the cake is good-*tasting* in some sense. After all, the speaker cares about how the cake will taste to those who will eat it and not about some other type of goodness. (It is possible to say *The cake tastes good* and be talking about a more taste-independent kind of goodness. Say we're playing a prank and want a cake that looks delicious but actually tastes like cardboard. One could then taste a cake, find it extremely bland and unpleasant, and say that it tastes good in the sense that it tastes like it'll be good for the purposes of the prank. But this wasn't the non-phenomenal reading in our original case, and we want to be able to account for that one too.)

What, then, makes (28) in context B still fall short of being used phenomenally? The answer, I propose, is that the embedded adjective, *good*—although it is being heard as *good-tasting*—is also being used *exocentrically*, as opposed to *autocentrically* (Lasersohn, 2005). That is to say, the individual whose assessment of good-tastingness matters is not the speaker herself, as it usually is by default, but rather someone else or some other group.

The possibility of both autocentric and exocentric uses is typically associated with the *judge-dependence* of the predicates in question. When the application of a predicate can vary from one judge to another, then the possibility also arises that the judge, though by default the speaker—giving rise to autocentric uses—can be shifted in some contexts to someone else—giving rise to exocentricity. Standard examples make use of PPTs, as in (29).

(29) a. The new cat food is tasty. (Amber gobbles it all up right away.)
      b. The roller coaster was fun. (I didn't set foot on it, but the kids couldn't get enough.)

There are many questions about how a judge enters into the interpretation of such predicates and, indeed, whether a judge is needed in the semantics at all (e.g., Pearson, 2013; Muñoz, 2019; Moltmann, this volume). These questions are orthogonal to my interests here. I will here take judge-dependence simply as a stand-in for whatever it is about the meaning of these predicates that gives rise to the perspectival differences across autocentric and exocentric uses. The key point is that such a phenomenon is widely recognized in cases that do not involve appearance language. My suggestion here is that this fact, combined with the non-phenomenal interpretation of appearance verbs from 3.3 as well as the dimension-sensitivity discussed in 4.2, predicts the availability of phenomenal and non-phenomenal readings of sensory-evaluative predicates.

The non-phenomenal reading of the *taste good* sentence in context B arises because it is used to convey, in effect, that the taste of the cake suggests that it is good-tasting *to the wedding guests*. By contrast, a phenomenal reading arises when the sentence is used to convey that the taste of the cake suggests that it is good-tasting *to the speaker*. Thus, the canonical examples of "phenomenal" appearance sentences, on this approach, are ones in which the embedded adjective is not only interpreted along the dimension of the appearance verb but is also used autocentrically.[26]

On the view I am presenting, there are in fact two different "loci" for perspective dependence in the sensory-evaluative constructions under examination. In 4.2, we said that, in the phenomenal case, the predicate *look splendid* is used to mean *look splendid-looking* and *taste good* to mean *taste good-tasting*. Now, we are adding that to truly predict the phenomenal reading, we also need the claim to be made autocentrically. But we should ask: Considering the case of *taste good*, must the speaker be the judge for the verb *taste*, for the adjective *good(-tasting)*, or both? That there can be different perspectives associated with these different pieces of the sentence can be shown from the fact that multiple experiencer prepositional phrases can co-occur:

(30) This treat tastes good-tasting for cats to me.

278   *Rachel Etta Rudolph*

This is a slightly odd sentence, since it implies that I have tasted the treat and judge, on the basis of its taste, that it would taste good to cats. There's no implication here that I enjoyed the treat. It's possible, then, for the verb *taste* to be used autocentrically but to evaluate good-tastingness as an exocentric property.[27] My sense is that this kind of use is non-phenomenal. Indeed, it's quite similar to the cake-sampling situation in context B, which we recently reviewed in (28). This shows that it's really the autocentricity or exocentricity of the embedded predicate that is determining whether a sentence with a sensory-evaluative predicate is phenomenal or non-phenomenal. All the cases we've been discussing are autocentric with respect to the verb.[28]

In sum, the "all in the adjective" approach leverages two key independently-motivated features of the adjectives embedded in sensory-evaluative constructions in order to explain the availability of phenomenal and non-phenomenal readings. First, the adjectives can be evaluated with respect to different dimensions; second, they are perspective-dependent, allowing for both autocentric and exocentric uses. Putting these together, we notice that phenomenal readings arise when the adjective is evaluated autocentrically and along the dimension of the appearance specified by the verb. On this approach, phenomenal readings are in some sense "epi-phenomenal". There's nothing especially unified about them, and they don't call for any special interpretive machinery. They simply arise due to a confluence of factors that can also show up separately and in many other linguistic contexts.

5.   Conclusion: Prospects for the Two Approaches

Let's step back and assess the prospects of the two approaches we have considered for analyzing sensory-evaluative predicates, like *look splendid* and *taste good*. The puzzle was to account for both their phenomenal and non-phenomenal readings, as distinguished in Section 2. The verbal ambiguity approach, discussed in Section 3, accounts for the distinction through two different argument structures for appearance verbs. The "all in the adjective" approach, discussed in Section 4, has the advantage of maintaining uniform semantics for appearance verbs while accounting for the distinction through independently-motivated features of adjective meaning. However, I would like to conclude by discussing a challenge that still faces this second view.

The challenge arises when we examine the relationship between sensory-evaluative predicates and other slightly different appearance constructions. Namely: Why is there such a felt difference between the sentences in (31)?

(31)   a.   The cake tastes good.
        b.   The cake tastes like it's good.

Differences of Taste 279

The "all in the adjective" approach can explain why (31a) can be interpreted either phenomenally or non-phenomenally. However, it leaves it mysterious why (31b) seems unable to be heard phenomenally. If the adjective *good* could, on its own, contain all the "phenomenal" material, why does (31b) seem only to have a non-phenomenal reading?

The most promising response on behalf of "all in the adjective" should appeal, I think, to competition between the different more and less complex surface syntactic forms. Assume that in (31a), proximity between the adjective *good* and the verb *taste* leads *good* by default to be evaluated along the dimension of taste; and assume, furthermore, that judge-dependent expressions are by default used autocentrically. These two assumptions have the result that (31a) by default gets interpreted phenomenally, with this only being overridden by a suitably special context (like context B from earlier). If we then take it that the more complex form in (31b) more readily lends itself to embedding the claim that something is good in other respects or for other judges, then we can understand why it would be rare, if not impossible, to use (31b) to convey the phenomenal claim. There is a simpler form, namely (31a), that will always do better in that the desired reading is the default for it.[29] While many details remain to be worked out, perhaps a pragmatic story along these lines can explain the felt difference between (31a) and (31b) without stipulating that the truth conditions available to each must, in principle, be different.

Still, given the challenge from (31), the verbal ambiguity approach may in the end be well-motivated. Nevertheless, it's worthwhile to work out the possibility of leveraging flexible adjective meanings to account for the different uses of appearance sentences. And importantly, in assessing whether we must depart from that view, we should consider not only the meaning of *taste good* and other sensory-evaluative predicates on their own but also the interpretive possibilities of these constructions in comparison to others.

Acknowledgments

For helpful discussion of this work, I wish to thank participants in the symposium on experiential language at the 2021 (virtual) Pacific APA, as well as audience members at the Dianoia Institute of Philosophy language workshop. Special thanks to Melissa Fusco, Dilip Ninan, Arc Kocurek, and Julia Zakkou for comments on earlier drafts of this chapter.

Notes

1. The literature dealing with PPTs is large and tends to center on two main phenomena and how they motivate relativist, contextualist, expressivist, or other semantic and pragmatic theories: first, faultless disagreement (as well as, to a lesser extent, retraction) (e.g., Kölbel, 2004; Lasersohn, 2005; Stephenson, 2007; Stojanovic, 2007; Egan, 2010; Sundell, 2011; MacFarlane, 2014; López de Sa, 2015; Anthony, 2016; Zeman, 2017; Wyatt, 2018; Zakkou,

280   *Rachel Etta Rudolph*

2019; Kneer, 2021); second, the acquaintance inference (e.g., Ninan, 2014, 2020; Anand & Korotkova, 2018; Franzén, 2018; Kennedy & Willer, 2016; Willer & Kennedy, 2020). Work that addresses both issues include Pearson (2013), Dinges (2017), Rudin and Beltrama (2019), Muñoz (2019).

2. The label "phenomenal" is based on Jackson (1977), though, as I'll discuss in what follows, my way of identifying such readings differs from his.

3. Moltmann (2010), for instance, uses the predicate *taste good* in discussing faultless disagreement and relativism—in contact with the literature on PPTs mentioned in footnote 1. MacFarlane (2014, p. 142) also notes that to the extent that *tasty* motivates truth relativism, so does *taste good*. For more discussion of the relationship between *tasty* and *taste good*, see Pearson (this volume).

4. PPTs like *tasty* can sometimes be used "exocentrically", i.e., from a perspective other than the speaker's, as opposed to "autocentrically", i.e., from the speaker's own perspective (Lasersohn, 2005). If *tasty* is used exocentrically, then it could be acceptable in context B. However, autocentricity is the default, and that is enough, I think, to get a contrast in the acceptability of *tasty* across the two contexts. In Section 4, I'll consider whether perspective dependence might play an important role in explaining the distinction of interest.

5. For discussion of this example, see Martin (2010, pp. 184ff); also Martin (2020, pp. 102–103). I will return to it in more detail in what follows.

6. See esp. Chisholm (1957, ch. 4), Jackson (1977, ch. 2). These authors and others following them often distinguish three uses of appearance verbs: phenomenal, comparative and epistemic. (Note: Chisholm's "non-comparative" lines up with Jackson's "phenomenal".) The data I am interested in most clearly motivates a two-way distinction, which is why I choose simply to speak in terms of phenomenal and non- phenomenal for now. I do not rule out that there may be good reason to draw further distinctions within my "non-phenomenal" category. The non-phenomenal category is unified in that a statement of this sort that something *appears so-and-so* cannot be paraphrased with a claim that just uses *so-and-so* as a property of things (Chisholm, 1957, pp. 44–47). The paraphrases in (6) can be used to test this. There is also some connection between the phenomenal/non-phenomenal distinction and the experiential/representational distinction in Charlow (2021).

7. While I focus on Jackson, others who have argued for a phenomenal sense of *look* along similar lines include Chisholm (1957), Byrne (2009), Brogaard (2014, 2015, 2018), Glüer (2017).

8. Note that Jackson considers explicitly relativized *look* sentences, i.e., with *to*-prepositional phrases specifying an experiencer. I omit these in my discussion, though it is worth considering whether any points that Jackson makes are more plausible about the relativized cases.

9. These are attempts to analyze the phenomenal in terms of his "comparative" and "epistemic" readings. I consider both to be versions of non-phenomenal readings on my taxonomy (see fn. 6).

10. Martin (2010, sec. 2) discusses the need to distinguish "evidential" and "non-evidential" uses of appearance statements, where the former have the conversational purpose of putting forward the embedded proposition. Jackson's epistemic cases (and my non-phenomenal ones) still need not be used evidentially in this sense. See also Gisborne and Holmes (2007).

11. See, among others, Pearson (2013), Ninan (2014, 2020), Anand and Korotkova (2018), Munõz (2019), Willer and Kennedy (2020).

12. As Martin (2010, p. 192) notes, it's not very convincing with *look red* either, since it seems we can compare things in way of looks even to merely hypothetical entities.

13. This example is used by Martin (2010, 2020) to defend a distinctively phenomenal use of *look splendid*, where it is the look itself that is characterized as

Differences of Taste 281

splendid. Note, however, that he claims to account for the difference between phenomenal and non-phenomenal readings without positing an ambiguity in the verb *look*. Thus, his approach is closer to the one I will discuss in Section 4 than to the verbal ambiguity view I'll outline in 3.3.

14. Ambiguity in appearance verbs is put forward by Chisholm (1957) and Jackson (1977, p. 49), when they specify different "senses" of *look*. It is also endorsed by Brogaard (2014, 2015, 2018), Glüer (2017). It is discussed, though not definitively endorsed, by Charlow (2021).

15. This is related to the "perceptual source" interpretation discussed by Asudeh and Toivonen (2012, 2017), Landau (2011), Rett and Hyams (2014), Rudolph (2019); however, those discussions focus on appearance sentences with *like*-complements, e.g., *The spread looks like it's splendid*.

16. One might question whether the infelicity in (31) is simply due to the acquaintance inference, which might be accounted for without a change in the semantics proposed in (12). However, the need for a semantic revision is supported by the difference between the sentences in (32), with the appearance constructions embedded under an operator that "obviates" the acquaintance inference (Anand & Korotkova, 2018).

  (32) a. The spread probably looks splendid.
      b. It probably looks like the spread is splendid.

17. For discussion of the nature of such "perceptual objects" and their role in the semantics of taste and appearance language, see Moltmann (this volume).

18. More evidence that something like this is needed, at least for *like*-complement constructions, comes from "copy-free" cases, as in (33).

  (33) a. Mary looks like John is upset.
      b. The cake tastes like the baker forgot the salt.

  See esp., Landau (2009, 2011).

19. The great flexibility of the adjective *good* is a theme in much work in metaethics, e.g., Moore (1903), Hare (1952).

20. Note that other than gradability, these features are not clearly present with adjectives like *red* that were the focus of the discussion of *look* from Jackson (1977) and others. Thus, the viability of the "all in the adjective" approach depends on something like Martin's 2010 comparative assimilation of apparently phenomenal uses of *look red* discussed in 3.2.

21. The view in Martin (2010, 2020) seems to be an example of the alternative approach. He explicitly disavows an ambiguity in *look* and takes the complement of *look* in all cases to in some way further characterize the look in question. However, in order to achieve the phenomenal/non-phenomenal readings, he does say that there is a structural ambiguity in the way the complement modifies the verb.

22. See Kennedy (2007, sec. 2.1), picking up on cases that Klein (1980, pp. 7–8) calls "nonlinear"; also McConnell-Ginet (1973), Kamp (1975). Solt (2018, p. 75) holds that adjectives like this are not multidimensional but instead display "dimensional ambiguity".

23. On multidimensionality, see also Kennedy (2013), Bylinina (2017), McNally and Stojanovic (2017), Solt (2018), Silk (2021), Soria-Ruiz and Faroldi (2020).

24. Note that I would predict (on either the view in this section or the last) that (34) is consistent:

  (34) The spread looks splendid, but it doesn't look splendid.

  I think this is right. And one can get the true reading with appropriate emphasis on *look* in the second conjunct. That it may be a bit hard to appropriately utter this sentence is not more mysterious than the difficulty of appropriately

282 *Rachel Etta Rudolph*

uttering *I went to the bank, but I didn't go to the bank*, talking about the two different kinds of banks.

Similarly, I predict that (35) can be acceptable, which I think is borne out with suitable emphasis on *good* (say, in a context in which the speaker is enjoying greasy fast food).

(35) This food is tasty, but it doesn't taste good.

25. An alternative explanation might appeal to comparison classes instead of dimensions. The idea would be to think of *look splendid* on the model of *splendid spread* when it comes to determining what kind of splendidness is at issue. Kennedy (2007) argues one should not take the comparison class to be an argument of the gradable adjective due to examples like (36).

(36) Alice's car is an expensive BMW, but it's not expensive for a BMW.

With just the first conjunct, one would naturally interpret the sentence to mean that the car is expensive *for a BMW*. But that is merely a pragmatic preference—as we can tell from the fact that the overall sentence in (36) is not a contradiction. Similarly, with *look splendid*, it may be especially natural to evaluate the spread as splendid *for a visually appearing thing*, which would give rise to the phenomenal reading. But just as with *expensive BMW*, this link is optional. Non-phenomenal readings arise when the context naturally supplies a different comparison class. Something like this is suggested by Martin (2020, p. 103) when he holds that adjectives like *splendid* "lack category restrictions", and so we can shift the comparison group from, say "splendid for the look of something" to "splendid for a platter of food." His way of characterizing things doesn't quite fit with my suggested analysis, on which *splendid* is always being attributed to the spread itself. Still, the possible role of shifting comparison classes is worth keeping in mind.

26. There is debate about the relationship between judge dependence and multi-dimensionality. I assume that there is a kind of experiential assessment associated with the judge in at least some cases, including with PPTs and adjectives like *splendid-looking*, that is distinct from multidimensionality as it arises with adjectives like *clever*. For related discussion, see, e.g., Bylinina (2017), Solt (2018), Kaiser and Herron Lee (2018), Soria-Ruiz and Faroldi (2020).

27. On related "perspective plurality" and its implications for an analysis of PPTs, see Kneer et al. (2016).

28. The phenomenal/non-phenomenal difference seems to persist even with exocentric uses of the main verb. For instance, imagine we are observing a bird that chews up food to feed to its young in addition to eating the food itself. And let's imagine that ornithologists have determined that the bird judges by taste whether some food is good for their young and chews this food in a distinctive way. Then, observing the bird chewing in this distinctive way, we might remark, *That food tastes good*, with the verb anchored exocentrically to the bird but the bird "judging" that the food is good for its young. This would be a non-phenomenal reading. By contrast, if we just observe the bird seeming to enjoy some food, we could utter that same sentence, again exocentrically, but this time with a phenomenal reading.

29. There may be some special contexts in which *good* in (36b) could be heard as *good-tasting to me*.

(37) This cake tastes like it's good, but it's not—it only tastes that way because we just ate miracle berries.

Miracle berries are fruits that make everything taste much sweeter than it normally would. With (37), it seems that the speaker is holding that the cake tastes

Differences of Taste 283

like it's good-tasting to them, but they doubt that it truly is good-tasting to them, since they think they wouldn't like its taste if they ate it without the influence of the berries. Thanks to Dilip Ninan for suggesting this case.

References

Anand, P., & Korotkova, N. (2018). Acquaintance content and obviation. In U. Sauerland & S. Solt (Eds.), *Proceedings of Sinn und Bedeutung*, 22. (pp. 55–72). ZAS. https://doi.org/10.18148/sub/2018.v22i1.65

Anthony, A. (2016). Experience, evaluation and faultless disagreement. *Inquiry: An Interdisciplinary Journal of Philosophy*, 59, 686–722. https://doi.org/10.1080/0020174X.2016.1208923

Asudeh, A., & Toivonen, I. (2012). Copy raising and perception. *Natural Language & Linguistic Theory*, 30, 321–380. https://doi.org/10.1007/s11049-012-9168-2

Asudeh, A., & Toivonen, I. (2017). A modular approach to evidentiality. In M. Butt & T. H. King (Eds.), *Proceedings of the LFG '17 conference* (pp. 45–65). CSLI Publications.

Barker, C. (2002). The dynamics of vagueness. *Linguistics and Philosophy*, 25, 1–36.

Brogaard, B. (2014). The phenomenal use of "look" and perceptual representation. *Philosophy Compass*, 9/7, 455–468. https://doi.org/10.1111/phc3.12136

Brogaard, B. (2015). Perceptual reports. In M. Matthen (ed.), *The Oxford handbook of philosophy of perception*. Oxford University Press. https://doi.org/10.1093/oxfordhb/9780199600472.013.005.

Brogaard, B. (2018). *Seeing and saying: The language of perception and the representational view of experience*. Oxford University Press.

Bylinina, L. (2017). Judge-dependence in degree constructions. *Journal of Semantics*, 34, 291–331. https://doi.org/10.1093/jos/ffw011

Byrne, A. (2009). Experience and content. *The Philosophical Quarterly*, 59, 429–451. https://doi.org/10.1111/j.1467-9213.2009.614.x

Charlow, N. (2021). *Experiential content* [Manuscript].

Chisholm, R. (1957). *Perceiving: A philosophical study*. Cornell University Press.

Dinges, A. (2017). Relativism, disagreement and testimony. *Pacific Philosophical Quarterly*, 98, 497–519. https://doi.org/10.1111/papq.12191

Egan, A. (2010). Disputing about taste. In R. Feldman & W. Ted (Eds.), *Disagreement* (pp. 247–286). Oxford University Press.

Franzén, N. (2018). Aesthetic evaluation and first-hand experience. *Australasian Journal of Philosophy*. https://doi.org/10.1080/00048402.2018.1425729

Gisborne, N., & Holmes, J. (2007). A history of English evidential verbs of appearance. *English Language and Linguistics*, 11, 1–29. https://doi.org/10.1017/S1360674306002097

Glüer, K. (2017). Talking about looks. *Review of Philosophy and Psychology*, 8, 781–807. https://doi.org/10.1007/s13164-017-0350-7

Hare, R. M. (1952). *The language of morals*. Clarendon Press.

Jackson, F. (1977). *Perception: A representative theory*. Cambridge University Press.

Jackson, F. (1982). Epiphenomenal qualia. *Philosophical Quarterly*, 32, 127–136. https://doi.org/10.2307/2960077

Jackson, F. (1986). What Mary didn't know. *Journal of Philosophy*, 83, 291–295. https://doi.org/10.2307/2026143

Kaiser, E., & Herron Lee, J. (2018). Predicates of personal taste and multidimensional adjectives: An experimental investigation. In W. G. Bennett, L. Hracs, & D.

284   *Rachel Etta Rudolph*

R. Storoshenko (Eds.), *Proceedings of the 35th West Coast conference on formal linguistics* (pp. 224–231). Somerville, MA: Cascadilla Proceedings Project.

Kamp, H. (1975). Two theories of the adjective. In E. Keenan (Ed.), *Formal semantics of natural language* (pp. 123–155). Cambridge University Press.

Kennedy, C. (2007). Vagueness and grammar: The semantics of relative and absolute gradable adjectives. *Linguistics and Philosophy*, *30*, 1–45. https://doi.org/10.1007/s10988-006-9008-0

Kennedy, C. (2013). Two sources of subjectivity: Qualitative assessment and dimensional uncertainty. *Inquiry*, *56*, 258–277. https://doi.org/10.1080/0020174X.2013.784483

Kennedy, C., & Willer, M. (2016). Subjective attitudes and counterstance contingency. In M. Moroney, C.-R. Little, J. Collard, & D. Burgdorf (Eds.), *Semantics and Linguistic Theory (SALT)*, *26*. (pp. 913–933). CLC. https://doi.org/10.3765/salt.v26i0.3936

Klein, E. (1980). A semantics for positive and comparative adjectives. *Linguistics and Philosophy*, *4*, 1–45.

Kneer, M. (2021). Predicates of personal taste: Empirical data. *Synthese*. https://doi.org/10.1007/s11229-021-03077-9

Kneer, M., Vicente, A., & Zeman, D. (2016). Relativism about predicates of personal taste and perspective plurality. *Linguistics and Philosophy*, *40*, 37–60. https://doi.org/10.1007/s10988-016-9198-z

Kölbel, M. (2004). Faultless disagreement. *Proceedings of the Aristotelian Society*, *104*, 53–73. https://doi.org/10.1111/j.0066-7373.2004.00081.x

Landau, I. (2009). This construction looks like a copy is optional. *Linguistic Inquiry*, *40*, 343–346. https://doi.org/10.1162/ling.2009.40.2.343

Landau, I. (2011). Predication vs. aboutness in copy raising. *Natural Language & Linguistic Theory*, *29*, 779–813. https://doi.org/10.1007/s11049-011-9134-4

Lasersohn, P. (2005). Context dependence, disagreement, and predicates of personal taste. *Linguistics and Philosophy*, *28*, 643–686. https://doi.org/10.1007/s10988-005-0596-x

López de Sa, D. (2015). Expressing disagreement: A presuppositional indexical contextualist relativist account. *Erkenntnis*, *80*, 153–165. https://doi.org/10.1007/s10670-014-9664-3

MacFarlane, J. (2014). *Assessment sensitivity: Relative truth and its applications*. Oxford University Press.

Martin, M. G. F. (2010). What's in a look? In B. Nanay (Ed.), *Perceiving the world* (pp. 160–225). Oxford University Press.

Martin, M. G. F. (2020). Variation and change in appearances. In K. M. Vogt & J. Vlasits (Eds.), *Epistemology after Sextus Empiricus* (pp. 89–115).

McConnell-Ginet, S. (1973). *Comparative constructions in English: A syntactic and semantic analysis* [PhD thesis]. University of Rochester.

McNally, L., & Stojanovic, I. (2017). Aesthetic adjectives. In J. Young (Ed.), *The semantics of aesthetic judgment* (pp. 17–37). Oxford University Press.

Moltmann, F. (2010). Relative truth and the first person. *Philosophical Studies*, *150*, 187–220. https://doi.org/10.1007/s11098-009-9383-9

Moltmann, F. (2022). Tastes and the ontology of impersonal perception reports. In J. Wyatt, J. Zakkou, & D. Zeman (Eds.), *Perspectives on taste*. Routledge.

Moore, G. E. (1903). *Principia ethica*. Cambridge University Press.

Munõz, P. (2019). *On tongues: The grammar of experiential evaluation* [PhD thesis]. University of Chicago.

Ninan, D. (2014). Taste predicates and the acquaintance inference. In T. Snider, S. D'Antonio, & M. Weigand (Eds.), *Semantics and Linguistic Theory (SALT), 24*. (pp. 290–309). CLC. https://doi.org/10.3765/salt.v24i0.2413

Ninan, D. (2020). The projection problem for predicates of taste. In J. Rhyne, K. Lamp, N. Dreier, & C. Kwon (Eds.), *Semantics and Linguistic Theory (SALT), 30*. (pp. 753–778). CLC. https://doi.org/10.3765/salt.v30i0.4809

Pearson, H. (2013). A judge-free semantics for predicates of personal taste. *Journal of Semantics, 30*, 103–154. https://doi.org/10.1093/jos/ffs001

Pearson, H. (2022). Individual and stage-level predicates of personal taste: Another argument for genericity as the source of faultless disagreement. In J. Wyatt, J. Zakkou, & D. Zeman (Eds.), *Perspectives on taste*. Routledge.

Rett, J., & Hyams, N. (2014). The acquisition of syntactically encoded evidentiality. *Language Acquisition, 21*, 173–198. https://doi.org/10.1080/10489223.2014.884572

Rudin, D., & Beltrama, A. (2019). Default agreement with subjective assertions. In K. Blake, F. Davis, K. Lamp, & J. Rhyne (Eds.), *Semantics and Linguistic Theory (SALT), 29*. (pp. 82–102). CLC. https://doi.org/10.3765/salt.v29i0.4597

Rudolph, R. E. (2019). A closer look at the perceptual source in copy raising constructions. In M. T. Espinal et al. (Eds.), *Proceedings of Sinn und Bedeutung 23* (Vol. 2, pp. 287–305). Universitat Autònoma de Barcelona, Bellaterra (Cerdanyola del Vallès). https://doi.org/10.18148/sub/2019.v23i2.612

Sassoon, G. W. (2013). A typology of multidimensional adjectives. *Journal of Semantics, 30*, 335–380. https://doi.org/10.1093/jos/ffs012

Silk, A. (2021). Evaluational adjectives. *Philosophy and Phenomenological Research, 102*, 127–161. https://doi.org/10.1111/phpr.12635

Solt, S. (2018). Multidimensionality, subjectivity and scales: Experimental evidence. In E. Castroviejo, L. McNally, & G. W. Sassoon (Eds.), *The semantics of gradability, vagueness, and scale structure* (pp. 59–91). Springer.

Soria-Ruiz, A., & Faroldi, F. L. G. (2020). Moral adjectives, judge-dependency and holistic multidimensionality. *Inquiry: An Interdisciplinary Journal of Philosophy*. https://doi.org/10.1080/0020174X.2020.1855241.

Stephenson, T. (2007). Judge dependence, epistemic modals, and predicates of personal taste. *Linguistics and Philosophy, 30*, 487–525. https://doi.org/10.1007/s10988-008-9023-4

Stojanovic, I. (2007). Talking about taste: Disagreement, implicit arguments and relative truth. *Linguistics and Philosophy, 30*, 691–706. https://doi.org/10.1007/s10988-008-9030-5

Sundell, T. (2011). Disagreement about taste. *Philosophical Studies, 155*, 267–288. https://doi.org/10.1007/s11098-010-9572-6

Willer, M., & Kennedy, C. (2020). Assertion, expression, experience. *Inquiry*. https://doi.org/10.1080/0020174X.2020.1850338

Wyatt, J. (2018). Absolutely tasty: An examination of predicates of personal taste and faultless disagreement. *Inquiry, 61*, 252–280. https://doi.org/10.1080/0020174X.2017.1402700

Zakkou, J. (2019). Denial and retraction: A challenge for theories of taste predicates. *Synthese, 196*, 1555–1573. https://doi.org/10.1007/s11229-017-1520-y

Zeman, D. (2017). Contextualist answers to the challenge from disagreement. *Phenomenology and Mind, 12*, 62–73. https://doi.org/10.13128/Phe_Mi-21106

13 Individual- and Stage-Level Predicates of Personal Taste

Another Argument for Genericity as the Source of Faultless Disagreement

Hazel Pearson

> '*Who is the greatest Italian painter?*'
> '*Leonardo da Vinci, Miss Brodie*'
> '*That is incorrect. The answer is Giotto, he is my favourite*'.
> — *The Prime of Miss Jean Brodie*, Muriel Spark

1. Introduction

The following pairs of sentences appear to be truth-conditionally equivalent.

1a. This tea is tasty.
1b. This tea tastes good.
2a. St Paul's cathedral is beautiful.
2b. St Paul's cathedral looks beautiful.
3a. Ben is handsome.
3b. Ben looks handsome.

In this chapter, I argue that contrary to appearances, the simple predicates of personal taste in the (a)-sentences differ from their complex counterparts in the (b)-sentences along two dimensions.[1,2] Firstly, the simple PPTs are individual-level predicates (ILPs) in the sense of Carlson (1977), whereas the complex ones are stage-level predicates (SLPs).[3] Secondly, while both can take covert Experiencers, such arguments of simple PPTs obligatorily receive a generic interpretation; by contrast, the covert Experiencer of a complex PPT can receive a generic, bound variable or referential interpretation. I propose an analysis of these facts based on a novel proposal about the licensing of ILPs: all covert pronominal arguments of an individual-level predicate must be bound by the generic operator (and not only their situation arguments, *pace* Chierchia, 1995).[4] Finally, I show that generic construal of the Experiencer is a necessary condition for faultless disagreement. This is evidence in favour of treatments of

DOI: 10.4324/9781003184225-17

Predicates of Personal Taste 287

subjective meaning that appeal to genericity (Anand, 2009; Moltmann, 2010b, 2012; Pearson, 2013a; Snyder, 2013; Roeper, 2016; Keshet, 2020) and against relativism about PPTs.

2. Stage-Level and Individual-Level Predicates of Personal Taste

Evidence that PPTs are individual-level is presented in Anand (2009), Pearson (2013a) and Snyder (2013). But Pearson (2013b), citing an observation from Irene Heim (p.c.), argued that *tastes good* is stage-level. In this section, I present further evidence that complex PPTs are stage-level.[5]

SLPs, unlike ILPs, tolerate temporal and locative modifiers (Carlson, 1982).

4a. ??Ben is tall today/at the zoo.
4b. Ben is happy today/at the zoo.

Likewise complex PPTs allow such modification, but simple PPTs do not.

5a. ??This tea is tasty in a china cup.
5b. This tea tastes good in a china cup.
6a. ??St Paul's is beautiful today.
6b. St Paul's looks beautiful today.

Secondly, with bare plural subjects, modification of an ILP by *always* has little effect on truth conditions—unlike with SLPs.

7a. Firemen are altruistic.
7b. Firemen are always altruistic.
8a. Firemen are available.
8b. Firemen are always available.

Both (7a) and (7b) mean roughly 'All firemen are altruistic'. By contrast, while (8a) means 'there are currently some firemen available', (8b) can be paraphrased as 'there are always some firemen available'.

Similarly, both (9a) and (9b) report that all pineapples are tasty; (10a) seems to have this meaning too. But (10b) can mean that pineapples taste good in all circumstances; one could respond to (10b), but not (10a), by saying, 'That's not true. They taste horrible when you've just brushed your teeth'.

9a. Pineapples are tasty.
9b. Pineapples are always tasty.
10a. Pineapples taste good.
10b. Pineapples always taste good.

288   *Hazel Pearson*

Consider also the following pairs. (11a), (11b) and (12a) say roughly that all English churches are beautiful, whereas (12b) is the outlier: one could respond with, 'That's not true. They look terrible when it's dark and there are floodlights on'.

11a.   English churches are beautiful.
11b.   English churches are always beautiful.
12a.   English churches look beautiful.
12b.   English churches always look beautiful.

The next observation concerns perception sentences. ILPs cannot be embedded below a perception verb like *saw* (13a), but SLPs can (13b).

13a.   ??Emma saw Ben tall.
13b.   Emma saw Ben happy.

Again, simple PPTs pattern with ILPs, but complex PPTs pattern with SLPs.[6]

14a.   ??Emma saw St Paul's beautiful.
14b.   Emma saw St Paul's looking beautiful.

Next, consider what happens when an ILP occurs in a *when*-clause.

15a.   ??When Ben is tall, everyone feels good.
15b.   When Ben is happy, everyone feels good.

(15a) generates the odd inference that Ben is tall only sometimes, but since people's moods can vary over time, (15b) is perfect. Now compare *tasty* with *tastes good*.

16a.   ??When Barry and Frieda's wedding cake is tasty, the whole family enjoys it.
16b.   When Barry and Frieda's wedding cake tastes good, the whole family enjoys it.

(16b) feels odd out of the blue, but with a suitable context it improves. Suppose that Barry and Frieda have saved their wedding cake. Every year on their anniversary they share some with their family. How the cake tastes varies from year to year depending on how the flavours have matured, how it has been stored, etc. In this context (16b) is acceptable, but (16a) is still degraded.

The same point can be made by comparing *beautiful* with *looks beautiful*.

17a.   ??When St Paul's is beautiful, tourists like to photograph it.
17b.   When St Paul's looks beautiful, tourists like to photograph it.

Predicates of Personal Taste 289

Again, (17a) suggests that St Paul's is only beautiful sometimes—an inference that is perceived as odd. But (17b) generates an inference that St Paul's only *looks* beautiful sometimes; this inference is acceptable.

Now let's turn to counterfactuals. Kratzer (1989) observes that (18a) and (18b) are both true.[7]

Scenario: There are five people in the room, including Otto and Paula. Of those five, only Otto and Paula are tall.

18a. If Otto and Paula weren't in this room, none of the people who were in the room would be tall.
18b. If none of the people who were in the room were tall, Otto and Paula wouldn't be in the room.

Now let's replace *tall* with the SLP *bored*. Kratzer observes that the resulting (a) sentence is still true, but (b) is false.

Scenario: There are five people in the room, including Otto and Paula. Of those five, only Otto and Paula are bored.

19a. If Otto and Paul weren't in the room, none of the people who were in the room would be bored.
19b. If none of the people who were in the room were bored, Otto and Paula wouldn't be in the room.

Intuitively, (19b) is false because the antecedent of the conditional could be satisfied in virtue of Otto and Paula being in the room but not being bored: the proviso that none of the people in the room are bored is not sufficient to exclude Otto and Paula, despite our knowledge that they are in fact bored right now. But in (19a), we are reluctant to consider possibilities where shorter versions of Otto and Paula are in the room: the proviso that none of the people in the room are tall is sufficient basis to conclude that they can't be in the room.

This pattern is replicated with PPTs. Simple PPTs behave like *tall*:

20. Scenario: There are five desserts leftover from yesterday's party. The desserts are in the fridge, including a chocolate cake and a tiramisu. The chocolate cake and the tiramisu are the only desserts in the group that are tasty (according to the speaker).

   a. If the chocolate cake and the tiramisu weren't in the fridge, no dessert that is in the fridge would be tasty.
   b. If none of the desserts that were in the fridge were tasty, the chocolate cake and the tiramisu wouldn't be in the fridge.

But when *tasty* is replaced with *tastes good*, the (b) sentence becomes false:

21a. If the chocolate cake and the tiramisu weren't in the fridge, no dessert that is in the fridge would taste good.

290 *Hazel Pearson*

21b. If none of the desserts that were in the fridge tasted good, the chocolate cake and the tiramisu wouldn't be in the fridge.

To see that (21b) is false, notice that whether or not a dessert that is in the fridge tastes good may depend on whether chilling it improves its flavour. In the relevant scenario, the chocolate cake and the tiramisu taste good served cold, but the other desserts do not. Now, we can evaluate (21b) by considering counterfactual possibilities where *none* of the desserts responds well to being chilled. The sentence is true just in case all such possibilities are such that the chocolate cake and the tiramisu are not in the fridge. But this doesn't follow: intuitively, the antecedent is compatible with the chocolate cake and the tiramisu being in the fridge and not tasting good (in virtue of not responding well to being chilled). But (20b) is true: the antecedent of the conditional is concerned with counterfactual possibilities where none of the desserts in the fridge is tasty *tout court*—regardless of the effect of being in the fridge on its flavour. In such circumstances, the cake and the tiramisu cannot be in the fridge, since it has already been established that they are tasty.

We can make the same point by comparing *beautiful* and *looks beautiful*:

> Scenario: Five buildings in London are lit up right now, including St Paul's. St Paul's is the only building of the group that is beautiful (according to the speaker).

22a. If St Paul's weren't lit up, no building that is lit up would be beautiful. [*True*]
22b. If none of the buildings that were lit up were beautiful, St Paul's wouldn't be lit up. [*True*]

Replacing *beautiful* with *looks beautiful* changes the truth value of (22b):

> Scenario: 5 buildings in London are lit up right now, including St Paul's. St Paul's is the only building of the group that looks beautiful.

23a. If St Paul's weren't lit up, no building that is lit up would look beautiful. [*True*]
23b. If none of the buildings that were lit up looked beautiful, St Paul's wouldn't be lit up. [*False*]

In (23b), we can consider possibilities in which St Paul's is lit up but doesn't look beautiful—perhaps St Paul's only looks beautiful in natural light, for example. On this basis, the sentence can be judged false. But in (22b), it seems that we do not consider possibilities in which St Paul's is not beautiful and is lit up; hence the sentence is true.

I have presented an array of evidence that simple PPTs such as *tasty* and *beautiful* are ILPs, and complex PPTs like *taste good* and *look beautiful*

Predicates of Personal Taste 291

are SLPs. In the next section, I present evidence for a second difference between these two classes: when simple PPTs take a covert Experiencer, that argument obligatorily receives a generic interpretation. Complex PPTs are more liberal: covert Experiencers can either be read generically or receive bound variable or referential construals.

3. The Experiencer Argument of Stage- and Individual-Level PPTs

One point of disagreement in the PPTs literature concerns whether, when occurring without an overt Experiencer such as *to Mandy*, the predicate is one place (Lasersohn, 2005) or two place (Stephenson, 2007a, 2007b; Schaffer, 2009; Moltmann, 2010b, 2012; Pearson, 2013a, 2013b; Snyder, 2013; Bylinina, 2017). I follow the latter authors in assuming a uniform two-place semantics for PPTs, with bare uses of PPTs involving a covert pronoun in internal argument position:

24a. This tea is [tasty *pro*].
24b. This tea [tastes good *pro*].

I will argue that stage-level PPTs allow bound variable, referential and generic construals of this pronoun, whereas individual-level PPTs allow only generic construals. My evidence includes weak crossover effects and strict/sloppy ambiguity.[8]

3.1. Weak Crossover

Lasersohn (2005) argues that if a predicate can take a covert pronoun as an argument, then we should expect that pronoun to show so-called 'weak crossover' effects.[9] Consider (25).

25. ?Whom$_i$ did the fact that the tiramisu wasn't tasty to him$_i$ upset t$_i$?

On the intended reading (indicated by co-indexation of the wh-word *whom* and the pronoun *him*), the sentence asks, 'For which x did the fact that the tiramisu wasn't tasty to x upset x?' *Whom* starts off as the object of the verb *upset* (indicated by the co-indexed trace) and undergoes movement to the sentence-initial position where it is pronounced. In doing so, it crosses over a pronoun with which it is co-indexed, generating a configuration that the grammar rules out: the sentence is degraded.

We can check that the source of ungrammaticality is indeed the crossing over of the pronoun by *whom* by comparing (25) with (26):

26. Who$_i$ t$_i$ was upset that the tiramisu wasn't tasty to him$_i$?

Here too, we have movement of a wh-word, but its base-generated position is higher: it is a subject rather than an object and does not cross over *him* en route to its landing site. The sentence is accordingly grammatical.

Lasersohn notes that if a PPT takes a covert pronominal argument, we should expect the same weak crossover effects that we have just seen with overt Experiencer pronouns. But this is not quite right: since crossover only arises when the wh-word and pronoun co-vary, the prediction is that crossover effects will arise if a PPT takes a covert pronominal argument, *and* this argument is bindable by wh-words. If instead a PPT takes a covert *generic* argument, we should not expect to see crossover effects. This distinction will be crucial for what follows.

In any event, Lasersohn claims that the alleged prediction is not borne out: there seems to be no difference in grammaticality between (27a) and (27b):

27a. Whom$_i$ did the fact that the tiramisu wasn't tasty upset t$_i$?
27b. Who$_i$ t$_i$ was upset that the tiramisu wasn't tasty?

Suppose we replace *tasty* with *taste good*:

28a. Whom$_i$ did the fact that the tiramisu didn't taste good upset t$_i$?
28b. Who$_i$ t$_i$ was upset that the tiramisu didn't taste good?

Here too there initially seems to be no difference between (a) and (b), suggesting that there is no crossover effect. At this point, it is worth pausing to reflect on what these examples show. We know from (25) that crossover arises, in the appropriate structural configuration, when a PPT takes a pronominal argument whose value covaries with that of the wh-word. That we judge (27a) and (28a) grammatical suggests that either (i) PPTs cannot take such a pronominal argument or (ii) PPTs optionally take such a pronominal argument, but when speakers judge (27a) and (28b) to be grammatical, their judgment is based on a parse in which such a pronominal argument is not present. I will argue that (i) is the correct analysis of (27b) (with *tasty*) and (ii) is the correct analysis of (28a) (with *tastes good*).

The first step is to create a scenario that makes a specific individual salient as Experiencer of the PPT. Consider (29).

29. Scenario: Rob is suffering from the aftereffects of a virus. For him, these include an altered sense of taste. Everything tastes horrible to him now, including things that he would normally enjoy. He is looking forward to attending a friend's wedding at the weekend, at which will be served a specially made wedding cake, which by all accounts is expected to be delicious. Rob is disappointed to realise that the cake will taste horrible to him, though it's expected that everyone else will enjoy it—including others who have had

Predicates of Personal Taste 293

the virus, since Rob is the only known patient to have experienced this particular aftereffect.

In this context, we can check whether the following question/answer pairs are felicitous.

30. A: ?Who did the fact that the cake wouldn't taste good because of the virus upset?
    B: Rob.

31. A: Who was upset that the cake wouldn't taste good because of the virus?
    B: Rob.

A's question in (31) is well formed, and the dialogue is felicitous. But in (30), A's question is degraded. As we have seen, this contrast is characteristic of weak crossover. This indicates that on the intended interpretation, A's question in (30) has the structure in (32).

32. ?Who$_i$ did the fact that the cake wouldn't [taste good *pro*$_i$] because of the virus upset t$_i$?

So we have evidence that *tastes good* can take a covert pronominal argument that can be bound by a wh-word.

Now let's return to what happens when *taste good* is replaced by *tasty*. Earlier, we suggested that such cases do not give rise to crossover effects. We need to check whether this is so even when the sentences are judged against our richer context.

33. Scenario: Rob is suffering from the aftereffects of a virus. For him, these include an altered sense of taste. Everything tastes horrible to him now, including things that he would normally enjoy. He is looking forward to attending a friend's wedding at the weekend, at which will be served a specially made wedding cake, which by all accounts is expected to be delicious. Rob is disappointed to realise that the cake will taste horrible to him, though it's expected that everyone else will enjoy it—including others who have had the virus, since Rob is the only known patient to have experienced this particular aftereffect.

34. A: #Who did the fact that the cake wouldn't be tasty because of the virus upset?
    B: Rob.

35. A: #Who was upset that the cake wouldn't be tasty because of the virus?
    B: Rob.

(35) provides a baseline; since the wh-word doesn't cross over the putative internal argument of *tasty*, the sentence is expected to be grammatical. I believe that it is indeed grammatical but infelicitous in context: it presupposes that the cake wouldn't be tasty. Intuitively, in order for this presupposition to be met, there would need to be something wrong with the cake itself. But we are told that there is nothing wrong with the cake: it is only Rob's tastes that are temporarily faulty. A's question in (34) is also grammatical but infelicitous for the same reason. So unlike its counterpart with *taste good*, (34) does not show weak crossover, suggesting that *tasty* cannot take a covert internal argument that is bindable by *who*. I take it that *tasty* involves a generic construal with respect to the Experiencer, which is therefore not bindable by *who*. That is, I take the class of analyses proposed by Moltmann (2010b, 2012), Pearson (2013a), Snyder (2013) and Keshet (2020) to be along the right lines—at least as far as *tasty* goes.

Now let's check that these observations are replicated with other simple and complex PPT pairs. Take *beautiful* and *looks beautiful*.

36. Sarah is a newly qualified architect. There is a church in her hometown that she has always found beautiful (and everyone else agrees). Returning home after graduation, she discovers that with her trained eye, the church no longer looks beautiful to her.

37. A: ?Who did the fact that the church no longer looked beautiful because of her architectural training upset?
     B: Sarah

38. A: Who was upset that the church no longer looked beautiful because of her architectural training?
     B: Sarah

Once again, A's question in (37) is degraded with respect to the baseline in (38)—evidence of crossover.

Finally, notice that the questions in both (39) and (40) are odd: they suggest that a single person having trained as an architect could somehow affect whether or not the church is beautiful.

39. A: #Who was upset that the church was no longer beautiful because of her architectural training?
     B: Sarah.
40. A: #Who did the fact that the church was no longer beautiful because of her architectural training upset?
     B: Sarah.

Predicates of Personal Taste 295

If it is correct that stage-level PPTs are susceptible to weak crossover effects, then we should expect that in a language such as German that does not show weak crossover in general, counterparts of sentences like (32) should be acceptable.[10] This is precisely what we find:

41. Wen   hat   die   Tatsache, dass der   Kuchen
    Who.ACC has DET.NOM fact   that DET.NOM cake
    wegen   des   Virus nicht gut   schmecken würde, verärgert?
    because DET.GEN virus not   good taste   would   annoy
    'Who did the fact that the cake wouldn't taste good because of the virus annoy?'

42. Wer   war   darüber verärgert,   dass   der
    Who.NOM was   about it annoyed   that   DET.NOM
    Kuchen   wegen   des   Virus nicht gut   schmecken würde?
    cake   because DET.GEN virus not   good taste   would
    'Who was annoyed that the cake wouldn't taste good because of the virus?'

The native German speakers I consulted found both (41) and (42) acceptable in the context in (29), with Rob as the intended answer.[11] This is expected on our account given that for these speakers the counterpart of (41) with an overt pronoun is also acceptable:

43. Wen   hat   die   Tatsache, dass ihm   der   Kuchen
    Who.ACC has DET.NOM fact   that him DET.NOM cake
    wegen   des   Virus nicht gut   schmecken würde, verärgert?
    because DET.GEN virus not   good taste   would annoy
    'Who did the fact that the cake wouldn't taste good to him because of the virus annoy?'

This is striking evidence in favour of our claim that the source of the degraded status of (32) is weak crossover: in a language that does not show weak crossover with a variant of the sentence with an overt pronoun, so too is the counterpart of (32) acceptable in context. I should mention, however, that speakers' judgments about German counterparts of (34) and (35) were more surprising:

44. Wen   hat   die   Tatsache, dass der   Kuchen
    who.ACC has   DET.NOM fact   that DET.NOM cake
    wegen   des   Virus nicht lecker/schmackhaft sein würde, verärgert?
    because DET.GEN virus not   tasty   be   would annoy
    'Who did the fact that the cake wouldn't be tasty because of the virus annoy?'

296 *Hazel Pearson*

45. Wer   war   darüber   verärgert,   dass   der   Kuchen
Who.NOM   was   about it   annoyed   that   DET.NOM cake
wegen   des   Virus   nicht   lecker/schmackhaft   sein   würde?
because   DET.GEN   virus   not   tasty   be   would
'Who was annoyed that the cake wouldn't be tasty because of the virus?'

Both sentences were judged felicitous in the intended scenario, unlike what we saw earlier for (34) and (35). It may be that the German counterparts of *tasty* (*lecker* and *schmackhaft*) are not individual-level predicates; I leave it to future work to investigate this.

To summarise, crossover data indicates that stage-level PPTs like *taste good* and *look beautiful* can take a covert internal argument that is bindable by a wh-word, but individual-level PPTs cannot. We should therefore expect to find that stage-level PPTs but not individual-level ones show sloppy readings under ellipsis and are bindable by quantifiers. I present evidence for this in 3.2.

3.2. Strict/Sloppy Readings

Consider (46).

46. Everyone who was recovering from the virus was disappointed that the wedding cake didn't taste good to her.

In a scenario where (i) all of the guests found the cake delicious except those who were recovering from the virus and (ii) all of those recovering from the virus have an altered sense of taste and were disappointed to find that the cake didn't taste good to them, (46) has a true reading. On this reading, the pronoun *her* is bound by *everyone*:

47. Everyone who was recovering from the virus λx_1 [t_1 was disappointed that the wedding cake didn't taste good to her$_1$].

(48) also has a true reading in the same scenario.

48. Everyone who was recovering from the virus was disappointed that the wedding cake didn't taste good.

This suggests that (48) has an LF that is identical to that in (47), except that the bound pronoun is covert:

49. Everyone who was recovering from the virus λx_1 [t_1 was disappointed that the wedding cake didn't taste good *pro*$_1$].

Suppose that we replace *tastes good* with *tasty*:

50. Everyone who was recovering from the virus was disappointed that the wedding cake was not tasty.

Predicates of Personal Taste   297

Unlike in (48), there is no bound variable reading for the internal argument of the PPT in (50). A way to see this is to consider what happens when (46), (48) and (50) are followed with '. . . *Of course I found it delicious*'. This results in a felicitous discourse for (46) and (48) but not (50).

51a.   Everyone$_i$ who was recovering from the virus was disappointed that the wedding cake didn't taste good to her$_i$. Of course I found it delicious.
51b.   Everyone who was recovering from the virus was disappointed that the wedding cake didn't taste good. Of course I found it delicious.
51c.#Everyone who was recovering from the virus was disappointed that the wedding cake was not tasty. Of course I found it delicious.

Since *disappointed* is factive, (51a) carries a presupposition—namely, that everyone who was recovering from the virus was such that the cake did not taste good to them.[12] This is compatible with the speaker finding the cake delicious (assuming that she is not among the patients herself), and so (51a) is felicitous. (51b) patterns with (51a), as expected if the covert internal argument of *tastes good* is bound. But the discourse in (51c) is infelicitous: the assertion that the speaker found the cake delicious is felt to contradict the presupposed content of the first sentence. This suggests that the first sentence of (51c) presupposes that the group of people who did not enjoy the cake was not confined to the patients, contrary to what would be expected if the internal argument of *tasty* were bound by *everyone*. So (50) cannot have an LF parallel to (47).[13]

Now consider the pair *looks beautiful* and *(is) beautiful*. Suppose that everyone who has had architectural training has made the discovery that the church in Sarah's hometown that they once found beautiful no longer seems beautiful to them. Suppose further that the speaker, who has no expertise in the area of architecture, finds the church beautiful. (52) has a true reading in this scenario.

52.   Everyone who has had architectural training is disappointed that the church no longer looks beautiful.

Yet (53) is infelicitous:

53.   #Everyone who has had architectural training is disappointed that the church is no longer beautiful.

Further evidence comes from VP ellipsis. Suppose that Sarah and Emma have both had their sense of taste affected by the virus. Tasting the wedding cake, Sarah says, 'I'm sure the wedding cake is delicious, but it doesn't taste good to me'. Emma adds, 'I'm not enjoying it either, but I'm sure it's very tasty'. We can report this with the sentence in (54).

298   *Hazel Pearson*

54. Sarah said that the wedding cake didn't taste good to her, and Emma did too.

This is the 'sloppy' reading of the pronoun, which is generally taken as evidence for a bound variable reading. Suppressing the overt pronoun yields a sentence that is also true in this scenario:

55. Sarah said that the wedding cake didn't taste good, and Emma did too.

But (56), where *tastes good* is replaced by *tasty*, is false: the content conflicts with our knowledge that both Sarah and Emma said that they were sure that the cake must be tasty.

56. Sarah said that the wedding cake wasn't tasty, and Emma did too.

So we have further evidence for a covert pronominal argument for *taste good* that can receive a bound variable reading and that *tasty* does not take such an argument. In fact, we can go one step further: VP-ellipsis permits *strict* readings for pronouns as well as the sloppy ones we have just investigated. On this reading, the second conjunct of (56) reports that Emma said that the wedding cake didn't taste good to *Sarah*. We can check that this reading is available for (55) by considering the following scenario.

57. Only Sarah has had her sense of taste affected by the virus. Tasting the wedding cake, Sarah says, 'I'm sure the wedding cake is delicious, but it doesn't taste good to me'. Having overheard this, Emma later says to a friend, 'I haven't tried the cake, but I'm sure it's very tasty. Unfortunately it doesn't taste good to Sarah though because of the virus'.

(55) has a true reading in this scenario, unlike (56). Again, Sarah and Emma's assertion that the cake must be delicious is sufficient to render (56) false.

The facts replicate with the pair *looks beautiful* and *(is) beautiful*:

58. Sarah and Emma are newly qualified architects. Looking at the church, Sarah says, 'I know most people find the church beautiful, but it no longer looks beautiful to me'. Emma adds, 'Yes, it no longer looks beautiful to me too'.

(59) and (60) both have true readings in this scenario, but (61) does not.

59. Sarah said that the church no longer looked beautiful to her, and Emma did too.

Predicates of Personal Taste 299

60. Sarah said that the church no longer looked beautiful, and Emma did too.
61. Sarah said that the church was no longer beautiful, and Emma did too.

Moreover, the covert pronoun in (60) can receive a strict reading; (60) is true in the following scenario, but (61) is false.

62. Sarah is a newly qualified architect. Looking at the church, Sarah says, 'I know most people find the church beautiful, but it no longer looks beautiful to me'. Having overheard this, Emma later says to a friend, 'I haven't seen the church, but I'm sure it's very beautiful. Unfortunately it no longer looks beautiful to Sarah, because she sees all sorts of faults with it now that she is a trained architect'.

In general, it seems that stage-level but not individual-level PPTs can take a covert pronominal argument that can either receive a bound variable interpretation or be free. In the examples just discussed involving strict readings, the pronoun is free and is interpreted as a third-person pronoun referring to an individual who is salient in the discourse. I'll now show that this pronoun has a construal where it behaves like a first-person indexical.

3.3. *First-Person Indexical Readings*

To set things up, consider the following examples involving overt Experiencers for *tastes good*.

63a. When I've just brushed my teeth, pineapple juice doesn't taste good to me.
63b. #When I've just brushed my teeth, pineapple juice doesn't taste good to Emma.
63c. #When I've just brushed my teeth, pineapple juice doesn't taste good to people in general.

If I brush my teeth, I temporarily alter my (but no one else's) perception of taste. This is why (63b) and (63c) are infelicitous: the *when*-clause redundantly imposes a restriction to situations where the speaker has just brushed her teeth. (63a) is fine, since it is plausible to think that whether or not the speaker has just brushed her teeth may affect how the pineapple juice tastes to *her*.

We can use this to test whether *tastes good* can take a covert speaker-denoting argument. If so, then (63)'s counterpart with no overt Experiencer should be felicitous. This prediction is borne out:

300   *Hazel Pearson*

64. When I've just brushed my teeth, pineapple juice tastes good.

Further evidence for the possibility of a covert first-person indexical argument for *taste good* comes from the so-called 'acquaintance inference' (Pearson, 2013a; Ninan, 2014; Anand & Korotkova, 2018). (65) gives rise to the inference that the speaker has tasted pineapple juice.

65. Pineapple juice tastes good.

One piece of evidence for this is that negating this inference creates an infelicitous discourse.

66. #Pineapple juice tastes good, but I've never tasted it.

It is well known that the acquaintance inference can be suspended by epistemic *must* (Pearson, 2013a; Anand & Korotkova, 2018).

67. Pineapple juice must taste good, but I've never tasted it.

PPTs with overt Experiencers are also subject to an acquaintance requirement (68). This requirement cannot be suspended by adding *must*, however, as shown by (69) (Pearson, 2013a; Anand & Korotkova, 2018).

68. #Pineapple juice tastes good to me, but I have never tasted it.
69. #Pineapple juice must taste good to me, but I have never tasted it.

In fact, attempting to combine epistemic *must* with a first-person Experiencer produces infelicity, even without the continuations shown.

70. #Pineapple juice must taste good to me.

This seems to be because there is a conflict between the inference generated by *must* that the speaker is basing her statement on indirect evidence and the requirement imposed by *to me* that the speaker has tasted pineapple juice (Pearson, 2013a; Anand & Korotkova, 2018).[14]

Returning to our *when*-sentences, in these cases the acquaintance requirement takes the form of a condition that the Experiencer must have tasted pineapple juice under the circumstances described by the *when*-clause.[15]

71. #When I've just brushed my teeth, pineapple juice tastes good. But I've never tasted pineapple juice after brushing my teeth.
72. #When I've just brushed my teeth, pineapple juice tastes good to me. But I've never tasted pineapple juice after brushing my teeth.

Predicates of Personal Taste 301

(73) is odd due to the mismatch between the indirect experience inference associated with *must* and the acquaintance inference:

73. #When I've just brushed my teeth, pineapple juice must taste good to me.

Here then is the prediction: if *taste good* takes a covert speaker-denoting argument in an example like (64), then adding *must* should produce infelicity. (74) shows that this prediction is borne out.

74. #When I've just brushed my teeth, pineapple juice must taste good.

This is striking evidence that *tastes good* can take a covert speaker-denoting argument. One question that remains is why the acquaintance inference is suspended by epistemic *must* in (67), repeated in what follows.

75. Pineapple juice must taste good, but I've never tasted it.

Clearly *taste good* does not take a speaker-denoting argument in this case; if it did, the example would be infelicitous. Moreover, the sentence is acceptable without any other salient individual in the discourse to serve as an antecedent for a covert pronominal argument. I propose instead that in this case, *taste good* takes a pronominal argument akin to generic *one*. Evidence that such a pronoun is a possible argument for *taste good* comes from the example in (76).

76. When one has just brushed one's teeth, pineapple juice tastes good.

As we have seen, for these types of *when*-sentence to be felicitous, the subject of the *when*-clause and the Experiencer of *taste good* must co-vary. Now notice that (76) is felicitous even when *must* is added.

77. When one has just brushed one's teeth, pineapple juice must taste good.

I take this as evidence that when *taste good* takes generic *one* as its (covert) argument, it is rendered possible to suspend the acquaintance inference by means of adding epistemic *must*. This suggests that the reason (75) is felicitous is because here too, *taste good* takes *one* as an argument.

We have now presented evidence that when *taste good* does not take an overt Experiencer argument, there is a covert pronoun present in the structure that can be construed referentially, receive a bound variable reading or be a covert counterpart of generic *one*. Finally, let's check what happens when *tastes good* in (64) is replaced with *tasty*:

302 *Hazel Pearson*

78. #When I've just brushed my teeth, pineapple juice is tasty.

This indicates that *tasty*, unlike *taste good*, cannot take a covert speaker-denoting argument. Instead, I assume, following Moltmann (2010a, 2012), Pearson (2013a) and Keshet (2020), that its argument must be the covert counterpart of generic *one*.

This pattern is replicated for the pair *looks beautiful/is beautiful*. Take the following example.

79. When I wear 3D glasses, St Paul's looks beautiful.

Given the argument developed here, the fact that (79) is acceptable suggests that *looks beautiful* can take a covert speaker-denoting argument. This is supported by the fact that adding epistemic *must* renders the sentence infelicitous.

80. #When I wear 3D glasses, St Paul's must look beautiful.

Replacing *looks beautiful* in (79) with *is beautiful* also produces infelicity:

81. #When I wear 3D glasses, St Paul's is beautiful.

For now we can say that *looks beautiful* patterns with *tastes good* in permitting both covert speaker-denoting arguments and a covert counterpart of generic *one*, while the adjectival PPT *beautiful*, like *tasty*, can only take generic *one* as a covert argument.

Further evidence comes from the following contrasts, which are based on examples discussed in (Pearson, 2013b).

82a. Now that the recipe has changed, Nutella no longer tastes good.
82b. Now that I have lost my sweet tooth, Nutella no longer tastes good.
83a. Now that the recipe has changed, Nutella is no longer tasty.
83b. #Now that I have lost my sweet tooth, Nutella is no longer tasty.

(82) shows that whether a foodstuff counts as *tasting good* may change as a result of a change in that foodstuff (82a) or as a result of changes in the taste perception of whoever is eating it (82b). But the contrast between (83a) and (83b) indicates that whether something is considered *tasty* depends purely on the foodstuff itself. The judgments for (82) are unchanged if *taste good* takes an overt first-person pronoun as its argument:

84a. Now that the recipe has changed, Nutella doesn't taste good to me anymore.

Predicates of Personal Taste 303

84b. Now that I have lost my sweet tooth, Nutella doesn't taste good to me anymore.

But the contrast in (83) disappears when *to me* is added:

85a. Now that the recipe has changed, Nutella is no longer tasty to me.
85b. Now that I have lost my sweet tooth, Nutella is no longer tasty to me.

I take this as further evidence that *taste good* can take a covert first-person indexical pronoun as its argument, but *tasty* cannot.

These facts are replicated with *looks beautiful* and *(is) beautiful*:

86a. Now that modern architectural standards have declined, English churches no longer look beautiful.
86b. Now that I have a trained architect's eye, English churches no longer look beautiful.
87a. Now that modern architectural standards have declined, English churches are no longer beautiful.
87b. #Now that I have a trained architect's eye, English churches are no longer beautiful.

With *looks beautiful*, adding *to me* does not change the judgments:

88a. Now that modern architectural standards have declined, English churches no longer look beautiful to me.
88b. Now that I have a trained architect's eye, English churches no longer look beautiful to me.

But the (b) sentence is improved by the addition of an overt first-person Experiencer in the case of *(is) beautiful*:

89a. Now that modern architectural standards have declined, English churches are no longer beautiful to me.
89b. Now that I have a trained architect's eye, English churches are no longer beautiful to me.

The next piece of evidence for the availability of a covert speaker-denoting argument with *tastes good* and *looks beautiful* but not with *tasty* and *(is) beautiful* builds on an observation from Pearson (2013a) that not all taste claims exhibit faultless disagreement: (90) is simply false, even if sincerely asserted.

90. Soapy dishwater is tasty.

304 *Hazel Pearson*

On the other hand, if *to me* is added, then the sentence is true if sincerely asserted.

91. Soapy dishwater is tasty to me.

Pearson (2013b) builds on this observation to argue that *taste good* can take a covert first-person indexical argument:

92. That soapy dishwater tasted good.

Intuitively, (92) is not false, assuming that the speaker is sincere. In this respect, (92) patterns with (91). I take this as additional evidence that *tastes good* but not *tasty* can take a covert speaker-denoting argument.

3.4. *Interim Summary*

We have presented evidence that complex PPTs are more liberal than simple PPTs in the range of covert internal arguments they can take. A covert internal argument of a complex PPT may (i) receive a bound variable interpretation, (ii) be interpreted referentially or (iii) have a generic construal. Of these three options, only (iii) is available for simple PPTs. We have also seen that option (ii) includes the possibility of a speaker-denoting argument for the complex PPT—a possibility that has been rejected by relativists from Lasersohn (2005) onwards. One of the lessons of this chapter is that a first-person indexical analysis should be brought back into the fold, although only for a certain class of PPTs.

We also saw in Section 2 that simple PPTs are individual-level, while complex PPTs are stage-level. Taking the findings of Sections 2 and 3 together, we can state the following generalisation.

93. *The PPT-Experiencer Correlation:* A PPT *P* can take a covert Experiencer argument that can receive a bound variable, referential or generic construal iff *P* is stage-level. Otherwise, a covert Experiencer argument of *P* must receive a generic construal.

In the next section, I propose an analysis of simple versus complex PPTs that predicts this correlation.

4. Analysis

I have been assuming that both simple and complex PPTs are two place predicates. I will also assume that predicates take situation arguments. Here are two sample denotations.[16]

94. $[[tasty]]^g = \lambda x \lambda y \lambda s.$ y is tasty to x in s
95. $[[taste\ good]]^g = \lambda x \lambda y \lambda s.$ y tastes good to x in s

Tasty holds between a Stimulus y and an Experiencer x in a situation s just in case y is tasty to x in s. Likewise *taste good* holds between y and x in s just in case y tastes good to x in s. I assume that where there is no overt Experiencer, the argument slot is filled by a covert pronominal *pro*:

96. This cake is tasty/tastes good *pro*.

In principle, the following three options are available to determine the interpretation of *pro*. Firstly, *pro*, like ordinary overt pronouns, may be bound by a lambda abstractor that is present in the Logical Form; it then receives a bound variable interpretation. Secondly, it may be free, in which case it receives its interpretation under a variable assignment, which maps *pro*'s index to some contextually salient individual. In this respect too, it behaves like an ordinary overt pronoun. Thirdly, it may be bound by the generic operator GEN and receive an interpretation akin to generic *one*.

I assume, following Chierchia (1995), that ILPs are only licensed if GEN is present at LF, adjoined to the VP. Thus (97b) is ungrammatical.

97a. $[\lambda s_1 \ [s_1 \ \text{This cake}_i \ [\text{GEN} \ \lambda s_2 \ [s_2 \ t_i \ \text{is tasty } pro]]$
97b. $*[\lambda s_1 \ [s_1 \ \text{This cake}_i \ [t_i \ \text{is tasty } pro]]]$

We can think of GEN as a covert adverb of (quasi-)universal quantification—an unselective binder of free variables in its scope. In (97a), the variables in question are the main predicate's situation and individual arguments:[17]

98. $[[\ [\lambda s_1 \ [s_1 \ \text{This cake}_i \ [\text{GEN} \ \lambda s_2 \ [s_2 \ t_i \ \text{is tasty } pro]] \ ]]^g = \lambda s. \ \forall x, s'$
$[\text{Acc}(s, s') \ \& \ C(x, s')] \ [\text{tasty(this cake, x, s')}]$

(98) illustrates that GEN makes two further contributions in addition to universal quantification over situations and individuals. First, it restricts the situations quantified over to those that are accessible from the situation of evaluation s. What it takes for a situation to count as accessible is a context-dependent matter. In this case, a situation s' will only be accessible if for example the cake has the same ingredients in s' as it has in s. So if the cake contains 100g of dark chocolate in s then it does in s' too. Secondly, a contextual restriction C ensures that the individual-situation pairs quantified over <x, s'> are restricted to those that are relevant. In (97), <x, s'> is relevant only if x eats the cake in s'. Both the accessibility relation and the contextual restriction are standard components of an analysis of genericity and independently motivated (see e.g. Krifka et al., 1995 for discussion).

306   *Hazel Pearson*

Putting everything together, *This cake is tasty* is predicted to be true just in case for every <x, s'> that is a relevant individual-situation pair (e.g. such that x eats the cake in s'), this cake tastes good to x in s'. Crucially, I assume that binding of the pronominal argument *pro* of *tasty* by GEN is obligatory. I propose that this follows from the following constraint.

99. *ILP Licensing Condition:* If *P* is an individual-level predicate, then all null pronominal arguments of *P* must be bound by GEN.

This ensures that *pro* cannot receive a bound variable interpretation and that it cannot be referential (and hence cannot be an indexical).[18] I take it that the null hypothesis is that unpronounced pronouns not obligatorily bound by GEN can either be free or can be bound by GEN or some other operator; this is sufficient to derive the PPT-Experiencer Correlation.[19]

5.   Predictions

GEN may or may not be present in the syntactic structure of a clause. With ILPs, this operator is obligatory in order to satisfy the ILP Licensing Condition. With stage-level predicates, the operator is optional. Furthermore, the internal argument of a predicate of personal taste may or may not receive a generic construal. In principle, then, we have the following four logical possibilities for a taste statement containing a bare PPT.

100.   (i)   +GEN -generic Experiencer
       (ii)   +GEN +generic Experiencer
       (iii) -GEN -generic Experiencer
       (iv)   -GEN +generic Experiencer

As I will demonstrate in this section, the account correctly predicts that only (ii) is available for individual-level PPTs and that (i–iii) are available for stage-level PPTs. We have already encountered examples attesting to options (i–iii) for stage-level PPTs and showing that only option (ii) is attested for individual-level PPTs. I will review the evidence in this section.

Consider option (i) first. This arises when GEN is present, but the Experiencer is not generic. I propose that this is the proper analysis of (64), repeated in what follows.

101.   When I've just brushed my teeth, pineapple juice tastes good.

As shown in Section 3, in this example, *tastes good* takes a covert speaker-denoting argument. We also need to show that GEN is present. I assume, following Partee (1984) and Kratzer (1991), that *when*-clauses are restrictors of adverbs of quantification. In an example like (101) where there is no overt quantificational adverb, this role is fulfilled by GEN:[20]

Predicates of Personal Taste 307

102a. [When I've just brushed my teeth] [pineapple juice$_i$ [GEN t$_i$ tastes good *pro$_1$*]]

102b. [[102a]]$^{c, g}$ = λs. ∀x, s' [Acc(s, s') & Pineapple-juice(x, s') & C(x, s') & speaker(c) has just brushed speaker(c)'s teeth in s'] [tastes good(x, g(1), s')]

Pick an assignment function g such that g(1) = speaker(c). The sentence is predicted to be true just in case for every situation s' and individual x such that x instantiates the pineapple juice-kind in s' and the speaker has just brushed her teeth in s', x tastes good to the speaker in s'. Since this matches intuitions about the meaning of the sentence, I conclude that GEN is present in this sentence.

We also predict the contrast between (101) and (103) first observed in Section 3.

103. #When I've just brushed my teeth, pineapple juice is tasty.

104a. [When I've just brushed my teeth] [pineapple juice$_i$ [GEN t$_i$ is tasty *pro*]]

104b. [[104a]]$^{c, g}$ = λs. ∀x, y, s' [Acc(s, s') & Pineapple-juice(x, s') & C(x, y, s') & speaker(c) has just brushed speaker(c)'s teeth in s'] [tasty(x, y, s')]

Given the ILP Licensing Condition, *tasty*'s Experiencer must be generic as shown in (104b). As argued in Section 3, the assumption that the Experiencer of *tasty* is read generically is sufficient to explain the infelicity of (103).

Consider also the following examples.

105. Now that I have lost my sweet tooth, Nutella no longer tastes good.

106. #Now that I have lost my sweet tooth, Nutella is no longer tasty.

As argued in Section 3, *tastes good* in (105) takes a covert speaker-denoting argument, but *tasty* cannot do so, and (106) is therefore infelicitous. Additionally, I assume that (105) contains GEN: intuitively the sentence means 'for any relevant situation s' and sample of Nutella x, x does not taste good to me in s'. I leave it as an exercise to the reader to spell out the LF and truth conditions.

Now let's turn to option (ii), where GEN is present and the Experiencer is also generic. One example of this with the stage-level PPT *tastes good* is found in (107).

107. Pineapple juice must taste good, but no one has ever tasted it.

Recall that epistemic *must* can (under appropriate conditions) suspend the acquaintance inference with bare PPTs, but not when the Experiencer is

308   *Hazel Pearson*

overt. In Section 3 I concluded that in such cases, the covert Experiencer is construed generically. Indeed (107) is felicitous even though it asserts that no one has tasted pineapple juice. Here we have a modal entailment characteristic of generics: intuitively, the sentence means roughly 'if in a situation s' a person x were to taste pineapple juice, it would taste good to x in s"; this is compatible with no one having ever tasted pineapple juice in actuality. This too is evidence for the presence of GEN. Unsurprisingly, (107) is also acceptable when *taste good* is replaced with *tasty*:

108.   Pineapple juice must be tasty, but no one has ever tasted it.

Further evidence that both stage-level and individual-level PPTs can occur with GEN and take a generic Experiencer comes from the following examples.

109.   When one has just brushed one's teeth, pineapple juice tastes good.
110.   When one has just brushed one's teeth, pineapple juice is tasty.

We have already argued in Section 3 that the Experiencer is construed generically in the case of (109); the same reasoning holds for (110). And as we saw earlier, the *when*-clause in these types of example is the restrictor of GEN.

Now let's turn to option (iii), where the generic operator is absent and the covert Experiencer of the PPT is not construed generically. Our account predicts that this option is available for stage-level but not individual-level PPTs. Constructing cases where GEN is absent requires some care: Dinges and Zakkou (2020) argue that *tastes good* has a reading reminiscent of dispositionals, which should arguably involve appeal to GEN. Indeed, they argue that this is the most prominent reading out of the blue.[21] It can be seen, for instance, in the following example.

111.   The cake tastes good to me. I tried it yesterday.
                           [Dinges and Zakkou (2020), Example 15]

(111) shows that *The cake tastes good to me* may be true even when the speaker is not currently eating it. In this case it seems to mean roughly, 'Whenever I taste the cake, it tastes good to me'. Dinges and Zakkou argue that there is also an episodic reading, brought out in examples like the following.

112.   The cake is done, and when I dig in tomorrow, it will taste good to me.
                           [Dinges and Zakkou (2020), Example 23]

These are the types of examples that we need to show that stage-level PPTs can occur in non-generic environments. We also need to check whether

Predicates of Personal Taste 309

in such cases, the PPT can take a covert, non-generic Experiencer. To do this, I will adapt my strategy of using *when*-clauses:

113. When I had just brushed my teeth, the pineapple juice tasted good.

Given the discussion in Section 3, it seems plausible to assume that *taste good* takes a speaker-denoting argument in (113). Moreover, with this particular type of *when*-clause, there is no generic quantification. Instead, I assume that the *when*-clause contributes a definite time, on which the main clause past tense is anaphoric (Partee, 1984). The intuitively correct truth conditions relative to a context c are in (114). (To incorporate temporal reference I now assume that predicates take time interval arguments.)

114. $\lambda s \lambda t. \iota t'$ [t' < t & speaker(c)-has-just-brushed-speaker(c)'s-teeth(t', s)] [taste-good(the-pineapple-juice, speaker(c), t', s)]

The sentence asserts that at that past time t' at which the speaker had just brushed her teeth, the pineapple juice tasted good to her. Crucially, the claim that the pineapple juice tasted good is limited to a post-toothbrushing situation; no further inferences can be drawn about the taste of the pineapple juice in other situations. Consequently, no generic operator should be posited here.

What about individual-level PPTs? If one subscribes to the view that the characteristic behaviour of ILPs should be accounted for by postulating GEN, then the data concerning *tasty* and *beautiful* in Section 2 can be taken as evidence that these predicates cannot occur without the generic operator. But we can also check what happens when *tasted good* in (113) is replaced with *was tasty*. Sure enough, the result is infelicitous.

115. #When I had just brushed my teeth, the pineapple juice was tasty.

What has gone wrong here? By hypothesis, the only licit parse of (115) is that in (116).

116. [When I had brushed my teeth] [the pineapple juice$_i$ [GEN t$_i$ was tasty *pro*]]

I continue to assume that the main clause past tense is anaphoric on a definite time contributed by the *when*-clause. The truth conditions assigned to (115) are as follows.

117. $\lambda s \lambda t. \iota t'$ [t' < t & speaker(c)-has-just-brushed-speaker(c)'s-teeth(t', s)] [$\forall x$, s' [Acc(s, s') & C(the-pineapple-juice, x, t', s')] [tasty(the pineapple juice, x, t', s')]]

310 *Hazel Pearson*

This says roughly that at that past time at which the speaker had brushed her teeth, the generic sentence *The pineapple juice is tasty* was true. But whether or not the speaker has just brushed her teeth has no bearing on whether the pineapple juice is tasty to all relevant people in all relevant situations. So the restriction induced by the *when*-clause is redundant, and the sentence is infelicitous. I take it then that we have evidence that option (iii) is attested for stage-level but not individual-level PPTs: the former but not the latter can occur in episodic contexts (without GEN), and when they do, their covert internal argument need not be generic.

In fact, it turns out that in episodic contexts, stage-level PPTs *cannot* take generic Experiencers. Recall that epistemic *must* suspends the acquaintance inference when the PPT takes a covert generic argument but not when the internal argument is referential. Additionally, when a PPT takes a speaker-denoting argument, adding *must* results in a degraded sentence. Sure enough, when *must* is added to (113), infelicity results.

118. #When I had just brushed my teeth, the pineapple juice must have tasted good.

True, the example is ameliorated by considering a context where the speaker has forgotten what the pineapple juice tasted like after toothbrushing and is basing her conclusion on some sort of indirect evidence. But an outright denial of acquaintance is also infelicitous.

119. #When I had brushed my teeth, the pineapple juice must have tasted good. But I have never tasted pineapple juice after brushing my teeth.

I take this to show that a stage-level PPT can only take a covert generic Experiencer if it occurs in a generic context—GEN is needed to license the generic construal of the Experiencer. This is unsurprising given that on our semantics, the generic construal of the Experiencer comes about via binding of *pro* by GEN. Furthermore, it is also to be expected if this argument is the covert counterpart of generic *one*, which Malamud (2006) and Moltmann (2006) argue must be licensed by the generic operator.

In Section 4, I have proposed an account of the observation that the covert Experiencer of an individual-level PPT must be generic, whereas covert Experiencers of stage-level PPTs can also have bound variable or referential interpretations. I assume that both classes of PPT take a covert argument *pro*, which can in principle be generic or referential or receive a bound variable interpretation. Additionally, I adopt Chierchia's (1995) view that ILPs require local licensing by GEN, augmented with the assumption that *all* null pronominal arguments of an ILP (and not only its situation argument) must be bound by GEN. Finally, I assume that the generic Experiencer is a null counterpart of generic *one* and is

Predicates of Personal Taste   311

subject to the same licensing condition (binding by GEN). This minimal set of assumptions is sufficient to derive the PPT-Experiencer Correlation. In particular, it correctly predicts that of the four logically possible configurations in (99), only (ii) is attested for ILPs, whereas (i–iii) are attested for SLPs. In the next section, I argue that these findings present a challenge for relativism.

6.   Genericity, Not Judge Relativism, Explains Faultless Disagreement

The central character in relativist accounts of predicates of personal taste is the phenomenon of faultless disagreement, where two speakers express incompatible assertions, but neither says something false (Kölbel, 2002; Lasersohn, 2005). In (120), both Ethan and Sarah can be taken to have spoken truly, as long as each expressed their opinion sincerely.

120.   Ethan: Pineapple juice is tasty.
       Sarah: No, pineapple juice is not tasty.

An alternative to relativism takes it that the source of faultless disagreement is a generic construal of the Experiencer (Anand, 2009; Moltmann, 2010b, 2012; Pearson, 2013a; Snyder, 2013; Keshet, 2020). These authors differ on precisely how genericity gives rise to faultless disagreement; according to the account I favour, faultless disagreement is a consequence of a specific type of genericity that is 'first person oriented' in the sense of Moltmann's (2006, 2010a) analysis of generic *one*.[22] But regardless of the details, if the appeal to genericity is correct, then the current proposal predicts that faultless disagreement will arise only when the PPT takes a generic Experiencer (Moltmann, 2010b, 2012; Pearson, 2013a; Keshet, 2020). More specifically, it will arise if either (a) the PPT is individual-level or (b) the PPT is stage-level, co-occurs with GEN and takes a generic Experiencer. It will not arise if (a) the PPT is stage-level, co-occurs with GEN and takes a covert non-generic Experiencer argument or (b) the PPT is stage-level and occurs in an episodic context. I will demonstrate that this prediction is borne out.

We have already seen in (120) that faultless disagreement can arise with the individual-level PPT *tasty*; I take it that this is uncontroversial. Next, let's show that faultless disagreement also arises with stage-level PPTs (e.g. *taste good*) and a generic Experiencer argument. Take the following dialogue.

121.   Ethan: When one has just brushed one's teeth, pineapple juice tastes good.
       Sarah: No, when one has just brushed one's teeth, pineapple juice does not taste good.

312   *Hazel Pearson*

We saw in Section 5 that in these sentences, *taste good* occurs in a generic context and takes a generic Experiencer. Sure enough, the disagreement between Ethan and Sarah is faultless: so long as each sincerely reports their opinion of the taste of pineapple juice post-toothbrushing, neither has said something false.

Now let's consider an example where *taste good* occurs in a generic environment, but its Experiencer is not generic. We have seen that (101), repeated in what follows, is such a case.

122. Ethan: When I've just brushed my teeth, pineapple juice tastes good.

There is no possible response to (122) that creates faultless disagreement. In (123), the content of Ethan's assertion has been negated, generating a disagreement.

123. Sarah: No, when you've just brushed your teeth, pineapple juice does not taste good.

The disagreement is not faultless: either Ethan or Sarah has said something false. (More likely Sarah, since Ethan has privileged access to information about how something tastes to him.) This is expected: in (123), *taste good* takes a covert addressee-denoting argument. Sure enough, a counterpart of (123) with an overt second-person Experiencer fails to generate faultless disagreement:

124. Sarah: No, when you've just brushed your teeth, pineapple juice does not taste good to you.

That indexical pronouns do not generate faultless disagreement has long been considered an argument against analyses of PPTs that appeal to hidden indexicals (Lasersohn, 2005). What to my knowledge has not been noticed before is that (i) there are taste statements with bare PPTs that *cannot* yield faultless disagreements, even though they would seem to involve an autocentric interpretation, and (ii) these include those taste statements that involve a covert indexical argument.

Finally, we need to show that there is no faultless disagreement with stage-level PPTs in episodic contexts. Consider again (113), repeated here as uttered by Ethan.

125. Ethan: When I had just brushed my teeth, the pineapple juice tasted good.
     Sarah: No, when you had just brushed your teeth, the pineapple juice did not taste good.

Predicates of Personal Taste 313

We again have a disagreement where only one of Ethan and Sarah can be speaking truly (again, most likely Ethan). This is again expected if in Sarah's reply, the argument of *taste good* is a second-person pronoun.

This is convincing evidence that faultless disagreement arises only when the PPT takes a generic Experiencer—exactly as one would expect if (first person–oriented) genericity is the source of faultless disagreement. I'll now say more about why judge-based accounts will have difficulty dealing with these facts.

By 'judge-based', I have in mind accounts that posit an individual parameter as part of the evaluation index (in addition to a situation or world parameter) and assign truth conditions such as the following.

126. [[Pineapple juice tastes good]]^{s,j,g} = 1 iff Pineapple juice tastes good to j in s

In what Lasersohn calls an 'autocentric' context, the value of the judge is set to the speaker. In such a context, Ethan speaks truly by uttering (125) just in case pineapple juice tastes good to him. Likewise, Sarah speaks truly in an autocentric context by uttering 'Pineapple juice does not taste good' just in case pineapple juice does not taste good to her. The contents expressed are incompatible, but since the judge parameter has a different value in each case, both utterances may turn out to be true.

On this view, faultless disagreement is derived without assuming that the Experiencer of the PPT is generic. So to account for the observation that faultless disagreement arises only with a generic Experiencer, one might give up Lasersohn's assumption that faultless disagreement arises in autocentric contexts and instead assume that it comes about when the judge parameter is set to something like an 'arbitrary' or 'ideal' Experiencer, thereby mimicking the effects that we have discussed in this chapter. But to make this work, one would need a story about why the judge is set to this value (i) obligatorily when the PPT is individual-level and (ii) optionally when the PPT is stage-level. Even supposing that this difficulty can be overcome, notice that on this account, the explanation for faultless disagreement is quite different from traditional relativism. This time, Ethan speaks truly by uttering (120) just in case pineapple juice is tasty to an arbitrary Experiencer, and Sarah speaks truly by saying 'Pineapple juice is not tasty' just in case it is not tasty to an arbitrary Experiencer. This explains disagreement (since the contents are incompatible), but one needs to say something more to explain faultlessness (since the judge has the same value in both cases). The move to a relativist semantics is then no longer motivated—it does not in and of itself account for faultlessness. Rather, faultlessness must be explained by appeal to genericity itself. But if genericity, not judge relativity, is necessary to explain faultlessness, then we no longer have an argument (from PPTs at least) for the radical claim

314 *Hazel Pearson*

that the truth values of sentences with identical contents may vary from speaker to speaker.

7. Conclusion

Whether or not Nutella tastes good to me may vary depending on one of two things: properties of Nutella (e.g. how much sugar it contains) and properties of me (e.g. whether or not I like sweet things). If over time there is a change along either of these dimensions, then the truth value of *Nutella tastes good to me* might change: I might then be in a position to assert, 'Nutella used to taste good to me, but it doesn't any more', for example. This is also true of certain sentences where *tastes good* does not take an overt Experiencer—namely, those where it instead takes a covert speaker-denoting argument. It is not, however, true of any sentences where *tastes good* is replaced by *tasty*. Nor is it true of sentences where *tastes good* takes a covert generic Experiencer. For the latter two classes of sentence, only a change in the properties of Nutella itself results in a change in truth value. And notice that it is precisely the latter two classes of sentence that give rise to faultless disagreement, and hence it is precisely these that the relativist should otherwise expect to analyse in terms of relativisation of truth to the speaker.

These facts are surprising from a relativist point of view, according to which the truth value (in an autocentric context) of *Nutella is tasty* depends on whether or not the property of being an individual to whom Nutella is tasty is true of the speaker. But they are not surprising from the point of view of analyses that explain faultless disagreement by appeal to a generic Experiencer. Relativisation of the interpretation function to a judge is neither necessary nor sufficient to explain the full range of facts concerning faultless disagreement with predicates of personal taste.

Acknowledgments

The initial impetus to consider that predicates of personal taste may come in both stage-level and individual-level flavours was a remark from Irene Heim about a decade ago; I also presented some tentative remarks on this topic to an audience at ZAS, Berlin. I thank Julia Zakkou for extensive comments on an earlier version of this chapter that resulted in significant improvements. Thanks for English judgments to David Adger, Elizabeth Cheshire, Daniel Harbour and Keren Rubner and for German judgments to Clemens Mayr, Frank Sode and Julia Zakkou. I am responsible for all remaining errors.

Notes

1. In English, a simple PPT is an adjective, which co-occurs with the copula, while a complex PPT consists of an appearance predicate such as *taste* or

Predicates of Personal Taste 315

look plus an adjectival complement. For more on appearance predicates, see Rudolph (this volume).

2. Throughout this chapter, I focus on gustatory and visual cases for reasons of space. However, Julia Zakkou (p.c.) has pointed out to me that the core observations seem to extend beyond these cases to pairs like *is pleasant/sounds pleasant* and *is cosy/feels cosy*.

3. An individual-level predicate (ILP) denotes a (quasi-)permanent property, e.g. *tall* or *old*. A stage-level predicate (SLP) denotes a temporary property, such as *hungry* or *bored*.

4. Here I build on Anand (2009), Pearson (2013a) and Snyder (2013), who all appeal to the idea that ILPs are inherent generics in their analyses of PPTs.

5. I ignore the adjectival PPT *fun* throughout this chapter, since it has no complex counterpart. It would be interesting to consider the tests discussed in this chapter in light of the contrast that Anthony (2016) identifies between 'dispositional' and 'experiential' construals of *fun*. Cf. Pearson (2013b), which tentatively suggests that *fun* may be stage-level.

6. I ignore *tasty/tastes good* for the purpose of this test, since they do not denote properties that can be detected through visual or aural perception.

7. It is crucial to this test that the noun phrases be construed de dicto. I have adapted Kratzer's examples to exclude the de re reading by using subjunctive morphology throughout.

8. A precedent for the use of strict/sloppy ambiguity as a probe for the properties of PPTs is found in Snyder (2013). His example involves *fun*.

9. Lasersohn's original examples involved *fun* rather than *tasty*.

10. The empirical landscape concerning weak crossover in German is complex; it may be that there is more than one dialect in this domain. See, for example, Müller (1995).

11. One speaker reported that (41) but not (42), suggests that there is more than one wedding guest whose taste has been affected by the virus. I suspect that this is due to the different presuppositional inferences induced by *die Tatsache, dass* . . . ('the fact that . . . ') in (41) and *verärgert, dass* . . . ('annoyed that . . . ') in (42) rather than having to do with the properties of the covert argument of *taste good*. This is supported by the fact that this speaker reported the same thing for (41)'s counterpart with an overt pronoun (43).

12. I assume that presuppositions project universally under universal quantifiers (Heim, 1983).

13. Julia Zakkou (p.c.) has pointed out to me that this claim is at odds with views found in Cappelen and Hawthorne (2009), Schaffer (2009) and MacFarlane (2014). Schaffer, for instance, claims that 'Everyone got something tasty' can be true in a situation in which each of the Smiths had a different flavour of ice cream and each one liked the flavour of ice cream that she had, but none of them liked any of the other flavours. I believe this is compatible with the internal argument of *tasty* being generically quantified rather than bound by *everyone*: as pointed out by Pearson (2013a), generic construal brings with it a restriction to *relevant* tasters. One necessary condition for being a relevant taster is that one must have tasted the item in question; since this condition is only met by one member of the family per flavour, the effects of binding by the universal quantifier are mimicked.

14. Although (70) is infelicitous out of the blue, it becomes acceptable if used by an amnesiac who, after a long stay in hospital, finds a lot of empty pineapple juice bottles in her home. Such a context provides an explanation for how on the one hand, the speaker could have tasted pineapple juice, while on the other, she is forced to base her statement on indirect evidence. Thanks to Julia Zakkou (p.c.) for pressing me on this.

316 *Hazel Pearson*

15. As far as I know this is a novel observation. I won't speculate on how best to account for it.
16. As Moltmann (this volume) points out, ultimately one should give a compositional treatment of complex PPTs like *tastes good*. I leave this to future work.
17. I assume that subjects reconstruct in VP-internal position, where they are base generated.
18. Notice that (99) also predicts that the situation argument of the predicate (itself a null pronoun) is obligatorily bound by GEN, thus subsuming Chierchia's analysis.
19. I have no account of why it should be simple PPTs that are individual-level and complex PPTs that are stage-level. I leave this for future work. See also Moltmann (this volume) for critical comments in this vein.
20. I continue to assume that null situation pronouns (and their binders) are represented in the syntax, although from now on I omit these for readability.
21. Ultimately, Dinges and Zakkou replace dispositions with what they call 'tendencies'. The details of this need not concern us here.
22. This view says roughly that when Ethan says that pineapple juice is tasty, he makes a generic claim about the tastiness of pineapple juice to anyone who might taste it, based on his own experience of drinking pineapple juice, together with the assumption that his tastes are representative of the set of (potential) pineapple juice drinkers. The role of first-person experience in taste claims ensures that the assertion is faultless as long as it sincerely represents Ethan's own experience. That Ethan's and Sarah's assertions involve generalisation across the same population ensures that the propositions they express are incompatible and hence that there is genuine disagreement. Note that merely treating the null Experiencer argument of a PPT as an individual pronoun bound by GEN (e.g., as in (98)) is not in itself sufficient to derive this result; in addition the first-person orientation is obtained by positing an individual variable bound by an operator in the left periphery of the clause:

(i) $[[[\lambda x_1 \lambda s_2 [s_2 \text{ This cake}_i [\text{GEN } \lambda s_3 [s_3 \text{ t}_i \text{ is tasty } one_1]]]]^{s, g} = \lambda x \lambda s. \forall y, s'$
$[\text{Acc}(s, s') \& C(y, s') \& I(x, y)] [\text{tasty}(\text{this cake}, y, s')]$

References

Anand, P. (2009). *Kinds of taste* [Ms]. UCSC.

Anand, P., & Korotkova, N. (2018). Acquaintance content and obviation. In U. Sauerland & S. Solt (Eds.), *Proceedings of Sinn und Bedeutung 22* (pp. 55–72). ZAS Papers in Linguistics 60, Leibniz-Centre General Linguistics, Berlin.

Anthony, A. (2016). Experience, evaluation and faultless disagreement. *Inquiry*, 59(6), 686–722.

Bylinina, L. (2017). Judge-dependence in degree constructions. *Journal of Semantics*, 34(2), 291–331.

Cappelen, H., & Hawthorne, J. (2009). *Relativism and monadic truth*. Oxford University Press.

Carlson, G. N. (1977). *Reference to kinds in English* [Doctoral dissertation]. University of Massachusetts, Amherst.

Carlson, G. N. (1982). Generic terms and generic sentences. *Journal of Philosophical Logic, 11*, 145–181.

Chierchia, G. (1995). Individual level predicates as inherent generics. In G. Carlson & J. Pelletier (Eds.), *The generic book* (pp. 176–223). University of Chicago Press.

Dinges, A., & Zakkou, J. (2020). Taste, traits and tendencies. *Philosophical Studies, 178*, 1183–1206.

Heim, I. (1983). On the projection problem for presuppositions. In D. Flickinger et al. (Eds.), *Proceedings of the second West Coast conference on formal linguistics* (pp. 114–125).

Keshet, E. (2020). A matter of taste. In C. Lee & J. Park (Eds.), *Evidentials and modals* (pp. 69–81). Brill, Current Research in the Semantics/Pragmatics Interface, Vol. 39 [Manuscript date 2005].

Kölbel, M. (2002). *Truth without objectivity*. Routledge.

Kratzer, A. (1989). An investigation of the lumps of thought. *Linguistics and Philosophy, 12*, 607–653.

Kratzer, A. (1991). Conditionals. In A. von Stechow & D. Wunderlich (Eds.), *Semantics: An international handbook of contemporary research* (pp. 639–650). de Gruyter.

Krifka, M., Pelletier, F. J., Carlson, G. N., ter Meulen, A., Chierchia, G., & Link, G. (1995). Genericity: An introduction. In G. N. Carlson & F. J. Pelletier (Eds.), *The generic book* (pp. 1–124). University of Chicago Press.

Lasersohn, P. (2005). Context dependence, disagreement, and predicates of personal taste. *Linguistics and Philosophy, 28*, 643–686.

MacFarlane, J. (2014). *Assessment sensitivity: Relative truth and its applications*. Oxford University Press.

Malamud, S. (2006). *Semantics and pragmatics of arbitrariness* [Doctoral dissertation]. University of Pennsylvania.

Moltmann, F. (2006). Generic one, arbitrary PRO, and the first person. *Natural Language Semantics, 14*, 257–281.

Moltmann, F. (2010a). Relative truth and the first person. *Philos Stud, 150*, 187–220. https://doi.org/10.1007/s11098-009-9383-9

Moltmann, F. (2010b). Generalizing detached self-reference and the semantics of generic one. *Mind and Language, 25*, 440–473.

Moltmann, F. (2012). Two kinds of first-person-oriented content. *Synthese, 184*, 157–177.

Müller, G. (1995). *A-bar syntax: A study in movement types*. Mouton de Gruyter.

Ninan, D. (2014). Taste predicates and the acquaintance inference. In *Proceedings of SALT 24* (pp. 290–309). Linguistic Society of America.

Partee, B. (1984). Nominal and temporal anaphora. *Linguistics and Philosophy, 7*(3), 243–286.

Pearson, H. (2013a). A judge-free semantics for predicates of personal taste. *Journal of Semantics, 30*(1), 103–154. https://doi.org/10.1093/jos/ffs001

Pearson, H. (2013b). *The sense of self: Topics in the semantics of de se expressions* [Doctoral dissertation]. Harvard University.

Roeper, T. (2016). Propositions and implicit argument carry a default general point of view: Acquisition evidence against relativism and subjectivity. In C. Meier & J. van Wijnbergen-Huitink (Eds.), *Subjective meaning* (pp. 201–226). de Gruyter.

Schaffer, J. (2009). Perspective in taste predicates and epistemic modals. In A. Egan & B. Weatherson (Eds.), *Epistemic modality* (pp. 179–226). Oxford University Press.

Snyder, E. (2013). Binding, genericity, and predicates of personal taste, *Inquiry*, 56(2–3), 278–306. https://doi.org/10.1080/0020174X.2013.784485

Stephenson, T. (2007a). Judge dependence, epistemic modals, and predicates of personal taste. *Linguistics and Philosophy*, 30, 487–525.

Stephenson, T. (2007b). *Towards a theory of subjective meaning* [PhD thesis]. MIT.

14 Tastes and the Ontology of Impersonal Perception Reports

Friederike Moltmann

Introduction

This chapter is about what I will call *impersonal taste reports* as in (1) as well as other *impersonal perception reports* such as (2):

(1) a. Chocolate tastes good.
    b. Chocolate is delicious.
(2) a. The photo looks good.
    b. The violin sounds strange.
    c. The perfume smells as if it was from Guerlain.
    d. It feels as if it is going to rain.

The standard semantic view about such sentences is that the predicates stand for a subjective relation of experience or evaluation between objects and experiencers (judges). This relation is generally used to explain the possibility of faultless disagreement about judgments of personal taste. It underlies standard contextualist and relativist accounts of the semantics of taste sentences as well as the generic version of the semantics of such sentences proposed in Moltmann (2010a, 2012).

This chapter will argue for a different semantics of impersonal taste reports and impersonal perception reports in general. This semantics is based on a richer ontology of what I will call *taste occurrences* and *taste objects* and more generally *perceptual occurrences* and *perceptual objects*. Perceptual occurrences involve a particular experiencer and depend on a particular perceptual experience; perceptual objects won't. The proposed semantics will not invoke experiencers or judges as implicit arguments of the perceptual relations expressed by the predicates in (1) and (2), let alone as arguments that would be syntactically realized by silent elements (*pro*). It thus avoids the problems for implicit experiencer arguments pointed out by Collins (2013).

The ontological distinction between perceptual occurrences and perceptual objects is reflected in semantic differences between impersonal perception verbs and the corresponding nouns: impersonal perception verbs

DOI: 10.4324/9781003184225-18

320 *Friederike Moltmann*

(*taste, look, sound, smell, feel*) take perceptual occurrences as arguments; the corresponding nouns take perceptual objects as arguments. Thus, the verb *taste* takes a taste occurrence as an implicit argument, whereas the noun *taste* as in *the taste of coffee* describes a taste object. Similarly, the nouns in *the look of the statue, the sound of the violin, the smell of the perfume*, and *the feel of the fabric* describe perceptual objects.

The ontology of taste occurrences and objective tastes allows dispensing with implicit experiencer arguments. Perceptual occurrences are entities that by nature have an experiencer and in their choice of an experiencer show a particular first-person orientation. More precisely, impersonal perception verbs show a logophoric behavior, which parallels that of generic *one*: the experiencer is understood either as the speaker, the described attitude bearer, or anyone the speaker or described attitude bearer identifies with or simulates (on the generic reading).

Not just perceptual occurrences have such a first-person orientation, but also the objects of perception themselves may, namely *agent-centered situations* of the sort that sentences like (2d) are about.

In contrast to taste occurrences, taste objects are 'objective' or public and do not involve a particular individual as experiencer. They are not only the sorts of things we refer to explicitly with NPs like *the taste of coffee*, but are also involved in the semantics of taste adjectives such as *delicious* or *tasty*. Given the semantic involvement of taste objects, faultless disagreement of sentences such as (1b) resides in the first person–based evaluation of a taste object rather than the perceptual experience itself.

The chapter will first briefly present standard semantic views of sentences about personal taste and address semantic differences between impersonal perception verbs and corresponding nouns and adjectives. It will then outline the ontology of perceptual occurrences and perceptual objects as well as the semantics of impersonal perception reports with the two sorts of predicates. At the end, it will address the sorts of predictions the present approach makes regarding faultless agreement.

1. Standard Semantics of Sentences Expressing Personal Taste

The general assumption is that taste predicates express a subjective, experiential relation that holds between an object (or kind of object) and an agent a, the experiencer or 'judge', so that (3a) has the logical form in (3b):[1]

(3) a. Coffee tastes good.
    b. tastes good(coffee, a)

Doubts whether such simple contextualist or relativist analyses can explain the phenomenon of faultless disagreement have motivated a more

Ontology of Impersonal Perception Reports 321

complex analysis of (3a) in terms of first person–based genericity, involving simulation (Moltmann, 2010a, 2012). A simplified version of that analysis is given for (3a) as follows, where, Gn is a suitable generic operator:

(4) a. Everyone as someone the speaker identifies with has a good-tasting experience of coffee.

  b. λx[Gn y taste good to(coffee, y qua someone x identifies with y)]

Thus, (3a) expresses a property, which needs to be self-applied by anyone accepting the content of the sentences.

Support for the involvement of genericity in taste statements such as (1a) comes from the possibility of co-variation of the 'judge' with generic *one* or arbitrary PRO, as in (5a) and (5b), respectively:

(5) a. When *one* drinks milk cold, it tastes *pro* good.

  b. It is pleasant *pro* PRO$_{arb}$ to sit on the sofa.

In what follows, I will assume that taste sentences such as (3a) display both a generic reading, along the lines of (4), as well as a first person–oriented nongeneric reading on which the speaker (or described agent) just conveys her own taste judgment. The latter, given the standard assumption about taste predicates and a Lewisian account of *de se*, would be represented as follows:

(4) c. λx[tastes good(coffee, x)].

2. Verbal, Adjectival, and Nominal Taste Predicates

2.1. *An Individual-Level/Stage-Level Distinction Among Taste Predicates*

Judgments of taste take different linguistic forms, which go along with somewhat different readings. In particular, *verbal taste predicates* as in (6a) display different readings from *adjectival taste predicates* as in (6b):

(6) a. The coffee tastes delicious.

  b. The coffee is tasty.

Pearson (this volume) points out that complex taste predicates as in (6a) permit both a generic reading and two sorts of nongeneric readings, namely a first-person referential reading and a bound-variable reading. This, for Pearson, is due to the fact that complex taste predicates are 'stage level'. By contrast, simple taste predicates display only a generic reading, which for Pearson means that they are 'individual level'.

322   Friederike Moltmann

Pearson lists various manifestations of the individual-level/stage-level distinction among taste predicates.[2] One of them is the readings of the floated quantifier *all*, which with complex taste predicates gets a reading on which it ranges over situations, as in (7a), but with simple taste predicates only has a reading on which it ranges over the relevant individuals, as in (7b):

(7)   a. Pineapples always taste good.
       b. Pineapples are always tasty.

The same contrast holds for other impersonal perception verbs and the corresponding adjectives. In (8a), *always* ranges over situations (broadly speaking, including times of the day); in (8b), *always* can range only over churches:

(8)   a. English churches look always beautiful.
       b. English churches are always beautiful.

Another diagnostic is the acceptability of *when*-clauses:

(9)   a. When the landscape looks beautiful, people photograph it.
       b. ?? When the landscape is beautiful, people photograph it.

Stage-level predicates can occur in a *when*-clause, but not individual-level predicates.

Yet another diagnostic is the ability for stage-level predicates to occur as small-clause predicates of *see*, as opposed to individual-level predicates:

(10)   a. Emma saw St Paul's looking beautiful.
       b. ??? Emma saw St Paul's beautiful.

For Pearson, simple taste predicates being 'individual level' means that they are always generic, involving a generic operator with just scope over the predicate at logical form (Chierchia, 1995). Thus, whereas (11a) has a first-person referential reading as in (11b) as well as a generic reading involving a wide-scope generic operator as in (11c), (12a) requires a generic operator taking scope just over the predicate as in (12b):

(11)   a. This cake tastes good.
       b. [tastes good (to)](this cake, speaker)
       c. Gn_i [this cake tastes good (to) pro_i]

(12)   a. This cake is tasty.
       b. This cake [Gn_i [is tasty pro_i]]
       c. For any entity d, [Gn_i [is tasty pro_i](d) = 1 iff x is tasty to everyone in any (relevant) situation.

Ontology of Impersonal Perception Reports 323

There are several issues, however, that arise for this account of simple and complex taste predicates.

First of all, the account does not give a compositional semantics of complex taste predicates like *taste good* and in particular fails to give justice to the contribution of the secondary predicate *good* in such predicates. In fact, the distinction between complex and simple predicates does not align well with the individual-level/stage-level distinction. Complex predicates with taste nouns such as *has a bitter taste* classify as individual level, not stage level (Section 4.1.)

Second, the account does not explain the stage-level/individual-level correlation with the two sorts of predicates. The simple predicates that Pearson considers are all adjectives, but adjectives themselves are not generally individual level. *Available, apparent, unwell, happy* are stage level, for example. There are also adjectives that can be used for taste judgments that fail to be individual-level, for example *terrible* and *stimulating*, predicates that focus on the effect on the experiencer. Such adjectives pattern with stage-level predicates given the various diagnostics:

(13) a. When I drank it at room temperature, the wine was terrible.
      b. When I drink coffee in the morning, it is stimulating; when I drink it at night, it puts me to sleep.

Third, the account fails to carry over to the semantics of taste nouns and other nouns denoting perceptual objects: *the taste of coffee, the look of St Paul's, the smell of the perfume, the sound of the violin* display only a sort of generic reading, not a reading relating to a particular perceptual occurrence. In the next section, we will discuss in greater detail the nominal construction, whose semantics can also shed light on the first and second issue with Pearson's account.

Fourth, the account hinges on treating taste predicates in impersonal taste reports as involving an experiencer argument, syntactically realized by a silent element *pro*. However, there is little if any syntactic evidence for judge or experiencer arguments of predicates in impersonal taste sentences, as Collins (2013) has argued in relation to criteria such as variable binding, obligatory arguments, and ellipsis. This also holds for other predicates of perception in impersonal perception reports.

Finally, Pearson's account fails to capture the first-person orientation of impersonal perception verbs, an issue I will turn to now.

2.2. *The Logophoric Nature of Verbal Taste Predicates*

Verbal taste predicates differ from adjectival ones not only in their stage-level as opposed to individual-level behavior but also in displaying a particular first person–orientation or logophoric character. Pearson (this

324   *Friederike Moltmann*

volume) notices that a first-person covert indexical reading is available for verbal taste predicates as in (14a) but not adjectival ones as in (14b), an observation that generalizes to all impersonal perception verbs, as in (15):

(14) a. When I am hungry, beans taste good.
     b. ?? When I am hungry, beans are tasty.

(15) a. When put in a long vase, a single rose looks nice.
     b. ?? When put in a long vase, a single rose is nice-looking.

A related observation is that a first-person bound-variable reading with generic *one* as antecedent is available only with verbal taste predicates and not adjectival ones:

(16) a. When one is hungry, beans taste good.
     b. ?? When one is hungry, beans are tasty.

Impersonal perception verbs need not relate to the speaker, though. In contexts embedded under attitude verbs, they will relate to whoever is the described agent. They may do so displaying a referential reading (17a) or a bound-variable reading (17b):

(17) a. John found that the cake tasted good.
     b. Everyone who ordered wine was upset that the wine did not taste good.

Taste occurrences still relate to the speaker when the taste predicate is not embedded under an attitude verb, as in (18):

(18) Everyone is drinking wine that tastes good.

The same generalization holds for impersonal perception verbs of other perceptual modes, illustrated by the following contrast where *look good* can relate to everyone in (19a), but only to the speaker in (19b):

(19) a. Everyone who looked at the picture from the entrance was angry that the picture did not look good.
     b. Everyone stood next to a picture that did not look good.

With respect to the perceptual occurrences they describe, impersonal perception verbs thus behave like logophoric pronouns, and also generic *one*, in relating to the speaker or else whoever is the bearer of the relevant described attitude. Impersonal perception verbs differ in that respect from ordinary perception verbs (*see, hear,* etc.), which fail to display such logophoricity. Capturing the latter is an important condition for an adequate semantics of impersonal perception verbs.

Ontology of Impersonal Perception Reports   325

3. Taste Occurrences and Other Perceptual Occurrences

3.1. The Linguistic Form of Impersonal Verbal Perceptual Reports

On the present view, taste verbs denote relations between entities and taste occurrences, and adjectival taste predicates relations between entities and taste objects. Neither involves experiencers as arguments. That is because the ontology of taste objects and other perceptual objects permits dispensing with experiencer arguments. Perceptual occurrences are dependent on or directed toward a particular experiencer. If impersonal verbs of perception denote relations between entities and perceptual occurrences, they won't require experiencer arguments for semantic reasons. By contrast, perceptual objects do not depend on particular experiencers. If adjectival perception predicates denote relations between entities and perceptual objects, an obligatory generic reading of adjectival predicates will follow without making use of experiencers.

If impersonal perception predicates denote relations between entities and perceptual occurrences or perceptual objects, such as tastes, looks, sounds, and smells, this permits a compositional semantics of complex predicates such as *taste good* and *look nice*. But first, a few remarks are in order about such predicates.

Impersonal perceptual reports with a verbal predicate are of the form DP V XP, where V is an impersonal perception verb (*look, sound, smell*) and XP is an obligatory adverbial modifier or secondary predicate. Though obligatory, the secondary predicate occupies the very same position as other adverbial modifiers. The secondary predicate can be any expression that can also act as an adverbial. On the present view, it always expresses a property to be predicated of the perceptual occurrence. Impersonal perception reports then will involve existential quantification over perceptual occurrences and predication of the secondary predicate of the perceptual occurrences. For an impersonal taste report such as (20a), this is given in (20b):

(20)   a. The cake tastes good.
        b. $\exists d(taste(\text{the cake}, d) \ \& \ good(d))$

In (20b), no use was made of event arguments. That is because the issue of event arguments is rather independent of the argument in favor of perceptual occurrences and perceptual objects.

The sort of analysis in (20b) will also be the semantics of impersonal perceptual reports of other perceptual modes.

The generic reading of verbal impersonal perceptual reports does not involve a distinct entity but rather a generic operator, which, one may assume, ranges just over situations suitably restricted. Thus, on the generic reading, the logical form of (20a) will be:

326 *Friederike Moltmann*

(20) c. Gn s ∃d(taste$_s$(the cake, d) & good$_s$(d))

There is an issue whether generically quantified sentences of this sort require actual instances. The potential truth of sentences like (21) indicates that they don't (McGrath, p.c.):[3]

(21) I'm sure the garden looks beautiful today, since it's such a nice day, so it's a shame they've closed off the place to all visitors, so that no one can see it.

The distinction between perceptual occurrences and perceptual objects is of course compatible with the generic operator not requiring actual instances.

(20a) actually has two readings (Jackson, 1977; Rudolph, this volume): a phenomenal reading on which *good* applies to the appearance, the taste occurrence, and a nonphenomenal reading on which it applies to the stimulus. On the second reading, the taste occurrence indicates that the cake is good rather than *good* qualifying the taste as such. I will not discuss the second reading in greater detail in this chapter but just suggest an ontological account of the two readings. Whereas on the first reading, the secondary predicate applies to the taste occurrence itself, on the second reading, it applies to the *epistemic modal object* generated by the taste occurrence.[4] Unlike a taste occurrence, a modal object has truth or satisfaction conditions, which may be specified by the content of various sentences (or small clauses). The modal object generated by a taste object d then has as part of its content the content of [*the cake good*] just in case d is evidence for the truth of [*the cake good*]. Given this proposal, the ambiguity between the phenomenal and the nonphenomenal reading is traced to the semantics of impersonal perception verbs, more precisely, the ontology that goes along with them, that is, the ontology of perceptual occurrences and the modal objects they generate.

The secondary predicate of impersonal perception reports may also be an *as if*-clause, an *as though*-clause, or a *like*-clause, which generally can fill in the position of optional as well as selected adverbials:[5]

(22) a. John walks as if he was drunk.
      b. John behaves like he was being hunted.

(23) a. This looks/tastes/smells/sounds as though it was very old.
      b. The landscape looks like it had not rained for weeks.

The semantics of *as if*-clauses and *like*-clauses is more complex, of course (see Bledin and Srinivas (forthcoming) for a recent discussion and possible worlds–based analysis). The ontology of perceptual occurrences promises

Ontology of Impersonal Perception Reports   327

a new analysis along the following lines, where X is a definite NP, ~ a suitable relation of similarity, and f a function mapping the set [S] of situations described by the sentence S to a matching kind of perceptual occurrences:

(24) a. X looks as if S.
   b. For a perceptual occurrence d, look([X], d) and d is similar to the kind of perceptual occurrence that matches the situational content of S.
   c. ∃d(look([X], d) & d ~ f([S],[X], *look*))

How the relation of a set of situations to a kind of perceptual occurrences is to be understood needs to be elaborated, of course. But as it is marginal to the main theme of this chapter, this can be left for another occasion. Note that (24b) captures only the nongeneric reading of (24a). The generic reading arguably does not require there to be an actual perceptual occurrence.[6]

3.2.   *The Nature of Taste Occurrences*

Taste occurrences are concrete qualities borne by taste experiences. Taste occurrences are thus dependent on the experience and its experiencer. The identity and existence of taste occurrences obviously depends on the agent. If I did not taste the coffee, the coffee did not taste good to me. The properties of taste occurrences are different though from the experience itself. The experience, for example, has temporal properties, but the taste occurrence won't. A taste experience can occur unintentionally or by mistake, but this is not what one would attribute to the taste occurrence. The taste occurrence only has qualitative properties, such as being sour, bitter, or sweet, which one would not attribute to the taste experience itself.

It is not obvious how exactly the relation between a taste occurrence and a taste experience should be conceived and how their relation should possibly be reflected in the semantic analysis of impersonal taste sentences. The relation could perhaps be conceived as one between an event and its result, as is suggested by German resultative morphology for taste occurrences (*schmecken*—to taste, *Geschmack*—taste).[7] In this chapter, I will set aside taste experiences and take impersonal taste predicates to only take a taste occurrence as an argument.

Other perceptual modes likewise come with perceptual occurrences besides perceptual experiences. Subjective looks are qualities borne by visual experiences, sound occurrences are qualities borne by auditory experiences, smell occurrences are qualities borne by olfactory experiences. Again, the properties of the occurrences are obviously different from those of the corresponding experiences.

(20c) does not yet capture all there is to the semantics of impersonal perception verbs. In particular, it does not account for [1] the logophoric

328 Friederike Moltmann

character of impersonal perception verbs and [2] the possibility of generic readings, and in particular covariation with generic *one*.

Impersonal perception verbs describe perceptual occurrences that relate either to the speaker or, in contexts embedded under attitude verbs, to the attitude bearer. They thus relate to a context that is centered on an intentional agent and can be shifted under embedding under attitude verbs. In this chapter, I will make use only of very basic, familiar tools of semantic analysis, leaving a possibly more accurate semantic analysis of the phenomenon to a future occasion. I will assume that sentences are evaluated with respect to two contexts: a context u, the utterance context, and a context c, the context of evaluation that may be shifted for sentences embedded under attitude verbs. Both contexts, for present purposes, are identified with a triple consisting of a situation or world s, a time t, and an agent a. Thus, for a context c s_c will be the situation in c, t_c the time in c, and a_c the agent in c. Attitude reports shift the context c to one in which the agent is the described attitude holder, as indicated in what follows for *believe*, making use, for present purposes, of a Hintikka-style semantics of belief reports:

(25) For contexts u and c and an individual a',
      $[believe\ that\ S\ ]^{u,\ c}(a') = 1$ iff for all s', s' $R_{believe,ac}$ s_c $[S]^{u,\ c'} = 1$,
      where c' is like c except that $s_c = s'$ and $a_c = a'$.

Let us take H to be the relation of 'having' or bearerhood that holds between an agent and a perceptual occurrence. Then impersonal perception verbs will be subject to the following condition:

(26) <u>Logophoric condition on impersonal perception verbs</u>
      For an impersonal verb of perception V,
      for contexts u and c, $[V]^{u,c} = \{\ x\ |\ \exists d\ (<x,\ d> \in [V]^{u,\ c}\ \&\ H(d,\ a_c))\}$

(20a) will now have the following truth conditions:

(27) $[The\ cake\ tastes\ good]^{u,\ c} = 1$ iff $\exists d(([the\ cake]^{u,\ c}(d) \in [tastes]^{u,\ c}\ \&\ H(d,\ a_c)\ \&\ d \in [good]^{u,\ c})$

Let us then turn to the generic reading of impersonal perception reports as well as the semantics of generic *one*. I will assume that on the generic reading, impersonal perception reports will involve a generic operator Gn, which will shift not only the situation s_c of the context of evaluation c but also the agent a_c in c This is given as follows, where R is a suitable relation restricting the situations of evaluation:

(28) <u>The generic reading of impersonal perception reports</u>

Ontology of Impersonal Perception Reports   329

For an impersonal perception verb V, a definite NP Y, and a modifier X,

[Gn Y V X]$^{u, c}$ = 1 iff for all situations s' such that s' R s_c, there is a perceptual occurrence d such that <[Y], d> ∈ [V]$^{u, c'}$ & d ∈ [X]$^{u, c'}$, where c' is like c, except that $s_{c'}$ = s' and $a_{c'}$ = the agent in s'.

Generic *one* involves the same type of logophoricity as impersonal perception verbs, which means that generic-*one* sentences will relate to the agent of the shiftable context c. On my previous account (Moltmann, 2006, 2010b), generic *one* ranges over individuals (in the relevant group) qua individuals the speaker identifies with or simulates. For present purposes, I will adopt that account; but in addition, I will assume that generic *one* goes along with a change in the context c, shifting the speaker (or attitude bearer) in c to the individuals generic *one* ranges over:

(29) The semantics of generic *one*
       [*one* VP]$^{u, c}$ = 1 iff for all a', a' [qua a_c I a'] ∈ [VP]$^{u, c'}$, where c' is like c except that $a_{c'}$ = a'.

Here, I is the relation of identification or simulation, which ensures that with generic *one*, a predicate is applied to an individual a' on the basis of the speaker putting herself into the shoes of a'— or simulating a' (Moltmann, 2006, 2010b).

Covariation of generic *one* with the experiencer associated with an impersonal perception verb is made possible through the presence of a single generic operator in the sentence, an operator that will trigger a shift of the context c to contexts c' such that the agents of the contexts c' are the individuals the generic operator ranges over. This is indicated for conditionals in what follows (using a very simplified semantics):

(30) For contexts u and c, a definite NP Y, an impersonal perception verb V, and a modifier X,

       [*If one* VP, *then* Y V X]$^{u, c}$ = 1 iff: for all a', if a' [qua a_c I a'] ∈ [VP]$^{u, c'}$, then ∃d (<[Y], d> ∈ [V]$^{u, c'}$ & d ∈ [X]$^{u, c'}$), where is c' is like c except that $a_{c'}$ = a'.

The same analyses apply to impersonal perception verbs of other modes. The sentences that follow will be about visual, auditory, olfactory, and tactile occurrences with the same first-personal orientation or logophoric status as the taste occurrences described by the verb *taste*:

(31) a. When I saw the picture this morning, it looked great.
       b. When I listened to it this morning, the piano sounded good.
       c. When I touched the fabric this morning, it felt good.

330   *Friederike Moltmann*

Impersonal verbs of perception thus describe simple relations between entities and perceptual occurrences, and it is their logophoric status that restricts those perceptual occurrences to those whose experiencers are the 'agents' of the current contexts of evaluation.

4.   Taste Objects and Other Perceptual Objects

4.1.   *Taste Nouns and Nouns for Other Perceptual Objects*

The noun *taste* enables reference to a taste object, an entity that is independent of particular taste experiences and in particular does not depend on a particular experiencer. Nominal taste predicates in the constructions that follow share the same apparent generic reading of adjectival taste predicates, as opposed to verbal predicates. That is, (32a) and (32b) only have the reading of (32c), not of (32d):

(32)   a. The coffee has a good taste.
        b. The taste of the coffee is good.
        c. The coffee is tasty.
        d. The coffee tastes good.

The application of relevant diagnostics supports that, for example the acceptability of *when*-clauses:

(33)   a. When I am really hungry, plain rice tastes good.
        b. ?? When I am really hungry, plain rice is tasty.
        c. ?? When I am really hungry, the taste of plain rice is good.

The nominal constructions display a reading on which *good* does not evaluate a particular tasting experience or rather taste occurrence but the taste of the coffee/plain rice as something objectual or public. This is obvious from the way epistemic predicates apply. The taste of coffee is treated as an object of knowledge, recognition, and differentiation:

(34)   a. Mary knows the taste of coffee.
        b. Bill recognizes the taste of cigarettes.
        c. Bill cannot distinguish the taste of coffee from the taste of chocolate.

Similarly, there are nouns for objects of other perceptual modes, such as looks, sounds, smells, which also provide objects of knowledge:

(35)   John knows the look/sound/smell of cats.

   Apart from the semantics of nouns for perceptual objects and of impersonal perception reports, looks as entities have been motivated for purely

Ontology of Impersonal Perception Reports 331

philosophical reasons as well, namely for perceptual justification. Entities that are looks, McGrath (2017, 2018) has argued, act as the reasons for perceptual beliefs.

There are actually two uses of nouns for tastes and other perceptual objects that need to be distinguished: a relational use and a nonrelational use. The relational use is restricted to reference to taste objects, as in (36a), whereas the nonrelational use serves for reference to taste occurrences and kinds of them, as in (36b, c):[8]

(36) a. I know the taste of coffee.
      b. I don't know this taste.
      c. I have never experienced this taste.

Only the construction *the taste of* applies to an entity mapping it to the 'objective' taste object that is associated with it.

For a given entity, there need not be a single perceptual object for a particular perceptual mode, but rather a distinction may have to be made between viewpoint-relative looks and what I will call 'overall looks' ('looks in the round', cf. McGrath, 2021). The relational noun *look* can be used for both, as (37a) and (37b) illustrate:

(37) a. The statue has different looks depending on the light and where one stands.
      b. I like the look of the statue.

With nominal taste predicates, it depends on the nature of the property expressed by the adjective whether faultless agreement arises: evaluative predicates like *good* give rise to faultless agreement, as is possible in (38 a, b); predicates like *bitter* as in (39 a, b) don't, an issue I will come back to in Section 6:

(38) a. Coffee has a good taste.
      b. The taste of coffee is good.

(39) a. Coffee has a bitter taste.
      b. The taste of the coffee is bitter.

In this chapter, I will not give a full ontological account of taste objects and other perceptual objects. Rather, it will have to suffice to characterize them in terms of some of their linguistically reflected properties.[9] First of all, taste objects are ontologically dependent on an entity, and thus they cannot be conceived as properties. But taste objects might be conceived as particularized properties, more precisely, particularized response-dependent properties. The entities on which a taste depends may inherit properties from the taste. Coffee is bitter because its taste is bitter, for example. But this does not hold for all properties. The taste of the wine may be unusual while the

332   *Friederike Moltmann*

wine is not unusual. Objective tastes are to be distinguished from tastes that pertain to particular taste experiences, that is, 'taste occurrences'. A taste object might be construed as a kind of taste occurrence, that is, a kind whose instances are particular taste occurrences. However, taste objects do not appear to require actual instances, an intuition that is even clearer with related entities such as looks, as we will see.

4.2.   *The Semantics of Nominal and Adjectival Taste Predicates*

Tastes as entities with the distinction between taste occurrences and taste objects allow for a straightforward semantics of verbal and nominal taste predicates. Verbs like *taste* take particular taste occurrences as arguments, whereas the relational noun *taste (of)* takes taste objects as arguments. Thus the logical form of (40a) will be as in (40b), where the relational noun *taste* is taken to denote a function from entities to taste objects:

(40)   a.   The taste of the coffee is good.
      b.   good(taste(the coffee))

The individual-level status of taste adjective such as *tasty* can now be attributed to the implicit presence of taste objects, along the lines of the following equivalence:

(41)   tasty(the coffee) iff good(taste(the coffee))

This carries over to other perceptual relational nouns (*smell, sound, feel*) and perceptual adjectives.

    The distinction between taste occurrences and taste objects generalizes to other modes of perception, though with different extents to which the objects are experience-dependent. With sounds, the distinction between experience dependence and object dependence is particularly intuitive. One may hear a particular sound, and one may hear/know/recognize the sound of a particular flute. Verbal taste predicates display an experience-dependent reading, as in (42a); relational uses of nouns display an object-dependent reading, as in (42b, c):

(42)   a.   This flute sounds unusual.
      b.   This flute has an unusual sound.
      c.   The sound of the flute is unusual.

The sound of a flute clearly is independent of a particular experience. It is less obvious that sounds are dependent on the object that produces them. Intuitively, the very same sound could have been produced by a different flute. Moreover, objects on which sounds depend do not generally inherit

Ontology of Impersonal Perception Reports 333

properties from the sounds. Thus, evaluative predicates, when applied to musical instruments, generally evaluate their physical shape, not their sounds. *Deep* cannot be applied to a contrabass even if the sound of it is deep, and *deep* applies to voices, not to the people that make the sounds.

Both predicates give rise to faultless disagreement with evaluative adjectives (See Section 6):

(43) a. This flute sounds nice.
      b. This flute has a nice sound.
      c. The sound of the flute is nice.

Smells display the very same pattern, allowing for verbal and nominal predicates, as in (44), and displaying faultless disagreement with evaluative predicates, as in (45) (Section 6):

(44) a. The perfume smells fruity.
      b. The perfume has a fruity smell.

(45) a. The perfume smells nice.
      b. The perfume has a nice smell.

Properties of smells are inherited by entities only if the entities are of the very same nature (perfumes). Whereas properties of looks (properties of shape, size) are inherited from the entities that have the looks, properties of sounds, smells, tastes are not inherited from the entities that have them.

4.3. The Ontology of Perceptual Objects

What is the ontological status of perceptual objects? Do they depend on experiences, or are they mind-independent? McGrath (2017, 2021), who argued that looks play a role both in perceptual justification and in the semantics of looks reports, argues against subjectivist and dispositionalist accounts of looks. First of all, looks do not require experiences by agents; they are 'public' entities. This holds for both viewpoint-relative looks and overall looks.[10] Linguistically, this reflected in the acceptability of the sentences that follow:

(46) a. The statue would look the same even if no one had looked at it.
      b. The statue would have the same looks from the different angles even if no one had looked at it.

McGrath also argues against dispositionalist accounts of looks for ontological reasons: we do not 'see' or 'recognize' dispositions when we see or recognize a look. Ontologically, McGrath (2018) proposes to identify looks with sets

334   *Friederike Moltmann*

of sensible properties. An alternative that one might pursue is to take them to be kinds of (collections of) response-dependent tropes. Both views, though, still have to elaborate the distinction between viewpoint-relative and overall looks.[11]

To what extent can the arguments for experience-independence be generalized to perceptual objects of other modes? The contrasts that follow indicate that they apply also to taste objects, as opposed to taste occurrences, at least with nonevaluative predicates:

(47)   a. ? If one can no longer drink coffee, coffee can no longer taste bitter.
       b. If one can no longer drink coffee, coffee would still have a bitter taste.

(48)   a. ? If one can no longer drink coffee, coffee can no longer taste good.
       b. If one can no longer drink coffee, coffee would still have a good taste.

The arguments do not carry over to all perceptual objects, though, in particular not to those that can hardly be separated from the experience itself, such as physical and emotional feelings (as in *the massage feels great, the praise felt good*).[12] Feelings come with verbal predicates describing occurrences as well as nominal predicates describing feelings as objectual, 'public' entities. The latter, again, are able to act as objects of knowledge:

(49)   a. I don't know what it feels like to be praised by everyone.
       b. I know the pleasure of good company.

That 'feelings' can hardly be dissociated from the experiences appears to be reflected linguistically, namely in the choice of the light verb with the nominal construction. Whereas tastes, looks, smells, and sounds are selected by the light verb *have*, feelings are selected by the light verb *give* indicating feelings as causal effects on an experiencer:

(50)   a. This thing has/?? gives a nice taste/look/smell/sound.
       b. The massage gives/??? has a strange feeling.

Thus, at least some perceptual objects are individuated on the basis of experiences themselves.

5.   Implicit Agent-Centered Situations as Objects of Perception

Not only individuals or kinds of them may serve as referents of the subject of impersonal perceptual reports. The very same types of impersonal

Ontology of Impersonal Perception Reports   335

perception reports allow for what I call *agent-centered situations* as the objects of perception. These are perceptual reports with the pronoun *it* as apparent expletive or dummy subject:[13]

(51) a. It is nice/hot/dark here.
      b. It smells nice here.

(52) a. It looks like it is going to rain.
      b. It sounds like there will be a tempest.
      c. It smells like there is a fire nearby.
      d. It felt as if it was going to rain.

In (50a, b), *here* obviously gives the speaker's location. Other location modifiers are possible only if they specify the location of the speaker (or described attitude bearer) at another time as in (53a, b) and (54) or if the sentence has a generic reading, as in (55):[14, 15]

(53) a. It was nice in Germany.
      b. It will be interesting in Beijing.

(54) There it looked like it was going to rain.
(55) It is pleasant in Paris in spring.

With agent-centered situations, the copula *be* can take the place of the perception verb, as in the first stanza of the most famous German romantic poem:

(56) Es war, als hätt' der Himmel die Erde still geküßt, daß sie im Blütenschimmer von ihm nun träumen müßt'. (Josef von Eichendorff *Mondnacht* 'Moonlight')
      'It was as though Heaven had softly kissed the Earth, so that she in a gleam of blossom had only to dream of him.' (translation Richard Stokes)

The agent-centered situations appear to have the very same 'logophoric' status as the perceptual occurrences of impersonal perception verbs. In contexts embedded under attitude verbs with a different agent, the situation will be centered on the other agent, as in (57a); but such a shift is not available without an attitude verb, as in (57b), where *pleasant* can relate only to the speaker:

(57) a. John was happy that it was so pleasant in Germany.
      b. John met me while it was still so pleasant in Berlin.

Agent-centered situations may also figure in generic-*one* sentences. In the following sentences, the *when*-clauses restrict the agent-centered situations the

336   *Friederike Moltmann*

implicit generic quantifier ranges over and that are also the objects of evaluation for the main clause:

(58)   a. It is unbearable when one has just lost a parent.
       b. It is like that when one is completely unprepared.

The agent-centered situations as the entities that impersonal perception reports are about relate to the shiftable context c, just like the perceptual occurrences described by impersonal perception verbs. For the semantics of impersonal perception reports with agent-centered situations, I will assume, as is plausible, that *it* in subject position stands for the relevant agent-centered situation. Then the semantics in a first approximation will be as follows:

(59)   <u>Semantics of impersonal perception reports with agent-centered situations</u>
       For an impersonal perception verb V, a modifier X, and contexts u and c,

       $[It\ V\ X]^{u,\,c} = 1$ iff $\exists d(<[it]^{u,\,c}, d> \in [V]^{u,\,c}$ & $d \in [X]^{u,\,c})$, where $[it]^{u,\,c}$ is a situation centered on a_c.

There are two further observations to be made about impersonal perception reports with agent-centered situations.

First, there are cases in which the situation that an (independent) impersonal perception sentence is about is in fact not the speaker-centered situation but a contextually relevant one that the speaker projects herself onto. These are examples:

(60)   a. It looks like the TV presenter is distracted.
       b. It sounds like you are exhausted.
       c. There it looks like no one had cleaned up.

Putting oneself in another situation (simulating being the center of another situation) is an option that is similarly available with generic *one* and impersonal verbal taste reports, when a speaker projects herself onto another agent (*This tastes good* when speaking to a baby).

Second, with verbs like *seem* and *look*, the agent-centered situations may also be epistemic situations, constituted by the evidence that presents itself in the context:

(61)   a. It seems as if there is no solution to the problem.
       b. It looks as if John is innocent.

Seem and *look* as impersonal epistemic verbs belong to the same class as impersonal perception verbs, though of course they will not take perceptual occurrences as arguments.

Ontology of Impersonal Perception Reports 337

6. Faultless Disagreement With Impersonal Perception Reports

Sentences expressing judgments of personal taste are at the center of a recent philosophical debate about faultless disagreement, the possibility for two agents maintaining (62a) and (62b) respectively being both right:

(62) a. Olives are tasty.
      b. Olives are not tasty.

Given my previous views, faultless disagreement is due to the sentence expressing first person–based genericity, involving simulation (Moltmann, 2010a, 2010b, 2012), as in (63) for (62a):

(63) λx[Gn y taste good to(olives, y qua someone x simulates)]

This is still a relativist account, in the sense that the property in (62) needs to be self-applied by anyone accepting the content of the sentences. However, unlike standard relativist accounts, it is first-person genericity that is crucial for explaining faultless disagreement. What matters for agreement or disagreement about taste judgments is whether agents can project themselves onto (or simulate) the same range of people on the basis of their first-person experience (or simulated experience). Two agents disagree about a taste judgments due to their ability or inability to attribute the taste judgment to anyone in the group on the basis of such identification.

Assuming first-person genericity to be the grounds for faultless disagreement, the present semantics of impersonal perception reports makes certain predictions as to when it will arise. First of all, the genericity of taste sentences with adjectival or nominal predicates is due to the involvement of a taste object, not first person–based genericity. This means that with non-evaluative predicates such as *bitter*, *sweet*, *unusual*, no faultless disagreement should arise, which appears to be correct for sentences such as the following:

(64) a. The taste of coffee is bitter.
      b. This coffee is bitter.

However, a taste object may itself be that subject of first-person based genericity, which arguably is part of the lexical meaning of evaluative predicates such as *delicious* or *mediocre*. With evaluative predicates, faultless disagreement clearly does arise:

(65) a. The taste of coffee is delicious.
      b. Coffee is delicious.

A different prediction is made for verbal taste predicates. The genericity of verbal taste predicates is first person–based genericity (even if the

338 *Friederike Moltmann*

present proposal gives a more complex semantics of generic *one*, explicitly involving simulation). Thus verbal taste predicates should always give rise to faultless disagreement, which seems to accord with intuitions:

(66) a. This drink tastes bitter.
     b. The cake tastes unusual.

The same contrast appears to hold for other perceptual predicates:

(67) a. The perfume smells fruity.
     b. The smell of the perfume is fruity.

In contrast to (67a), (67b) does not seem to give rise to faultless disagreement.

7. Conclusion

This chapter has argued for a novel semantics of impersonal perceptual reports based on an ontology of perceptual occurrences and perceptual objects. Perceptual occurrences display the same sort of 'logophoric' first-person orientation as generic *one*, as do agent-centered situations as the objects of perception in impersonal perception reports with dummy subjects. 'Objective' perceptual objects are the source of genericity of perceptual reports with nominal and adjectival predicates, which is thus a distinct kind of genericity from the first person–based genericity available for perceptual reports with verbal predicates.

Acknowledgments

I would like to thank John Collins, Hazel Pearson, Matthew McGrath, Rachel Etta Rudolph, and Dan Zeman for comments on a previous version of this chapter. For very stimulating discussions, I would also like to thank the audience of an online presentation of the material of this chapter at the University of Oslo in August 2021 (project Sarah Zobel 'Impersonal Pronouns in Norwegian, Swedish, and German').

Notes

1. There is another view, namely on which the experiencer or judge is part of the context of assessment, requiring reassessment by anyone evaluating the sentences as true or false (McFarlane, 2014; Lasersohn, 2005). Then, with judges acting as parameters of evaluation, *tasty* denotes a property of objects, as follows:

   (i) $[tasty(coffee)]^{w, t, a}$ = true iff coffee is tasty to a in w at t.

2. Pearson also lists the possibility of adverbial modifiers with stage-level predicates but not with individual-level predicates, using the following examples:

Ontology of Impersonal Perception Reports   339

(i)   a.   This tea tastes good in a china cup.
      b.   ??? This tea is tasty in a china cup.
(ii) a.   St Paul's looks beautiful today.
      b.   ??? St Paul's is beautiful today.

However, it appears that speakers do not generally agree with the judgments.
3. But see Dinges and Zakkou (2021) for arguments that they do.
4. For more on modal objects, see Moltmann (2017, 2018), where modal objects are taken to have a truthmaker-based content and play a central role in the semantics of modal sentences.
5. *As if*-clauses also permit co-variation of generic *one* with the experiencer of the described perceptual occurrences:

(i)   The massage feels as if one was being tortured.

6. Thus, McGrath (p.c.) points out the potential truth of (i), when the speaker knows that no one is looking at the house now:

(i)   I wonder if his house still looks as if it is about to fall down, which it did last time I saw it.

7. If taste occurrences are regarded as results of taste experiences, this would match the view that judgments are results of acts of judging and conclusions results of acts of concluding (Moltmann, 2017). Given such a view, the logical form of (19a) would be as follows:

(i) $\exists e(\text{taste}(e, \text{the coffee}) \ \& \ \text{good}(\text{result}(e$

8. A similar distinction holds for the noun *color* (Moltmann, 2013 chap. 6.6.). (ia) has a reading involving reference to kinds of color occurrences, which is unavailable in (ib):

(i)   a.   I have never seen this color.
      b.   ? I have never seen the color of this car.

In (ib), *color of* is used relationally, referring to the color that pertains to a particular object.
9. In fact, a semanticist should not have to decide how tastes are to be conceived ultimately; this rather is a matter for the philosopher of mind or metaphysician to decide. See the discussion of the distinction between foundational and naïve or descriptive metaphysics (which comprises natural language ontology) in Fine (2017) and Moltmann (2019).
10. McGrath (2018) distinguishes those from 'subjective looks', which would fall under perceptual occurrences in the present sense.
11. McGrath (2021) proposes that viewpoint-relative looks be conceived as properties of presenting light of a certain character to the viewpoint. Moreover, looks on the round (overall looks) are what it is about an object that grounds the possibilities of its viewpoint-relative looks. This proposal obviously does not carry over to perceptual objects of other perceptual modes.
12. Feeling of this sort needs to be distinguished from tactile feels, which are as experience-independent as tastes, looks, and sounds:

(i)   a.   The fabric feels rough.
      b.   The feel of the fabric is rough.

340 *Friederike Moltmann*

13. Not all perception verbs that can occur in impersonal perception reports allow for agent-centered situations. German *wirken* 'appear', for example, cannot:

(i) a. Hans wirkt muede.
'Hans appears tired.'
b. Hans wirkt, als haette er nicht geschlafen.
'John appears as if he had not slept.'
c. * Es wirkt, als wuerde es regnen.
'It appears as if it was going to rain.'

14. Sentences reporting weather (*it is raining*) belong to the same syntactic class, though they are less directly related to perception.
15. (53a), (53b), and (54) also have a generic reading on which they do not require the speaker's (or anyone's) presence at the location in question.

References

Bledin, J., & Srinivas, S. (forthcoming). Descriptive *as ifs*. *Linguistics and Philosophy*.

Chierchia, G. (1995). Individual-level predicates as inherent generics. In G. Carlson & J. Pelletier (Eds.), *The generic book* (pp. 176–223). University of Chicago Press.

Collins, J. (2013). The syntax of personal taste. *Philosophical Perspectives*, 27(1), 51–103.

Dinges, A., & Zakkou, J. (2021). Taste, traits and tendencies. *Philosophical Studies*, *178*, 1183–1206.

Fine, K. (2017). Naïve metaphysics. *Philosophical Issues*, 27(1), 98–113.

Jackson, F. (1977). *Perception: A representative theory*. Cambridge University Press.

Lasersohn, P. (2005). Context dependence, disagreement, and predicates of personal taste. *Linguistics and Philosophy*, *28*, 643–686.

MacFarlane, J. (2014). *Assessment relativity: Relative truth and its applications*. Oxford University Press.

McGrath, M. (2017). Knowing what things look like. *The Philosophical Review*, *126*(1), 1–41.

McGrath, M. (2018). Looks and perceptual justification. *Philosophy and Phenomenological Research*, *96*(1), 110–133.

McGrath, M. (2021). *The metaphysics of looks* [Manuscript]. Rutgers University.

Moltmann, F. (2006). Generic *one*, arbitrary PRO, and the first person. *Natural Language Semantics*, *14*, 257–281.

Moltmann, F. (2010a). Generalizing detached self-reference and the semantics of generic "one". *Mind and Language*, *25*(4), 440–473.

Moltmann, F. (2010b). Relative truth and the first person. *Philosophical Studies*, *150*, 187–220.

Moltmann, F. (2012). Two kinds of first-person-oriented content. *Synthese*, *184*, 157–177.

Moltmann, F. (2017). Cognitive Products and the Semantics of Attitude Verbs and Deontic Modals. In F. Moltmann & M. Textor (Eds.), *Act-Based Conceptions of*

Propositional Content. Contemporary and Historical Perspectives (pp. 254–290). Oxford University Press.

Moltmann, F. (2018). An Object-Based Truthmaker Semantics for Modals. *Philosophical Issues*, 28(1), 255–288.

Moltmann, F. (2019). Natural Language and its Ontology. In A. Goldman & B. McLaughlin (Eds.), *Metaphysics and Cognitive Science* (pp. 206–232). Oxford University Press.

Pearson, H. (this volume). Individual and stage-level predicates of personal taste. To appear in J. Wyatt, J. Zakkou & D. Zeman (Eds.), *Perspectives on Taste*. Routledge.

Rudolph, R. (this volume). Differences of Taste. An Investigation of Phenomenal and Non-phenomenal Appearance Sentences. To appear in J. Wyatt, J. Zakkou & D. Zeman (Eds.), *Perspectives on Taste*. Routledge.

Stephenson, T. (2007). Judge dependence, epistemic modals, and predicates of personal taste. *Linguistics and Philosophy*, 30, 487–525.

Notes on Contributors

Constant Bonard is a postdoctoral researcher in philosophy at the Institut Jean Nicod (École Normale Supérieure, Paris), grantee of the Swiss National Science Foundation. He works on emotion, on communication, and especially on the intersection of these two topics.

Florian Cova is Assistant Professor in Philosophy at the University of Geneva. His main research areas are moral psychology and experimental philosophy of aesthetics. He is the co-editor of *Advances in Experimental Philosophy of Aesthetics* (Bloomsbury, 2018). His research has also appeared in philosophy, psychology, and linguistics journals. These include *Philosophical Studies, Journal of Aesthetics and Art Criticism, Mind and Language, Philosophy Compass, The Monist, Review of Philosophy and Psychology, Philosophical Psychology,* and *Ethical Theory and Moral Practice; Cognition and Emotion, Personality and Social Psychology Bulletin, Behavioral and Brain Sciences,* and *Semantics and Pragmatics.*

Alexander Dinges is Lecturer in Theoretical Philosophy at Friedrich-Alexander-Universität Erlangen-Nürnberg. He works primarily in epistemology (especially on knowledge ascriptions) and the philosophy of language (especially on subjective language and context sensitivity). His work has appeared in *Philosophers' Imprint, Philosophical Studies, Analysis, Australasian Journal of Philosophy, Synthese, Erkenntnis, Pacific Philosophical Quarterly, Mind and Language, Journal of Pragmatics, Episteme,* and *Philosophical Psychology,* as well as *Skeptical Invariantism Reconsidered* (Routledge, 2021). He is a co-editor of the *Inquiry* special issue *Semantic Variability* (forthcoming), and his monograph *Knowledge, Stakes, and Error: A Psychological Account* was published by Klostermann in 2019.

Steve Humbert-Droz is a Ph.D. student at the University of Geneva (Switzerland). He is currently working on a taxonomy of imagination in light of the mode/content distinction. His other interests concern aesthetic values and organic unities as well as the philosophy of emotions.

Notes on Contributors 343

Elsi Kaiser is Associate Professor of Linguistics at the University of Southern California. Her current research focuses mostly on psycholinguistics, especially on interface issues related to semantics and pragmatics. She has published in journals such as *Cognition, The Journal of Memory and Language*, and *Language, Cognition and Neuroscience* and has received funding from the U.S. National Science Foundation and the National Institutes of Health.

Christopher Kennedy is William H. Colvin Professor of Linguistics at the University of Chicago. His work is geared toward discovering the principles that are involved in relating linguistic forms to meanings, determining how properties of the linguistic system and properties of the context of utterance interact in achieving this mapping, and understanding the extent to which structural and typological features of language can be explained in terms of meaning. He has published articles in *Mind, Linguistics and Philosophy, Inquiry, Synthese, Language, Semantics and Pragmatics, Journal of Semantics, Linguistic Inquiry, Natural Language and Linguistic Theory* and elsewhere. He is the author of *Projecting the Adjective: The Syntax and Semantics of Gradability and Comparison* (Garland, 1999), the editor (with Louise McNally) of *Adjectives and Adverbs: Syntax, Semantics, Discourse* (Oxford, 2008), and he is a general editor (with Chris Barker) of the Oxford University Press series *Studies in Semantics and Pragmatics* and *Surveys in Semantics and Pragmatics.*

Markus Kneer is Research Associate and Director of the *Reading Guilty Minds* Research Group at the University of Zurich. He works primarily in the philosophy of language and mind, as well as ethics broadly conceived, including moral psychology. His research has appeared in *Linguistics and Philosophy, Review of Philosophy and Psychology,* and *Cognition,* as well as *Oxford Studies in Experimental Philosophy* (Oxford, forthcoming) and *Advances in Experimental Philosophy of Aesthetics* (Bloomsbury, 2019).

Dan López de Sa is ICREA Research Professor at Universitat de Barcelona. He works mainly in social metaphysics and social philosophy of language and in particular on social groups, terminological ethics, evaluative disagreement, the metaphysics of gender, the reclamation of slurs, and the philosophy of sex and sexualities. He has published papers in *Analysis, Erkenntnis, Mind, Noûs, Philosophers' Imprint, Philosophical Studies, Proceedings of the Aristotelian Society,* and *Synthese,* among other venues, as well as in the collections *Relative Truth* (Oxford, 2008), *Cuts and Clouds* (Oxford, 2010), *A Companion to Relativism* (Blackwell, 2011), and *Semantics of Aesthetic Judgements* (Oxford, 2017), among others.

Irene Martínez Marín is a Ph.D. candidate in aesthetics at the Department of Philosophy at Uppsala University. Her thesis work concerns

344 *Notes on Contributors*

the relations between emotions, reasons, and value within aesthetic judgement. She was awarded the Fabian Dorsch ESA Essay prize in 2019. She is also the coordinator of the Nordic Network for Women in Aesthetics.

Friederike Moltmann is Research Director at Centre Nationale de la Recherche Scientifique (CNRS-IHPST). Her main research interests lie at the interface between natural language semantics and philosophy. Among these are natural language ontology, sentence meaning and the nature of propositions, plural reference, the distinction between mass nouns and count nouns, and the semantics of parts and wholes. She is the author of *Parts and Wholes in Semantics* (Oxford, 1997), *Abstract Objects and the Semantics of Natural Language* (Oxford, 2013), and *Individuation und Lokalitaet. Studien zur Ereignis- und Nominalphrasensemantik*, (Fink Verlag, 1992). She also has two forthcoming books: *Objects and Attitudes* and *Plural Reference and Syntactic Three-Dimensionality* (both with Oxford University Press). She has published articles in venues such as *Noûs, Mind, Philosophical Studies, Synthese, Thought, Canadian Journal of Philosophy, Journal of Semantics, Linguistics and Philosophy, Theoretical Linguistics*, and *Natural Language Semantics*, as well as in numerous edited volumes.

Hazel Pearson is Senior Lecturer in Linguistics at Queen Mary University of London. She works in formal semantics, with additional interests in experimental semantics, linguistic fieldwork, and philosophy of language. She has published in venues including *Journal of Semantics, Natural Language and Linguistic Theory, Natural Language Semantics,* and *Semantics and Pragmatics*, as well as the collections *Syntax and Its Limits* (Oxford, 2013) and *The Wiley Blackwell Companion to Semantics* (Wiley Blackwell, forthcoming). She is also currently working on a monograph called *Perspective and the Self in Natural Language: The Grammar of the De Se* (under contract with Oxford University Press). She is an associate editor of *Semantics and Pragmatics*.

Jon Robson is Assistant Professor in Philosophy at the University of Nottingham. He mainly researches topics in aesthetics, epistemology, and the philosophy of religion. He is co-editor of *Aesthetics and the Sciences of Mind* (Oxford, 2014) and *The Aesthetics of Videogames* (Routledge, 2018) as well as co-author of *A Critical Introduction to the Metaphysics of Time* (Bloomsbury, 2016). His articles have appeared in venues such as *Philosophy and Phenomenological Research, Philosophers' Imprint, Australasian Journal of Philosophy, Synthese, Philosophy Compass, Pacific Philosophical Quarterly, Journal of Aesthetics and Art Criticism, The British Journal of Aesthetics*, and *WIREs Cognitive Science*.

Rachel Etta Rudolph is Assistant Professor in Philosophy at Auburn University. Her main research areas are philosophy of language and metaethics. Her papers have appeared in *Philosophical Studies, Philosophers' Imprint*, and *Proceedings of Sinn und Bedeutung*.

Elisabeth Schellekens is Chair Professor of Aesthetics at the Department of Philosophy at Uppsala University and Fellow of the Royal Society of the Humanities. Her research interests include aesthetic normativity and obligation; the relations between aesthetic, moral, and cognitive value in art; non-perceptual art and theories of perception; Hume's and Kant's aesthetics; and the philosophy of cultural heritage. She is the author of *Aesthetics and Morality* (Continuum, 2007) and co-author of *Who's Afraid of Conceptual Art?* (Routledge, 2009). She is also a co-editor of *Philosophy and Conceptual Art* (Oxford, 2007), *The Aesthetic Mind: Philosophy and Psychology* (Oxford, 2011), and *Aesthetics, Philosophy, and Martin Creed* (Bloomsbury, 2019). Her articles have appeared in *Philosophy Compass, Behavioral and Brain Sciences, Journal of Consciousness Studies, Acta Analytica*, and *Theoria*, as well as in many edited collections.

Isidora Stojanovic is Research Director for the Centre National de la Recherche Scientifique (CNRS) at the Institut Jean-Nicod. Her main research topics are context dependence, the semantics–pragmatics interface, indexicals, the *de se*, and evaluative discourse. She is the author of *What Is Said: An Inquiry into Reference, Meaning and Content* (VDM, 2008) and a co-editor of *Context-Dependence, Perspective, and Relativity* (de Gruyter, 2010). Her articles have appeared in venues such as *Erkenntnis, Philosophy Compass, Synthese, Southern Journal of Philosophy, Linguistics and Philosophy*, and *Inquiry*, as well as numerous edited collections.

Kevin Sweeney is Professor Emeritus of Philosophy at the University of Tampa. He is particularly interested in gustatory aesthetics and has recently published *The Aesthetics of Food: The Philosophical Debate About What We Eat and Drink* (Rowman & Littlefield, 2018). Earlier contributions include "Hunger Is the Best Sauce: The Aesthetics of Food," *The Philosophy of Food*, ed. David Kaplan (University of California Press, 2012), pp. 52–68; "Is There Coffee or Blackberry in My Wine?" *Wine & Philosophy: A Symposium on Thinking and Drinking*, ed. Fritz Allhoff (Blackwell, 2008), pp. 205–218; "Can a Soup Be Beautiful? The Rise of Gastronomy and the Aesthetics of Food," *Food & Philosophy: Eat, Think and be Merry*, eds. F. Allhoff and D. Monroe (Blackwell, 2007), pp. 117–132; and "Alice's Discriminating Palate," *Philosophy and Literature*, 23, 1 (April, 1999): 17–31.

Rebecca Wallbank is a Ph.D. candidate in aesthetics at the Department of Philosophy at Uppsala University. Her research encompasses wide-ranging debates in aesthetics and epistemology, and she specializes in issues pertaining to aesthetic expertise, and our reasons to trust in such

346   *Notes on Contributors*

experts. She is a contributor to *The Philosophy of Rhythm: Aesthetics, Music, Poetics* (Oxford, 2019) and *Epistemic Duties: New Arguments, New Angles* (Routledge, 2020).

Malte Willer is Associate Professor in the Department of Philosophy and the College at the University of Chicago. His main areas of interest are the philosophy of language and philosophical logic. He has published in journals such as *Philosophical Review*, *Journal of Philosophy*, *Philosophers' Imprint*, *Semantics and Pragmatics*, and *Linguistics and Philosophy*, and he has papers published or forthcoming in *Deontic Modality* (Oxford, 2016) and *Oxford Studies in Philosophy of Language Volume II* (Oxford, forthcoming). Together with Olivier Roy and Allard Tamminga, he edited *Reasons, Argumentation and Justification: DEON 2016 Special issue* (Journal of Logic and Computation, 2019). He is currently an associate editor at *Semantics and Pragmatics* and an area editor at *Ergo*, as well as a member of the DEON Steering Committee.

Jeremy Wyatt is Senior Lecturer in Philosophy at the University of Waikato. His main research interests are the philosophy of language, truth, metaphysics, and experimental philosophy. He is a co-editor of *Pluralisms in Truth and Logic* (Palgrave Macmillan, 2018) and *The Nature of Truth: Classic and Contemporary Perspectives*, 2nd ed. (MIT Press, 2021) and the editor of the *Synthese* special issue *Truth: Concept Meets Property* (2021). His articles have appeared in *Philosophical Studies*, *The Philosophical Quarterly*, *Synthese*, *American Philosophical Quarterly*, and *Inquiry*.

Julia Zakkou is Assistant Professor in Philosophy at Bielefeld University. Her research focus is on the philosophy of language and epistemology. Her book *Faultless Disagreement* was published in 2019 with *Klostermann*, and her articles have appeared in venues such as *Philosophers' Imprint*, *Philosophical Studies*, *Synthese*, *Semantics and Pragmatics*, *Mind and Language*, *Philosophy Compass*, *Inquiry*, and *Thought*. She is also a co-editor of the *Inquiry* special issue *Semantic Variability* (forthcoming).

Dan Zeman is Adjunct Professor in Philosophy at the University of Warsaw. His research area is the philosophy of language, in particular the semantics of various natural language expressions. His monograph *Disagreement in Semantics* (co-authored with Mihai Hîncu) is forthcoming with *Routledge* in 2022. He has published in *Thought*, *Dialectica*, *Linguistics & Philosophy*, *Philosophia*, *Critica*, *Inquiry*, and *Theoria* and has contributed to *Context-Dependence, Perspective, and Relativity* (de Gruyter, 2010), *Subjective Meaning: Alternatives to Relativism* (de Gruyter, 2016), *Meaning, Context, and Methodology* (de Gruyter, 2017), *The Architecture of Context and Context-Sensitivity*

(Springer, 2020), and *The Routledge Handbook of Philosophy of Relativism* (Routledge, 2020). He is a co-editor of the *Southern Journal of Philosophy* special issue *Relativism about Value* (2012), the *Grazer Philosophische Studien* special issue *Non-Derogatory Uses of Slurs* (2020), the *Synthese* topical collection *New Work on Disagreement* (forthcoming) and is the editor of the *Organon F* special issue *Value in Language* (2021).

Index

acquaintance: acquaintance inference 253, 266, 281n16, 300–301, 307, 310; Acquaintance Principle 41–44; acquaintance requirement 300
Addison, Joseph 59
aesthetic appreciation 2–3, 40–54
aesthetic attribution 60–62; aesthetic adjective 234, 237; aesthetic predicate 211, 214
aesthetic belief 44–50
aesthetic evaluation 60–62, 65–66, 70
aesthetic judgement 21–24, 40–45, 47–49, 53n1, 54n9, 54n13, 60–62
aesthetic objectivism 3–4, 62–63, 77, 96, 106
aesthetic perception 60–67
aesthetic pleasure 59–62, 71n18, 72n22, 72n35
aesthetic subjectivism 3–4, 62–63, 79–80, 82, 85, 90, 94–96, 105–106
aesthetic taste 1–4, 58–72, 77–106; affect-based accounts of 63, 65; emotional sensibility 60–71; epistemological ambivalence in the notion of 58, 59, 66–67, 70; good *vs.* bad 77–106; holistic approach to the functional roles of 60–61, 63; improvement of 101–104; nature of 3, 58–72, 78–82; normativity of 64; paradox of 4, 78–80, 95–96, 105; perception-based accounts of 63, 65–66; perceptual discernment 60–71; *see also* taste of reflection
aesthetic testimony 41–42, 45–53; aesthetic optimism *vs.* aesthetic pessimism 45–46, 48; social value of 50–53
appearance: appearance-independent 276; appearance language 261,

281n17; appearance verb 261–264, 268–269, 275, 277–278, 280n6, 281n14
arousal rating 246–252
assertion 110–111, 114–115, 128, 130–132, 194–203, 204n10, 220; norm/norm of 1, 5, 7, 110–112, 114–115, 128, 132, 194–195, 198; permissible 194, 197–200; retract an 110, 194–195, 197, 201–202
assessment relativism 7–8, 146, 193, 195–200, 203, 204n1, 204n4
at issue, non-at-issue 219, 224
attunement 3–4, 60, 67–71; as emotional understanding 69–70; Ludwig Wittgenstein on 67; Martin Heidegger on 67; Rita Felski on 68–69; Stanley Cavell on 67–68

Bailey, Olivia 51
Baldy, Marian 30–31
Beddor, Bob 116, 134n10
beneficiary argument 234
Berchoux, Joseph 24
Bonard, Constant 3–4, 71n14
bound variable interpretation 299, 304–306, 310
Bourdieu, Pierre 81, 98, 101, 105
Brillat-Savarin, Jean-Anthelme 2, 24–31, 35, 37n21
Brysbaert, Marc 245–246
Budd, Malcolm 40
Burke, Edmund 80, 97, 104–105
Bylinina, Lisa 211, 226n5

Canberra Plan 6–7, 164–169, 175–178, 180, 181n6
Carroll, Noël 71n21, 72n26, 80, 104–105

Index 349

character trait predicate 211, 214
Chisholm, Roderick 280n6
circumstance of evaluation 109, 193–195, 200–201
Cohen, Ted 72n35
context of use 194–195, 197–203, 204n3, 204n7
context of utterance 109–110, 112–113, 116, 118, 120, 123, 125, 127, 132
color predicate 271
context dependence 243, 261, 305
contextualism *see* predicates of personal taste (PPT)
contextualism/relativism debate 111–112, 114, 132
contingency: contingency requirement 208; counterstance contingency 214–225
coordination 151, 173–174, 216–217, 215–217
Coppock, Elizabeth 208–209, 225
Cova, Florian 3–4, 6, 71n14, 170–172, 183n18
crossover effect 291–296

Darley, John 235
deontic term 237
Dickie, George 40
dimension-sensitivity 274, 277
Dinges, Alexander 5, 7–8, 111, 117–120, 122, 124–127, 134nn4–5, 155, 159n14, 308
Direction Effect 118, 121–122, 124, 133n4
disagreement: in attitude 143, 149–151, 158n12; dispute 5; doxastic 6; faultless 233–237, 238, 253n3, 254n6, 254n9, 279n1, 280n3, 286, 303, 311–314, 316n2; metalinguistic 235, 255n17; platitudes about 6; pluralism about 7; and preferences 6; about taste 5–7, 9, 10
Douven, Igor 128
doxastic: doxastic alternative 209, 214, 219, 223; doxastic state 215–216, 218, 222; doxastic verb 214
Dummett, Michael 128

Egan, Andy 116, 134n10, 155, 158n13
Elgin, Catherine 70

ellipsis 296–298
embedding 207, 209–214, 217–219, 223–225, 226n3, 233, 236, 253n3, 266, 273, 275–279, 281n16, 288
emotional adjective 237
epistemic term 237
evaluation: evaluative adjective 261–263, 266, 271–273, 275; evaluative character 231; evaluative component 211; evaluative term 232, 274; evaluative vocabulary 261
Even Split 118–119, 121–125, 134n4
exclusionary/nonexclusionary contents 5, 147–149, 151–152, 154, 158n7
experiencer-sensitive adjectives 234, 236
experiential: predicates 157n2, 266, 315n5, 320; states 41–43
experiential/representational distinction 280n6
experimental aesthetics 3–4, 77–107
expressivism *see* predicates of personal taste (PPT)

faultless disagreement *see* disagreement
first person: -based genericity 9–10, 321, 337–338; bound variable 324; experience 316n22; experiencer 300, 303; indexical 299–300, 303–304, 324; orientation 311, 313, 320–321, 323, 329, 338; pronoun 302; referential reading 321–322
folk aesthetics *see* experimental aesthetics

gastronomy 24–25, 37n21
genericity: GEN 295–296, 305–311, 316n18, 316n22; generic construal 286, 291, 294, 304, 306, 310–311, 315n13; generic interpretation 286, 291; generic *one* 301–302, 305, 310–311
Ginsborg, Hannah 72n22
Goodwin, Geoffrey 235
Gorodeisky, Keren 45
gradable adjective 232, 261, 272, 274, 276, 282n25
Grahm, Randall 34–35
gustatory experience 19–37; taste map theory of 30
gustatory taste 2, 19–37, 255n19, 260, 262; good *vs.* bad 98–101; and

350 *Index*

smell 19–20, 24–26, 30, 37n32; *see also* gustatory experience; taste of sense
gustatory trajectory 2, 19, 29–36

Howell, Robert 55n16
Humbert-Droz, Steve 3–4, 71n14
Hume, David 4, 21, 24, 62, 69–70, 71n18, 78–80, 95–97, 104–106
Hutcheson, Francis 71n4

impersonal taste reports 9, 319, 323
implicature 227n7, 241–242
indeterminacy 209, 274–275
individual-level predicate (ILP) 286–288, 290, 296, 305–307, 309–311, 315nn3–4
Iseminger, Gary 54n2

Jackson, Frank 165, 264–267, 280n2, 280nn6–8, 280n10, 281n14, 281n20
judge: judge argument 207–208, 211–212, 214, 226n3; judge-dependent 209, 269, 277, 279, 282n26; judge PP 211; judge-sensitive 208, 225
judgments of taste 231–232, 254n9

Kaiser, Elsi 8–9, 235
Kant, Immanuel 2, 4, 21–26, 29, 35, 36nn15–17, 37n28, 59, 62, 71n18, 72n22, 77–78, 81, 98, 100, 104–105
Kaplan, David 109, 201
Kennedy, Christopher 8, 209–210, 214–218, 226n7, 227n9
Khoo, Justin 130–133, 149
Kneer, Markus 4–5, 112–113, 134n10
Knobe, Joshua 5, 111–115, 118, 127–131, 133, 149
Kölbel, Max 147, 198, 253n2, 311
Konigsberg, Amir 54n4
Korsmeyer, Carolyn 41, 63, 78
Kramer, Matt 33–35
Kratzer, Angelika 289
Kuperman, Victor 245–246

La Reynière, Alexandre Grimod de 24, 37n21
Lasersohn, Peter 204n2, 207–209, 233, 253n2, 261, 276, 280n4, 291–292, 304, 311–313

Lewis, David 109, 151, 154, 158n8, 165, 204n10, 321
linguistic denial: felicity of 146, 152, 154–155, 157, 158n12, 158n13, 160n17
Lizardo, Omar 81
locationism 8, 200–204
logophoricity 320, 323–324, 327–330, 335, 338
López de Sa, Dan 5–6, 145, 159n13
Lord, Errol 40–41, 46–47

MacFarlane, John 109, 111–112, 114–115, 128–129, 132–133, 143, 145–146, 151, 156, 157n4, 157n5, 184, 196, 198–199, 204n3, 280n3
McGrath, Matthew 331, 333, 339n6, 339n11
McIver Lopes, Dominic 41–44, 54n6
McShane, Paddy 48
Marcus, Eric 45
Martin, Michael 267, 280n10, 280n12, 280n13, 281n21, 282n25
Martínez Marín, Irene 3–4
measure function 273–274
Mistake Principle 166, 168, 171, 177, 181n7, 182n13, 184n27
Moltmann, Friederike 9–10, 280n3, 281n17, 311, 316nn16, 19, 321, 329, 337
moral: moral predicate 211, 214; moral term 236
multidimensionality 212, 261, 272, 274–275, 281nn22–23, 282n26

neutral 231–232, 238–243, 245–253, 225nn19–20, 257n45
Nguyen, C. Thi 47, 49, 51–52
Ninan, Dilip 194–196, 199, 253n3
non-indexical contextualism *see* predicates of personal taste (PPT)
normative force 111, 128, 133

objective predicate 212
outlook-based semantics 225, 228n17

Pain, Nicolas 6, 170–172, 183n18
paralysis inducement 6, 178–180
Pearson, Hazel 9–10, 287, 302–304, 315n13, 321–323, 338n2
perception 264, 271; impersonal perception reports 9, 319–320, 323, 325–326, 328, 330, 336–338, 340n13; impersonal perception

verb(s) 10, 319–320, 322–329, 335–336; perception of taste 299, 302; perception sentence 288; perception verb 288; perceptual objects 281n17, 319–320, 323, 325–326, 330–331, 333–334, 338, 339n11; perceptual occurrences 319–320, 324–328, 330, 335–336, 338, 339n5

perspective: autocentric 276–279, 280n4, 312–314; exocentric 276–278, 280n4, 282n28; perspectival argument 207, 209–210; perspectival content 209, 212–214, 218, 221, 224–225, 228n17; perspective-dependent/ perspective dependent 261, 272, 277–278, 280n4; perspectival meaning 207, 210; perspectival nature 207, 226n1; perspectival predicate 207, 209; perspective-sensitive 209–210

phenomenal, non-phenomenal 260–262, 264–279, 280n2, 280n6, 280nn9–10, 280n13, 281nn20–21, 282n25, 282n28

Plato 20

Plunkett, David 156

predicates of personal taste (PPT): absolutism about 7, 228n17; adjectival 321, 325, 330, 332; contextualism about 207, 225n1, 228n17, 279n1; experimental results on 4–5; expressivism about 6–7, 231, 254n3, 254n9, 257n45; indexical contextualism about 5, 7–9, 109; nominal 321, 330–334, 337–338; non-indexical contextualism about 7–8, 193, 195–200, 203–204; relativism about 5, 7–9, 207–209, 217–218, 225, 225n1, 226n2, 228n16, 279n1, 280n3, 287, 304, 311, 313–314; and retraction 5, 7–8, 279n1; and truth assessment 5

presupposition 207, 209, 214–217, 220, 222–224, 226n2, 227n7, 227n12, 294, 297, 315n11; of commonality 6, 154–156, 158n13, 159n14

problem of lost disagreement 5, 143, 146–151, 153–154, 157

projection 210, 214, 218, 220, 226n2, 227n6, 227n12, 315n12

pronoun: covert pronominal argument 286, 292–293, 298–299, 301; covert pronoun 291, 299, 301; indexical pronoun 303, 312; *pro* 291, 293, 296, 305–307, 309–310

Proust, Marcel 64–66

psychological adjective 234, 237

Raffman, Diana 146

Ransom, Madeleine 46

referential interpretation 286

relativism *see* predicates of personal taste (PPT)

relativistic effects 143–145, 153, 157n2

retraction 5, 7–8, 110–114, 116, 127–133, 134n10, 145–146, 157n4, 159n15, 195–196, 199, 201–203; data 159n15, 193, 196–200, 202–203, 204n4; norm/ norm of 7–8, 111, 116, 132, 134n5, 194–197, 199, 203; Retraction Rule 110–112, 128–129

Richard, Mark 168–169, 182n13, 200

Robson, Jon 2–3, 47, 54n15

Rudin, Deniz 235

Rudolph, Rachel 9, 144–145, 153, 157nn2–3, 326

Sæbø, Kjell Johan 8, 207–210, 213–214, 218, 223–224, 225n1, 226n2

Schaffer, Jonathan 315n13

Schellekens, Elisabeth 3–4, 78

senses *see* gustatory taste

sensory: sensory-evaluative construction 261, 272, 275–278; sensory-evaluative predicate 261–262, 264, 266, 268, 276–279

Sibley, Frank 59, 62

Silk, Alex 155–156, 159n16, 226n2, 254n7

stage-level predicate (SLP) 286–291, 295–296, 299, 304, 306–308, 310–314, 315n3, 316n19

Stalnaker, Robert 154–155, 220

standard-relativity 207, 238

Stevenson, Charles 150–151

stipulation: coordination by stipulation 216–217

Stojanovic, Isidora 8–9, 234, 236, 238

352 *Index*

strict/sloppy ambiguity 291, 296, 298, 315n8
subjectivity: ordering subjectivity 274; subjective adjective 232, 234, 253; subjective attitude verb 207, 209–210, 212–214, 217, 219–220, 222–224, 226n2, 253n3; subjective predicate 233, 235, 253n2; subjective term 232, 237–238
Sundell, Tim 156, 160n17
Sweeney, Kevin 2

taste: nouns 323, 330; objects 10, 319–320, 325, 330–332, 334; occurrences 9, 319–320, 324–325, 327, 329, 331–332, 334, 339n7; *see also* aesthetic taste; gustatory taste
taste of reflection 2, 21–22
taste of sense 2, 21
taste predicates *see* predicates of personal taste (PPT)
temporalism 8, 200–203
terroir 2, 19, 33–36
Todd, Cain 54n13
truth-assessment 5, 111–113, 116, 118–120, 122, 125, 127, 132, 134n5
Truth Rule 110–112, 114, 118
type-noncotenability 6, 164, 174–180
type-noncotenable preferences 175, 177–178

Umbach, Carla 253n3
underdetermination 215–216
underspecification 231, 246, 249, 252–253

vagueness 261
valence rating 239, 245–251
Väyrynen, Pekka 238, 254n8
View of Delft 64–66
Voltaire 22, 24

Wallbank, Rebecca 2–3
Warriner, Amy Beth 245–246
Willer, Malte 8, 209–210, 214–218, 226n7, 227n9
Williamson, Timothy 128
wine 19, 27, 31–36, 38n35; *see also terroir*
Wollheim, Richard 41–44, 54nn6–7, 54nn9–10
Wright, Crispin 145–147, 152, 182n13
Wyatt, Jeremy 6–7, 181n7, 183n15, 184nn31–34

Yalcin, Seth 5, 111–115, 118, 127–131, 133, 134n10

Zakkou, Julia 5, 111, 117–120, 122, 124–127, 134nn4–5, 159n15, 202–203, 308, 315n2, 315n13, 315n14

Printed in the United States
by Baker & Taylor Publisher Services